CALIFORNIA Real Estate PRACTICES

Practical Information for the Real Estate Professional.

Walter Hub

etc...
Educational Textbook Company
P.O. Box 3597
Covina, California 91722
(818) 339-7733

3rd Edition

By Educational Textbook Company, Inc.
P. O. Box 3597
Covina, CA 91722
1(818) 339-7733 FAX 1(818) 332-4744

ISBN: 0-916772-26-8

PRINTED IN CANADA

TABLE OF CONTENTS

Section One

Business Practices

Chapter One

Introduction to Agency

The Broker-Principal Relationship

The agency relationship between the broker and his or her principal is normally created by a written contract and is therefore subject to the rules of both agency and contract law. It is important, though, to recognize the distinction. The broker's right to compensation is based on contract but the broker's duties and potential liabilities are grounded both in agency and contract. The broker must have a valid written contract (listing agreement) in order to enforce a claim for a commission. However an agency may be created, and fiduciary duties thereby imposed, without either consideration or a written agreement (or, in fact, without any express agreement at all). It is possible, then, for a real estate broker to be subject to all the fiduciary obligations inherent in a principal-agent relationship, even though the broker has no enforceable right to a commission. A broker without a right to be paid could still be held liable to the principal for damages resulting from breach of a fiduciary duty and could still be subject to discipline by the Real Estate Commissioner.

Fiduciary Relationship

The broker's fiduciary duties usually arise when the agency is created, which may be prior to or even in the absence of a formal employment contract. The agency is considered to terminate when the property is sold, but fiduciary obligations may extend after close of escrow. For example, the duty to maintain the confidentiality of information received from the principal may arise prior to signing the listing agreement and may continue after the sale has closed.

Unlike the usual business or contractual relationship in which the parties bargain with each other looking to their own self interests, in a fiduciary relationship, the parties are considered to be able to trust and confide in each other and to have the confidential information protected. Fiduciaries are bound to look toward the best interests of the other(s). A fiduciary may not take advantage of the other party or parties but must, instead, act for the benefit of the other(s).

The fiduciary position held by a real estate broker requires the broker to meet a standard of utmost good faith in all dealings with his or her principal, a much higher standard of good faith and honest dealing than is required in a normal business transaction. The fiduciary duties of a real estate agent to his or her client have been compared to those owed by a trustee to the beneficiary of the trust and have been stated in numerous court decisions. Some of those pronouncements were summarized by the Supreme Court of California as follows:

> . . . "The law imposes on a real estate agent 'the same obligation of undivided service and loyalty that it imposes on a trustee in favor of his beneficiary.' . . . This relationship not only imposes upon him the duty of acting in the highest good faith toward his principal but precludes the agent from obtaining any advantage over the principal in any transaction had by virtue of the agency. . . ." A real estate licensee is "charged with the duty of fullest disclosure of all material facts concerning the transaction that might affect the principal's decision."

The strict legal standards applied to the duties of a fiduciary have led to a large number of lawsuits involving real estate brokers and their clients.

Consequences of breach of fiduciary duties.

Consequences to an agent for breach of his or her fiduciary duties may include: loss of the commission, liability for civil damages and/or disciplinary action by the Real Estate Commissioner. If the agent's breach of his or her fiduciary duties to the principal results in any monetary damages suffered by the principal, the principal may hold the agent liable for those damages. Even if there are **no damages** suffered by the principal, a court may hold that the agent is not entitled to compensation and may allow the principal to recover any commission which has already been paid. Further, the Real Estate Law requires real estate licensees to follow their fiduciary obligations, and breach of an agent's fiduciary duty may lead to disciplinary action by the Commissioner even in cases where the client has suffered no apparent financial damages and has made no complaint.

For example, a licensee may be subject to disciplinary action for failing to advise the seller that the licensee or some member of the licensee's family or business associate of the licensee is the buyer, even though the full listing price is paid, the seller is satisfied with the sales price and the seller makes no complaint to the Commissioner. In one California case, a broker's license was suspended even though his principal was apparently satisfied with the whole transaction.

In that case, the broker arranged to sell the property to his sister without disclosing to the seller that the buyer would be the broker's sister. The transaction was closed and the seller received the agreed upon price.

Disciplinary action was commenced against the broker for failing to disclose to the seller that the buyer was a close relative of the broker. Following a hearing, the broker's license was suspended even though the seller had made no complaint and had apparently suffered no injury. To the contrary, the seller seemed to be perfectly satisfied with the agent's performance even after being informed that the property had been sold to the agent's sister without prior disclosure. The seller testified later that he had received his full asking price and that he did not care whether the property was sold to the broker's sister or wife since he had gotten what he wanted for the property.

Notwithstanding the principal's satisfaction with the transaction and even though the broker's actions did not amount to fraud under the common law, they were a violation of the broker's fiduciary duties to the principal and constituted fraud and dishonest dealing under the real estate license law. As such, the broker was properly subjected to disciplinary action. The Real Estate Law exists to protect the public by requiring certain standards and conduct on the part of real estate licensees. Failure to meet those standards may result in disciplinary action (with the intent of protecting the public), even though the particular principals or customers involved in the transaction may not have suffered any damages and may have been satisfied with the agent's performance.

Fiduciary Duties

The nature of an agent's fiduciary obligations in general require the agent to represent and serve the best interests of the principal. Some specific duties include the duty to exercise reasonable skill and care in performing the agency, to properly account for client funds, and to make a full disclosure to the principal of all material facts.

Reasonable care and skill.

A real estate agent must exercise reasonable care and skill in acting for the principal and may be held liable to the principal for any damages suffered as a result of the agent's negligence or failure to act in a timely and diligent fashion. In addition to the civil liability for damages, negligence or incompetence while acting as a licensee is grounds for license suspension or revocation under the Real Estate Law. Most listing agreement forms contain an express agreement by the broker to exercise due diligence in attempting to find a buyer. For an example, see the California REALTORS® exclusive right to sell listing form in the listing agreement materials (page 63).

Because real estate brokers are professionals who hold themselves out as having particular knowledge and expertise in real estate matters, they are held to a higher standard of competence and knowledge than would be expected of ordinary buyers and sellers without special training or experience in real estate. This means that in deciding whether or not a real estate agent is negligent or has failed to act in a reasonably diligent and careful manner, the court compares the agent's behavior and knowledge to that which would be expected of a reasonably competent real estate professional, not what would be expected of the average citizen. Although a real estate broker or salesperson would probably be held liable for negligence in giving incorrect legal advice or negligently preparing a deposit receipt or other document, most of the cases in this area have concerned negligence in advising the principal as to the value of property, the condition of title or the financial ability of the buyer.

A real estate broker may be held responsible for giving the seller an incorrect opinion as to the value of the seller's property or of property to be received in exchange, if that inaccurate opinion causes the seller some monetary damage, and if a reasonably competent real estate professional would have rendered a more accurate opinion of value which would not have resulted in the owner losing any money. This is particularly true if the broker makes any express representations that he or she can give the owner a professional opinion of value.

In one case, real estate agents were sued for giving the sellers incorrect advice as to the value of their home and the length of time it would take to sell it. The sellers contacted the agent and told her that they were interested in selling their home and buying another. They indicated that their decision to buy another house would be dependent upon how much they could get for their current home and that they really did not know much about real estate values. The sellers wanted to know the minimum that they could expect to get for their property.

The agent told the sellers that she had the experience and professional expertise to be able to tell them what they could expect to sell their home for and how long it would take to sell it. She inspected the home and told them that she thought the home should be listed for $168,000 and that they could expect to sell it very quickly for between $162,000 and $163,000.

Based on the agent's advice, the sellers entered an agreement to buy another house and then listed their home for a price of $167,500 with the firm which had given them the opinion of value. Unfortunately their home failed to sell during the three month listing. The inability of the sellers to obtain cash from the sale of their home resulted in their being forced to sell their new home at a substantial loss.

In the subsequent lawsuit against the real estate broker and salesperson, independent appraisals indicated the property was worth about $20,000 less than the opinions given by the real estate agents. In finding liability for negligence on the part of the real estate agents, the court stated that anyone who undertook to perform a task, such as giving a professional opinion would be required to perform that task with reasonable skill and competence. In this particular case, the broker and salesperson had made repeated statements that they had the professional expertise necessary to give the sellers an accurate opinion of value. They had also given the sellers a pamphlet which contained a list of reasons they should employ a real estate agent. One of the reasons listed was that professional real estate agents knew market value and could ensure that the property would be priced right to sell quickly for full value.

In other cases, brokers have been held liable for negligent advice regarding the value of exchange property or property being offered as collateral, or the income from income property, and for negligently recommending that the principal sell the property to a buyer financially unable to complete the purchase. Brokers have also been held liable for incorrect advice concerning the existence of encumbrances, or the impact on value of an easement, and for failing to advise the buyer to obtain a title search after incorrectly telling the buyer that there was only one encumbrance when there were, in fact, two trust deeds on the property.

In questionable situations where the broker or salesperson feels that he or she does not have the information or expertise to give accurate advice, as may sometimes arise in title matters or questions regarding taxes or law, it is best to recommend that the party or parties obtain the advice of an attorney or other expert. In one case where the broker was sued for failing to advise the client as to the income tax consequences of a particular transaction, the broker was held not liable in part because he had advised the client to seek professional counsel regarding the tax question.

Due diligence and the listing agreement. If a broker fails to act in a diligent manner in representing the principal, the principal has grounds for revoking an exclusive agency or exclusive right to sell listing agreement. Failure of the broker to act diligently constitutes failure to perform under the contract and gives the other party, the principal, the right to terminate the listing without liability for the commission. Determination of whether the agent has acted with due diligence is a question of fact to be decided based on the circumstances of the particular case. If the broker has acted with proper diligence in attempting to find a buyer, revocation of an exclusive listing agreement containing a withdrawal from sale clause prior to the termination date of the listing would entitle the broker to the commission even if a buyer had not yet been found (see the listing agreement materials).

Proper accounting for client funds.

A real estate broker must account for and maintain accurate records of all funds received on behalf of a principal and may not convert those funds to his or her use or commingle them with the broker's own funds. California real estate license law requires real estate licensees to place fiduciary funds (such as the deposit accompanying an offer to buy) in a neutral escrow, trust account or in the hands of one of the principals no later than the end of the next banking day after receipt.

Disclosure of all material facts.

A real estate broker or salesperson must make a full and complete disclosure to his or her principal of any and all facts material to the transaction. A material fact is anything which might affect the principal's decision, in the usual real estate transaction, anything which might have affected the seller's decision to sell on the price and terms involved (or, if the buyer is the principal, any fact which might have influenced the buyer's decision to buy on the price and terms involved). An agent must disclose to the principal any material fact which is in the agent's knowledge. A material fact, as defined in the Restatement of Agency and quoted in several California court decisions, "is one which the agent should realize would be likely to affect the judgment of the principal in giving his consent . . . or is likely to have a bearing upon the desirability of the transaction from the standpoint of the principal." Examples of material facts which would have to be disclosed to the principal would include: all offers to buy the property; information relating to the value of the property, including how to increase the market value or marketability of the property; the buyer's financial status; the agent's role as a buyer; and any dual agency.

Offers. Any offer to buy the property must be presented to the seller, regardless of whether the offer conforms to the terms set out in the listing agreement or whether the agent believes that the offer is a good one. A California licensee is under an obligation to continue presenting any bona fide offers to the seller even after the seller has accepted an offer, if the offer is received prior to closing. According to the California Code of Ethics and Professional Responsibility, it is unlawful for a listing broker to fail to present or to cause to be presented to the owner any offer which is received **prior to closing**, unless the broker has been instructed by the owner not to present such an offer, or unless the offer is patently frivolous. Failure of the agent to advise the principal of an offer is considered to be the same as representing that no offers have been received.

Value and marketability. Advice concerning the market value of the property, the best price obtainable in the current market and, in the appropriate case, how to increase the marketability of the property or the best obtainable price, is probably one of the main reasons that sellers employ real estate brokers and is one of the most important professional services offered by brokers. Accordingly, real estate agents must disclose to the principal any information regarding the value of the property or steps or actions which could be taken to improve the market value or marketability of the property, such as repairs, improvements, subdivision, or other development. For example, if there are some cosmetic repairs or maintenance which could be performed at relatively low cost and which would significantly increase the value of the property or its appeal to the average buyer, the agent should so inform the owner. If a higher price can be obtained by subdividing the property and selling it in separate parcels, the owner should be so advised.

The broker's advice may or may not be followed by the owner. The owner may be aware, either as a result of the agent's advice or otherwise, that the property would be more attractive if the exterior were repainted or that more money could be obtained by dividing it into lots and selling the lots individually, but may not have the money, the time or the inclination to do the necessary work. Whether or not the owner decides to take action based on the broker's advice, it is important for the broker to make a full disclosure of any actions which could be taken to increase the value or marketability of the property. This is especially important if the agent intends to buy the property for him or herself. An agent who buys the principal's property, performs some repairs or additions, without having previously advised the principal of the effect of those actions, and quickly resells the property at a substantial profit may be found to have breached his or her fiduciary duties to the principal and to be liable in the amount of any profit realized. See the discussion below on self dealing and secret profits.

Buyer's financial status. Any information obtained by the seller's agent concerning the buyer's financial status and financial ability to complete the purchase would be considered material information and should be disclosed to the seller. It is common practice for real estate agents to interview prospective purchasers regarding their available cash and other assets, monthly income and monthly obligations in order to arrive at an estimate of the type and amount of loan(s) for which the buyers could qualify and, consequently, the general price range of homes they could afford. This process is often called "prequalifying" the buyer, in reference to the loan qualifying procedure employed by lending institutions in considering loan applications.

This information bearing on the amount of downpayment and monthly house payment the buyer could afford would of course be of importance to the seller in deciding whether or not to accept an offer. If it appears that the buyer would have little difficulty qualifying for a loan, the seller would probably be more likely to accept a low offer. The seller would usually be less favorably inclined to accept an offer and take the home off the market or reduce its marketability if the offer were from a buyer who appeared to have a marginal chance of obtaining the necessary financing to buy the house. In transactions in which seller financing is contemplated (as opposed to financing from lending institutions), the seller might be even more interested in whether the buyer has the available cash to make the downpayment called for in the deposit receipt and the income to make the monthly payments required under the contemplated purchase money note and trust deed.

In a recent case from Wisconsin, the court held that a broker and salesperson (the salesperson was also the buyer), were required to give the seller information regarding the agent/buyer's financial ability even if the seller said it was not necessary. In that case, a salesperson working for the listing broker wanted to buy the property for himself. At the time of presenting the offer, the salesman disclosed to the seller that he was buying the property for his own account and offered to provide the seller with financial information. The seller declined the offer of information, saying, in effect, that he knew the broker and the fact that the salesman was working for the broker was good enough for him.

Unfortunately, the seller's optimistic trust in the salesman's financial status was unfounded. The salesman had made about $10,000 the year of the sale and expected to make about the same the next year. The purchase money financing required payments of $325 per month during the first year and $625 per month in subsequent years. The salesman defaulted after about ten months and the seller foreclosed. The seller later sued the broker, the listing agent and the selling agent/buyer to recover the commission and the costs of foreclosure and resale.

At trial and on appeal, it was held that the agents had a duty to disclose the information regarding the buyer's income. The information concerning the buyer's financial ability was obviously material and would have affected the owner's decision to sell and it was within the knowledge of the broker and sales agent (judgment against the listing agent was reversed by the appeals court, apparently on the theory that he did not know the other salesman's income). It was not enough to offer to disclose the financial information, the agents had to actually give it to the seller even if the seller said that disclosure was not necessary.

Self dealing. If the agent acquires an interest in the property, either directly or indirectly through another entity or person, it must be disclosed. The agent would be required to disclose if he or she were acquiring the property, if a member of the agent's family were buying the property, or if a business entity in which the agent was a partner, shareholder or other participant, were acquiring the property. A broker or salesperson should disclose to the seller any relationship he or she has with a partnership or corporation buying the property, even if only as a limited partner or minority shareholder. The disclosure made to the seller must be full and complete so that the seller understands the true state of affairs and the economic reality of the transaction.

For example, in one case the broker told the seller that he was the president of the corporation buying the property. However, he did not tell the seller that he and his wife were the only two shareholders in the corporation and that they had paid the purchase price out of their own pocket. The agent had, in effect, misled the seller into believing that a corporation in which the broker held an interest was buying the property when, in fact, the broker was dealing for his own account and being paid a commission at the same time. The court considered the broker's disclosure to be inadequate.

It is, of course, permitted for an agent to purchase listed property for his or her own account, provided that a full disclosure of all material facts is made. Under the applicable law, it is presumed that in any transaction where the agent buys the principal's property, the principal has entered the agreement without sufficient consideration and under undue influence. In any subsequent dispute, then, the agent will be required to present proof that the transaction was fair and that a full disclosure was made. A real estate broker or salesperson who purchases the principal's property should take care to document the disclosures. This can be done by putting all disclosures in a letter, or other writing, to the principal and retaining a copy. It should be noted that in any case where an agent buys the principal's property and resells it a short time later at a substantial profit, it is likely to be extremely difficult for the agent to convince a judge and/or jury that a full disclosure was made of all material facts. See the following discussion of secret profits.

Secret profits. Controversies and lawsuits arising out of transactions involving self dealing by real estate agents often include allegations of secret profits. A real estate licensee, while acting as an agent, is not allowed to receive any benefit from the transactions other than the agreed upon commission or other compensation, without the prior knowledge and consent of the principal. Any profit or financial benefit obtained by the agent as a consequence of the agency which has not been authorized by the principal is a secret profit. The agent is liable to the principal for any secret profit, regardless of whether the transaction was otherwise fair. Although there are endless variations, the most common examples of secret profits involve self dealing. The agent directly or indirectly acquires the property and then markets it for a substantial profit. In these cases the agent has used his or her superior knowledge regarding real estate for his or her own profit rather than for the principal's profit. This is a breach of the duty of loyalty and utmost good faith to the principal.

If the agent intends to acquire the property and to market it for profit, the seller should be fully advised of any profit the agent expects to receive and how that profit is to be achieved. For example, if the agent is of the opinion that some minor repairs or alterations would substantially increase the market value of the property, the agent would be obliged to advise the seller of that at the time the offer is made. Similarly, if the agent feels that the property would be worth substantially more if subdivided, and if the agent intends to subdivide and develop the property, the seller should be so informed.

Anyone in the real estate profession should rid him or herself of the false impression that a real estate license is a great opportunity to learn about and to buy underpriced property to his or her own profit and gain. It should be clearly understood that, in essence, the legal standard requires the broker to do everything possible and to render the seller any advice or knowledge the broker has which would result in the seller's obtaining the best possible price. It is not proper for the agent to use his or her special knowledge and expertise for his or her own profit at the expense of the principal. If the property is undervalued or if steps could be taken to increase its market value, the agent should advise the seller.

Under the law, all benefits acquired by an agent in the course of performing the agency are deemed to have been obtained by the agent for the principal, except for the agent's agreed upon compensation. Therefore, an agent will be required to pay over to the principal any profit or other benefit derived from the transaction unless the agent can prove that the nature and amount of the expected profit was fully disclosed to the principal **before** the principal made the decision to enter the transaction. The fact that the transaction was fair or that the principal received exactly the asking price (or, if the principal is the buyer, that he or she paid no more than was intended) or that the principal was not damaged is not relevant; if a full disclosure is not made, the agent is liable to the principal for the entire profit received.

Under California law, an agent may be held liable to the principal not only for profits received by the agent but also for secret profits received by a third party. Similarly, under the California Real Estate Law, a licensee may be required to disgorge secret profits even in a transaction where the licensee is not acting as an agent. In one case, a real estate broker misrepresented to a prospective buyer that he had an exclusive listing on a particular piece of property. The property was, in fact, listed with another broker. The prospective buyer was induced to make an offer for the property at a price of $5,000 per acre. Instead of presenting this offer to the seller or listing broker, the broker arranged to buy the property for $4,000 per acre and resell it to the buyer for $5,000 per acre, pocketing a profit of $1,000 per acre or a total of a little over $72,000. Even though the court agreed that the broker was not acting as agent for either the buyer or seller in this transaction and even though there was no evidence to suggest the property was not worth $5,000 per acre, the broker was held to be liable to the buyer for the $1,000 per acre secret profit. This liability was based primarily on the Real Estate License Law requirement that real estate licensees treat members of the public honestly and fairly. In this case, the broker had acted dishonestly by falsely informing the buyer that he had a listing on the property, failing to convey the buyer's offer to the seller, and deceiving both buyer and seller as to his role as principal (buyer/seller) in the transaction. The broker was required to pay over to the buyer the approximately $72,000 profit even though there was no indication that the buyer had any monetary damages since there was no proof that the property was worth less than the $5,000 per acre that the buyer paid for it.

In addition to liability to the principal for the amount of the profit, the agent may lose the right to compensation and may be subject to discipline by the Real Estate Commissioner, as it is a violation of the Real Estate Law for a licensee to take an undisclosed profit.

Dual agency. Any time a broker acts as agent for more than one party in a transaction, a full disclosure must be made to all parties. Failure to do so is a violation of the Real Estate Law and may subject the licensee to disciplinary action by the Commissioner. Similarly, a full disclosure must be made in any case where the agent has an interest which is adverse to that of the principal or where it may appear that the agent has an adverse interest which may interfere with the agent's duty of undivided loyalty to the principal. In this regard, any family or business connection between the agent and the buyer should be disclosed.

It is not always completely clear whose agent the broker is. In most cases, the broker's commission is paid by the seller and, absent other factors, payment of the commission is an indication that the broker is the agent of the person paying the commission. In some transactions the broker may be retained under a formal employment agreement with the buyer. Even in transactions where the broker is employed under a listing agreement with the seller and acting as agent for the seller, the broker may be considered the agent of the buyer for some purposes. For example, if the broker assumes the role of assisting the buyer in obtaining financing the broker may be the buyer's agent for that purpose; the broker may be considered the buyer's agent for the purpose of transmitting an offer or counteroffer or escrow instructions; or the broker who assumes to advise the buyer regarding exceptions on a title report may be considered the buyer's agent for that purpose. This type of situation in which the broker may be treated as the seller's agent for one purpose and the buyer's agent for another purpose is often a source of confusion and may result in disputes and unintentional breaches of fiduciary duties.

An agent should be cautious of situations where it may appear that he or she has undertaken to represent both the buyer and the seller without making a full disclosure to both parties. Such situations frequently arise in multiple listings and in transactions involving offers and counter-offers. A multiple listing agreement normally authorizes the listing broker to cooperate with other brokers within the multiple listing service to market the seller's property, and authorizes those cooperating brokers to act as subagents in the efforts to procure a buyer. The effect of this express authorization is that the cooperating brokers are subagents of the seller owing the customary fiduciary duties to the seller as principal. If a cooperating broker undertakes to locate and show property to a prospective buyer, he or she may be regarded as the buyer's agent, owing fiduciary duties to the buyer, and at the same time, the subagent of the seller, owing fiduciary duties to the seller. Listing and cooperating agents should be aware of the potential for breaches of fiduciary duties owed to one or both of the principals that exist in these subagency relationships. Care should be taken to ensure that all principals are fully advised of the agent's position and activities with respect to representing or acting on behalf of the buyer and/or seller.

In addition to being subject to disciplinary action by the Commissioner, an agent who fails to make a full disclosure of a dual agency relationship may also lose the right to the commission and may be held liable for any monetary damages suffered by the principal. Further, if there is an undisclosed dual agency, a principal who is unaware of the undisclosed dual agency may be permitted to rescind the purchase and sale agreement.

To avoid some of the confusion regarding who is representing whom, California statutes require real estate agents to give an agency disclosure form to buyers and sellers in residential transactions. A listing agent is to give the seller the disclosure form prior to entering into the listing agreement. A selling agent is to give the seller the form prior to presenting the seller with an offer to purchase. A selling agent is to provide the buyer with the form as soon as practicable prior to execution of the buyer's offer to purchase. An example of such a disclosure form is shown on the following pages.

Agent's Duties to Buyer

A real estate agent's duties to the buyer may arise out of an express or implied agency relationship with the buyer, out of the general obliga-

DISCLOSURE REGARDING REAL ESTATE AGENCY RELATIONSHIPS

(As required by the Civil Code)

CALIFORNIA ASSOCIATION OF REALTORS® (CAR) STANDARD FORM

When you enter into a discussion with a real estate agent regarding a real estate transaction, you should from the outset understand what type of agency relationship or representation you wish to have with the agent in the transaction.

SELLER'S AGENT

A Seller's agent under a listing agreement with Seller acts as the agent for the Seller only. A Seller's agent or a subagent of that agent has the following affirmative obligations:

To the Seller:

(a) A Fiduciary duty of utmost care, integrity, honesty, and loyalty in dealings with the Seller.

To the Buyer & the Seller:

(a) Diligent exercise of reasonable skill and care in performance of the agent's duties.
(b) A duty of honest and fair dealing and good faith.
(c) A duty to disclose all facts known to the agent materially affecting the value or desirability of property that are not known to, or within the diligent attention and observation of, the parties.

An agent is not obligated to reveal to either party any confidential information obtained from the other party which does not involve the affirmative duties set forth above.

BUYER'S AGENT

A selling agent can, with a Buyer's consent, agree to act as agent for the Buyer only. In these situations, the agent is not the Seller's agent, even if by agreement the agent may receive compensation for services rendered, either in full or in part from the Seller. An agent acting only for a Buyer has the following affirmative obligations.

To the Buyer:

(a) A fiduciary duty of utmost care, integrity, honesty, and loyalty in dealings with the Buyer.

To the Buyer & Seller:

(a) Diligent exercise of reasonable skill and care in performance of the agent's duties.
(b) A duty of honest and fair dealing and good faith.
(c) A duty to disclose all facts known to the agent materially affecting the value or desirability of the property that are not known to, or within the diligent attention and observation of, the parties.

An agent is not obligated to reveal to either party any confidential information obtained from the other party which does not involve the affirmative duties set forth above.

AGENT REPRESENTING BOTH SELLER & BUYER

A real estate agent, either acting directly or through one or more associate licensees, can legally be the agent of both the Seller and the Buyer in a transaction, but only with the knowledge and consent of both the Seller and the Buyer.

In a dual agency situation, the agent has the following affirmative obligations to both the Seller and the Buyer:

(a) A fiduciary duty of utmost care, integrity, honesty and loyalty in the dealings with either Seller or the Buyer.
(b) Other duties to the Seller and the Buyer as stated above in their respective sections.

In representing both Seller and Buyer, the agent may not, without the express permission of the respective party, disclose to the other party that the Seller will accept a price less than the listing price or that the Buyer will pay a price greater than the price offered.

The above duties of the agent in a real estate transaction do not relieve a Seller or a Buyer from the responsibility to protect their own interests. You should carefully read all agreements to assure that they adequately express your understanding of the transaction. A real estate agent is a person qualified to advise about real estate. If legal or tax advice is desired, consult a competent professional.

Throughout your real property transaction you may receive more than one disclosure form, depending upon the number of agents assisting in the transaction. The law requires each agent with whom you have more than a casual relationship to present you with this disclosure form. You should read its contents each time it is presented to you, considering the relationship between you and the real estate agent in your specific transaction.

This disclosure form includes the provisions of article 2.5 (commencing with Section 2373) of Chapter 2 of Title 9 of Part 4 of Division 3 of the Civil Code set forth on the reverse hereof. Read it carefully.

I/WE ACKNOWLEDGE RECEIPT OF A COPY OF THIS DISCLOSURE.

BUYER/SELLER____________________ Date____________ TIME________ AM/PM

BUYER/SELLER____________________ Date____________ TIME________ AM/PM

AGENT ________________ (Please Print) By________________ (Associate Licensee or Broker-Signature) Date____________

A REAL ESTATE BROKER IS QUALIFIED TO ADVISE ON REAL ESTATE. IF YOU DESIRE LEGAL ADVICE, CONSULT YOUR ATTORNEY.

FORM AD-11

OFFICE USE ONLY
Reviewed by Broker or Designee ________
Date __________

EQUAL HOUSING OPPORTUNITY

SF-Oct-87

CHAPTER 2 OF TITLE 9 OF PART 4 OF DIVISION 3 OF THE CIVIL CODE

Article 2.5. Agency Relationships in Residential Real Property Transactions

2373. As used in this article, the following terms have the following meanings:

(a) "Agent" means a person acting under provisions of this title in a real property transaction, and includes a person who is licensed as a real estate broker under Chapter 3 (commencing with Section 10130) of Part 1 of Division 4 of the Business & Professions Code, and under whose license a listing is executed or an offer to purchase is obtained.

(b) "Associate licensee" means a person who is licensed as a real estate broker or salesperson under Chapter 3 (commencing with Section 10130) of Part 1 of Division 4 of the Business & Professions Code and who is either licensed under a broker or has entered into a written contract with a broker to act as the broker's agent in connection with acts requiring a real estate license and to function under the broker's supervision in the capacity of an associate licensee.

The agent in the real property transaction bears responsibility for his or her associate licensees who perform as agents of the agent. When an associate licensee owes a duty to any principal, or to any buyer or seller who is not a principal, in a real property transaction, that duty is equivalent to the duty owed to that party by the broker for whom the associate licensee functions.

(c) "Buyer" means a transferee in a real property transaction, and includes a person who executes an offer to purchase real property from a seller through an agent, or who seeks the services of an agent in more than a casual, transitory, or preliminary manner, with the object of entering into a real property transaction. "Buyer" includes vendee or lessee.

(d) "Dual agent" means an agent acting, either directly or through an associate licensee, as agent for both the seller and the buyer in a real property transaction.

(e) "Listing agreement" means a contract between an owner of real property and an agent, by which the agent has been authorized to sell the real property or to find or obtain a buyer.

(f) "Listing agent" means a person who has obtained a listing of real property to act as an agent for compensation.

(g) "Listing price" is the amount expressed in dollars specified in the listing for which the seller is willing to sell the real property through the listing agent.

(h) "Offering price" is the amount expressed in dollars specified in an offer to purchase for which the buyer is willing to buy the real property.

(i) "Offer to purchase" means a written contract executed by a buyer acting through a selling agent which becomes the contract for the sale of the real property upon acceptance by the seller.

(j) "Real property" means any estate specified by subdivision (1) or (2) of Section 761 in property which constitutes or is improved with one to four dwelling units, any leasehold in this type of property exceeding one year's duration, and mobilehomes, when offered for sale or sold through an agent pursuant to the authority contained in Section 10131.6 of the Business & Professions Code.

(k) "Real property transaction" means a transaction for the sale of real property in which an agent is employed by one or more of the principals to act in that transaction, and includes a listing or an offer to purchase.

(l) "Sell," "sale," or "sold" refers to a transaction for the transfer of real property from the seller to the buyer, and includes exchanges of real property between the seller and buyer, transactions for the creation of a real property sales contract within the meaning of Section 2985, and transactions for the creation of a leasehold exceeding one year's duration.

(m) "Seller" means the transferor in a real property transaction, and includes an owner who lists real property with an agent, whether or not a transfer results, or who receives an offer to purchase real property of which he or she is the owner from an agent on behalf of another. "Seller" includes both a vendor and a lessor.

(n) "Selling agent" means a listing agent who acts alone, or an agent who acts in cooperation with a listing agent, and who sells or finds and obtains a buyer for the real property, or an agent who locates property for a buyer for the property for which no listing exists and presents an offer to purchase to the seller.

(o) "Subagent" means a person to whom an agent delegates agency powers as provided in Article 5 (commencing with Section 2349) of Chapter I. However, "subagent" does not include an associate licensee who is acting under the supervision of an agent in a real property transaction.

2374. Listing agents and selling agents shall provide the seller and buyer in a real property transaction with a copy of the disclosure form specified in Section 2375, and, except as provided in subdivision (c), shall obtain a signed acknowledgement of receipt from that seller or buyer, except as provided in this section of Section 2374.5, as follows:

(a) The listing agent, if any, shall provide the disclosure form to the seller prior to entering into the listing agreement.

(b) The selling agent shall provide the disclosure form to the seller as soon as practicable prior to presenting the seller with an offer to purchase, unless the selling agent previously provided the seller with a copy of the disclosure form pursuant to subdivision (a).

(c) Where the selling agent does not deal on a face-to-face basis with the seller, the disclosure form prepared by the selling agent may be furnished to the seller (and acknowledgement of receipt obtained for the selling agent from the seller) by the listing agent, or the selling agent may deliver the disclosure form by certified mail addressed to the seller at his or her last known address, in which case no signed acknowledgement of receipt is required.

(d) The selling agent shall provide the disclosure form to the buyer as soon as practicable prior to execution of the buyer's offer to purchase, except that if the offer to purchase is not prepared by the selling agent, the selling agent shall present the disclosure form to the buyer not later than the next business day after the selling agent receives the offer to purchase from the buyer.

2374.5 In any circumstance in which the seller or buyer refuses to sign an acknowledgement of receipt pursuant to Section 2374, the agent, or an associate licensee acting for an agent, shall set forth, sign and date a written declaration of the facts of the refusal.

2375.5 (a) As soon as practicable, the selling agent shall disclose to the buyer and seller whether the selling agent is acting in the real property transaction exclusively as the buyer's agent, exclusively as the seller's agent, or as a dual agent representing both the buyer and the seller and this relationship shall be confirmed in the contract to purchase and sell real property or in a separate writing executed or acknowledged by the seller, the buyer, and the selling agent prior to or coincident with execution of that contract by the buyer and the seller, respectively.

(b) As soon as practicable, the listing agent shall disclose to the seller whether the listing agent is acting in the real property transaction exclusively as the seller's agent, or as a dual agent representing both the buyer and seller and this relationship shall be confirmed in the contract to purchase and sell real property or in a separate writing executed or acknowledged by the seller and the listing agent prior to or coincident with the execution of that contract by the seller.

(c) The confirmation required by subdivisions (a) and (b) shall be in the following form.

______________________________ is the agent of (check one):
(Name of Listing Agent)

[ ] the seller exclusively; or
[ ] both the buyer and seller.

______________________________ is the agent of (check one):
(Name of Selling Agent if not the same as the Listing Agent)

[ ] the buyer exclusively; or
[ ] the seller exclusively; or
[ ] both the buyer and seller.

(d) The disclosures and confirmation required by this section shall be in addition to the disclosure required by Section 2374.

2376. No selling agent in a real property transaction may act as an agent for the buyer only, when the selling agent is also acting as the listing agent in the transaction.

2377. The payment of compensation or the obligation to pay compensation to an agent by the seller or buyer is not necessarily determinative of a particular agency relationship between an agent and the seller or buyer. A listing agent and a selling agent may agree to share any compensation or commission paid, or any right to any compensation or commission for which an obligation arises as the result of a real estate transaction, and the terms of any such agreement shall not necessarily be determinative of a particular relationship.

2378. Nothing in this article prevents an agent from selecting, as a condition of the agent's employment, a specific form of agency relationship not specifically prohibited by this article if the requirements of Section 2374 and Section 2375.5 are complied with.

2379. A dual agent shall not disclose to the buyer that the seller is willing to sell the property at a price less than the listing price, without the express written consent of the seller. A dual agent shall not disclose to the seller that the buyer is willing to pay a price greater than the offering price, without the express written consent of the buyer.

This section does not alter in any way the duty or responsibility of a dual agent to any principal with respect to confidential information other than price.

2380. Nothing in this article precludes a listing agent from also being a selling agent, and the combination of these functions in one agent does not, of itself, make that agent a dual agent.

2381. A contract between the principal and agent may be modified or altered to change the agency relationship at any time before the performance of the act which is the object of the agency with the written consent of the parties to the agency relationship.

2382. Nothing in this article shall be construed to either diminish the duty of disclosure owed buyers and sellers by agents and their associate licensees, subagents, and employees or to relieve agents and their associate licensees, subagents, and employees from liability for their conduct in connection with acts governed by this article or for any breach of a fiduciary duty or a duty of disclosure.

tions of a real estate licensee to deal fairly and honestly, or out of specific common law or statutory requirements to make certain disclosures to prospective buyers.

Buyer agency.

A broker may enter a written exclusive agency agreement with the buyer in which the broker agrees to represent the buyer in attempting to find property of the nature and price sought by the buyer. Under a buyer listing agreement the buyer may agree to compensate the broker if the broker is successful or, in some contracts, may agree to pay the broker on an hourly or other basis even if the buyer does not ultimately purchase any property located through the broker's efforts (see the discussion on representing the buyer in Chapter 3). In transactions of this type where the broker acts as the buyer's agent under an express agreement, the broker owes the normal fiduciary duties to the buyer which have been discussed above in the coverage of fiduciary duties to the seller: to act in a competent and diligent manner, to disclose to the buyer all material information, and to loyally represent and further the buyer's best interests.

In general, the broker's objectives in representing the buyer would be the opposite of those in representing the seller. Instead of giving the seller advice and negotiating on the seller's behalf to best market the property for the highest obtainable price and on the best terms for the seller, the broker would employ his or her skill, professional knowledge, expertise and negotiating abilities in an effort to obtain the desired property for the buyer at the **lowest** price and best terms for the buyer.

Disclosure requirements to buyer.

Even in transactions where there is no express agreement to represent or to act on the buyer's behalf and there is, instead, an express written agreement to represent and act on behalf of the seller, circumstances frequently arise in which the real estate agent has important duties to the buyer as well as to the seller. As was noted above in the Dual Agency section, any time an agent undertakes to perform some action on the buyer's behalf, such as assisting the buyer in obtaining financing, or any time the particular facts of the transaction would support an inference that a relationship of trust and confidence had developed between the buyer and broker or salesperson, the law may hold that the agent owes fiduciary duties to the buyer at least to the extent of carrying out the particular function or task involved.

Even in transactions where no express or implied agency or fiduciary relationship exists between the licensee and the buyer, there are obligations owed to the buyer, both statutory and common law (based on court decisions). Under the Real Estate Law, a broker or salesperson is subject to discipline for any action which would constitute fraud or dishonest dealing, whether or not an agency or fiduciary relationship exists between the licensee and the other party, whether or not the other party has suffered any damages and whether or not the licensee's actions or omissions would amount to fraud under general civil law.

Most problems and disputes which arise are based on the broker's failure to make necessary disclosures to the buyer. In some cases, the broker's position as seller's agent imposes on the broker the obligation to make disclosures which are required of the seller. For example, in sales of one- to four-unit residential property, the seller and the seller's agent are required to provide the buyer with a written disclosure form, called a Real Estate Transfer Disclosure Statement, setting out representations of the seller concerning the condition of the property and the results of the agent's inspection of the property. A sample of the form is shown in Chapter 4. If the transaction includes seller financing, the broker is required to make certain disclosures to both the buyer and seller (see Chapter 9 for details of the disclosure requirements).

The most common omission leading to legal liability is failure to make proper disclosure(s) regarding the physical condition or other characteristics of the property. Occasionally, though, a broker or salesperson is held liable for failure to make some other sort of disclosure, such as a secret profit. For example, in one case (discussed above in the section on secret profits) a broker was required to disgorge to the buyer a profit of $1,000 per acre made by the broker because the broker had concealed his true position as principal in the transaction. This liability was imposed even though the court specifically found that the broker was not an agent of the buyer or seller, did not owe fiduciary duties to the buyer and was dealing at arms length with the buyer in the transaction.

Physical condition or other characteristics of the property.

California court decisions and statutes provide California buyers with greater protection and impose greater disclosure burdens on licensees than is true in most other states. Under the Real Estate Law, it is unlawful conduct for a licensee to fail to disclose to a prospective buyer or lessee any facts known to the licensee which materially affect the value or desirability of the property, when the licensee has reason to believe that such facts are not known to or readily discoverable by the buyer or lessee. This regulation essentially sets out the common law rule created by a line of California court decisions prior to 1984.

Under the regulation and case law, a licensee was required to disclose any facts that materially affected the value or desirability of the property, if the facts were known to the licensee and not readily discoverable by the buyer. The agent was not required to inspect the property (although see discussion below for the change in this rule) or to disclose defects which were readily observable by the buyer, such as broken windows. Examples of facts which California courts have ruled materially affect value or desirability, and therefore must be disclosed, include: that a home was constructed on filled land; that improvements had been made in violation of building codes; that a building was termite infested; and the correct net income for a piece of income property.

In one case, the court even held that if it could be shown that the property's history had a significant impact on market value, then that history had to be disclosed to the buyer. In that case, a mother and her four children had been murdered in the house ten years before it was sold to the buyer. The owner and the real estate agent were aware of the murder but did not mention it to the buyer. The owner, in fact, asked neighbors to keep the matter quiet. Nonetheless, one of the neighbors told the story to the buyer shortly after she bought the property. She then sued the broker for failing to disclose a fact which materially affected the value of the property. The buyer claimed she paid more for the property than she or anyone else would have paid had they known the gruesome history of the house. The court held that if the buyer could show the murders really did affect the market value then she had a right to recover from the broker.

Partly in response to that decision, and partly in response to the AIDS crisis, in 1986 the California legislature passed a law limiting the duty to disclose information about deaths on a property. Under this statute, a seller or a real estate agent cannot be sued for failing to disclose to a buyer that the property was occupied by someone who had AIDS or died from AIDS. The statute also provides that if someone died on the property more than three years earlier—from any cause—neither the seller nor the agent can be held liable for failing to tell the buyer about the death.

The basic obligation to disclose defects or other facts known to the agent was expanded by the results of *Easton v. Strassburger,* a lawsuit decided in 1984 and by a statute later passed by the legislature in response to the court decision. Now the agent is not only required to disclose information known to the agent but also to conduct an inspection in order to discover material facts for the buyer, if the property is one- to four-unit residential property.

The facts of the *Easton* case are, briefly, as follows: In 1976, a broker took a listing to sell property which included a 3,000 square foot home, a guest house and one acre of land. The home had been built on improperly compacted fill. The sellers had experienced two earth slides while they owned the property, but did not inform the listing broker or the buyer of the prior soil problems. Two agents with the listing broker inspected the property. Evidence indicated that one or both of them knew the house was built on fill, saw netting on a slope which had been placed there following a slide, and saw that the floor in the guest house was not level. In short, there were indications of problems associated with soil slippage and settling, termed "red flags" by the court. Despite these "red flags," neither of the agents ordered soil tests, conducted any more extensive investigation or mentioned anything to the buyer.

The buyer purchased the property for $170,000 without knowledge of the soil slippage problems. After she took possession, there were additional large slides and the buyer suffered substantial damages. Later appraisals indicated the property might be worth only $20,000 in its damaged condition and that repairs might cost over $200,000. The buyer sued the listing broker, the sellers, and the builders. The jury found all defendants liable in varying amounts (sellers 65%, builder 25%, listing agent 5%, selling agent 5%).

In deciding against the listing broker in his appeal, the Court of Appeals held that a real estate broker representing a seller of residential property has a duty to conduct a reasonable and diligent inspection of the property and to disclose to prospective purchasers all facts materially affecting the value or desirability of the property that would be revealed by such an inspection.

The decision in that case created substantial doubt among California brokers and salespersons as to exactly what was required of them. It also generated some uncertainty among professional liability insurance companies, some of which began excluding from coverage any losses caused by licensees' failing to meet the standard set by the court. Accordingly, the State Legislature passed a statute in 1985 with the intent to codify and clarify the holding in the case and to establish duties, standards, and exceptions to the duty of care created by the court decision.

The statute requires a licensee involved in the marketing of one- to four-dwelling residential property to conduct a reasonably competent and diligent visual inspection of the property and to disclose to prospective buyers any facts which would materially affect the value or desirability of the property which would be revealed by such an inspection. The duty to inspect the property for the benefit of the buyer is imposed upon cooperating brokers as well as the listing broker ("a broker who acts in cooperation with" the listing broker to find a buyer). Subsections of the statute spell out, to some degree, the nature of the obligation to inspect. The broker's visual inspection need not include areas which are not reasonably accessible to a visual inspection. If the property is a condominium or cooperative apartment, the inspection need be of the unit only.

The statute says that the standard of competence and care to be applied in the broker's inspection is that of a reasonably prudent real estate licensee and is measured by the degree of knowledge, acquired through education, experience and examination, that is required to obtain a license. It is somewhat unclear exactly what the legislature means by this since none of the course subjects listed in the license law as satisfying the mandatory education requirement for real estate brokers deal specifically with the inspection of existing buildings to determine the soundness of construction, soil conditions, or other investigations aimed at uncovering defects in the property.

In any event, it is clear that a real estate licensee marketing residential property containing one to four dwellings must conduct a reasonably competent inspection of the property with an eye to discovering facts which would be of interest to the buyer. Anything discovered must then be disclosed to the buyer. The disclosure would most often be made in the appropriate section of the form containing the seller's representations and disclosures which must be provided to the buyer in any transfers of one- to four-unit residential property.

"As is."

The obligation to disclose facts materially affecting the value of the property cannot be escaped by an "as is" clause or other provisions attempting to disclaim liability for defects in the property. In one case the property was advertised as a "fixer upper" and the broker clearly stated on the purchase and sale agreement that the buyer agreed to take the property "as is" and expressly disclaimed in the deposit receipt any warranties "as to any condition having to do with city regulations or zoning or any other municipal conditions . . ." Nevertheless, the broker was still found liable for failing to tell the seller that the property was in violation of several building code requirements and was, in effect, condemned. If there is an obligation to disclose to the buyer any facts which materially affect the value or desirability of the property, that obligation cannot be circumvented by simply putting a clause in the contract that says, in effect, that the seller or broker is not responsible for his or her own fraudulent misrepresentations. In the particular case, the broker's license was revoked for dishonest dealing and the broker was held responsible to the buyer for damages.

Liability of Agent

The most common complaints brought against real estate agents are based on fraud, that is, untrue statements or failure to make a disclosure required by law. A real estate broker may be held liable not only for intentional misrepresentations, that is, making a false statement which the broker knows is false, but also for negligent misrepresentation (making a false statement without taking proper steps to ascertain whether it was true or not) and for concealing information which the law requires the agent to disclose (matters affecting the desirability or value of the property).

For example, an agent may be held liable for telling the buyer that a lot contains 35,000 square feet when the agent has measured it and knows that it contains only 30,000 square feet. This would be intentional fraud. The agent may also be held liable for telling the buyer that the lot contains 35,000 square feet when the agent has not measured it and does not know whether it contains 35,000 square feet or not. This would be negligent fraud. Finally, an agent may also be held liable if the agent knows that the house has plumbing or electrical problems and fails to disclose those problems to the potential purchaser. This would be concealment. All three situtations would constitute actionable fraud or deceit under California law.

It is frequently stated that an agent will not be held legally liable for statements, even untrue statements, which may be classified as **opinions, predictions or puffing**. One reason that these types of misrepresentations are not considered to be actionable fraud is based on the common law elements of fraud. The elements which are necessary in order to prove fraud may be summarized as follows:

1) one party makes a statement of a material fact or conceals a material fact which he or she has a legal duty to disclose;
2) if a statement is made (rather than a concealment), the statement is false;
3) the party making the false statement knows that it is false or should know that it is false;
4) the statement or the concealment is made with the intent of inducing another person to enter a transaction;
5) the other person does rely upon the statement or lack of knowledge of the information which has been concealed and is induced to enter the transaction;
6) the other person is damaged as a result of entering the transaction.

In order to prevail in a lawsuit based on allegations of fraud, it is necessary to show that the person defrauded relied on the misrepresentation. Opinions, predictions and puffing are not considered to be the type of statements that a reasonable person would justifiably rely upon in making a decision to buy property and are, therefore, not a proper basis for a suit in fraud. Opinions, predictions and puffing are not considered to be material facts. Note, however as was mentioned earlier in the discussion of the case involving an inaccurate appraisal, if the agent holds him or herself out as being an expert in a particular area, then the agent may be held liable for the consequences if another person relies upon an erroneous opinion.

DISCRIMINATION

There are a number of laws, both state and federal, which have been enacted over the years to prohibit discriminatory behavior. Federal legislation includes the Civil Rights Act of 1866 and the Federal Fair Housing Law of 1968. State legislation includes the Unruh Civil Rights Act, the Housing Financial Discrimination Act of 1977 and the Fair Employment and Housing Act. The California License Law also prohibits real estate licensees from acting in a discriminatory manner (such acts are grounds for disciplinary action), so the real estate agent must be aware of these laws and the types of actions that are prohibited.

Federal laws

The Civil Rights Act of 1866. This act provides that all citizens of the United States shall have the same right, in every state and territory, as enjoyed by white citizens to inherit, purchase, lease, sell, hold and convey real and personal property. The act prohibits any discrimination based on race and was upheld in 1968 by the United States Supreme Court in the landmark case of *Jones v. Mayer*. The court ruled that the 1866 federal law "prohibits all racial discrimination, private or public, in the sale and rental of property" and was constitutional based on the 13th Amendment to the U.S. Constitution, which prohibits slavery.

The Federal Fair Housing Act. Contained in Title VIII of the Civil Rights Act of 1968, this law took the 1866 act one step further, making it illegal to discriminate on the basis of race, color, religion, handicap, children, sex, or national origin in the sale or lease of residential property or in the sale or lease of vacant land for the construction of residential buildings.

Some residential sales and leases are **exempt** from the provisions of the Fair Housing Law. The owner of a single-family home is exempt if three conditions are met:

1. the owner does not own more than three such homes at one time;
2. there is no real estate broker or agent involved in the transaction; and,
3. there is no discriminatory advertising.

This exemption is limited to one transaction in any 24-month period, unless the owner was the most recent occupant of the home which is sold or rented.

The rental of a unit or a room in an owner-occupied dwelling which contains four units or less is exempt from the Fair Housing Law, provided rental advertisements are not discriminatory and a real estate broker is not used to locate tenants. This is called the **Mrs. Murphy exemption**.

Religious discrimination is permitted with respect to rentals in dwellings owned by religious organizations; lodgings in private clubs are also exempt from the law if the club is truly private and non-commercial.

The Fair Housing Law **prohibits specific acts if they are done on the basis of race, color, religion, handicap, children, sex, or national origin.** These prohibited acts include the following: refusing to sell, rent or negotiate the sale or lease of residential property; changing the terms of a sale or lease for different people; discriminating in advertising; making false representations regarding the availability of certain property for sale or lease; blockbusting; steering; and limiting participation in a multiple listing service or similar device.

Blockbusting is the process by which a person induces property owners in a neighborhood to sell their property by predicting the entry of minorities into the neighborhood. The persons buys the property from the owners and then resells it, for a profit, or lists the property and collects a commission on the sale.

Steering is the channeling of various applicants to specific areas in order to maintain or change the character of those neighborhoods.

In addition to the above, Title VIII makes it unlawful to discriminate in **lending practices.** For example, it is illegal to refuse to grant a loan or alter the terms of a loan because of the borrower's race, color, religion, sex or national origin. Also, racial redlining is prohibited. Racial redlining is the refusal to make loans on property located in a particular area for discriminatory reasons. The prohibition against redlining is enforced by the **Home Mortgage Disclosure Act** which requires large institutional lenders to file an annual report of all loans made during that year. The loans are categorized according to the locations of the various properties so that cases of redlining will be more easily discovered.

State laws

Unruh Civil Rights Act. This act states that all persons are entitled to the full use of any services provided by a business establishment. Of course, the act applies to real estate brokers, since a brokerage firm is considered to be a business establishment. Thus the act prohibits a broker from discriminating in the performance of his or her work. (The California License Law also prohibits real estate licensees from acting in a discriminatory manner.)

Fair Employment and Housing Act. This act generally prohibits all housing discrimination in California. It makes it illegal to discriminate in selling, leasing, or financing housing because of race, color, religion, sex, marital status, national origin, or ancestry. It applies to sellers, landlords, property managers, real estate agents, and lenders. The act specifically prohibits a seller or landlord from asking about the race, color, religion, sex, marital status, national origin, or ancestry of any prospective buyer or tenant. It also prohibits them from making any statement or using advertising that indicates an intent to discriminate.

There are very limited exceptions to the Fair Employment and Housing Act. It does not apply to rental of a portion of a single-family, owner-occupied home. It also does not apply to accommodations operated by nonprofit religious, fraternal, or charitable organizations.

Housing Financial Discrimination Act. This law (often called the Holden Act) states that it is against public policy to deny residential mortgage loans or give stricter terms for loans because of neighborhood characteristics unrelated to the creditworthiness of the borrower or the value of the real property. The act applies to all California institutional lenders, and to all loans for the purchase, construction, rehabilitation, improvement, or refinancing of housing.

The Holden Act prohibits a lender from considering neighborhood characteristics in evaluating a loan application, unless the lender can demonstrate they must be considered to avoid an unsound business practice. The act does not prevent a lender from taking the fair market value of the property into consideration, however.

Commissioner Regulations. The state Business and Professions Code prohibits discriminatory conduct by anyone holding a state business license. Three regulations issued by the Real Estate Commissioner implement this provision by addressing the duties of real estate agents with respect to unlawful discrimination based on race, color, sex, religion, ancestry, physical handicap, marital status or national origin. Regulation 2780 lists a number of actions or types of conduct which are grounds for disciplinary action. Regulation 2781 concerns panic selling or blockbusting. Regulation 2782 describes the duty of a broker to supervise agents so that they are familiar with the requirements of federal and state civil rights laws.

Regulation 2780 is an explanatory regulation intended to give licensees some guidance as to the types of discriminatory conduct that are prohibited and the kinds of actions that are permissible, even though they may involve discriminatory treatment. The regulation takes the form of several pages of examples of prohibited and permissible conduct. The examples are intended to be merely illustrative of some, not all prohibited actions. A few of these examples are listed below:

- refusing to negotiate for the sale, rental or financing of real property;
- refusing to show, rent, sell or finance real property;
- refusing or failing to provide information regarding real property;
- channeling or steering a person away from real property;
- discriminating in the terms or conditions of sale, rental or financing of the purchase of real property;
- representing that real property is not available for inspection, sale or rental when it is in fact available;
- processing an application more slowly or otherwise acting to delay or hinder a sale, rental or financing of real property;
- making any effort to encourage other persons to discriminate in showing, renting, selling or financing the purchase of real property;
- refusing or failing to cooperate with or assist another real estate licensee because of the prospect's race, color, sex, religion, ancestry, physical handicap, marital status or national origin;
- refusing to accept a listing;
- entering an agreement or carrying out explicit or "understood" instructions not to show, lease, sell or finance the purchase of real property;

It is important to remember that the regulation is only intended to provide some examples of prohibited practices, not to list all prohibited acts. Other discriminatory acts may also constitute unlawful conduct and be grounds for license suspension or revocation.

In certain situations, some discriminatory conduct is permitted, such as failing to show, rent or sell property because of a person's physical handicap if the property has characteristics which would render it dangerous or inaccessible to the physically handicapped. Affirmative action programs are also permissible.

Regulation 2781 is directed to panic selling (blockbusting). As does Regulation 2780, this regulation lists several types of prohibited behavior: a licensee may not solicit listings by making any written or oral statements, warnings or threats, or taking any other actions to induce owners to sell or lease property because of present or anticipated entry in the neighborhood of one or more persons of another race, color, sex, religion, ancestry, marital status or national origin.

Regulation 2782 concerns the supervisory duties of real estate brokers in connection with civil rights laws. The regulation imposes on brokers a duty to take reasonable steps to familiarize themselves and their employed salespersons with state and federal discrimination laws and regulations.

Chapter Two

Broker – Salesperson Employment Contracts

A salesperson who is actively engaged in professional real estate activities must be employed by a licensed real estate broker. Under the California Real Estate Law, a salesperson may not deal directly with the public except through or on behalf of the licensed broker employing the salesperson. A salesperson cannot be employed by or paid for professional real estate services by anyone other than the broker with whom the salesperson is licensed at the time. Nor may a salesperson pay compensation to any other real estate licensee, except through his or her employing broker.

The employment contracts between broker and salesperson usually identify the salesperson as an **independent contractor**, but this characterization of the salesperson as an independent contractor is not necessarily controlling and the salesperson may still be considered an employee. Because of provisions of the Real Estate Law which require brokers to supervise and control their salespersons, salespersons are regarded as **employees**, not independent contractors, for purposes of the Real Estate Law regardless of any contractual agreement between the salespersons and their employing brokers. Similarly, as between the broker and third persons, the salesperson is the broker's agent and the broker is liable to third persons for the salesperson's activities, again regardless of any agreement between the broker and salesperson or any common law rules which might apply in other principal-agent or independent contractor-employee cases. The reasoning behind this is that, since a salesperson can act only for or on behalf of the broker under whom he or she is licensed and cannot act independently, then the salesperson cannot really be classified as an independent contractor.

The salesperson may be treated as an independent contractor for income tax purposes, though. A real estate salesperson may be classified as an independent contractor if the following three conditions are met:

1) the salesperson is a licensed real estate agent;
2) there is a written agreement between the salesperson and broker which provides that the agent is an independent contractor for tax purposes; and,
3) the agent's compensation is based on sales commissions, as opposed to salary or hourly wages.

Classification of the salesperson as an independent contractor for tax purposes means that the broker need not withhold income and social security taxes from the compensation paid to the salesperson. The salesperson operating as an independent contractor for tax purposes files his or her own returns and pays his or her own income taxes. Independent contractor status allows the agent more liberal expense deductions for income taxes than is permitted employees.

The remainder of this chapter will be an overview of a broker-salesperson employment contract. There are a number of different employment contract forms in use in California. The California Association of Realtors® standard form for an independent contractor agreement will be used as an example in this text since it contains most of the types of provisions found in these contracts and it is widely distributed and used throughout the state. No endorsement or criticism of this or any other form is intended by using this particular form for illustrative purposes.

Heading. This is called a *Broker-Associate Licensee Contract* because a broker can use it in hiring either a salesperson or an associate broker. The subheading indicates that it's an independent contractor form, one that will make the associate licensee an independent contractor for tax purposes. The first few lines contain blanks for the date of the contract and the names of the broker and the associate licensee.

(1) Broker. This paragraph provides information about the broker's business. The broker states that he or she is licensed as a real estate broker in California. Then there is a blank for the firm name (the name under which the broker does business). Next, the broker checks one of three boxes to specify how the brokerage is organized: as a sole proprietorship, a partnership, or a corporation. There are also blanks for the names of the Realtors® associations and multiple listing services the broker belongs to.

(2) Associate Licensee. In this paragraph, the associate licensee states that he or she holds a California real estate license, and indicates whether it's a broker's license or a salesperson's license. If the associate licensee has used any names during the past five years other than the one he or she is currently using, they should be listed here.

Both the broker and the associate licensee agree to keep their licenses current while this contract is in effect. The associate licensee also agrees to satisfy continuing education requirements and provisional license requirements (license restrictions, or conditions for holding a special type of license).

(3) Listing and Sales Activities. This paragraph contains several agreements regarding the working relationship between the broker and the associate licensee. In the first sentence, the broker generally agrees to make all his or her current listings available to the associate licensee, who will share them on equal footing with other associate licensees in the office. However, the broker reserves the right to assign particular listings to one of the associate licensees, or a specified group of them, exclusively. Nothing in this provision (or in the rest of the contract) guarantees the associate licensee access to a minimum number of listings.

The next sentences give the associate licensee a significant amount of freedom in working for the broker. The licensee has the right to refuse to handle any current or prospective listing, or to refuse to work with any particular person (an obnoxious customer, for example). The broker agrees not to restrict the licensee's sales activities to a particular territory. The broker also won't direct or limit the licensee's work in regard to "hours, leads, open houses, opportunity or floor time, production, prospects, sales meetings, schedule, inventory, time off, vacation, or similar activities." In other words, the licensee can choose when and how to work at selling

BROKER-ASSOCIATE LICENSEE CONTRACT

(Independent Contractor)

THIS IS INTENDED TO BE A LEGALLY BINDING CONTRACT — READ IT CAREFULLY.

CALIFORNIA ASSOCIATION OF REALTORS® (CAR) STANDARD FORM

☐

THIS AGREEMENT, made this ________________ day of ________________, 19____, by and between ____ (hereinafter "Broker") and ____ (hereinafter "Associate Licensee").

IN CONSIDERATION of the respective representations and covenants herein, Broker and Associate Licensee agree and contract as follows:

1. **BROKER:** Broker represents that he/she/it is duly licensed as a real estate broker by the State of California, ☐ doing business as ________________________ (Firm name), ☐ a sole proprietorship, ☐ a partnership, ☐ a corporation. Broker is a member of the ________________________ Board(s)/Association(s) of REALTORS®, and a Participant in the ________________________ multiple listing service(s).
2. **ASSOCIATE LICENSEE:** Associate Licensee represents that, (a) he/she is duly licensed by the State of California as a ☐ real estate broker, ☐ real estate salesperson, and (b) he/she has not used any other names within the past five years except ________________________. Broker shall keep his/her/its license current during the term of this agreement. Associate Licensee shall keep his/her license current during the term of this agreement, including satisfying all applicable continuing education and provisional license requirements.
3. **LISTING AND SALES ACTIVITIES:** Broker shall make available to Associate Licensee, equally with other licensees associated with Broker, all current listings in Broker's office, except any listing which Broker may choose to place in the exclusive servicing of Associate Licensee or one or more other specific licensees associated with Broker. Associate Licensee shall not be required to accept or service any particular listing or prospective listing offered by Broker, or to see or service particular parties. Broker shall not restrict Associate Licensee's activities to particular geographical areas. Broker shall not, except to the extent required by law, direct or limit Associate Licensee's activities as to hours, leads, open houses, opportunity or floor time, production, prospects, sales meetings, schedule, inventory, time off, vacation, or similar activities. In compliance with Commissioner's Regulation 2780, et seq. (Title 10, California Code of Regulations, §2780, et seq.), Broker and Associate Licensee shall at all times be familiar with, and act in compliance with, all applicable federal, California and local anti-discrimination laws.
4. **BROKER SUPERVISION:**
   (a) Associate Licensee shall submit for Broker's review:
      i. All documents which may have a material effect upon the rights and duties of principals in a transaction, within 24 hours after preparing, signing, or receiving same. Broker may exercise this review responsibility through another licensee provided the Broker and the designated licensee have complied with Commissioner's Regulation 2725 (Title 10, California Code of Regulations, §2725).
      ii. Any documents or other items connected with a transaction pursuant to this agreement, in the possession of or available to Associate Licensee, (i) immediately upon request by Broker or Broker's designated licensee, and/or (ii) as provided in Broker's Office Policy Manual, if any.
      iii. All documents associated with any real estate transaction in which Associate Licensee is a principal.
   (b) In addition, without affecting Associate Licensee's status, Broker shall have the right to direct Associate Licensee's actions to the extent required by law, and Associate Licensee shall comply with such directions. All trust funds shall be handled in compliance with Business and Professions Code §10145, and other applicable laws.
5. **OFFICE FACILITIES:** Broker shall make available for Associate Licensee's use, along with other licensees associated with Broker, the facilities of the real estate office operated by Broker at ____ and the facilities of any other office locations made available by Broker pursuant to this agreement.

6. **ASSOCIATE LICENSEE'S EFFORTS:** Associate Licensee shall work diligently and with his/her best efforts, (a) to sell, exchange, lease, or rent properties listed with Broker or other cooperating Brokers, (b) to solicit additional listings, clients, and customers, and (c) to otherwise promote the business of serving the public in real estate transactions to the end that Broker and Associate Licensee may derive the greatest benefit possible, in accordance with law.

7. **UNLAWFUL ACTS:** Associate Licensee shall not commit any act for which the Real Estate Commissioner of the State of California is authorized to restrict, suspend, or revoke Associate Licensee's license or impose other discipline, under California Business and Professions Code Sections 10176 or 10177 or other provisions of law.

8. **LISTING COMMISSIONS:** Commissions shall be charged to parties who desire to enter into listing agreements and other contracts for services requiring a real estate license, with Broker,

☐ as shown in "Exhibit A" attached which is incorporated as a part of this agreement by reference, or

☐ as follows: ____

____

____.

Any proposed deviation from that schedule must be reviewed and approved in advance by Broker. Any permanent change in commission schedule shall be disseminated by Broker to Associate Licensee.

9. **COMPENSATION TO ASSOCIATE LICENSEE:** Associate Licensee shall receive a share of commissions which are actually collected by Broker, on listings and other contracts for services requiring a real estate license which are solicited and obtained by Associate Licensee, and on transactions of which Associate Licensee's activities are the procuring cause,

☐ as shown in "Exhibit B" attached which is incorporated as a part of this agreement by reference, or

☐ as follows: ____

____

____

____

____.

The above commissions may be varied by written agreement between Broker and Associate Licensee before completion of any particular transaction. Expenses which must be paid from commissions, or are incurred in the attempt to collect commissions, shall be paid by Broker and Associate Licensee in the same proportion as set forth for the division of commissions.

10. **DIVIDING COMPENSATION WITH OTHER LICENSEES IN OFFICE:** If Associate Licensee and one or more other licensees associated with Broker both participate on the same side (either listing or selling) of a transaction, the commission allocated to their combined activities shall be divided by Broker and paid to them according to the written agreement between them which shall be furnished in advance to Broker.

11. **COMMISSIONS PAID TO BROKER:** All commissions will be received by Broker. Associate Licensee's share of commissions shall be paid to him/her, after deduction of offsets, immediately upon collection by Broker or as soon thereafter as practicable, except as otherwise provided in (a) Paragraph 9, above, (b) Broker's Office Policy Manual, or (c) a separate written agreement between Broker and Associate Licensee. Broker may impound in Broker's account Associate Licensee's share of commissions on transactions in which there is a known or pending claim against Broker and/or Associate Licensee, until such claim is resolved.

12. **UNCOLLECTED COMMISSIONS:** Neither Broker nor Associate Licensee shall be liable to the other for any portion of commissions not collected. Associate Licensee shall not be entitled to any advance payment from Broker upon future commissions.

EQUAL HOUSING OPPORTUNITY
M-SC-SEP-90

13. **ASSOCIATE LICENSEE EXPENSES; OFFSETS:** Associate Licensee shall provide and pay for all professional licenses, supplies, services, and other items required in connection with Associate Licensee's activities under this agreement, or any listing or transaction, without reimbursement from Broker except as required by law. If Broker elects to advance funds to pay expenses or liabilities of Associate Licensee, Associate Licensee shall repay to Broker the full amount advanced on demand, or Broker may deduct the full amount advanced from commissions payable to Associate Licensee on any transaction without notice.

14. **INDEPENDENT CONTRACTOR RELATIONSHIP:** Broker and Associate Licensee intend that, to the maximum extent permissible by law, (a) this agreement does not constitute a hiring or employment agreement by either party, (b) Broker and Associate Licensee are independent contracting parties with respect to all services rendered under this agreement or in any resulting transactions, (c) Associate Licensee's only remuneration shall be his/her proportional share, if any, of commissions collected by Broker, (d) Associate Licensee retains sole and absolute discretion and judgment in the methods, techniques, and procedures to be used in soliciting and obtaining listings, sales, exchanges, leases, rentals, or other transactions, and in carrying out Associate Licensee's selling and soliciting activities, except as required by law or in Broker's Office Policy Manual, (e) Associate Licensee is under the control of Broker as to the results of Associate Licensee's work only, and not as to the means by which those results are accomplished except as required by law, or in Broker's Office Policy Manual, if any, (f) this agreement shall not be construed as a partnership, (g) Associate Licensee has no authority to bind Broker by any promise or representation unless specifically authorized by Broker in writing, (h) Broker shall not be liable for any obligation or liability incurred by Associate Licensee, (i) Associate Licensee shall not be treated as an employee with respect to services performed as a real estate agent, for state and federal tax purposes, and (j) the fact the Broker may carry worker compensation insurance for his/her/its own benefit and for the mutual benefit of Broker and licensees associated with Broker, including Associate Licensee, shall not create an inference of employment.

15. **LISTINGS AND OTHER AGREEMENTS PROPERTY OF BROKER:** All listings of property, and all agreements for performance of licensed acts, and all acts or actions requiring a real estate license which are taken or performed in connection with this agreement, shall be taken and performed in the name of Broker. All listings shall be submitted to Broker within 24 hours after receipt by Associate Licensee. Associate Licensee agrees to and does hereby contribute all right and title to such listings to Broker for the benefit and use of Broker, Associate Licensee, and other licensees associated with Broker.

16. **TERMINATION OF RELATIONSHIP:** Broker or Associate Licensee may terminate their relationship under this agreement at any time, on 24 hours written notice, with or without cause. Even after termination, this agreement shall govern all disputes and claims between Broker and Associate Licensee connected with their relationship under this agreement, including obligations and liabilities arising from existing and completed listings, transactions, and services.

17. **COMMISSIONS AFTER TERMINATION AND OFFSET:** If this agreement is terminated while Associate Licensee has listings or pending transactions that require further work normally rendered by Associate Licensee, Broker shall make arrangements with another licensee associated with Broker to perform the required work, or shall perform the work him/herself. The licensee performing the work shall be reasonably compensated for completing work on those listings or transactions, and such reasonable compensation shall be deducted from Associate Licensee's share of commissions. Except for such offset, Associate Licensee shall receive his/her regular share of commissions on such sales or other transactions, if actually collected by Broker, after deduction of any other amounts or offsets provided in this agreement.

18. **ARBITRATION OF DISPUTES:** All disputes or claims between Associate Licensee and other licensee(s) associated with Broker, or between Associate Licensee and Broker, arising from or connected in any way with this agreement, which cannot be adjusted between the parties involved, shall be submitted to the Board of REALTORS® of which all such disputing parties are members for arbitration pursuant to the provisions of its Bylaws, as may be amended from time to time, which are incorporated as a part of this agreement by reference. If the Bylaws of the Board do not cover arbitration of the dispute, or if the Board declines jurisdiction over the dispute, then arbitration shall be pursuant to the rules of the American Arbitration Association, as may be amended from time to time, which are incorporated as a part of this agreement by reference. The Federal Arbitration Act, Title 9, U.S. Code, Section 1, et seq., shall govern this agreement.

19. **PROPRIETARY INFORMATION AND FILES:** Associate Licensee shall not use to his/her own advantage, or the advantage of any other person, business, or entity, except as specifically provided in this agreement, either during Associate Licensee's association with Broker or thereafter, any information gained for or from the business or files of Broker. All files and documents pertaining to listings and transactions are the property of Broker and shall be delivered to Broker by Associate Licensee immediately upon request or upon termination of their relationship under this agreement.

20. **INDEMNITY AND HOLD HARMLESS:** All claims, demands, liabilities, judgments, and arbitration awards, including costs and attorney's fees, to which Broker is subjected by reason of any action taken or omitted by Associate Licensee in connection with services rendered or to be rendered pursuant to this agreement, shall be:

☐ Paid in full by Associate Licensee, who hereby agrees to indemnify and hold harmless Broker for all such sums, or

☐ Other: ____

____

____.

Associate Licensee shall pay to Broker the full amount due by him/her on demand, or Broker may deduct the full amount due by Associate Licensee from commissions due on any transaction without notice.

21. ADDITIONAL PROVISIONS: ______________________________

____

____

22. DEFINITIONS: As used in this agreement, the following terms have the meanings indicated:

(a) "Listing" means an agreement with a property owner or other party to locate a buyer, exchange party, lessee, or other party to a transaction involving real property, a mobile home, or other property or transaction which may be brokered by a real estate licensee, or an agreement with a party to locate or negotiate for any such property or transaction.

(b) "Commission" means compensation for acts requiring a real estate license, regardless of whether calculated as a percentage of transaction price, flat fee, hourly rate, or in any other manner.

(c) "Transaction" means a sale, exchange, lease, or rental of real property, a business opportunity, or a mobile home which may lawfully be brokered by a real estate licensee, or a loan secured by any property of those types.

(d) "Associate Licensee" means the real estate broker or real estate salesperson licensed by the State of California and rendering the services set forth herein for Associate Licensee.

23. NOTICES: All notices under this agreement shall be in writing. Notices may be delivered personally, or by certified U.S. mail, postage prepaid, or by facsimile, to the parties at the addresses noted below. Either party may designate a new address for purposes of this agreement by giving notice to the other party. Notices mailed shall be deemed received as of 5:00 P.M. on the second business day following the date of mailing.

24. ATTORNEY FEES:

In any action, proceeding, or arbitration between Broker and Associate Licensee arising from or related to this agreement, the prevailing party shall, in the discretion of the court or arbitrator, be entitled to reasonable attorney fees in addition to other appropriate relief.

25. ENTIRE AGREEMENT; MODIFICATION: All prior agreements between the parties concerning their relationship as Broker and Associate Licensee are incorporated in this agreement, which constitutes the entire contract. Its terms are intended by the parties as a final and complete expression of their agreement with respect to its subject matter, and may not be contradicted by evidence of any prior agreement or contemporaneous oral agreement. This agreement may not be amended, modified, altered, or changed in any respect whatsoever except by a further agreement in writing duly executed by Broker and Associate Licensee.

BROKER:		ASSOCIATE LICENSEE:	
(Signature)		(Signature)	
(Name Printed)		(Name Printed)	
(Address)		(Address)	
(City, State, Zip)		(City, State, Zip)	
(Telephone)	(Fax)	(Telephone)	(Fax)

NOTE: (1) Broker and Associate Licensee should each receive an executed copy of this agreement.

(2) Attach commission schedules Exhibits A and B if applicable.

This form is available for use by the entire real estate industry. The use of this form is not intended to identify the user as a REALTOR®. REALTOR® is a registered collective membership mark which may be used only by real estate licensees who are members of the NATIONAL ASSOCIATION OF REALTORS® and who subscribe to its Code of Ethics.

EQUAL HOUSING

real estate. There's an important limitation here, however: the broker will not direct the licensee's activities "except as required by law."

This is the first of several provisions in the contract intended to establish that the associate licensee is an independent contractor and not an employee. The underlying question in independent contractor-employee cases is the degree of control the hiring party has over the person hired. So a number of this contract's provisions emphasize that the associate licensee operates independently, and the broker has no right to control the associate licensee's activities—except to the extent required by law. But as explained above, the Real Estate Law does require brokers to supervise their salespersons and exercise considerable control over them. Contract provisions cannot relieve the broker from that responsibility, or limit the broker's liability for the salesperson's actions.

(4) Broker Supervision. In contrast to Paragraph 3, this paragraph focuses on the ways in which the broker will supervise the associate licensee's work. Subparagraph 4a requires the associate licensee to submit certain documents to the broker for review—including documents connected with any transaction in which the associate licensee is a principal, whether or not the property is listed with the broker.

Subparagraph 4b specifically gives the broker the right to direct the associate licensee's actions to the extent required by law. The associate licensee also agrees to follow the broker's directions to that extent. The provision says the broker will exercise this degree of control "without affecting Associate Licensee's status"—in other words, without making the associate licensee an employee rather than an independent contractor.

(5) Office Facilities. Here the broker agrees to allow the licensee to use the broker's office facilities, sharing them with the broker's other associates. The blank is for the address of the office where the licensee will work; the broker may also permit the licensee to use other branch offices.

(6) Associate Licensee's Efforts. Paragraph 3 left how to go about selling real estate up to the associate licensee's discretion. Now in Paragraph 6, the licensee agrees to "work diligently and with his/her best efforts" to: sell properties listed with the broker and cooperating brokers; solicit listings, clients, and customers; and generally serve the public in real estate transactions. So, even though the licensee doesn't promise the broker specific actions ("forty cold calls per week") or specific results ("at least one closing per month"), he or she does promise to work hard and try to accomplish certain goals.

(7) Unlawful Acts. Here, the associate licensee simply agrees not to commit any act that would be grounds for restriction, suspension, or revocation of his or her real estate license.

Paragraphs 8 through 13 deal with receipt and payment of commissions, and with payment of expenses.

(8) Listing Commissions. In this paragraph, the broker sets forth his or her ordinary commission rates. The broker may attach a commission schedule to the contract ("Exhibit A"), or fill in the blanks, if they provide enough room. Under California law all commissions must be negotiated between client and broker, so the rates stated in this contract are merely those the broker usually requests when taking listings. The contract requires the associate licensee to get the broker's approval before agreeing to a commission rate that does not match the broker's rate schedule.

(9) Compensation to Associate Licensee. Like most broker-salesperson contract forms, this one provides that the associate licensee is entitled to a share of a commission only when the commission has actually been *collected* by the broker. If the broker is unable to collect a commission from the client, the broker does not have to compensate the licensee. Remember that a salesperson does not have the right to sue the client directly; a salesperson can deal with the public only in his or her broker's name. The broker is the one who is a party to the listing agreement and has a right to enforce payment. This contract (again, like most broker-salesperson contracts) does not obligate the broker to sue the client or otherwise try to enforce the listing agreement.

The associate licensee is entitled to a share of the collected commission if he or she obtained the listing or was the procuring cause of the sale. The amount of the licensee's share is either set forth in "Exhibit B" or in the blanks provided. The broker and the licensee may agree to share the commission for a particular transaction differently, but they must put that agreement in writing before the transaction is completed.

The broker and associate licensee also split any expenses that have to be paid from a commission, or that are incurred in trying to collect a commission. Each pays a share of those expenses proportionate to his or her respective share of the commission.

(10) Dividing Compensation with Other Licensees. This provision addresses the situation where two or more of the broker's salespersons work on the same transaction. The contract allows them to split the share of the commission that Paragraph 9 allocates to the associate licensee, but the question of who will get how much is left up to the salespersons involved. They are supposed to submit a written agreement to the broker in advance, asking the broker to divide the commission.

(11) Commissions Paid to Broker. Paragraph 11 first states that the broker will receive all commissions. (The Real Estate Law prohibits payment of a commission to anyone other than a licensed broker.) Unless otherwise agreed, the broker has to pay the associate licensee his or her share "immediately upon collection...or as soon thereafter as practicable." The broker is allowed to deduct offsets—amounts the licensee owes the broker—before paying the commission share. (See Paragraph 13, below.) The broker is also allowed to *impound* a commission if someone makes a claim against the broker or the licensee arising out of the transaction in which they earned the commission. That means the broker can hold onto the licensee's share until the claim is resolved.

(12) Uncollected Commissions. This paragraph expressly states that the broker is not personally responsible to the associate licensee for any share of a commission that hasn't been collected. (The associate licensee isn't responsible to the broker for uncollected commissions, either.) This paragraph also makes it clear that the associate licensee is not entitled to advances out of commissions he or she expects to earn.

(13) Associate Licensee Expenses; Offsets. Here the licensee agrees to pay all his or her own real estate expenses: license fees, supplies, and other costs. If the broker gives the licensee an advance to cover expenses, the broker can demand repayment at any time, or deduct the amount from the licensee's commission in any transaction (not just the one in which the expenses were incurred). The broker is not required to notify the licensee before making the deduction.

(14) Independent Contractor Relationship. This paragraph establishes the associate licensee's status as an independent contractor "to the maximum extent permissible by law." Clauses (a) through (e) each describe an aspect of the relationship between the broker and the licensee in terms showing that the licensee fits the legal definition of an independent contractor, rather than the legal definition of an employee. The licensee's only compensation will be a share of collected commissions—not wages or a salary. The associate licensee will have absolute discretion to choose what methods to use in his or her work. The broker will control only the results of the licensee's work, and not the means by which they are accomplished. However, these sweeping assertions are balanced by the phrase "except as required by law, or in Broker's Office Policy Manual, if any."

Clauses (f) through (h) clarify the limits of the relationship between the broker and the associate licensee. They are not business partners. The licensee can't bind the broker to a promise or a representation without specific authorization in writing. And the broker will not be liable for the licensee's debts (neither obligations, such as a bill for car repairs, nor liabilities, such as a judgment in a lawsuit arising out of a traffic accident). Of course, this provision cannot relieve the broker of liability for the salesperson's negligence or fraud in a real estate transaction.

Clauses (i) and (j) specifically address taxation and worker's compensation. The associate licensee will not be treated as an employee for state or federal tax purposes; so the broker is not required to withhold tax money from the associate licensee's compensation. If the broker chooses to provide worker's compensation insurance (to cover injuries in on-the-job accidents), that won't carry the implication that the associate licensee is an employee instead of an independent contractor.

(15) Listings and Other Agreements Property of Broker. Paragraph 15 deals with the issue of who really has the rights to the listings the associate licensee obtains. All listings (and other agreements for the performance of acts for which a real estate license is required) are taken and performed in the broker's name. The licensee is required to submit all listings to the broker within 24 hours after receiving them. The licensee also agrees to give up all right and title to the listings to the broker, for the benefit of the broker and the licensees associated with the broker.

(16) Termination of Relationship. This paragraph sets out the parties' agreement regarding termination of their relationship. Either the broker or the associate licensee may terminate the association by giving 24 hours' notice, in writing, to the other party. It can be terminated "with or without cause," which means that there doesn't have to be a good reason for ending the relationship. The broker can let the associate licensee go even if his or her performance has been completely satisfactory. If the broker and associate licensee have any unfinished business, it will still be settled according to the terms of this contract.

(17) Commissions After Termination and Offset. This provision covers the associate licensee's right to be paid after the relationship with the broker has ended. The broker still owes the associate licensee his or her share of any commissions collected (even if the broker had a good reason for firing the associate licensee).

If the associate licensee hasn't completed work on a transaction when the association is terminated, the broker can either assign that transaction to another salesperson or do the work him or herself. Whoever finishes the work is entitled to "reasonable compensation," and that will be deducted from the departing licensee's share of the commission.

(18) Arbitration of Disputes. Here the broker and the associate licensee agree that, if a dispute arises out of this contract and they are unable to settle it, they will submit it to arbitration. The arbitration will ordinarily be handled by the broker's Board of Realtors®. If the broker's board has no arbitration procedure or refuses to decide the dispute, the arbitration will be conducted according to the rules of the American Arbitration Association. (Almost all local boards have established arbitration procedures, which are set forth in their bylaws.)

This arbitration provision applies not only to disputes between the associate licensee and the broker, but also to disputes between the associate licensee and other licensees associated with the broker. So if two of the broker's salespersons are unable to agree on how to split their share of a commission (see Paragraph 10), that issue would be decided by an arbitrator—not by the broker.

(19) Proprietary Information and Files. In Paragraph 19, the associate licensee agrees not to use information gained for or from the broker's business or files to his or her own advantage, or to the advantage of another broker or business. (One example of the kind of information protected is a client or customer list.) This agreement applies while the licensee is working for the broker, and also afterwards. The licensee agrees to give the broker all files and documents pertaining to listings and transactions, either upon request or when their association ends.

(20) Indemnity and Hold Harmless. This paragraph concerns responsibility for liabilities or expenses the broker incurs as a result of the associate licensee's real estate activities. If the first box is checked, the licensee agrees to accept full responsibility. If the second box is checked, the parties fill in the blanks with a different arrangement (shared responsibility, for example). In most cases, the broker will check the first box.

Under this provision, the broker would still be liable to third parties, such as buyers or sellers, who were harmed by the licensee's actions. They could sue and obtain a judgment against the broker. But the broker could demand reimbursement from the licensee after paying off the judgment.

(21) Additional Provisions. These blank lines are for any terms or conditions that the broker and the associate licensee agree to make part of their contract, which aren't covered by its printed provisions.

(22) Definitions. This paragraph explains what the words "listing," "commission," "transaction," and "associate licensee" mean in the context of this contract. The definitions are broad. For example, "listing" covers exchanges and leases as well as sales, and agreements with buyers as well as with sellers. A "commission" is any form of compensation for acts requiring a real estate license; flat fees are covered as well as percentage commissions.

(23) Notices. Paragraph 23 sets forth the procedures the parties are required to follow when giving notice to the other party regarding any matter arising out of this contract. Notices must be in writing and delivered in person, mailed, or faxed to the other party's address given at the bottom of the form.

(24) Attorney Fees. Here, the broker and associate licensee agree that, if this contract leads to arbitration or a lawsuit, whoever loses will pay the winner's attorney fees (in addition to any other compensation the winner is entitled to). The arbitrator or judge has discretion to deny the award of attorney fees; in any case, the fees must be reasonable.

(25) Entire Agreement; Modification. The first two sentences in this paragraph are an "integration clause." The broker and licensee agree that this written contract contains their entire agreement in regard to its subject matter (their working relationship), and expresses that agreement in its final form. It replaces any earlier agreements they might have reached.

Because of the integration clause, in a legal proceeding neither party would be allowed to introduce evidence of an earlier agreement or an oral side agreement that changes the terms of this contract. For example, suppose that when they were filling out the contract, the broker told the associate licensee she would always pay him his share of a commission even when she couldn't collect the commission from the client. That promise did not get included in the written contract, however; the wording of Paragraph 9 was not altered, and nothing was added in Paragraph 21. If the associate licensee later sued the broker, the judge would not permit anyone to give testimony about the broker's unwritten promise. Only the written contract terms would be considered. So it's extremely important to make sure that all understandings between the broker and the associate licensee are written down on this form (or on a signed attachment to the form that is incorporated into it by reference).

The final sentence in Paragraph 25 provides that any changes to this contract can only be made by another written agreement signed by both parties. For example, six months after executing this contract, the broker might agree to increase the associate licensee's commission share. That modification of their contract would have to be put into writing and signed by the broker and the associate licensee.

Signatures and Addresses. At the bottom of the form, there are blanks for the signatures, addresses, and telephone numbers of the broker and the associate licensee. After they've both signed the form, the broker should give the licensee a copy and put a copy in his or her files.

Chapter Three

Broker – Client Employment Contracts

The employment contract which establishes the agency relationship between the broker and his or her client is called a listing agreement. The listing agreement, most often between the broker and the seller, gives the broker the authority to negotiate the sale or purchase of real property.

There are three major types of listing agreements, the open listing, the exclusive agency listing, and the exclusive right to sell listing. The distinctions between these three types of listings will be discussed shortly.

Prerequisites for Collecting a Commission

Entering into a written listing agreement is one of the prerequisites to collecting a commission. Under California law a broker who wants to recover a commission must be able to show that:

1) he or she was licensed at the time the services for which the commission is claimed were performed;

2) he or she has a written listing agreement signed by the seller(s); and,

3) he or she has performed the services and/or satisfied the conditions under that listing agreement which entitle the broker to compensation.

The basic performance required for the broker to earn a commission under a listing agreement is normally the procurement of a buyer who is is "**ready, willing and able**" to purchase the property on the seller's terms (as set out in the listing agreement or otherwise acceptable to the seller).

A real estate broker is the "**procuring cause**" of a sale if the broker finds a "ready, willing and able" purchaser and if the broker obtains a valid written offer to enter a binding contract. Even if the broker is unable to obtain a written offer from the buyer, the broker may still be considered the procuring cause if he or she brings the buyer and seller together so that they may enter into such a contract for the purchase and sale of the property. The broker is the procuring cause if he or she sets in motion a chain of events that proximately causes the buyer and seller to come to terms.

So, if the broker's efforts result in a meeting of the minds between the buyer and seller, the broker would still be entitled to a commission even though the final negotiations and agreement were conducted without the direct involvement of the broker. Whether the broker's efforts actually resulted in producing the buyer (whether the broker was the "procuring cause") is a question of fact which must be determined by examining all the circumstances surrounding the particular transaction.

To make matters even more complicated, depending on the type of listing agreement used, the broker may or may not need to "procure" the ready, willing and able buyer him or herself to be entitled to the commission. Under an open listing agreement, the broker must be the procuring cause; under an exclusive agency listing, the broker is entitled to a commission unless the seller is the procuring cause; and under an exclusive right to sell listing, the broker need not be the procuring cause at all. This will be discussed in greater detail later in the chapter.

Ready, willing and able buyer.

Courts across the country say that a broker has earned his or her commission when the broker has produced a buyer who is ready, willing and able to buy the property on the seller's terms as expressed in the listing agreement, or on other terms which are acceptable to the seller. This might give the impression that there is a uniform rule across the United States as to when a broker's commission is earned. This impression would be incorrect. Even though the same three descriptive words are used, "ready, willing and able," they do not mean the same thing in all places.

A ready and willing buyer is usually interpreted to mean one who is ready and willing to sign a binding agreement to buy the property. So the ready and willing requirement is met in most places (including California) when the buyer signs the purchase and sale agreement. It is not necessary that the buyer actually buy the property or stay ready and willing to buy the property right through escrow. It is the execution of the binding contract to buy that is crucial, not that the sale actually be consummated.

The usual rule is that the broker is entitled to compensation even though the buyer backs out of the transaction. The reasoning here is that the seller should be able to sue the buyer on the contract and recover damages. As a practical matter, in most cases, if the sale does not close, there is no money to pay the commission. Sellers rarely sue buyers for damages beyond the earnest money deposit (and in many cases do not even get the deposit). Brokers normally are satisfied to split the forfeited deposit, if any, with the seller; they seldom bring suit against the seller for the commission in transactions where the failure to close is due to the buyer's refusal to go through with the deal. Many standard purchase and sale forms specifically provide that in the event of a default by the buyer, the seller and broker will split the forfeited deposit, with the broker limited to receiving no more than what would have been paid as a commission if the transaction had been successfully consummated.

The third leg of the "ready, willing and able" requirement is a buyer who is able to buy. A buyer is able to buy if he or she has the financial resources necessary to make the downpayment and other closing costs associated with the transaction and to make the installment payments required under the planned financing arrangements; the buyer does not have to have the full price in cash in order to be an able buyer.

The typical situation in which disputes and lawsuits arise in this context is a transaction in which the buyer defaults either before closing or shortly after closing. The broker demands a commission based on the normal rule that he or she has earned a commission when the seller accepts the buyer's offer and a binding contract has been entered. The seller argues that the buyer was not "able" and that therefore the broker has not earned a commission.

There is a line of older cases which says that if the seller accepts the buyer's offer and enters a contract with the buyer, then the seller has accepted the buyer and it is not necessary for the broker to prove that the buyer was able. This rule has been modified or strictly limited in a number of more modern court decisions from several states. The decisions in these cases have been to the effect that the broker can only rely on the seller's acceptance of the buyer if the broker has scrupulously told the seller everything in the broker's knowledge relating to the buyer's financial ability, including information relating to the buyer's income, cash and other assets, and the buyer's credit history. A couple of cases have held, for example, that the broker should inform the seller if the broker is aware that the buyer has borrowed the deposit and/or downpayment. If the broker has any information relating to the buyer's financial status and fails to pass that information on to the seller or has in any way misled the seller regarding the buyer's financial ability, then the broker cannot base a claim for a commission on the bare fact that the seller accepted the buyer. That rule assumes that the broker has fully performed his or her fiduciary duties to keep the principal (seller) fully informed.

To summarize the rule: If the agent has fully and truthfully disclosed to the seller all information in the agent's knowledge concerning the buyer's financial ability, and the seller entered a binding agreement of sale with the buyer, then the seller would be obligated to pay the commission even if the transaction failed to close. The reasoning would be that the seller had accepted the buyer by entering the agreement and, therefore, could not later refuse to pay the commission because the buyer was not financially able. It would be especially likely that the seller would be found liable if the seller had taken any opportunity to independently evaluate the buyer's financial ability, such as by checking on the buyer's employment or credit rating.

On the other hand, if the broker has in any way misrepresented the buyer's financial ability, withheld information regarding the buyer's financial status, or in any other way misled the seller as to the buyer's financial ability, then the seller retains the right to object to paying the commission on the basis that the buyer was financially unable (the broker failed to produce a buyer who was ready, willing and able), even if the seller has entered a binding purchase and sale contract with the buyer.

In one case dealing with this issue, the agent actively misled the seller concerning the buyer's financial ability to purchase a laundromat. The agent told the seller that the buyer had a good job and that the buyer's wife would manage the business. The agent also told the seller that the buyer had enough stock in an oil company to pay off the seller at any time but did not want to liquidate his stock at this time. The agent was aware, though, that the buyer intended to resign his job and, in fact, could only raise the money for the downpayment by quitting his job and cashing out his retirement plan. The agent also knew that the buyer's total stock portfolio was worth only a little over $300.

The court held that the rule which entitled the broker to a commission when the seller accepted the buyer did not apply in a case such as this where the broker had fraudulently misled the seller as to the buyer's financial ability. The seller was able to recover the commission which had been paid.

Distinctions Between Types of Listing Agreements

The primary differences among open, exclusive, and exclusive right to sell listings are the conditions under which a seller is obligated to pay a commission and whether the seller has a right to list the property with more than one broker or to sell the property him or herself without liability for a commission. The type of listing agreement is determined by the terms in the contract itself.

Open listings are the only listings under which the seller is free to list the property with more than one broker at the same time. Under an open listing agreement, no exclusive rights or priorities are given to any one listing agent. A broker earns a commission only if he or she procures and presents to the owner an enforceable offer from a ready, willing and able buyer on the listing terms or other acceptable terms, **before** the property is sold by another agent, sold by the owner, or the listing expires or is revoked.

Under both **exclusive agency** and **exclusive right to sell** listing agreements, the seller is permitted to list the property with only one broker. The difference between these two is whether or not the seller has the right to market and sell the property on his or her own without the obligation for a commission. Under an exclusive right to sell, the owner has no such right. An exclusive right to sell listing, the most common type of listing for residential property, is an agreement which gives the agent a specified period of time in which to find a buyer. The broker is entitled to a commission if the property is sold during that period of time, regardless of who finds the buyer and effects the sale, or if the broker receives and presents to the owner an enforceable offer from a ready, willing and able buyer on the terms in the listing agreement or on other acceptable terms.

An exclusive agency listing agreement is the same as an exclusive right to sell, except that the owner reserves the right to market the property and sell it him or herself, but not through another real estate agent. If the owner is successful in finding a buyer without the assistance of a real estate agent, the owner need not pay the broker a commission.

To summarize, the exclusive right to sell listing is the only one which obligates the seller to pay a commission when the seller is the one who finds the buyer. Under open and exclusive agency listings, the seller is free to attempt to market the property on his or her own and, if successful in finding a buyer without the assistance of the broker, to sell the property without liability for a commission. There is, of course, enormous potential in these situations for disputes between the seller and broker as to who was the procuring cause of the sale. The exclusive right to sell listing eliminates such disputes because the seller is obligated to pay the commission regardless of who finds the buyer.

California Real Estate Law requires that any exclusive listing agreement (exclusive agency or exclusive right to sell agreements) must have a specified termination date. This requirement is met if you can tell from the listing agreement itself when the term will end. This can be done by setting a specific date for termination or by setting a beginning date and specifying a definite period of time for the term.

The Code of Ethics of the National Association of REALTORS® encourages the use of exclusive type listings whenever possible. This would include both exclusive agency and exclusive right to sell listing agreements. Theoretically, exclusive types of listings result in better service to the seller. Since the broker has a more secure claim for a commission if the property is sold, the broker is more likely to work harder to sell the property. With exclusive listings there is also less potential for dispute among competing brokers than is likely to occur if open listings are employed.

Seller's agreement to pay commission.

The circumstances under which a seller is obligated to pay the broker a commission are spelled out in the listing agreement. A typical California exclusive right to sell listing agreement form, such as the California REALTORS® form covered in the next chapter, would obligate the seller to pay a commission if:

1) a ready, willing and able buyer is found during the listing term or extensions of the listing term;
2) the owner withdraws the property from sale or makes it unmarketable; or,

3) the owner, within some specified period of time after termination of the listing, sells the property to a buyer with whom the broker or other cooperating agent first negotiated during the listing term.

A ready, willing and able buyer is procured. The first circumstance is the most common occurrence resulting in an obligation of the seller to pay a commission. The property is actually sold, or an enforceable offer is presented, during the listing term on the terms and conditions stated in the listing agreement or on other terms which have been accepted and agreed upon by the seller. Under an exclusive right to sell agreement, it makes no difference how the sale comes about or who finds the buyer: the listing broker, some other broker or real estate licensee, the owner or anyone else. If a buyer is found on the seller's terms, then a commission is owed to the broker.

Withdrawal from sale. A withdrawal from sale provision is the contract basis for a broker's claim to a commission if the listing is terminated and the property withdrawn from the market by the seller prior to the agreed upon termination date. Under such circumstances the seller is obligated to pay the broker the full commission.

Such clauses have been attacked as unenforceable penalty provisions by sellers in numerous jurisdictions. The general rule in contract law is that liquidated damages provisions must be an attempt, in situations where it would be difficult to calculate and prove the actual damages, to estimate and provide for damages which the parties contemplate will actually be suffered as a consequence of breach of the contract. If the "liquidated damages" clause is determined by a court to be nothing other than a provision to penalize one party for breaching the contract, rather than an attempt to provide for damages suffered, then it will normally not be enforced. The general American law is that penalty provisions in contracts are unenforceable; persons breaching contracts should be held liable for the damages caused by such breach but should not be required to pay excessive penalties on account of breaching a contract.

In most jurisdictions, however, clauses providing for payment of the commission if the seller terminates the listing and withdraws the property from sale without the broker's permission prior to the termination date generally have been upheld and enforced by the courts. In most jurisdictions this has been on the theory that the provisions are legitimate efforts to estimate the damages that would be incurred by the broker as a result of the breach (loss of the commission) and are not unenforceable penalty provisions.

The California courts have taken a completely different tack in upholding such clauses. Rather than getting bogged down in questions of whether the clauses provided for unreasonable penalties for breach (and would therefore be void under the California Civil Code), they have simply adopted the theory that the clauses are not intended to provide for liquidated damages in the event of breach but are, rather, intended to provide for payment of indebtedness upon the occurrence of a particular condition (withdrawal of the property from the market).

Under this theory, the clause gives the owner a choice or alternative: if, during the term of the exclusive right to sell contract, the owner changes his or her mind and decides that he or she does not wish to sell the property after all, the owner has the power to terminate the agent's otherwise exclusive right through the payment of a sum certain set forth in the contract.

According to the California Supreme Court, the listing agreement is freely negotiated by the parties (seller and broker) dealing at arms' length; neither enjoys a vastly superior bargaining position. The contract then gives the owner ". . . a realistic and rational choice in the future with respect to the subject matter of the contract." If the owner decides to have the broker discontinue efforts to sell the property, the owner may withdraw the property upon the payment of the sum certain provided for in the contract (the commission). "In these circumstances the contract is truly one which contemplates alternative performance, not one in which [there is] a penalty for failure to perform the main promise."

"Safety clause." A provision leading to the seller's obligation to pay a commission for a sale occurring after the termination of the listing is sometimes called a "safety" or "extender" clause. The intent of such a provision is to prevent the seller and buyer from conspiring to deny the broker the commission by agreeing to wait until the listing runs out before buying and selling the property. The California Civil Code specifically provides that an exclusive right to sell listing agreement may contain a clause which gives the listing broker a right to compensation if the property is sold during a specified period after termination of the listing to anyone with whom the agent had negotiations during the listing term. In order to establish a right to a commission under this type of clause, it is not necessary that the broker actually be the procuring cause of the sale, but the broker must be able to show some action or negotiations with the buyer beyond simply initially contacting the buyer. For example, in one case the broker was unable to collect a commission for a sale occurring one day after termination of the listing agreement when the broker's sole connection with the transaction was that the buyer had seen the broker's "For Sale" sign in front of the property.

Most California listing agreements with "safety" clauses include a requirement that the broker, at the termination of the listing, give the seller a list of names of persons that he or she has negotiated with during the listing term. This is intended to protect the seller from unknowingly selling the property to someone who had previously been shown the property by the broker and thus unexpectedly becoming liable for a commission. In the usual situation, the seller does not know all the people who may have been shown the property or negotiated with the agent during the listing term. Particularly in a multiple listing where a keybox is used, it is possible that many potential buyers may be shown the property by cooperating agents while the seller is not at home. The cooperating agents never advise the seller of names of such prospective purchasers because no offer is made.

Safety clauses also contain a potential for the owner to become liable for two commissions if the property is listed with a second broker following expiration of the first listing agreement. If the second broker procures a buyer who had first seen the property and negotiated with the first broker, the owner could be obligated to pay the first broker a commission under the safety clause and the second broker a commission as the procuring cause of the sale. In order to protect the seller in such situations, the CAR listing agreement form and many other forms include a provision that no commission will be owed under the safety clause if the property is listed with another licensed broker at the time of sale. Some forms have a provision that if the two brokers are members of the same multiple listing service, the commission will be split between them.

Conditions.

A seller may want to protect him or herself by placing conditions on the obligation to pay a commission. In general, these conditions are intended to limit the seller's obligation to those transactions where the deal actually closes and the seller receives the money. Since the listing agreement forms are normally prepared by attorneys representing real estate brokers, conditions of this type are rarely part of a form. The forms are intended to give the broker the widest possible right to a commission, not to limit or restrict that right. Any limit or restriction would have to be written in at the direction of the seller.

For example, the seller may direct that the listing agreement state that the seller will be obligated to pay a commission only "when and if the transaction closes," or the agreement may provide that the seller will pay the commission "out of the funds received from the buyer at closing." Such provisions are intended to protect the seller from being required to pay a commission in cases where the broker finds a buyer and a binding contract is entered but, for some reason (which is not the fault of the seller), the transaction is never successfully consummated and the seller does not receive the price. The seller does not want to find him or herself in a position of owing the broker several thousand dollars for a commission and not having any money with which to pay it.

In general, if the **deposit receipt** contains **conditions**, as most of them do, the broker does not become entitled to a commission until the conditions are met or waived. When all the conditions have been met or waived, the broker then becomes entitled to the commission, even if the transaction is not later consummated, unless payment of the commission has been conditioned on a successful closing (as in the examples directly above).

Multiple listing.

A "multiple listing" is not a particular type of listing agreement, it is simply a listing with a broker who belongs to a multiple listing service. A multiple listing service is an organization of real estate brokers who have banded together to share information relative to the properties that each has listed. The intention is to increase their marketing ability by increasing exposure to the public. The listing broker (listing agent) normally shares the commission received with the broker who actually finds the purchaser (selling agent).

In most cases, brokers who belong to multiple listing services utilize exclusive right to sell listings. However, in California, a multiple listing service may not require that all listing agreements be exclusive right to sell listing agreements. Such a requirement by a multiple listing service in California would be considered an unfair restraint of trade.

Brokers within a multiple listing service may not agree to set commissions at a certain rate. Commissions must be freely negotiated between the seller and the listing broker without restriction or limitations imposed by the multiple listing service to which the listing will be submitted.

California law requires that listing agreements for one to four unit residential property must contain a notice that commissions are negotiable and not set by law. For an **example** of such a notice, refer to the CAR listing agreement form in the next chapter.

Net listing.

A net listing is not a particular type of listing; it is a way of determining the amount of commission. A net listing arrangement can be part of an open, exclusive agency, or exclusive right to sell listing agreement. Instead of agreeing to pay a commission of a certain amount or percentage of the sales price (which is the most common arrangement), the owner agrees to pay the broker a commission of everything above a certain "net" to the seller.

There is a potential for fraud in net listings in that the broker normally has much more knowledge concerning property values and market conditions than does the owner. There is the opportunity for an unscrupulous broker to mislead the seller as to the expected selling price of the property and thereby obtain an unconscionably large commission.

For example, suppose an owner tells the broker that he would like to get at least $100,000 for his property, after paying commissions and closing costs. The broker believes that the property is worth nearly $200,000 and could probably be sold quickly for well over $150,000. The broker, however, does not advise the seller of this; he simply takes the listing at $100,000 net to seller. The broker then finds a buyer for $165,000 and quickly makes a commission of over $50,000, much of the commission at the expense of the owner.

Net listings are illegal in some states, but are not unlawful in California. A broker with a net listing must reveal the amount of the commission to the principal before the principal commits him or herself to the transaction. Failure to make the proper disclosure may expose the broker to civil liability and to possible disciplinary action by the Real Estate Commissioner.

Buyer - Broker Agreements

Although there has been an increasing awareness of and discussion of buyer representation, as opposed to the traditional notion that the broker represents the seller, the number of transactions in which the broker is actually employed by the buyer remains relatively small in comparison to the number of transactions in which the broker is employed by the seller. Questions of agency and fiduciary relationships are extremely complex. An agent may be representing the seller, the buyer or both, depending upon the facts in a particular transaction. Even an agent who is apparently working for the buyer may also be considered to be the subagent of the seller. The nature of fiduciary relationships and dual agency is discussed in the Agency chapter. At this point, the discussion is concerned only with those still relatively rare transactions where the broker has a written employment contract with the buyer.

Much of the discussion of seller-broker listing agreements is applicable to buyer-broker agreements. Such agreements must be in writing, must contain a bold print statement that the commission is negotiable if for residential property, and must be signed by the buyer. Some provisions which are normally found in broker-buyer agreements include: the term of the agency; general characteristics of the property the buyer wants; price range; conditions under which a commission will be earned; amount of commission; who is to pay the commission; a "safety" clause; and some description of the broker's duties.

Buyer agency agreements are normally "exclusive right to buy" agreements which obligate the buyer to pay a commission to the agent if the buyer purchases, exchanges or takes an option on property of the general nature described in the agreement during the term of the agreement or during the specified "safety" period after termination of the agreement, regardless of whether the buyer locates the property through the services of the broker, another broker or real estate agent, through anyone else or through his or her own efforts.

A section is usually included to set out the general characteristics of the property sought by the buyer, including type (e.g., single family residential, three bedroom, two bath), size, location (e.g., Mira Vista or Corona Dorado subdivisions, or Gwydion school district), price range, terms the buyer is able and willing to pay (e.g., VA only, 80% conventional loan, or seller financing with no more than 10% down, interest rate of not over 11% fixed, term not less than twenty years), and any other terms or conditions desired by the buyer or broker.

One significant problem with buyer agency agreements is that the typical buyer does not have any extra money at closing to pay a real estate broker's fee. The average buyer uses most or all of his or her available cash to buy the property. There simply is not enough extra to pay a five or six percent commission to the broker who located the property and negotiated the deal for the buyer. It is common in broker-buyer agreements to provide that the buyer's obligation to pay a commission will be eliminated if the broker is able to split with the listing broker the commission being paid by the seller. In most buyer agency transactions this is currently the way payment of the commission is arranged.

For example, the buyer's broker has an agreement under which she is entitled to a 6% commission. The seller's listing agreement also calls for payment of a 6% commission to the listing broker. The buyer's broker and seller's broker agree to split the seller's commission half and half. The seller's broker is in a position the same or similar to the position he or she would be in if the sale were arranged by a cooperating broker in the multiple listing service. The buyer's broker, by agreeing to accept half of the commission payable to the listing agent gives up the right to be paid directly by the buyer under the most common forms of buyer agency agreements.

Disclosures are particularly important when an agent is representing the buyer. A broker operating under a buyer agency agreement may, if he or she is a member of the same multiple listing association as the listing broker, appear to also be a subagent of the seller. The buyer's broker should then insure that the seller is informed that he or she is representing the buyer. If the buyer's broker is to be compensated by the seller or by splitting the fee with the seller's broker, it is necessary to make a full disclosure to the buyer. It is safest to include a written disclosure on the deposit receipt signed by the seller and buyer. (See Chapter 1 for a discussion and example of the disclosure form agents are required to give to their buyers and sellers.)

EXAMPLE:

> *"Seller acknowledges that (name of buyer's broker) is acting in this transaction as the agent for buyer."*

There should also be a disclosure on the deposit receipt regarding payment of the commission.

EXAMPLE IF COMMISSION PAID BY BUYER:

"Broker's commission in connection with this transaction will be paid by buyer."

EXAMPLE IF COMMISSION PAID BY SELLER:

"Broker's commission in connection with this transaction will if for residential property be paid by seller. The commission to be paid to broker by seller is part of the consideration for seller's contract with buyer and does not arise out of any agency relationship between seller and broker."

## Chapter Four

The CAR Listing Form

An exclusive right to sell listing agreement form promulgated by the California Association of Realtors® will be used for illustrative purposes in the following review and analysis of listing agreement provisions and clauses. A copy of that form is reproduced on the next four pages.

Use of this particular form for illustration is not intended as an endorsement or criticism of it or any other particular form. The CAR form contains elements common to most exclusive right to sell forms by multiple listing services across the state but it may, of course, differ from the particular form you use in your daily business. Careful review and analysis of this form, coupled with contrasting and comparing it to your own form should assist you to achieve a greater level of understanding and professional competence in dealing with listing agreements.

Another form, a Real Estate Transfer Disclosure Statement, which sets out the seller's representations as to the condition of the property and the existence of any conditions which might affect the desirability or marketability of the property, is filled out in accord with the clause in the listing agreement (paragraph 11).

Title and Heading

The title at the top of the form, "EXCLUSIVE AUTHORIZATION AND RIGHT TO SELL," indicates that this is an exclusive right to sell listing agreement form. The CAR form for an exclusive agency contract is titled "EXCLUSIVE AGENCY AUTHORIZATION AND RIGHT TO SELL" and the form for an open listing agreement is titled "NONEXCLUSIVE

EXCLUSIVE AUTHORIZATION AND RIGHT TO SELL

MULTIPLE LISTING AUTHORIZATION

THIS IS INTENDED TO BE A LEGALLY BINDING AGREEMENT — READ IT CAREFULLY.

CALIFORNIA ASSOCIATION OF REALTORS® (CAR) STANDARD FORM

☐

1. **EXCLUSIVE RIGHT TO SELL:** I hereby employ and grant ______________ hereinafter called "Broker," the exclusive and irrevocable right commencing on ______________, 19____, and expiring at midnight on ______________, 19____, to sell or exchange the real property situated in the City of ______________, County of ______________, California described as follows: ______________

2. **TERMS OF SALE:** The purchase price shall be ______________ ($______________), to be paid as follows ______________

The following items of personal property are included in the above stated price: ______________

3. **MULTIPLE LISTING SERVICE (MLS):** Broker is a Participant of ______________ ASSOCIATION/BOARD OF REALTORS® Multiple Listing Service (MLS) and this listing information will be provided to the MLS to be published and disseminated to its Participants in accordance with its Rules and Regulations. Broker is authorized to cooperate with other real estate brokers, to appoint subagents and to report the sale, its price, terms and financing for the publication, dissemination, information and use by authorized Association/Board members, MLS Participants and Subscribers.
4. **TITLE INSURANCE:** Evidence of title shall be a California Land Title Association policy of title insurance in the amount of the selling price.

Notice: The amount or rate of real estate commissions is not fixed by law. They are set by each Broker individually and may be negotiable between the Seller and Broker.

5. **COMPENSATION TO BROKER:** I hereby agree to compensate Broker, irrespective of agency relationship(s), as follows:
   (a) ____ percent of the selling price, or $______________, if the property is sold during the term hereof, or any extension thereof, by Broker or through any other person, or by me on the terms herein set forth, or any other price and terms I may accept, or ____ percent of the price shown in 2, or $______________, if said property is withdrawn from sale, transferred, conveyed, leased, or rented without the consent of Broker, or made unmarketable by my voluntary act during the term hereof or any extension thereof.
   (b) The compensation provided for in subparagraph (a) above if property is sold, conveyed or otherwise transferred within ______ calendar days after the termination of this authority or any extension thereof to anyone with whom Broker has had negotiations prior to final termination, provided I have received notice in writing, including the names of the prospective purchasers, before or upon termination of this agreement or any extension hereof. However, I shall not be obligated to pay the compensation provided for in subparagraph (a) if a valid listing agreement is entered into during the term of said protection period with another licensed real estate broker and a sale, lease or exchange of the property is made during the term of said valid listing agreement.
   (c) I authorize Broker to cooperate with other brokers, to appoint subagents, and to divide with other brokers such compensation in any manner acceptable to brokers.
   (d) In the event of an exchange, permission is hereby given Broker to represent all parties and collect compensation or commissions from them, provided there is full disclosure to all principals of such agency. Broker is authorized to divide with other brokers such compensation or commissions in any manner acceptable to brokers.
   (e) Seller shall execute and deliver an escrow instruction irrevocably assigning Broker's compensation in an amount equal to the compensation provided in subparagraph (a) (above) from the Seller's proceeds.
6. **DEPOSIT:** Broker is authorized to accept and hold on Seller's behalf a deposit to be applied toward purchase price.
7. **HOME PROTECTION PLAN:** Seller is informed that home protection plans are available. Such plans may provide additional protection and benefit to a Seller and Buyer. Cost and coverage may vary.

*8. **KEYBOX:** I authorize Broker to install a KEYBOX: (Initial) **YES** (____/____) **NO** (____/____)
Refer to reverse side for important keybox information.

9. **SIGN:** Authorization to install a FOR SALE/SOLD sign on the property: (Initial) **YES** (____/____) **NO** (____/____)
10. **PEST CONTROL:** Seller shall furnish a current Structural Pest Control Report of the main building and all structures of the property, except ______________. (Initial) **YES** (____/____) **NO** (____/____)
11. **DISCLOSURE:** Unless exempt, Seller shall provide a Real Estate Transfer Disclosure Statement concerning the condition of the property. I agree to save and hold Broker harmless from all claims, disputes, litigation, and/or judgments arising from any incorrect information supplied by me, or from any material fact known by me which I fail to disclose. (Initial) (____/____)

* 12. **TAX WITHHOLDING:** Seller agrees to perform any act reasonably necessary to carry out the provisions of FIRPTA (Internal Revenue Code §1445) and California Revenue and Taxation Code §§18805 and 26131, and regulations promulgated thereunder. Refer to the reverse side for withholding provisions and exemptions.

13. **EQUAL HOUSING OPPORTUNITY:** This property is offered in compliance with federal, state, and local anti-discrimination laws.

* 14. **ARBITRATION OF DISPUTES: Any dispute or claim in law or equity arising out of this contract or any resulting transaction shall be decided by neutral binding arbitration in accordance with the rules of the American Arbitration Association, and not by court action except as provided by California law for judicial review of arbitration proceedings. Judgment upon the award rendered by the arbitrator(s) may be entered in any court having jurisdiction thereof. The parties shall have the right to discovery in accordance with Code of Civil Procedure §1283.05. The following matters are excluded from arbitration hereunder: (a) a judicial or non-judicial foreclosure or other action or proceeding to enforce a deed of trust, mortgage, or real property sales contract as defined in Civil Code §2985, (b) an unlawful detainer action, (c) the filing or enforcement of a mechanic's lien, (d) any matter which is within the jurisdiction of a probate court, or (e) an action for bodily injury or wrongful death, or for latent or patent defects to which Code of Civil Procedure §337.1 or §337.15 applies. The filing of a judicial action to enable the recording of a notice of pending action, for order of attachment, receivership, injunction, or other provisional remedies, shall not constitute a waiver of the right to arbitrate under this provision.**

"NOTICE: BY INITIALLING IN THE SPACE BELOW YOU ARE AGREEING TO HAVE ANY DISPUTE ARISING OUT OF THE MATTERS INCLUDED IN THE 'ARBITRATION OF DISPUTES' PROVISION DECIDED BY NEUTRAL ARBITRATION AS PROVIDED BY CALIFORNIA LAW AND YOU ARE GIVING UP ANY RIGHTS YOU MIGHT POSSESS TO HAVE THE DISPUTE LITIGATED IN A COURT OR JURY TRIAL. BY INITIALLING IN THE SPACE BELOW YOU ARE GIVING UP YOUR JUDICIAL RIGHTS TO DISCOVERY AND APPEAL, UNLESS THOSE RIGHTS ARE SPECIFICALLY INCLUDED IN THE 'ARBITRATION OF DISPUTES' PROVISION. IF YOU REFUSE TO SUBMIT TO ARBITRATION AFTER AGREEING TO THIS PROVISION, YOU MAY BE COMPELLED TO ARBITRATE UNDER THE AUTHORITY OF THE CALIFORNIA CODE OF CIVIL PROCEDURE. YOUR AGREEMENT TO THIS ARBITRATION PROVISION IS VOLUNTARY."

"WE HAVE READ AND UNDERSTAND THE FOREGOING AND AGREE TO SUBMIT DISPUTES ARISING OUT OF THE MATTERS INCLUDED IN THE 'ARBITRATION OF DISPUTES' PROVISION TO NEUTRAL ARBITRATION."

(Initial) **BROKER (________) SELLER (_______/_______)**

15. **ATTORNEY'S FEES:** In any action, proceeding or arbitration arising out of this agreement, the prevailing party shall be entitled to reasonable attorney's fees and costs.

16. **ADDITIONAL TERMS:** ____

17. **ENTIRE AGREEMENT:** I, the Seller, warrant that I am the owner of the property or have the authority to execute this agreement. The Seller and Broker further intend that this agreement constitutes the complete and exclusive statement of its terms and that no extrinsic evidence whatsoever may be introduced in any judicial or arbitration proceeding, if any, involving this agreement.

I acknowledge that I have read and understand this agreement, including the information on the reverse side, and have received a copy.

Date ____________________, 19 ____ ____________________, California

Seller ____________________ Address ____________________

Seller ____________________ City ____________ State ____ Zip ______

In consideration of the above, Broker agrees to use diligence in procuring a purchaser. Phone __________

Real Estate Broker ____________________ By ____________________

Address ____________________ City ____________ Date __________

THIS STANDARDIZED DOCUMENT FOR USE IN SIMPLE TRANSACTIONS HAS BEEN APPROVED BY THE CALIFORNIA ASSOCIATION OF REALTORS® IN FORM ONLY. NO REPRESENTATION IS MADE AS TO THE APPROVAL OF THE FORM OF ANY SUPPLEMENTS NOT CURRENTLY PUBLISHED BY THE CALIFORNIA ASSOCIATION OF REALTORS® OR THE LEGAL VALIDITY OR ADEQUACY OF ANY PROVISION IN ANY SPECIFIC TRANSACTION. IT SHOULD NOT BE USED IN COMPLEX TRANSACTIONS OR WITH EXTENSIVE RIDERS OR ADDITIONS.

A REAL ESTATE BROKER IS THE PERSON QUALIFIED TO ADVISE ON REAL ESTATE TRANSACTIONS. IF YOU DESIRE LEGAL OR TAX ADVICE, CONSULT AN APPROPRIATE PROFESSIONAL.

This form is available for use by the entire real estate industry. The use of this form is not intended to identify the user as a REALTOR®. REALTOR® is a registered collective membership mark which may be used only by real estate licensees who are members of the NATIONAL ASSOCIATION OF REALTORS® and who subscribe to its Code of Ethics.

* REFER TO REVERSE SIDE FOR ADDITIONAL INFORMATION.

REVIEWED 2/91

FORM A-14

OFFICE USE ONLY
Reviewed by Broker or Designee ________
Date __________

EQUAL HOUSING OPPORTUNITY

8. **KEYBOX:** A keybox designed as a repository of a key to the above premises, will permit access to the interior of the premises by Participants of the Multiple Listing Service (MLS), their authorized licensees and prospective buyers. If property is not seller occupied, seller shall be responsible for obtaining occupants' written permission for use of the keybox. Neither listing nor selling broker, MLS or Board of REALTORS® is an insurer against theft, loss, vandalism or damage attributed to the use of keybox. SELLER is advised to verify the existence of, or obtain appropriate insurance through their own insurance broker.

12. **TAX WITHHOLDING:** (a) Under the Foreign Investment in Real Property Tax Act (FIRPTA), IRC §1445, every Buyer of U.S. real property must, unless an exemption applies, deduct and withhold from Seller's proceeds 10% of the gross sales price. The primary FIRPTA exemptions are: No withholding is required if (i) Seller provides Buyer with an affidavit under penalty of perjury, that Seller is not a "foreign person," or (ii) Seller provides Buyer with a "qualifying statement" issued by the Internal Revenue Service, or (iii) Buyer purchases real property for use as a residence and the purchase price is $300,000 or less and Buyer or a member of Buyer's family has definite plans to reside at the property for at least 50% of the number of days it is in use during each of the first two 12-month periods after transfer. (b) In addition, under California Revenue and Taxation Code §§18805 and 26131, every Buyer must, unless an exemption applies, deduct and withhold from the Seller's proceeds 3⅓% of the gross sales price if the Seller has a last known street address outside of California, or if the Seller's proceeds will be paid to a financial intermediary of the Seller. The primary exemptions are: No withholding is required if (i) the Seller has a homeowner's exemption for the subject property, for local property taxes, for the year in which the title transfers, or (ii) the property is selling for $100,000 or less, or (iii) the Franchise Tax Board issues a certificate authorizing a lower amount or no withholding, or (iv) the Seller signs an affidavit stating that the Seller is a California resident or a corporation qualified to do business in California. (c) Seller and Buyer agree to execute and deliver as directed any instrument, affidavit, or statement reasonably necessary to carry out those statutes and regulations promulgated thereunder.

14. **ARBITRATION:** Arbitration is the referral of a dispute to one or more impartial persons for final and binding determination. It is private and informal, designed for quick, practical, and inexpensive settlements. Arbitration is an orderly proceeding, governed by rules of procedure and standards of conduct prescribed by law.

ENFORCEMENT OF ARBITRATION AGREEMENTS UNDER CALIFORNIA CODE OF CIVIL PROCEDURE SECTIONS 1281, 1282.4, 1283.1, 1283.05, 1287.4 & 1287.6

§ 1281. A written agreement to submit to arbitration an existing controversy or a controversy thereafter arising is valid, enforceable and irreversible, save upon such grounds as exist for the revocation of any contract.

§ 1282.4. A party to the arbitration has the right to be represented by an attorney at any proceeding or hearing in arbitration under this title. A waiver of this right may be revoked; but if a party revokes such waiver, the other party is entitled to a reasonable continuance for the purpose of procuring an attorney.

§ 1283.1. (a) All of the provisions of Section 1283.05 shall be conclusively deemed to be incorporated into, made a part of, and shall be applicable to, every agreement to arbitrate any dispute, controversy, or issue arising out of or resulting from any injury to, or death of, a person caused by the wrongful act or neglect of another.

(b) Only if the parties by their agreement so provide, may the provisions of Section 1283.05 be incorporated into, made a part of, or made applicable to, any other arbitration agreement.

§ 1283.05. To the extent provided in Section 1283.1 depositions may be taken and discovery obtained in arbitration proceedings as follows:

(a) After the appointment of the arbitrator or arbitrators, the parties to the arbitration shall have the right to take depositions and to obtain discovery regarding the subject matter of the arbitration, and, to that end, to use and exercise all of the same rights, remedies, and procedures, and be subject to all of the same duties, liabilities, and obligations in the arbitration with respect to the subject matter thereof, as provided in Chapter 2 (commencing with Section 1985) of, and Article 3 (commencing with Section 2016) of Chapter 3 of, Title 3 of Part 4 of this code, as if the subject matter of the arbitration were pending in a civil action before a superior court of this state, subject to the limitations as to depositions set forth in subdivision (e) of this section.

(b) The arbitrator or arbitrators themselves shall have power, in addition to the power of determining the merits of the arbitration, to enforce the rights, remedies, procedures, duties, liabilities, and obligations of discovery by the imposition of the same terms, conditions, consequences, liabilities, sanctions, and penalties as can be or may be imposed in like circumstances in a civil action by a superior court of this state under the provisions of this code, except the power to order the arrest or imprisonment of a person.

(c) The arbitrator or arbitrators may consider, determine, and make such orders imposing such terms, conditions, consequences, liabilities, sanctions, and penalties, whenever necessary or appropriate at any time or stage in the course of the arbitration, and such orders shall be as conclusive, final, and enforceable as an arbitration award on the merits, if the making of any such order that is equivalent to an award or correction of an award is subject to the same conditions, if any, as are applicable to the making of an award or correction of an award.

(d) For the purpose of enforcing the duty to make discovery, to produce evidence or information, including books and records, and to produce persons to testify at a deposition or at a hearing, and to impose terms, conditions, consequences, liabilities, sanctions, and penalties upon a party for violation of any such duty, such party shall be deemed to include every affiliate of such party as defined in this section. For such purpose:

(1) The personnel of every such affiliate shall be deemed to be the officers, directors, managing agents, agents, and employees of such party to the same degree as each of them, respectively, bears such status to such affiliate; and

(2) The files, books, and records of every such affiliate shall be deemed to be in the possession and control of, and capable of production by, such party. As used in this section, "affiliate" of the party to the arbitration means and includes any party or person for whose immediate benefit the action or proceeding is prosecuted or defended, or an officer, director, superintendent, member, agent, employee, or managing agent of such party or persons.

(e) Depositions for discovery shall not be taken unless leave to do so is first granted by the arbitrator or arbitrators.

§ 1287.4. If an award is confirmed, judgment shall be entered in conformity therewith. The judgment so entered has the same force and effect as, and is subject to all the provisions of law relating to, a judgment in a civil action; and it may be enforced like any other judgment of the court in which it is entered.

§ 1287.6. An award that has not been confirmed or vacated has the same force and effect as a contract in writing between the parties to the arbitration.

AUTHORIZATION AND RIGHT TO SELL." This particular form is intended for use by brokers who belong to a multiple listing service and plan to disseminate the listing through that service. There is then a notice that the form is intended to create a binding contract and that therefore the parties should read it carefully before signing. At the end of the heading is a simple identification that this printed contract form is a California REALTORS® standard form.

Paragraph 1. Exclusive Right to Sell

The initial paragraph in the listing agreement contract sets out four extremely important elements of the agreement. Clauses in Paragraph 1:

1) identify the broker who is employed;
2) specifically employ the broker and describe the type of authority given to the broker;
3) show the beginning and ending dates of the listing term; and,
4) identify the property which is listed with the broker.

The broker's name as licensed would be written in the blank on the first line.

This first sentence contains the all-important words necessary for an enforceable listing agreement which specifically employs the broker, paraphrased as follows:

> "I hereby **employ and grant** . . . (the broker) . . . **the exclusive and irrevocable right** . . . **to sell or exchange** the real property . . . described as follows . . ."

In order to satisfy the California Statute of Frauds, the written listing agreement must show the employment of the broker by the principal in language which clearly gives the broker authority to act as agent for the principal.

The grant of authority in the clause above indicates that the broker in this agreement is given an exclusive right to sell listing which is irrevocable during its term. For an exclusive agency listing agreement, the appropriate CAR form contains the following grant of authority:

> "I hereby employ and grant . . . (*broker*) . . . the **exclusive and irrevocable Agency right** . . . to sell or exchange . . ."

For an open listing, the appropriate CAR form uses the following language in the grant of authority clause in the form's first paragraph:

> "I hereby employ and grant . . . (*broker*) . . . the **nonexclusive and revocable right** . . . to sell or exchange . . ."

The titles at the tops of the particular forms and these clauses in the initial paragraphs are indications of the type of listing agreement which is intended: exclusive right to sell, exclusive agency or open. As was discussed earlier, characterization of a listing agreement as an exclusive right to sell, exclusive agency or open listing is determined by the agreement as to when the broker is entitled to a commission. The conditions under which the seller becomes liable for a commission are set out in Paragraph 5 of this contract form (Paragraph 3 of the CAR exclusive agency and open listing agreement forms). That paragraph relating to compensation will be covered later.

Even though these clauses state that the broker is given the right to sell or exchange the property, this statement is somewhat misleading. The broker is in fact given no such authority. The broker is really only authorized to show the property to prospective buyers and to present offers to the seller who then accepts or rejects the offer. The actual authority to enter an agreement to sell the property and to convey it (the right to really sell or exchange the property) would normally be granted in a power of attorney, not in a listing agreement.

There are blanks to indicate the beginning and ending dates of the listing term. In California, exclusive right to sell and exclusive agency listing agreements must have a definite termination date.

The final blank lines in Paragraph 1 provide space to enter the description of the property. The California Statute of Frauds does not require a full legal description of the property in order to have an enforceable listing agreement; however, the property must be described with enough clarity to permit it to be identified. Therefore, accuracy is essential, whether a street address or legal description is used. If there is any reason to believe that the street address may not accurately or unambiguously describe the property, then the exact legal description should be used. If there is not enough space in the blank on the form, then the legal description may be attached as an exhibit which is referenced in this blank. The attached exhibit would be dated and signed by the parties. Often, the agent filling out the deposit receipt form relies on the listing agreement for the property description so it is doubly important that the listing agreement contains an accurate and sufficient description. The enforceability of two contracts may depend on it.

The last line in Paragraph 1 refers to an attached information sheet. Many multiple listing associations have computerized services to provide accurate and timely information regarding available listings. This information is normally entered in the computer (and displayed by the computer) in a standardized form.

Paragraph 2. Terms of Sale

The second paragraph sets out the price and terms which the seller would accept and lists any personal property which the seller intends to include in the sale.

The total purchase price is entered in the first blank. This is the so-called "listing price." The seller often relies upon the agent's expertise and knowledge of the market in setting the listing price. The agent should render competent professional advice to the owner. Sometimes, in order to convince the owner to list the property with him or her, an agent inflates the value of the property and lists it at an unreasonably high figure. This is not only a disservice to the client, it is an unethical practice under the Commissioner's regulations.

Next are blanks for the terms which are acceptable to the seller. For example, the seller might be willing to accept all cash to be paid from the purchaser's cash downpayment and the proceeds of a conventional loan, or the seller might be willing to sell to an FHA or VA buyer. The seller might also be willing to carry back a purchase money deed of trust for all or part of the purchase price on certain specified terms (interest rate, monthly payments, loan term) or might even be willing to sell only on a seller financed installment basis because of tax planning considerations. If the property is income property for the owner, the seller might require an exchange instead of a sale for income tax planning purposes.

Care should be taken in discussing acceptable terms with the seller and accurately describing those terms in the listing agreement. The broker's right to a commission normally hinges on producing a buyer who is ready, willing and able to buy the property on the seller's terms as expressed in the listing agreement. Failure to accurately describe acceptable terms here may make it difficult for the broker to establish a right to a commission if the seller later becomes uncooperative and unwilling to accept any offers from potential buyers.

Example:

> 2. **TERMS OF SALE:** The purchase price shall be *One hundred thousand dollars* ______________ ($ *100,000.00*), to be paid as follows *All cash to seller at close of escrow from buyer's cash resources and/or proceeds of Conventional loan* .

The final sentence and blank lines in the paragraph permit the seller to indicate any personal property items, such as household appliances, which are included in the price. The agent should review with the seller the relevant paragraph from the deposit receipt form which will be used for the purchase and sale contract so that the seller is aware of which items are normally included as part of the standard printed contract. Most standard deposit receipt forms have a paragraph or paragraphs relating to items included in the sale, usually titled "INCLUDED ITEMS," "FIXTURES," "PERSONAL PROPERTY INCLUDED IN SALE" or some similar designation. If the seller is willing to include items in the sale which are not listed in that standard paragraph on the deposit receipt, they should be listed here. If there is anything in the paragraph(s) in the deposit receipt which the seller intends to remove, that should be listed on the listing agreement form, probably in the ADDITIONAL TERMS paragraph at the bottom of the form or in an addendum. The seller should be cautioned to insure that the same items are also listed as exceptions on the deposit receipt form when an offer is accepted.

It is important to emphasize at this point that the listing agreement is an employment contract between the owner and the broker; the buyer is not a party to that contract. The agreement between the buyer and seller is the purchase and sale agreement (the deposit receipt); terms included in the listing agreement, such as an agreement that the seller can remove the TV antenna, are not a part of the contract between the buyer and seller and are not binding on the buyer.

Paragraph 3. Multiple Listing Service (MLS)

Paragraph 3 serves to advise the seller that the broker is a member of a multiple listing service, named in the blank provided, and authorizes the broker to place the listing in that multiple listing service, to cooperate with other brokers, to appoint subagents and to publish and disseminate all relevant information regarding the listing and any subsequent sale to participants in the MLS. Under California law, a real estate broker may not place a listing in a multiple listing service unless authorized or directed to do so by the property owner as in this provision. There is a similar paragraph in the CAR deposit receipt form which authorizes the broker to disseminate the information regarding the sale.

Paragraph 4. Title Insurance

Paragraph 4 is an agreement that evidence of the owner's title shall be provided in the form of a California Land Title Association policy. This clause does not specify whether standard or extended coverage will be provided. (Standard coverage insures against defects that could be discovered by a thorough search of the public record, such as an invalid deed; extended coverage also insures against defects that could be discovered in an inspection or survey of the property.) This clause also does not commit the seller to paying for the policy. The title insurance costs are usually allocated between the seller and the buyer in the deposit receipt (see paragraph 5 in the CAR standard deposit receipt form, discussed in Chapter 18).

Notice That Commission is Negotiable

Following the TITLE INSURANCE paragraph is a bold print notice that commissions are not set by law; the commission is negotiable between the seller and broker. This bold print notice is required on any printed or form listing agreement for mobile homes or one- to four-unit residential property. It is against the law for the broker to include the amount or rate of the commission as part of the printed form; the commission must be decided on and written in at the time the listing agreement is entered. It is also prohibited for brokers to work together in an attempt to fix commissions at a certain level or to establish minimum commission rates.

Paragraph 5. Compensation to Broker

Paragraph 5 governs payment of the commission; it sets forth the seller's agreement to compensate the broker, the amount or rate of compensation and the conditions under which the commission becomes payable. We will cover each of the five subparagraphs individually.

Subparagraph 5(a) has two separate provisions addressing payment of the commission on account of occurrences **during the listing term** or extensions of the term. Under the first provision, the seller is obligated to pay the commission specified in the blank (either a percentage of the sales price or specified amount) if the property is sold by the broker, the owner or anyone else during the listing term or any extensions. This clause establishes this listing agreement as an exclusive right to sell agreement, as the listing broker is entitled to compensation if the property is sold during the listing term on the terms set forth in the listing agreement or on other terms acceptable to the seller, no matter who effects the sale.

The second provision is a so-called "withdrawal from sale" clause. Under this provision, the seller is obligated to pay the broker a commission if the seller withdraws the property from the market, transfers or rents it without the consent of the broker or does anything which renders the property unmarketable during the listing term. Provisions of this type have been upheld and enforced by California courts under the theory that the seller is given a true option or alternative under the listing contract. The owner can either leave the property on the market and give the broker an opportunity to earn the commission by finding a buyer, or, if the owner decides not to sell the property, he or she can pay the broker the agreed upon compensation and withdraw the property from sale.

Subparagraph 5(b) is a "safety" or "extender" clause which allows the broker to recover a commission under certain circumstances if a sale occurs **after** the listing term. The general purpose and effect of this type of clause was discussed earlier. This particular safety clause entitles the broker to compensation if the buyer who buys within the specified number of days after the end of the listing term (the number of days is usually somewhere between 90 and 365) is someone with whom the broker "**negotiated**" during the listing term. Other forms may give the broker a right to compensation only if the broker is the cause of the sale or allow the broker a commission for merely introducing the buyer to the property. Under this form, the broker does not have to have been the procuring cause of the sale in order to satisfy that requirement but it is likely that the broker would have to have actually held discussions with the buyer. The mere fact that the buyer saw a "For Sale" sign, for example, would probably not entitle the broker to compensation under this contract.

There are two restrictions on the broker's right to a commission for sales during the "protection period:"

1) the broker must provide the owner with a list of names of prospective purchasers on or before the termination of the listing agreement or any extension; and,

2) no commission will be owed for a sale, lease or other transfer during the safety period if the seller has the property listed with another licensed broker at the time.

The requirement that the broker give the seller a list of names of potential buyers with whom the broker has negotiated is intended to protect the seller from unknowingly selling the property during the protection period to someone with whom the broker had negotiated and thereby becoming liable for a commission. Often, the seller has no other way of knowing who has been shown the property by real estate agents. This is especially true in multiple listings where a key box has been installed to permit the property to be shown by a large number of agents when the owner is not at home. The limitation that a commission is not owed to this listing broker if a sale or other transfer is arranged while the property is listed with another broker protects the owner from the potential liability of two commissions: one under the safety clause and one to the broker who arranged the sale. Some listing agreement forms do not have this limitation or the limitation applies only if the sale is arranged during the protection period by another broker within the same multiple listing service.

This provision, then, would most likely result in a commission payable to the broker in cases where the owner arranges a sale after expiration of the listing to a buyer named on the broker's list and without the assistance of another licensed broker. The broker should take care to explain the effect of this clause at the time the listing agreement is entered and again at the time the list of names is given to the owner, in order to avoid later disputes and claims by the owner that he or she was unaware that a commission might be owed for a sale arranged after the listing.

Subparagraph 5(c) has two clauses relating to subagents and cooperating brokers. The first is a specific authorization for the listing broker to cooperate with other brokers and appoint subagents (such as an associate broker employed by the listing broker). The second clause concerns splitting the commission. In the opening line of Paragraph 5, the owner agrees to compensate the listing broker; in this clause, the owner in a sense leaves the question of division of that commission to the broker(s). The listing broker is authorized to divide the commission among any cooperating brokers in any way that the brokers can agree on. The last paragraph in the CAR deposit receipt form contains a couple of clauses wherein the seller and broker(s) agree as to how the commission is to be paid and direct the escrow agent to make payment accordingly to the broker(s) entitled to the commission or portions of it. (See the discussion of the deposit receipt form, ACCEPTANCE paragraph.)

Subparagraph 5(d) is applicable only in exchanges. If the broker arranges an exchange, the broker is authorized to represent all parties and to be paid by all parties, as long as the broker makes a full disclosure to all parties of the agency role(s) he or she is playing in the transaction. Exchanges often involve three, and sometimes more, properties and owners. The complexity in finding the right types of property (including purpose, value, underlying encumbrances and other factors) in order to satisfy the requirements of the listing seller and the owner(s) of the exchange property or properties often requires that one agent be familiar with the requirements of all owners who are potential parties to the exchange. It is, therefore, much more common in exchanges than in sales for one broker to deal with and even represent several parties in order to get the deal together.

If other brokers are involved in arranging the trade, the listing broker is authorized to split the commission with them in any way that can be agreed upon by the cooperating brokers.

The last provision in the compensation paragraph is an agreement by the seller to execute escrow instructions assigning the compensation to the broker from the funds due to the seller at close of escrow. The escrow agent would then pay the broker directly from the funds available at closing; the broker would not have to rely upon being paid by the seller. There is, in the CAR deposit receipt form, a clause to this effect. The sentence in the ACCEPTANCE paragraph at the end of the deposit receipt reads: "Seller shall execute and deliver an escrow instruction irrevocably assigning the compensation for service in an amount equal to the compensation agreed to above."

Paragraph 6. Deposit

This paragraph authorizes the broker to accept the buyer's deposit on behalf of the seller, thus making the broker the seller's agent in handling the deposit. Without such express authorization, the broker would hold the deposit as the buyer's agent. The distinction is important in deciding who stands the loss in the event that the deposit is lost or misappropriated. If the broker holds the deposit as the buyer's agent (the normal situation absent an express authorization to accept it for the seller), the buyer would bear the risk of loss. On the other hand, if the broker accepts and holds the deposit on the seller's behalf (as provided by this authorization), the risk of loss is with the seller.

Paragraph 7. Home Protection Plan

The seller is advised by this clause that home warranty insurance plans are available. Such policies cover the costs of major and/or minor repairs to the structure, systems, and/or appliances for some time after transfer of title to the buyer. They are intended to take care of the matter of who should pay for correcting certain problems, such as a malfunctioning furnace, that come up within the first year or two after the sale and thereby avoid disputes and lawsuits involving the buyer, seller and/or broker. There is a similar provision in the CAR deposit receipt form. See the coverage of Subparagraph 16(h) HOME PROTECTION PLAN, in the deposit receipt materials.

Paragraph 8. Keybox

Paragraph 8 and the associated blanks for initials allow the seller to indicate whether or not the broker is permitted to install a keybox so that he or she and other cooperating agents can gain admittance to the property when the owner is not present. If the seller does authorize a keybox, then the keybox paragraph on the reverse side of the listing agreement becomes a part of the contract.

The keybox provisions on the reverse side of the contract explain that the keybox will serve to hold a key to the property. Members of the multiple listing service have keys which allow them to open the keybox to get the key to the house. If the property is rental property, the seller is to obtain the written permission of the tenants for the keybox.

The last part of this keybox paragraph concerns liability for loss or damage which may be traced to use of the keybox. The brokers and the MLS disclaim any liability for any theft, damage or other loss and advise the seller to make sure that he or she is properly insured against the possibility of such losses.

Paragraph 9. Sign

Paragraph 9 provides blanks for the seller's initials to indicate whether or not the broker is given permission to install a "FOR SALE/SOLD" sign on the property.

Paragraph 10. Pest Control

In this paragraph, the seller has the opportunity to agree to furnish the buyer with a Structural Pest Control Report on all the structures on the property, except for those buildings which are specifically excluded.

Paragraph 11. Disclosure

In the disclosure paragraph, the seller agrees to provide a Real Estate Transfer Disclosure Statement containing the seller's representations regarding the condition of the property, unless the transaction is exempt from that legal requirement. The CAR standard Real Estate Transfer Disclosure Statement form will be covered following the listing agreement form materials.

Paragraph 11 also includes an agreement by the seller to hold the broker harmless from any claims, litigation or judgment arising out of incorrect information given to the broker by the seller or information withheld by the seller. In effect, this means that if the seller misleads the broker as to the condition of the property and the broker subsequently misleads the buyer, the seller will be responsible for any claims made against the broker and will pay any judgment or reimburse the broker for the broker's liability to the buyer. There are then blanks for the seller's initials to show that the seller has been advised of and has specifically assumed this responsibility and liability.

The seller's disclosure obligations, which are also incumbent on the seller's agent, are also discussed in the materials covering the deposit receipt form. See the discussion of subparagraphs 16(a), (b), and (c) of the CAR deposit receipt form.

Paragraph 12. Tax Withholding

Paragraph 12 and the related information on the back of the form are intended to inform the seller of certain federal and state income tax requirements that apply to some real estate transactions. Under federal law, buyers must withhold 10% of the sales price if the seller is a foreign person. State law requires buyers to withhold 3⅓% of the price if the money is being collected by an intermediary or if the seller has an out-of-state address. (Many residential transactions are exempt from both the federal and state laws, however.) A similar provision is found in paragraph 14 on the CAR deposit receipt form.

Paragraph 13. Equal Housing Opportunity

Paragraph 13 is of little legal consequence. It simply states that the property is offered in compliance with local, state and federal anti-discrimination laws. Since compliance with these laws is mandatory, inclusion of this paragraph is little more than a notice and reminder to the parties that there may be several anti-discrimination laws which apply to this particular transaction.

Paragraph 14. Arbitration of Disputes

This arbitration provision only becomes a part of the contract if the broker and seller initial it in the blanks provided. If they do so, any dispute or legal claim based on the listing agreement will be decided through binding arbitration instead of a court action. In other words, if the seller and the broker are unable to resolve a disagreement concerning the commission or any other aspect of the broker's agency, they will have to submit the matter to an arbitrator. Neither party will be able to sue the other. The arbitration will be conducted according to the rules of the American Arbitration Association.

To comply with state law, paragraph 14 includes a notice in large, boldface type. The law requires that this notice be included in any listing agreement or deposit receipt that provides for binding arbitration. (That rule also applies to real estate marketing contracts, land contracts, and some leases.) The notice warns the parties that by initialling the arbitration provision, they are giving up their right to have a dispute litigated in a court or jury trial. It also warns that they may be compelled to submit to arbitration.

Several excerpts from the California Code of Civil Procedure are listed on the reverse side of the form, for the seller's information. These statutory provisions establish the enforceability of arbitration clauses like the one included in this listing agreement and explain the parties' rights in arbitration. Section 1282.4 provides that either party may be represented by a lawyer in the proceedings. Section 1283.05 sets forth the discovery procedures that may be used in connection with the arbitration, including depositions and requests for document production. Section 1287.4 provides that if the arbitrator's award is confirmed by a court, it will have the same legal effect as a court decision, and a judgment may be entered against the losing party. Under section 1287.6, an unconfirmed award has the legal effect of a contract between the parties.

Paragraph 15. Attorney's Fees

This is an attorney's fees provision similar to those found in most printed contract forms. In any legal action or proceeding (including arbitration) arising out of disputes concerning this contract, whoever wins will be entitled to recover the reasonable amount of attorney's fees and other costs, as well as their damages.

Paragraph 16. Additional Terms

There is a blank line provided to insert any additional terms desired by the broker or seller which are not part of the printed form or to reference an attached addendum with such term(s). For example, a cautious seller who wanted to avoid having to pay a commission even if the buyer defaulted and the transaction never closed might want to include a provision that no commission would be payable if the sale failed to close through no fault of the seller.

Example:

> *"Seller shall be obligated to pay the compensation referenced in subparagraph 5(a) only on close of escrow and recording of a deed to buyer or on failure to close if the failure to close is due to the seller's default or failure to act in good faith."*

Paragraph 17. Entire Agreement

The ENTIRE AGREEMENT paragraph deals with three matters. First, there is a warranty by the seller(s) that he or she (or they) is (are) the owner(s) of the property or otherwise have the authority to list the property for sale with a broker.

Next, there is an "entire agreement" or "integration" clause. This type of clause is found in most printed form contracts and provides that this written contract sets forth the entire agreement and understanding of the parties, that there are no other oral agreements, and that in any dispute no other evidence (other than this written contract) may be presented to show what the agreement between the parties is.

Third, there is an acknowledgment by the seller that he or she has read the entire listing agreement, including the provisions on the reverse, and has been given a copy of the agreement. The broker is required to give the owner a copy of any listing agreement at the time of signature.

In order to avoid later disputes regarding authority to sell the property and agreement to pay a broker's commission, the broker should have all owners of the property sign the listing agreement.

Due Diligence

Just above the signature lines for the broker, usually signed by a salesperson who would then sign in the "by" line as an agent of the broker, is a promise by the broker to use due diligence in attempting to procure a buyer. Failure of the broker to in fact exercise due diligence in actively marketing the property may give the owner the right to revoke the listing without liability for a commission.

Notice and Disclaimer

There is finally, at the bottom of the form, a notice and disclaimer. The seller is advised that the real estate broker is an expert in real estate matters, but not necessarily in legal or tax matters. A competent attorney or tax accountant should be consulted for legal or tax advice. There is a disclaimer that no guarantee is made that this particular form is adequate for any particular transaction.

Real Estate Transfer Disclosure Statement

The Real Estate Transfer Disclosure Statement form reproduced on the following pages contains provisions and blanks to provide several disclosures required under California law, including the seller's disclosure of structural changes or alterations made without appropriate permits, seller's and broker's disclosure of facts that would materially affect the property and that are not readily discoverable by the buyer, and the broker's disclosure of material facts known or discoverable to the broker from a reasonably diligent inspection of the property. The form consists of five sections, Section II containing information provided by the seller and Sections III and IV concerning the listing and selling agents' inspections of the property. The contents of the form are prescribed by statute (section 1102 of the Civil Code).

The first sentence of the form gives the property address and recites that the statement is a disclosure of the condition of the property as of the specified date.

The sentence directly below states, somewhat curiously, that the information is not intended as a warranty of any kind on the part of the agent or seller and is not to be a substitute for the buyer's own inspection(s). This disclaimer is particularly odd in view of the statement, contained at the beginning of the "SELLER'S INFORMATION" section of the form, that even though the disclosure is not intended as a warranty, the seller authorizes the agent to give a copy of the disclosure to any prospective buyer and acknowledges that the information may be relied upon by a buyer in deciding whether or not to buy the property. Under such circumstances, where a party makes certain representations with the understanding or expection that another party will rely upon them in making a decision, liability would be imposed for damages incurred if the representations prove to be material and false.

Section I allows the seller to indicate what other disclosures have been made in connection with the transaction which may also satisfy the disclosure obligations on this form. Then another bold print disclaimer appears before the actual disclosures begin. It is stated that the information set out in the SELLER'S INFORMATION section of the form are representations by the seller, not by the agent and that the representations are not intended to be part of the purchase and sale agreement.

After a statement of whether or not the property is currently occupied by the seller, is a section for the seller to check off items which are located on the property or services connected to the property.

After the checklist of amenities and other items is a statement for the seller to complete to indicate whether or not everything is in working order, as far as the seller is aware. If not, the seller is to provide further explanation in the space provided or on additional sheets if that is insufficient.

REAL ESTATE TRANSFER DISCLOSURE STATEMENT

(CALIFORNIA CIVIL CODE 1102, ET SEQ.)

CALIFORNIA ASSOCIATION OF REALTORS® (CAR) STANDARD FORM

☐

THIS DISCLOSURE STATEMENT CONCERNS THE REAL PROPERTY SITUATED IN THE CITY OF ________________ ________________, COUNTY OF ________________, STATE OF CALIFORNIA, DESCRIBED AS ________________.

THIS STATEMENT IS A DISCLOSURE OF THE CONDITION OF THE ABOVE DESCRIBED PROPERTY IN COMPLIANCE WITH SECTION 1102 OF THE CIVIL CODE AS OF ________________, 19____. IT IS NOT A WARRANTY OF ANY KIND BY THE SELLER(S) OR ANY AGENT(S) REPRESENTING ANY PRINCIPAL(S) IN THIS TRANSACTION, AND IS NOT A SUBSTITUTE FOR ANY INSPECTIONS OR WARRANTIES THE PRINCIPAL(S) MAY WISH TO OBTAIN.

I
COORDINATION WITH OTHER DISCLOSURE FORMS

This Real Estate Transfer Disclosure Statement is made pursuant to Section 1102 of the Civil Code. Other statutes require disclosures, depending upon the details of the particular real estate transaction (for example: special study zone and purchase-money liens on residential property).

Substituted Disclosures: The following disclosures have or will be in connection with this real estate transfer, and are intended to satisfy the disclosure obligations on this form, where the subject matter is the same: ________________

____

____

____

(LIST ALL SUBSTITUTED DISCLOSURE FORMS TO BE USED IN CONNECTION WITH THIS TRANSACTION)

II
SELLER'S INFORMATION

The Seller discloses the following information with the knowledge that even though this is not a warranty, prospective Buyers may rely on this information in deciding whether and on what terms to purchase the subject property. Seller hereby authorizes any agent(s) representing any principal(s) in this transaction to provide a copy of this statement to any person or entity in connection with any actual or anticipated sale of the property.

THE FOLLOWING ARE REPRESENTATIONS MADE BY THE SELLER(S) AND ARE NOT THE REPRESENTATIONS OF THE AGENT(S), IF ANY. THIS INFORMATION IS A DISCLOSURE AND IS NOT INTENDED TO BE PART OF ANY CONTRACT BETWEEN THE BUYER AND SELLER.

Seller ☐ is ☐ is not occupying the property.

A. The subject property has the items checked below (read across):

☐ Range	☐ Oven	☐ Microwave
☐ Dishwasher	☐ Trash Compactor	☐ Garbage Disposal
☐ Washer/Dryer Hookups	☐ Window Screens	☐ Rain Gutters

☐ Burglar Alarms	☐ Smoke Detector(s)	☐ Fire Alarm
☐ T.V. Antenna	☐ Satellite Dish	☐ Intercom
☐ Central Heating	☐ Central Air Conditioning	☐ Evaporator Cooler(s)
☐ Wall/Window Air Conditioning	☐ Sprinklers	☐ Public Sewer System
☐ Septic Tank	☐ Sump Pump	☐ Water Softener
☐ Patio/Decking	☐ Built-in Barbeque	☐ Gazebo
☐ Sauna	☐ Pool	☐ Spa ☐ Hot Tub
☐ Security Gate(s)	☐ Automatic Garage Door Opener(s)*	☐ Number of Remote Controls ______
Garage: ☐ Attached	☐ Not Attached	☐ Carport
Pool/Spa Heater: ☐ Gas	☐ Solar	☐ Electric
Water Heater: ☐ Gas	☐ Solar	☐ Electric
Water Supply: ☐ City	☐ Well	☐ Private Utility ☐ Other ______
Gas Supply: ☐ Utility	☐ Bottled	

Exhaust Fan(s) in ______________ 220 Volt Wiring in ______________

Fireplace(s) in ______________ ☐ Gas Starter

☐ Roof(s): Type: ______________ Age: ______________ (approx.)

☐ Other: ______________

Are there, to the best of your (Seller's) knowledge, any of the above that are not in operating condition? ☐ Yes ☐ No If yes, then describe. (Attach additional sheets if necessary.): ______________

____

____

B. Are you (Seller) aware of any significant defects/malfunctions in any of the following? ☐ Yes ☐ No If yes, check appropriate space(s) below.

☐ Interior Walls ☐ Ceilings ☐ Floors ☐ Exterior Walls ☐ Insulation ☐ Roof(s) ☐ Windows ☐ Doors ☐ Foundation ☐ Slab(s) ☐ Driveways ☐ Sidewalks ☐ Walls/Fences ☐ Electrical Systems ☐ Plumbing/Sewers/Septics ☐ Other Structural Components

(Describe: ______________

____

______________)

If any of the above is checked, explain. (Attach additional sheets if necessary): ______________

____

____

____

*This garage door opener may not be in compliance with the safety standards relating to automatic reversing devices as set forth in Chapter 12.5 (commencing with Section 19890) of Part 3 of Division 13 of the Health and Safety Code.

Buyer and Seller acknowledge receipt of copy of this page, which constitutes Page 1 of 2 Pages.

Buyer's Initials (________) (________) Seller's Initials (________) (________)

IN COMPLIANCE WITH CIVIL CODE SECTION 1102.6 / EFFECTIVE JULY 1, 1991.

OFFICE USE ONLY
Reviewed by Broker or Designee ________
Date ________

EQUAL HOUSING OPPORTUNITY

REAL ESTATE TRANSFER DISCLOSURE STATEMENT (TDS-14 PAGE 1 OF 2)

C. Are you (Seller) aware of any of the following:

1. Substances, materials, or products which may be an environmental hazard such as, but not limited to, asbestos, formaldehyde, radon gas, lead-based paint, fuel or chemical storage tanks, and contaminated soil or water on the subject property. ☐ Yes ☐ No
2. Features of the property shared in common with adjoining landowners, such as walls, fences, and driveways, whose use or responsibility for maintenance may have an effect on the subject property. ☐ Yes ☐ No
3. Any encroachments, easements or similar matters that may affect your interest in the subject property. ☐ Yes ☐ No
4. Room additions, structural modifications, or other alterations or repairs made without necessary permits. ☐ Yes ☐ No
5. Room additions, structural modifications, or other alterations or repairs not in compliance with building codes. ☐ Yes ☐ No
6. Landfill (compacted or otherwise) on the property or any portion thereof. ☐ Yes ☐ No
7. Any settling from any cause, or slippage, sliding, or other soil problems. ☐ Yes ☐ No
8. Flooding, drainage or grading problems. ☐ Yes ☐ No
9. Major damage to the property or any of the structures from fire, earthquake, floods, or landslides. ☐ Yes ☐ No
10. Any zoning violations, nonconforming uses, violations of "setback" requirements. ☐ Yes ☐ No
11. Neighborhood noise problems or other nuisances. ☐ Yes ☐ No
12. CC&R's or other deed restrictions or obligations. ☐ Yes ☐ No
13. Homeowners' Association which has any authority over the subject property. ☐ Yes ☐ No
14. Any "common area" (facilities such as pools, tennis courts, walkways, or other areas co-owned in undivided interest with others). ☐ Yes ☐ No
15. Any notices of abatement or citations against the property. ☐ Yes ☐ No
16. Any lawsuits against the seller threatening to or affecting this real property. ☐ Yes ☐ No

If the answer to any of these is yes, explain. (Attach additional sheets if necessary.): ____________

Seller certifies that the information herein is true and correct to the best of the Seller's knowledge as of the date signed by the Seller.

Seller ____________ Date ____________

Seller ____________ Date ____________

III
AGENT'S INSPECTION DISCLOSURE

(To be completed only if the seller is represented by an agent in this transaction.)

THE UNDERSIGNED, BASED ON THE ABOVE INQUIRY OF THE SELLER(S) AS TO THE CONDITION OF THE PROPERTY AND BASED ON A REASONABLY COMPETENT AND DILIGENT VISUAL INSPECTION OF THE ACCESSIBLE AREAS OF THE PROPERTY IN CONJUNCTION WITH THAT INQUIRY, STATES THE FOLLOWING:

____

Agent (Broker Representing Seller) ____________ (PLEASE PRINT) By ____________ (ASSOCIATE LICENSEE OR BROKER-SIGNATURE) Date ____________

IV

AGENT'S INSPECTION DISCLOSURE

(To be completed only if the agent who has obtained the offer is other than the agent above.)

THE UNDERSIGNED, BASED ON A REASONABLY COMPETENT AND DILIGENT VISUAL INSPECTION OF THE ACCESSIBLE AREAS OF THE PROPERTY, STATES THE FOLLOWING:

____

____

____

Agent (Broker
obtaining the Offer) ____________ (PLEASE PRINT) By ____________ (ASSOCIATE LICENSEE OR BROKER-SIGNATURE) Date ________

V

BUYER(S) AND SELLER(S) MAY WISH TO OBTAIN PROFESSIONAL ADVICE AND/OR INSPECTIONS OF THE PROPERTY AND TO PROVIDE FOR APPROPRIATE PROVISIONS IN A CONTRACT BETWEEN BUYER AND SELLER(S) WITH RESPECT TO ANY ADVICE/INSPECTIONS/DEFECTS.

I/WE ACKNOWLEDGE RECEIPT OF A COPY OF THIS STATEMENT.

Seller ____________ Date ______ Buyer ____________ Date ______

Seller ____________ Date ______ Buyer ____________ Date ______

Agent (Broker
Representing Seller) ____________ (PLEASE PRINT) By ____________ (ASSOCIATE LICENSEE OR BROKER-SIGNATURE) Date ________

Agent (Broker
obtaining the Offer) ____________ (PLEASE PRINT) By ____________ (ASSOCIATE LICENSEE OR BROKER-SIGNATURE) Date ________

A REAL ESTATE BROKER IS QUALIFIED TO ADVISE ON REAL ESTATE. IF YOU DESIRE LEGAL ADVICE, CONSULT YOUR ATTORNEY.

Page 2 of ______ Pages.

OFFICE USE ONLY
Reviewed by Broker or Designee ______
Date ______

EQUAL HOUSING OPPORTUNITY

REAL ESTATE TRANSFER DISCLOSURE STATEMENT (TDS-14 PAGE 2 OF 2)

DISCLOSURE

Sellers of real property should be aware of their disclosure obligations under the California Court Cases, Statutes and Real Estate Law commentaries excerpted or paraphrased below:

SELLER DISCLOSURE OBLIGATIONS UNDER CIVIL CODE SECTION 1102, ET SEQ.

Effective January 1, 1987, a transferor (seller) of real property including a residential stock cooperative containing 1 to 4 residential units (unless exempted under §1102.1) must supply a transferee (buyer) with a completed Real Estate Transfer Disclosure Statement in the form prescribed in Civid Code §1102.6.

EXEMPTED TRANSFERS: Summary of exempted transfers (Civil Code Section 1102.1) where Real Estate Transfer Disclosure Statement is **not** required:

a. Transfers requiring "a public report pursuant to §11018.1 of the Business & Professions Code" and transfers pursuant to §11010.4 of Business & Professions Code where no public report is required;
b. "Transfers pursuant to court order" (such as probate sales, sales by a bankruptcy trustee, etc.);
c. Transfers by foreclosure (including a deed in lieu of foreclosure and a transfer by a beneficiary who has acquired the property by foreclosure or deed in lieu of foreclosure);
d. "Transfers by a fiduciary in the course of the administration of a decendent's estate, guardianship, conservatorship, or trust."
e. "Transfers from one co-owner to one or more co-owners."
f. "Transfer made to a spouse" or to a direct blood relative;
g. "Transfers between spouses" in connection with a dissolution of marriage or similar proceeding;
h. Transfers by the State Controller pursuant to the Unclaimed Property Law;
i. Transfers as a result of failure to pay property taxes;
j. "Transfers or exchanges to or from any government entity."

TIMING OF DISCLOSURE AND RIGHT TO CANCEL (CIVIL CODE SECTION 1102.2):

a. In the case of a sale, the disclosures to the buyer shall be made "as soon as practicable before transfer of title."
b. "In the case of transfer by a Real Property Sales Contract, (Installment Land Sales Contract). . . or, by a lease together with an option to purchase, or ground lease coupled with improvements, as soon as practical before. . . the making or acceptance of an offer."

   "If any disclosure, or any material amendment of any disclosure, required to be made by this article, is delivered after the execution of an offer to purchase, the transferee shall have three days after delivery in person or five days after delivery by deposit in the mail, to terminate his or her offer by delivery of a written notice of termination to the transferor or the transferor's agent."

SUBSTITUTED DISCLOSURES: (CIVIL CODE SECTION 1102.4)

a. Neither the transferor nor <u>any listing</u> or <u>selling</u> agent shall be liable for any error, inaccuracy, or omission of any information delivered pursuant to this article if the error, inaccuracy, or omission was not within the personal knowledge of the transferor or <u>that listing</u> or <u>selling</u> agent, was based on information timely provided by public agencies or by other persons providing information as specified in subdivision (c) that is required to be disclosed pursuant to this article, and ordinary care was exercised in obtaining and transmitting it.

b. The delivery of any information required to be disclosed by this article to a prospective transferee by a public agency or other person providing information required to be disclosed pursuant to this article shall be deemed to comply with the requirements of this article and shall relieve the transferor or any listing or selling agent of any further duty under this article with respect to that item of information.

c. The delivery of a report or opinion prepared by a licensed engineer, land surveyor, geologist, structural pest control operator, contractor, or other expert, dealing with matters within the scope of the professional's license or expertise, shall be sufficient compliance for application of the exemption provided by subdivision (a) if information is provided to the prospective transferee pursuant to a request therefor, whether written or oral. In responding to such a request, an expert may indicate, in writing, an understanding that the information provided will be used in fulfilling the requirements of Section 1102.6 and, if so, shall indicate the required disclosures, or parts thereof, to which the information being furnished is applicable. Where such a statement is furnished, the expert shall not be responsible for any items of information, or parts thereof, other than those expressly set forth in the statement.

OTHER DISCLOSURE REQUIREMENTS

I "... Where the seller knows of facts materially affecting the value or desirability of the property which are known or accessible only to him and also knows that such facts are not known to, or within the reach of the diligent attention and observation of the buyer, the seller is under a duty to disclose them to the buyer." Lingsch v. Savage, 213 Cal. App. 2d 729.

II "Concealment may constitute actionable fraud where seller knows of facts which materially affect desirability of property and seller knows such facts are unknown to buyer." Koch v. Williams, 193 Cal. App. 2d 537, 541.

III "Deceit may arise from mere nondisclosure." Massei v. Lettunich, 248 Cal. App. 2d 68, 72.

IV Failure of the seller to fulfill such duty of disclosure constitutes actual fraud. [Civil Code Section 1572(3)]

V **California Civil Code: §1709. Deceit—Damages** One who willfully deceives another with intent to induce him to alter his position to his injury or risk is liable for any damages which he thereby suffers. **§1710. Elements of Actionable Fraud** A deceit, within the meaning of the last section, is either: (1) The suggestion, as a fact, of that which is not true, by one who does not believe it to be true; (2) The assertion, as a fact, of that which is not true, by one who has no reasonable ground for believing it to be true; (3) The suppression of a fact, by one who is bound to disclose it, or who give information of other facts which are likely to mislead for want of communication of that fact; or (4) A promise, made without any intention of performing it.

VI "The maker of a fraudulent misrepresentation (seller) is subject to liability... to another (buyer) who acts in justifiable reliance upon it if the misrepresentation, although not made directly to the other (buyer), and that it will influence his conduct..." [parenthetical material added]. Restatement (2d) or Torts §533.

VII "The Seller may have an affirmative duty to disclose certain significant facts regarding the condition of his property. It is not enough for the seller to say nothing because he is not asked." California Real Estate Sales Transactions, §12.2, p.463 (Cal. C.E.B. 1967).

VIII "A buyer who has been defrauded by the seller has the choice of either: (A) Using the seller's fraud as a defense when and if the buyer refuses to follow through with his obligation under the contract; or (B) Using the seller's fraud as a basis for an action for affirmative relief in the form of an action for damages or for recission of the contract."

IX Exculpatory Clauses: "It is better for the seller to disclose the specific condition than to attempt to exculpate himself against its nondisclosure. In general, the exculpatory (e.g., "as is") clause provides little, if any, protection." California Real Estate Sales Transactions p.483 (Cal. C.E.B. 1967).

[The Above is a general statement of the seller disclosure obligations. Other disclosure may be required].

In Subsection B, the seller is to state whether or not he or she is aware of any defects or malfunctions in the basic structure or systems of the property. Again, if the seller has any knowledge of problems, a full explanation is to be provided in the blank lines provided on the form or on additional sheets.

The top of the second page of the disclosure statement has a section for the seller to disclose his or her knowledge regarding any conditions which could affect the value or desirability of the property, including environmental hazards, boundary line problems, structural additions or modifications made without permits or in violation of local codes, soil drainage or stability problems, lawsuits against the seller which might affect the property and even any "neighborhood noise problems or other nuisances." If the seller answers in the affirmative to any of the questions, a full explanation must be included or attached.

At the end of the seller's information section are signature lines for the seller(s) and a certification that the information provided is correct to the best of their knowledge as of the date of signature.

The third and fourth sections deal with the AGENT'S INSPECTION DISCLOSURE and are quite a bit shorter. An agent is to fill out one of the two provisions, depending on whether he or she is the listing agent or selling agent. Under California law, an agent is required to make a reasonably competent and diligent inspection of residential property with an eye to discovering any conditions or facts that would materially affect the value or desirability of the property. If any such facts are discovered, the agent must make a full disclosure to the buyer. This form recites that the inspection has been made and provides space for each agent to disclose any conditions or other matters that have been discovered that would materially affect the value or desirability of the property. These disclosure requirements are discussed in more detail in the Agency materials. Signature lines for the agents are provided.

The fifth sections states that the buyer and seller may want to get professional advice and/or inspection of the property and so provide in a deposit receipt. At the end of the form are signature lines for sellers and buyers to acknowledge receipt of their copies.

Chapter Five

Competitive Market Analysis

The foundation of all real estate transactions is the value placed upon each particular piece of property. The value of a home will affect its selling price, its financing terms, its rental rate, its income tax consequences, its property tax assessment, and its insurance coverage. Obviously, before buying or selling property, an individual will want to know what it's worth. Thus, while the real estate agent may never be called upon to perform a formal appraisal, he or she must be able to estimate value with a fair degree of accuracy. To do this, the agent must have a firm grasp of the principles of value, the various factors that influence value, and the methods by which value can be estimated. It is the purpose of this chapter to explain value and the valuation process to enable the agent to use this information in his or her real estate practice.

The Listing Presentation

One of the most important benefits of a working knowledge of property valuation is the ability to determine a competitive listing price. Presenting a reasonable, factually based listing price as part of your listing presentation demonstrates your professional competence. Helping the seller establish a competitive listing price avoids the frustration of trying to sell an unrealistically priced property. Overpriced listings rarely sell, arouse the ill will of the seller and harm your firm's reputation.

While it is the responsibility of the agent to advise and assist the seller, it is ultimately the seller who must determine a listing price for his or her own property. However, the average seller does not have the knowledge or expertise to arrive at a fair market price. This is where the agent's information and experience comes into play. A major benefit of a real estate agent's services is his or her ability to help establish a realistic listing price. Such a price can be determined with the aid of a competitive market analysis. At its most basic, a competitive market analysis is a comparison of the prices of recently sold homes that are similar in location, style, and amenities to the listed property. (If it is difficult to make comparisons because of the uniqueness of the property, a complete real estate appraisal may be necessary.)

Approaches to value. Over the years, agents have used a variety of methods to arrive at a listing price. Unfortunately, many of these methods result in inaccurate estimates of value, are too complicated for the owner to fully understand, or are difficult to support factually. Many owners expect to receive more for their property than it is worth due to market misinformation, inflated expectations of value, or their own personal attachment to the property. When an agent presents a much lower than expected figure as a reasonable listing price, the owner will want to know why. Unless the agent can back up his or her estimate with facts and figures that are easy to understand, the agent will lose credibility as well as the seller's good will. Thus, a simple method of valuing property that is easy to apply and explain is essential.

Many agents erroneously use the "eyeball" approach to determining a listing price. The agent simply walks through the property, observes the various features of the home and compares them to those observed in other properties. The agent then arrives at what he or she feels is a competitive price. A major problem with this method (aside from inaccuracy) is explaining the price (which is probably lower than expected) to the seller without offending the seller and/or losing the listing.

Other possible methods include the cost approach (determining what it would cost to build a similar home and then subtracting depreciation) and the income approach (determining value based on the potential income the property could bring in). These methods are complicated, time consuming to apply and more difficult for the seller to understand. The market data approach, or competitive market analysis, is the method most suited to setting a listing price for residential property. Some advantages of this method are:

1. It is the easiest method to learn and use.
2. It is particularly applicable to single-family residences (the bulk of real estate transactions).
3. It is easily understood by the non-licensee.

Before describing the process of determining value through competitive market analysis, we will first discuss the definition of value and describe some of the forces that affect value.

Value

Value is created by people. It is not the intrinsic qualities of an item that make it valuable, but rather people's attitudes towards that item. For example, if it were to begin raining gold instead of water, gold would become a nuisance and its value would disappear. However, its intrinsic qualities would be the same whether it was a rare and precious metal or a too common nuisance. In the same way, changes in fashions and technologies make certain items (e.g., steam boats, telegraphs) obsolete or practically useless.

Factors that influence value.

For people to accord value to a product or service it must have certain characteristics: 1) utility, 2) scarcity, 3) demand, and 4) transferability.

Utility. A product must be able to render a service or fill a need before it has value. However, utility must exist in conjunction with demand and scarcity or market value will not exist. For example, air has great utility (it is necessary for life), but since there is an abundance of air (no scarcity), it has no market value.

Scarcity. Generally, the more scarce an item, the greater its value. For example, if diamonds were to become much more plentiful, their value would decline.

Demand. There must not only be a need for the product or service, but also the ability to meet that need through purchasing power. Need alone does not constitute demand. No matter how great the need for something, if the item is not affordable, it will have no value.

Transferability. If an item cannot be transferred, market value cannot exist. Transferability refers to the ability to acquire possession and control of the rights that constitute ownership of property. For example, public properties that are not transferable have no market value.

Forces affecting value. There are three major forces that affect value. These are social ideals and customs, economic circumstances, and government regulations. These forces may act individually or collectively to affect the value of a particular piece of property. Examples of social ideals and customs include changes in architectural styles, changes in family size and the emergence of the two-car family. Economic circumstances include employment levels, interest rates and the availability of money. Government regulations include zoning ordinances and building codes.

Types of value.

Although one might assume that a piece of property has only one value, in fact, property may have a different value for each of a variety of different purposes. Some of the common types of value are as follows:

1. mortgage loan value
2. exchange value
3. leasehold value
4. insurance value
5. depreciated value
6. liquidated value
7. salvage value
8. tax value
9. use value
10. rental value

The idea of one piece of property having different values for different purposes may seem confusing at first. But consider this example. The value of a home for fire insurance purposes would be different than for financing purposes. With fire insurance, emphasis is placed on the replacement cost of the improvements that are subject to fire hazards, regardless of the marketability of the property. On the other hand, when determining a loan amount, the lender will place a great deal of emphasis on how much the property would sell for in case of mortgage default, not the actual cost to replace the property.

Market value. Most people referring to the "value" of property mean the market value. The commonly accepted definition of market value is as follows:

> "... the highest price in terms of money which a property will bring in a competitive and open market under all conditions requisite to a fair sale, the buyer and seller, each acting prudently, knowledgeably, and assuming the price is not affected by undue stimulus. Implicit in this definition is the consummation of a sale as of a specified date and the passing of title from seller to buyer under conditions whereby:
>
> 1. buyer and seller are typically motivated;
> 2. both parties are well informed or well advised, and each acting in what he [or she] considers his [or her] own best interest;
> 3. a reasonable time is allowed for exposure in the open market;
> 4. payment is made in cash or its equivalent;
> 5. financing, if any, is on terms generally available in the community at the specified date and typical for the property type in its locale;
> 6. the price represents a normal consideration for the property sold unaffected by special financing amounts and/or terms, services, fees, costs, or credits incurred in the transaction."

As you can see, the time and terms of the sale, the relationship of the parties, and knowledge about the property all influence market value.

Principles of value.

Several rules, or principles have been formulated to explain the effect of certain conditions on value. These are:

Principle of substitution. No one will pay more for a piece of property than they have to pay for an equally desirable substitute property, provided there would be no unreasonable or costly delay in acquisition.

Principle of highest and best use. The most profitable use is that which provides the greatest net return over time (net return includes both income and amenities, e.g., pleasure and satisfaction from owning the property). The highest and best use will depend on zoning or deed restrictions (e.g., a gas station cannot be the highest and best use for a piece of land which is zoned residential, even though it may be more profitable). Also, the highest and best use may change over time.

Principle of change. Property is in a constant state of change. It is the future that gauges the value of property, not the past. There are several phases in the life cycle of property: integration (development), equilibrium (stability), disintegration (decline), and rebirth (renovation).

Principle of contribution. This refers to the value an improvement or feature adds to the overall value of the property. Some improvements will add more value than the expense of making them (e.g., the addition of a second bathroom), others will add less (e.g., a remodeled basement).

Principle of increasing and decreasing returns. There is a point where any additional improvements to land will either have no effect or actually be detrimental to value. For example, if a homeowner keeps adding more and more amenities (e.g., a swimming pool, tennis courts) to a home in a low income neighborhood, the additions will not add any more value to the property because no one will want to pay for them.

Principle of conformity. Maximum land value may be achieved when there exists an acceptable degree of social and economic conformity in the area (this does not mean racial or ethnic homogeneity). With residential property this means similarities in the size and structural quality of homes. A home of noticeably lower quality will have a **regressive**, or negative, effect on the value of surrounding homes. Higher quality homes have a **progressive**, or positive, effect on the surrounding homes.

Determining Value

The **comparative market**, or **market data** method determines value by comparing the subject property with similar properties in the same locale that are either for sale or that have sold recently. Competitive forces influence prices and no informed buyer acting free of pressure will pay more for a particular property than he or she would have to pay for an equally desirable substitute property. Also, no informed property owner will sell for less than is necessary, and, if he or she is objective, the seller will base the pricing decision on the prices recently paid in the area for similar properties.

When establishing the value of property by using this method, it must be remembered that the prices paid for properties are better indications of values in the area than are list prices (asking prices) because they represent what buyers were actually willing to pay in a competitive marketplace. Asking prices represent the ceiling of values in the area (no buyer will pay more than the asking price).

Sources of market information.

As you begin your competitive market analysis, you will need to refer to various sources of information. You will need to obtain comprehensive market data — listing and sales prices of properties in the subject property's neighborhood, the financing terms of the sales transactions, and the physical characteristics of the properties. It is best to maintain a history file of real estate activity in your area so you can have a good deal of the information you will need at your fingertips. The most reliable sources of sales information are Multiple Listings Services, which operate in most communities. Such a service usually requires its active members to assemble and share complete records, not only of listing prices, but also of other useful data such as consummated sales, financing, and length of time on the market. Other sources include:

1. the past listings in the broker's own office;
2. real estate advertisements in the local newspapers (this provides listing prices only);
3. other brokers, salespersons, loan officers, escrow officers, and anyone else who is actively involved with the local real estate market; and,
4. practical, everyday experience gained from dealing in properties in a given locale for a reasonable period of time.

The valuation process.

There are several steps to completing a competitive market analysis. The first steps involve collecting and analyzing the data on both the subject property and the comparable properties. When all the necessary information has been gathered, the comparables are compared to the subject property and the market values of the comparables are weighted according to the distinctions and similarities between them and the subject property. Finally, a conclusion is drawn as to the market value of the subject property.

1. Analysis of the subject property.

Before seeking out comparable properties, you must first complete a detailed analysis of your subject property. The most critical elements to analyze are those that will have the greatest impact on value. If you know what is most likely to contribute to or detract from value, you will be able to arrive at the most accurate estimate of value. The important elements of comparison can be broken down into the general categories of neighborhood, site and improvement. Bear in mind that you will be analyzing these same elements in the properties you choose as comparables. It is by comparing the elements of properties whose values are known to the elements of the subject property that the value of the subject property can be estimated.

Neighborhood analysis.

A neighborhood is a geographical area wherein the properties share certain characteristics. Its boundaries are determined by physical elements such as highways and canals, land use patterns (e.g., residential versus commercial), or other characteristics such as age, the value of homes or the economic status of the residents.

There are various forms which can be used for gathering neighborhood information. One such form is shown on the following page. Careful consideration should be given to the neighborhood's physical qualities, social trends, economic characteristics and governmental influences. Physical qualities include location, land use, traffic patterns, nuisances and topographical aesthetics. Social trends include population patterns, income and vocational levels, socioeconomic compatibility and potential for value stability. Economic characteristics include percentage of rentals, vacancy levels and infiltration of another type of use (e.g., commercial uses into a residential neighborhood). Governmental influences include property taxes and zoning and building codes.

Some specific neighborhood characteristics to consider are:

Percentage of home ownership. Is there a high degree of owner occupancy or do rental properties predominate? Owner-occupied neighborhoods are generally better maintained and less susceptible to deterioration.

Vacant homes and lots. Is there an unusual number of vacancies in the neighborhood? Vacant homes and/or lots suggest a low level of interest in the area. If less than 25% of the lots are developed and/or occupied for residential use, the area is not considered desirable for residential lending purposes.

Rental rates. Where there is a prevalence of rental properties, how do the rents compare to other rental dominated neighborhoods?

Construction activity. Significant construction activity in a neighborhood signals strong current interest in the area and this has a positive effect on values.

NEIGHBORHOOD DATA FORM

Property Adjacent To:

North *Plum Boulevard, garden apartments*
South *Cherry Boulevard, single-family residences*
East *14th Avenue, single-family residences*
West *12th Avenue, single-family residences*

Population:

☐ increasing ☐ decreasing ☑ stable

Stage of Life Cycle:

☐ development ☑ equilibrium ☐ decline ☐ rebirth

Tax Rate:

☐ higher ☐ lower ☑ same as competing areas

Services:

☑ police ☑ fire ☑ garbage ☐ other

Average Family Size: *3.5*
Predominant Occupations: *white collar, skilled tradesman*

Distance from:

Commercial Area *3 miles*
Primary Schools *6 blocks*
Secondary Schools *1 mile*
Recreational Areas *2 miles*
Cultural Areas *3 miles*
Churches and Synagogues *Methodist, Catholic, Baptist*
Public Transportation *bus stops nearby, excellent service*
Freeways/Highways *10 blocks*

Typical Properties	% of	Age	Price Range	% Owner-Occupied
vacant lots	0			
single-family residences	80%	10 yrs.	$80,000-$95,000	93%
2- to 6-unit apartments	15%	15 yrs.		
over 6-unit apartments	5%	5 yrs.		
non-residential	0			

Nuisances in neighborhood (odors, noise, etc.) *none*
Hazards in neighborhood (chemical storage, pollution, etc.) *none*

Changing land use. Is the neighborhood in the midst of a transition from residential to some other use? If so, the properties within are probably losing their value as residences, even though the change promises higher values overall because of the potential for more productive use of the land in the future.

Size and shapes of lots. Rectangular lots are more useful than irregularly shaped lots. Street frontage and area of land are the most influential factors.

Contour of the land. Mildly rolling topography is preferred to flat, monotonous or excessively hilly terrain.

Street patterns. Do the neighborhood's streets have good access to main traffic arteries? Wide, gently curving streets are more appealing than narrow and/or straight streets. Streets should be hard surfaced.

Nuisances. Are there any nuisances present in or near the neighborhood that might be detrimental to its value? Nuisances include odors, industrial noises or pollutants and exposure to unusual winds, smog or fog.

Prestige. Is there a prestige factor that makes one neighborhood more valuable than another?

Proximity to city. How far is the neighborhood from important points, such as downtown, industrial (employment) regions and major shopping centers?

School district. What schools service the neighborhood? Are they highly regarded? Are they within walking distance? The quality of a school or school district can make a major difference with respect to value.

Public service. Is the neighborhood properly serviced by public transportation, police and fire units?

Government influences. Does zoning in and around the neighborhood promote residential use and insulate the property owner from nuisances like unpleasant sights, sounds and odors from nearby industrial lands? Are property taxes and special assessments equitable? How do they compare with the tax levels of other neighborhoods nearby?

A property's value is affected to a great degree by its location. No two neighborhoods can ever be exactly alike. The characteristics of a neighborhood put effective limits on a property's maximum and minimum values. A high quality property by itself cannot overcome the adverse influence of a poor quality neighborhood. On the other hand, the value of a relatively weak property can be enhanced by a desirable neighborhood.

Site analysis.

The data collected and evaluated in a site analysis includes data on the physical characteristics of the property and on the condition (marketability) of the title. Physical characteristics are all of the property's physical features, both within its boundaries and in relation to the neighborhood, including width, frontage, depth, shape, topography, utilities, and the site in relation to the area (e.g., is it a corner lot?).

SITE DATA FORM

Address *10157 - 13th Avenue*
Legal Description *(see attached description)*

Size *50' × 200'*
Shape *Rectangular*
Square Feet *10,000*
Street Paving *asphalt*
Landscaping *professional*
Topsoil *good*
Drainage *good*
Frontage ______

☐ corner lot ☒ inside lot

Utilities:

☒ water ☒ telephone
☐ gas ☒ sewers
☒ electricity ☒ storm drains

Improvements:

☒ sidewalks ☒ curbs
☒ alley ☒ driveway

Improvement analysis.

After examining the neighborhood and the site of the property, you must examine the improvement (or structure) built on the property. The various factors to analyze include layout and design, construction quality, age and condition, and special amenities. Use a form to aid your building analysis such as the one shown on the following page.

Design and layout. When examining a house for design and layout, bear in mind that comparisons between houses of different designs are generally invalid. For example, do not compare a one-story home with a two-story home.

The perfectly designed house is one that is the exact size, shape and design to produce the maximum value. As one might expect, most houses are not the perfect house for their neighborhood. However, you are not seeking the perfect house but are rather trying to identify design elements that adversely affect value. The following is a brief description of what is generally accepted as good design.

The interior space of a home may be divided into separate zones: the private/sleeping zone (bedrooms, bathrooms and dressing rooms), the living/social zones (living room, dining room, recreation room, den and enclosed porch) and the working/service zone (kitchen, laundry, pantry and other work areas). The three zones should be separated from each other so that activities in one zone do not interfere with those in another.

The private/sleeping zone should be located so that it is insulated from noise coming from the other two zones. One should be able to move from the bedrooms to the bathrooms without being seen from the other areas of the house. All the household activities are usually controlled from the working/service zone. From the kitchen, it should be possible to control the entrances, the activities in the private/sleeping zone and living/social zone, and the activities in the porch, patio and backyard areas. The guest entrance should lead into the center of the house. From

BUILDING DATA FORM

Address *10157 - 13th Avenue*
Age *7 yrs.* Square Feet *1,350*
Number of Rooms *7* Quality of Construction *excellent*
Style *ranch*

	Good	Bad	Fair
Exterior (general condition)	✓		
Foundation (slab/bsmt./crawl sp.)	✓		
Exterior (brick/frame/veneer/stucco/aluminum)	✓		
Windows (metal/frame/storm/screens)	✓		
Garage (attached/detached/single/double)	✓		
Patio, porch, shed, other	✓		
Interior (general condition)	✓		
Walls (dry wall/wood/plaster)	✓		
Ceilings	✓		
Floors (wood/tile/carpet/concrete)	✓		
Electrical wiring	✓		
Heating (electric/gas/oil/other)	✓		
Air conditioning	✓		
Fireplaces ([*1*] number)	✓		
Kitchen	✓		
Bathroom(s) ([*2*] number)	✓		
Bedrooms ([*3*] number)	✓		

Additional Amenities *none*
Design Advantages *convenient, sunny kitchen*
Design Flaws *none*
Energy Efficiency *insulation, weather-stipping, storm windows, heat pump*

	Living Rm.	Dining Rm.	Ktchn.	Bdrm.	Bath	Family Rm.
Basement						
1st Floor	✓	✓	✓	*3*	*2*	✓
2nd Floor						
Attic						

Depreciation:

Deferred Maintenance *normal wear*
Functional Obsolescence *none*
Economic Obsolescence *none*

here there should be direct access to the living areas. A noise and visibility barrier should exist between the guest entrance and the private/sleeping zone. The family entrance should be from the garage or carport into the kitchen or to a circulation area directly connecting to the kitchen. Traffic from this entrance should not have to pass through the work triangle of the kitchen (stove, refrigerator and sink) to enter the other rooms of the house. One should be able to move from the working/service zone to the private/sleeping zone, the living/social zone and both the guest and family entrances, without going through the living room or the kitchen work triangle.

The number of bedrooms and bathrooms in a house has a significant effect on value. Other things being equal, a three bedroom house is generally worth considerably more than a two bedroom house. The same is true for a two bathroom house versus a one bathroom house. If the number of bedrooms and bathrooms exceeds the norm required for the typical family size, however, the value of the house may decrease. For example, with today's small family size, a six bedroom house would not have as much appeal as a three bedroom house.

Design deficiencies. According to a national survey of homeowners, some of the most common floor plan deficiencies include the following items. These will vary depending on the geographical region and the size and value of the residence.

1. Front door entering directly into the living room.
2. No front hall closet.
3. No direct access from front door to kitchen, bath or bedroom without passing through other rooms.
4. Rear door not convenient to kitchen and difficult to reach from the street, driveway and garage.
5. No comfortable area in or near the kitchen for family to eat.
6. A separate dining area or room not easily accessible from the kitchen.
7. Stairways off of a room rather than in a hallway or foyer.
8. Bedrooms and baths that are visible from the living room or foyer.

9. Recreational or family room poorly located (not visible from kitchen).
10. No access to the basement from outside the house.
11. Walls between bedrooms not soundproof (separation by a bathroom or closet will accomplish soundproofing).
12. Outdoor living areas not accessible from the kitchen.

Construction quality. Is the quality of the materials and craftsmanship good, average or poor?

Age/condition. When the subject property and comparables are in similar condition, a difference in age of up to five years is generally inconsequential. Older properties will maintain their value if the bath(s), kitchen, plumbing and electrical facilities are up to code and of a quality acceptable to typical purchasers and renters in the area.

When visually inspecting the property, make a list of the items that need repair or that are in poor condition (deferred maintenance). Immediate repairs may include touching up exterior paint, fixing plumbing leaks, rehanging loose gutters, and making minor electrical repairs. Items that are in poor condition may include floor finishes, exterior paint, interior paint, electric fixtures, hot and cold water pipes, carpeting, and kitchen appliances.

Additional amenities. The presence or absence of an **air conditioning** system is more critical in hot regions than regions with milder climates. With spiraling energy costs, an **energy efficient** home is more valuable than a comparable one which is not. Examples of energy efficient items include clock controlled thermostats, insulation wrapped water heaters, insulated ducts and pipes in unheated areas, adequate insulation for floors, walls and attic, and weather stripping for doors and windows.

2. Selection and analysis of comparable properties.

After analyzing the subject property, the next step is to select other properties having the same or nearly the same characteristics as the subject property. Properties are selected for comparison that have been bought and sold in the open market (no "forced sales"). Other useful sources of information includes listings or offers to sell, offers to purchase, and rentals.

Sales used as a basis for comparison must be truly comparable in the areas of greatest importance. When evaluating a sale to see if it qualifies as a legitimate comparable, you should be concerned with five issues:

1. **Date of comparable sale.** The sale should be recent, within the last six months if possible (sales more than one year old are not very reliable). Recent sales more accurately indicate what is happening in today's marketplace. Market conditions that change over time include present and anticipated sales prices, rental prices, availability of financing, volume of transfers, preferences for various types of properties, and construction costs. Other related conditions include the level of earnings in the community and the costs of operating expenses.

   If the market has been inactive and there are not enough valid comparable sales from the past six months (at least three), it is possible to go back further but adjustments must be made for the time factor, allowing for inflationary or deflationary trends or any changes that may have affected prices in the area during that period.

2. **Location of comparable sale.** Whenever possible, comparables should be selected from the neighborhood of the subject property. If there are no legitimate comparables in the neighborhood, comparables from other neighborhoods may be used, but the neighborhoods must also be comparable. (Refer to neighborhood analysis above.) If a comparable is in an inferior neighborhood it is probably less valuable than the subject property, even if structurally identical. The converse is true of a comparable from a superior neighborhood. It is generally conceded that location contributes more to the value of real estate than any other characteristic.

Some of the factors that affect the quality of the neighborhood include: a) the general reputation of the neighborhood or district; b) the desirability of the area as a place to live; c) the presence or absence of adverse conditions (e.g., odors, noise); d) tax rates and assessments; e) zoning, building and traffic regulations; f) police and fire protection; and g) public improvements, e.g., streets, utilities, schools, and related facilities.

3. **Physical characteristics.** To qualify as a comparable, a property should have physical characteristics that are similar to the subject property, including size, style, layout and design, materials of construction, and condition of the building.

4. **Terms of the sale.** With the increase in seller participation in financing today, the terms of sale have become a significant factor when estimating value. Buyers are often willing to pay top prices (possibly inflated prices) to sellers who are willing to sell their properties on attractive terms, which often include extended repayment periods and low interest rates. The effect the terms of sale had on the price paid for the comparable must be taken into account.

5. **Must be arm's length transaction.** Finally, before a comparable sale can be relied upon as in indication of what the subject property is worth, it must have been an arm's length transaction. This means the buyer and seller were informed and acting free of unusual pressure, and the property was offered for sale and tested on the open market.

3. Comparison of subject and selected properties.

Proper comparison of the subject and comparable properties is vital to an accurate estimate of value. Remember that the value of comparables will decrease for such conditions as poor repair, poor design, and existing nuisances, and increase for cleanliness, good design, special features, view, landscaping, and the like. Unless the sales being compared are of recent date, consideration must also be given to adjusting the values in keeping with the general economic conditions.

Comparisons are made on the basis of the major elements listed above: 1) time of sale, 2) physical factors, including both land and buildings; 3) location, and 4) terms of the sale.

Of course, the more similar the comparables, the easier the comparison. A comparable that is identical in design, neighborhood, site characteristics, and condition (e.g., a house in the same housing development as the subject property) which sold under the usual financing terms the previous month will give an excellent indication of the market value of the subject property. However, in the absence of housing development conditions, finding comparables of such similarity is a rarity. It is more likely that there will be at least a few significant differences between the comparables and the subject property. When this happens, proper adjustments must be made to the values of the comparables.

For example, the agent has found a comparable that is very similar to the subject property except that it has three bedrooms and the subject property has only two. The comparable recently sold for $94,000. If the agent knows that a third bedroom is worth approximately $3,000, the value of the comparable is reduced by $3,000. This adjusted price reflects the difference in number of bedrooms. **The agent must remember that the selling price of the comparable is adjusted to indicate the probable market value of the subject property.** The adjustment will be an addition (+) if the feature (e.g., number of bedrooms) represents a higher value for the subject property and a subtraction (-) if it represents a lower value for the subject property. A completed comparison chart is shown on the next page which illustrates this principle.

One of the greatest difficulties with the market data method is determining the value of the differences between the comparables and the subject property. How do you know how much an extra bathroom or bedroom or proximity to a good elementary school is really worth?

COMPARABLE SALES COMPARISON CHART

	Subject Property	Comparables			
		1	2	3	4
Sales price		*$91,750*	*$96,500*	*$87,000*	*$88,500*
Location	*quiet street*				
Age	*7 yrs.*				
Lot Size	*50' × 200'*				
Construction	*frame*			*+6,000*	
Style	*ranch*				
# of Rooms	*7*		*-5,000*		
# of Bedrooms	3				
# of Baths	*2*	*+3,500*		*+3,500*	*+3,500*
Square Feet	*1,350*				
Exterior	*good*				
Interior	*good*				
Garage	*1 car attached*				
Other Improvements		*-4,000*			
Financing					
Date of Sale			*-3,000*		
Net Adjustments		*-1,000*	*-8,000*	*+9,500*	*+3,500*
Adjusted Value		*$90,250*	*$88,500*	*$96,500*	*$92,000*

The value of distinguishing features is also arrived at by comparison. For example, you have two properties, A and B. They are virtually identical except A has one bathroom and B has two. A sold for $87,000 and B sold for $91,500. Since the number of the bathrooms is the only real difference between the two properties, the value of the second bathroom is $4,500. By looking at many different properties, you will be able to place a value on several individual features. A sample sales price adjustment chart is shown on the next page. As you examine this chart, note that a few of the properties had no variables, so they were used as the standard against which the value of each distinguishing feature was measured.

SALES PRICE ADJUSTMENT CHART

COMPARABLES

	A	B	C	D	E	F	G	H
Sales Price	$92,500	$89,000	$92,500	$97,500	$97,000	$92,500	$87,500	$82,500
Location	resid.	resid.	resid.	resid.	resid.	resid.	resid.	highway
Age	8 yrs.	7 yrs.	8 yrs.	6 yrs.	8 yrs.	7 yrs.	6 yrs.	7 yrs.
Lot Size	50' × 200'	50' × 200'	50' × 200'	50' × 200'	50' × 200'	50' × 200'	50' × 200'	50' × 200'
Construction	frame	frame	frame	frame	brick	frame	frame	frame
Style	ranch	ranch	ranch	ranch	ranch	ranch	ranch	ranch
# of Rooms	7	7	7	8	7	7	6	7
# of Bedrooms	3	3	3	4	3	3	2	3
# of Baths	2	1	2	2	2	2	2	2
Square Feet	1,300	1,300	1,300	1,425	1,300	1,300	1,250	1,300
Exterior	good	good	good	good	good	good	good	good
Interior	good	good	good	good	good	good	good	good
Garage	2-car att.	2-car att.	2-car att.	2-car att.	2-car att.	2-car att.	2-car att.	2-car att.
Other	basement	basement	basement	basement	basement	basement	basement	basement
Financing	70% S/L	70% S/L	75% bank	75% bank	70% S/L	70% S/L	75% S/L	70% bank
Date of Sale	2 mo.	7 wk.	6 wk.	2 mo.	5 wk.	7 wk.	6 wk.	9 wk.
Typical House Value	$92,500	$92,500	$92,500	$92,500	$92,500	$92,500	$92,500	$92,500
Variable Feature		1 less bath		extra bdrm.	brick		1 less bdrm.	poor loc.
Adjustment Value For Variable		$3,500		$5,000	$4,500		$5,000	$10,000

4. Formulating an indicated market value estimate from the direct market method.

You have developed market value figures from the comparables in the previous step. From these, a final estimate of market value is arrived at by evaluating the reliability of each comparable. Obviously, those sales most like the subject property and those with the fewest adjustments offer the best (most reliable) indication of market value. This use of a judgment or weighting process produces a final estimate of market value from the direct market method. For example, you have three comparables with the following values:

	A	B	C
Selling Price	$96,500	$101,150	$119,050
extra bedroom	- 3,000	- 3,000	- 3,000
two-car garage			- 2,300
waterfront property			- 14,000
aluminum siding		- 2,750	- 2,750
Final Value	$93,500	$95,400	$97,000

Obviously, comparable C has a significant number of variables, which makes it less reliable as a comparable. A and B are much more similar, with A being most like the subject property. Therefore, the market value of A should be given the most weight and C the least. In this situation, the market value of the subject property might be estimated at $94,000.

Competitive Market Analysis in Review

We will now take a few minutes to review the principles just discussed by going through the steps of a competitive market analysis. Note that while the steps taken here will be the same as those you will take when preparing your own competitive market analysis, the data we present is more abbreviated.

Susan Green has informed you that she will give you the listing on her property if you can present her with a sound listing price.

The first step is to gather data on the subject property, the Green home. After viewing the property, speaking with the owner, and studying the neighborhood, you determine the following: the house is located in Cedar Hills which is a small, middle-income, stable neighborhood three miles north of the business district of Jeffersville. The house has three bedrooms, two full bathrooms, a dining room and a large, well landscaped backyard. It is a ranch-style house with a double garage. The house is four years old and is in excellent condition.

The next step is to select and gather information on comparable properties. After referring to your history files and your local multiple listing association, you discover the properties described below. After analyzing them as to date of sale, location, physical characteristics, and terms of sale, you determine them to be comparable. All are located in the Cedar Hills neighborhood.

> A — a ranch-style, three bedroom, two bathroom home with a single garage. This house has a dining room, a large yard, is 3½ years old and in excellent condition. It sold five months ago for $93,500.
>
> B — a single-story home with two bedrooms, two bathrooms, a dining room, a large side yard and a double garage. It is four years old and in excellent condition. It sold two months ago for $90,700.
>
> C — a single-story home with three bedrooms, one bathroom, a large back yard, and a single garage. It has no dining room. It is 3½ years old and in excellent condition. It sold seven months ago for $91,700.

You must now compare the comparables to the subject property. Of course, you quickly determine that there are some differences between the comparables and the subject property that will require some adjustments. These are:

1. a single versus a double garage
2. two bedrooms versus three bedrooms
3. one bathroom versus two bathrooms
4. the absence of a dining room

Before you can make the adjustments, you must determine the adjustment value of each distinguishing feature. Again referring to your history file (as well as other sources), you find the following properties:

- D and E are virtually identical except for the fact that D has a double garage and E has a single garage. D sold for $89,500 and E sold for $88,700. From this you determine that a double garage is worth $800 more than a single garage.

- F and G are virtually identical except for the fact that F has three bedrooms and G has two bedrooms. F sold for $97,500 and G sold for $93,000. Thus you determine that the third bedroom is worth $4,500.

- H and I are virtually identical except for the fact that H has two bathrooms and I has only one. H sold for $94,550 and I sold for $89,000. The second bathroom is worth $5,550.

- J and K are virtually identical except for the fact that J has a dining room and K does not. J sold for $97,000 and K sold for $94,800. The dining room is worth $2,200.

(NOTE: you are unlikely to find such straightforward comparables in the real world and you will need more than one or two comparables to determine the adjustment value of the various distinguishing features.)

Based on these comparables, you have a general idea how each of the variables should be valued. Now you make the adjustments for each of these features as follows:

Subject Property	A	Comparables B	C
Market Value	$93,500	$90,700	$91,700
double garage	+ $800	X	+ $800
three bedrooms	X	+ $4,500	X
two bathrooms	X	X	+ $5,500
dining room	X	X	+ $2,200
Total Adjustments	+ $800	+ $4,500	+ $8,500
Total Adjusted Value	$94,300	$95,200	$100,200

You now have the adjusted market values for the three comparables and can formulate an opinion on the subject property's market value. You examine each comparable to determine its reliability. Comparable C has the most distinguishing features and thus the most adjustments. Therefore, it is the least reliable. Comparables A and B each have only one adjustment, but the variable between comparable A and the subject property (the single garage) is the least vital to the property's overall value. Comparable A is probably the most reliable (but note how close the market values of A and B are anyway). A reasonable opinion of market value for the subject property might be $94,500.

You present your estimate of value and the supporting data to Ms. Green and impressed with your professional competence, she gives you the listing on her property.

The Competitive Market Analysis Form

The real estate agent might find it helpful to use a competitive market analysis form such as the one shown on the following pages when making the listing presentation to the seller.

COMPETITIVE MARKET ANALYSIS

Property Address *10157 - 13th Avenue*

Address	Sugg. Sales Price	Age	Lot Size	Style	Exterior	# of Rooms	Square Feet	Bdrms.
SUBJECT PROPERTY	*$91,500*	*7 yrs.*	*50' × 200'*	*ranch*	*frame*	*7*	*1,350*	*3*
ON MARKET NOW								
3952 Maple	*90,000*	*8 yrs.*	*45' × 190'*	*ranch*	*frame*	*6*	*1,250*	*3*
1725 Sycamore	*89,700*	*12 yrs.*	*40' × 180'*	*ranch*	*brick*	*7*	*1,350*	*3*
10372 - 18th Ave.	*91,500*	*10 yrs.*	*50' × 200'*	*ranch*	*brick*	*7*	*1,420*	*3*
9950 - 8th Ave.	*86,000*	*5 yrs.*	*50' × 200'*	*ranch*	*frame*	*6*	*1,415*	*2*
SOLD PAST 12 MONTHS								
3256 Oak	*87,500*	*10 yrs.*	*50' × 180'*	*ranch*	*frame*	*7*	*1,270*	*3*
1892 Larch	*86,000*	*6 yrs.*	*50' × 200'*	*ranch*	*brick*	*6*	*1,400*	*3*
10521 - 9th Ave.	*90,250*	*7 yrs.*	*50' × 180'*	*ranch*	*brick*	*7*	*1,300*	*3*
EXPIRED LAST 12 MONTHS								
2782 Cherry	*96,800*	*6 yrs.*	*50' × 200'*	*ranch*	*frame*	*6*	*1,150*	*2*
10012 - 16th Ave.	*99,800*	*4 yrs.*	*50' × 180'*	*ranch*	*brick*	*7*	*1,300*	*3*

Location *centrally located, convenient to business/cultural center and public transportation*

Assets *excellent condition, professionally landscaped yard*

Drawbacks *no basement*

Market Conditions *market is very competitive, sales price within 2% of market value*

Financing Terms *cash*

General Comments

Probable Market Value *$91,500*

Date *September*

# of Baths	Garage	Condition	Other Improvements	Terms	$ Per Sq. Foot	Comments	Date Listed	Date Sold
2	*1-car att.*	*excellent*	—	*cash*	*$68*			
1	*1-car att.*	*excellent*	*basement*	*seller*	*$72*		*July*	
2	*1-car att.*	*good*	—	*assume*	*$66*		*August*	
2	*2-car att.*	*good*	*basement*	*cash*	*$64*		*August*	
2	*1-car att.*	*good*	—	*cash*	*$61*		*June*	
2	*2-car att.*	*good*	—	*seller*	*$69*		*March*	*May*
1	*1-car att.*	*excellent*	—	*cash*	*$61*		*Feb.*	*April*
2	*1-car att.*	*good*	—	*cash*	*$69*		*April*	*June*
2	*1-car att.*	*good*	—	*assume 1st*	*$84*		*Jan.*	
2	*2-car att.*	*excellent*	—	*seller*	*$77*		*March*	

Company *Smith Realty*
Agent *Susan James*
Phone *714-8811*

The form is easy to explain and understand — you do not have to be an appraiser to use it. A major advantage to this form is that it illustrates to the seller what buyers can pay, will pay, and will not pay for a home in his or her neighborhood. Another reason such a form is effective is that it helps you plan your presentation in a logical sequence. Of course, as with any form, it is only useful if the information contained in it is accurate and current.

The form has spaces for 15 homes that are comparable to the seller's home. Of course, the more alike the comparables are to the seller's home, the more likely the seller is to accept your estimate of value.

The first section of the form calls for homes that are for sale now. This is what a buyer *could* pay on the open market. You should select five homes from your current listing files that are the most comparable to the seller's property. List the address, age, style, number of rooms, number of bedrooms and baths, condition, financing terms, date listed and other characteristics of the property.

The next section is for homes that have sold in the past 12 months. This is what a buyer *did* pay. You should choose five homes from your history file that are the most recent and most comparable to the seller's property and fill in the pertinent information. Of course, the most vital information is how much it sold for and the terms under which it sold.

The next section deals with listings that have expired in the past 12 months. This is what a buyer *would not* pay. List all of the information called for on the form.

Other items to be listed on the form include information on the subject property's location, assets, drawbacks, market conditions, financing and general comments.

All the information you have gathered and analyzed on the seller's property and the comparable properties should be presented to the seller, along with your explanation of how this information determines market value. Using this form in your listing presentation enables the seller to *see* what you are saying, not just hear what you are saying. The information presented in the form can correct any misconception the seller has regarding the current market conditions in his or her neighborhood and forces a more realistic approach to pricing. The form also helps make the listing presentation more organized, reasonable and logical — your estimate of value is obviously based on facts, not personal opinion.

Request for Reconsideration of Value

A firm grasp of the competitive market analysis will also be invaluable to you in your efforts to help a potential buyer obtain financing. One of the most prevalent of all real estate selling problems is the low appraisal, an estimate of value that is below (sometimes a good deal below) the actual selling price. No one gets through an entire career without facing the appraisal problem at least a few times. A sale is written and one to three weeks later the appraiser gives the agent the unfortunate news. The lender bases the loan amount on the sales price or the appraised value, *whichever is lower.* When an appraised value is below the sales price, the buyer will be unable to get the amount of financing that he or she expected.

When an appraisal comes in below the sales price, there are five options:

1. reduce the sales price to the appraised value.
2. keep the price as is and have the buyer make up the difference in cash.
3. strike a compromise price somewhere between the appraised value and the initial selling price.
4. ask for a reconsideration of the appraised value in the hope it will be increased to a level more acceptable to the buyer and seller.
5. terminate the sale.

Once a seller has become accustomed to a certain selling figure, he or she gives it up very reluctantly. If the seller is agreeable to a price reduction, the first option is the simplest and quickest solution, but do not be surprised if your seller resists a price reduction.

Options two and three are the least likely of the solutions because buyers have understandably always been reluctant to pay more for a property than a professional appraiser has told them it is worth. Where a transaction is dependent on financing, the buyer does not have to complete the sale if the appraisal comes in low. Transactions are infrequently salvaged by buyers agreeing to pay over value.

Option four — a request for reconsideration of value — is viable if done properly. The correct way to request reconsideration of value will be explained subsequently.

Finally, where there is a significant gap between the sales price and the appraised value, option number five — a termination of the sale — is the solution more than 70% of the time.

Of course the best way to eliminate the problems created by low appraisals is to avoid them in the first place by pricing properties realistically. A seller should not be given an unrealistic estimate of the property's worth. Even if a buyer can be persuaded to pay the inflated price, the appraisal will come back low and the real problems of trying to keep the sale together will begin.

Request for reconsideration of value. Regardless of how objective an appraiser might try to be, subjective considerations and conclusions are a part of every appraisal, and in the end the appraiser's findings can only be termed an opinion of value. If you are affected by a low appraisal and sincerely believe the appraiser made a mistake, there is a chance you can appeal the decision and, with proper documentation, get the appraisal increased, possibly to the figure originally requested.

The Market Data Analysis portion of a residential appraisal is the heart of the appraisal. It shows what informed buyers have been willing to pay for properties like the subject property in the recent past, and the lender can only presume that the indicated value is what informed buyers will be willing to pay for the subject property if it is foreclosed and resold.

If you disagree with an appraisal and plan to ask the lender to reconsider the appraisal amount, you will have to support your request by submitting for the lender's review at least three comparable sales that indicate a higher value estimate is in order. If you are to persuade the lender to accept your comparables over the appraiser's, they must be at least as similar to the subject property as the comparables contained in the initial appraisal report. A typical market data analysis that would be included in a request for reconsideration is shown below.

MARKET DATA ANALYSIS

412 Acme Drive

Item	Subject Property	Comparables 1	Comparables 2	Comparables 3
Address	*412 Acme Drive*	*131 Skip Rd.*	*221 Sutter St.*	*168 Bow Rd.*
Sales Price	*$135,000*	*$141,000*	*$134,500*	*$129,500*
Data Source	*sales contract*	*present owner*	*MLS*	*selling broker*
Date of Sale	*9/1/90*	*6/29/90*	*7/14/90*	*5/17/90*
Location	*hi-qual.suburb*	*same*	*same*	*same*
Site/View	*inside lot*	*corner lot*	*corner lot*	*inside lot*
Design/Appeal	*rambler/exc.*	*same*	*same*	*same*
Constr. quality	*good*	*good*	*good*	*good*
Age	*7 yrs.*	*6 yrs.*	*8 yrs.*	*8 yrs.*
Condition	*good*	*good*	*good*	*good*
# of Rooms	*8*	*7*	*7*	*6*
# of Bedrooms	*4*	*4*	*3*	*3*
# of Baths	*2½*	*2½*	*2*	*2*
Liv.Area(sq.ft.)	*2,700*	*3,300*	*2,350*	*2,150*
Garage/Carport	*2-car att.*	*same*	*same*	*same*
Patio,pool,etc.	*15'×21'patio*	*15'×26'patio*	*18'×16'patio*	*15'×17'patio*
Additional Data	*2 fireplaces range, oven D/W,disposal central air*	*2 fireplaces range, oven D/W central air*	*1 fireplace range, oven D/W central air*	*1 fireplace range, oven D/W*
Comments	*Subject has superior energy efficiency to comps 2 and 3 and is at least equal in this respect to comp 1. Principal difference between comps 1 and 2 is square footage.*			

Sometimes appraisers get careless and when this happens, their findings can be successfully challenged. If your request for reconsideration of value contains well researched, properly documented information and is presented in a professional manner, your chances of success will increase dramatically. By using the same methods you would use to prepare a competitive market analysis for listing purposes — proper data collection, analysis and comparison — you will be able to submit a convincing case for reconsidering the value of the property.

Chapter Six

Advertising

For many real estate offices, advertising is the only way they communicate their existence to potential buyers and sellers. Advertising is their only avenue to public recognition and the business that name identification brings. They use advertising to promote the idea of home (or other real estate) ownership, to persuade prospects to come to *them* for real estate services, and to create interest in the properties they are trying to sell. According to a New York Times attitudinal study, real estate brokers get up to 84% of their buyers and 43% of their sellers through newspaper advertisements alone!

Yet, in spite of the importance of advertising to the real estate business, many offices fail to give it the time and attention it deserves. Advertisements may be written and placed according to how other offices do it instead of according to sound advertising principles. Unfortunately, advertising that does not reach the targeted audience or fails to convince prospects to respond represents wasted advertising dollars. This chapter will attempt to explain some of the basic principles of advertising so that the agent can not only advertise, but advertise effectively.

Advertising Defined

Advertising is any type of paid, nonpersonal message communicated through selected media that promotes a product, service, or idea. Advertising is considered "nonpersonal" because it is aimed at specific groups of individuals with some common characteristic rather than any particular person. (This does not mean advertising should not carry a personal message.)

All advertising can be divided into two categories: product advertising and image (or institutional) advertising. The purpose of **product advertising** is to get the reader to purchase a particular item or service. It gives the reader information about the benefits and specific features of a product, for instance, an individual listing or groups of properties.

Image advertising communicates general information about a company or individual. Its purpose is to create a positive public image and increase name recognition. A company will use image advertising to differentiate itself from other companies in the same business. For example, a real estate office may advertise that it specializes in vacation and retirement properties. Image advertising may also be used to educate prospective buyers (e.g., that this is a good time to finance a house), to emphasize the friendliness or professionalism of an office, or to illustrate how the company has made the community a better place to live.

Many times, product and image advertising can be effectively combined in the same advertisement. Both purposes can thus be accomplished at little extra cost. For example, an ad may focus on an office's expertise in starter homes and then go on to describe three such homes currently listed with the office.

Advertising may be either classified or display. **Classified advertising** is the more inexpensive type. It consists of line ads (with no illustrations) which appear in a special section (the "classifieds") of the newspaper. For most firms, classified advertising is the most popular way to advertise real estate, especially residential real estate.

Display advertising is larger and often includes some type of visualization, either illustrations or photographs. Display advertising is more expensive than classified advertising and can appear in any section of the newspaper. Display ads may be used to advertise housing developments, industrial properties or shopping centers. Display ads may also be used to picture sales agents, announce sales records (perhaps using graphs for illustration) or present testimonials from satisfied customers.

Factors to Consider

Before discussing some of the steps necessary to develop an effective advertising strategy, it should be noted that the best results are usually achieved when one person is put in charge of the advertising program. While other members of the office can and should participate in the ad writing, the overall program should be overseen by one individual. This individual can give direction to the advertising program, watch the costs, control the volume of advertising, schedule advertising for the most effective exposure, compile and interpret sales data, evaluate the effectiveness of the advertising, and make sure that what needs to get done actually does get done. (For example, this person could take advantage of lower advertising rates by scheduling ads to appear for more than one consecutive day. See the chart on the following page, which shows the rates offered by a major California newspaper.) All ads should be channeled to this person to be checked for errors, omissions, and repetitious themes, and to ensure consistent quality and continuity. Putting one person in charge eliminates the confusion and waste that is caused by several people moving in conflicting directions.

Also remember that writing good advertisements takes time. Be sure to allot a sufficient amount of time to the actual task of designing the ad. Planning on spending an hour or more to write a two inch ad would not be unreasonable.

Any advertising program should not only reach the desired audience, but reach it in the most effective and efficient manner possible. This means that there must be sales information available to evaluate past advertising performance and to help determine where changes are needed. Some of the data that will be required include volume of sales per advertising dollar spent, the number and percentage of buyers and sellers you attract from each geographical area you serve, and the number and percentage of leads you get from each advertising source. A sample of the kind of form you can use to tabulate this type of information is shown on page 127.

CLASSIFIED ADVERTISING

FULL RUN CIRCULATION

LOCAL RATES

Per Line per Day
Published Daily
STRAIGHT CLASSIFIED

The following rates apply to all classified advertisements except Employment Advertising, (#5a), Legal Advertising, (#5b), Special Classifications (#5c), Private Party Prepaid Bonus Plans, (#5d).
For a description of circumstances and classifications charged at National Rates refer to #4, Policy Guidelines, paragraph E.

RATEHOLDER RATES

A rateholder advertiser is one who orders and maintains an advertisement for 30-or-more consecutive days. The following are rateholder local rates per line per day.

	Weekday	Sunday
RATEHOLDER (3 line minimum)	6.30	8.25
RATEHOLDER (2 line minimum)	6.85	9.00

ADS IN ADDITION TO RATEHOLDER

Rateholder advertisers will be billed the following rates per line per day for each additional advertisement.

3 LINE MINIMUM	Weekday	Sunday
4 or more consecutive days	6.30	8.25
3 consecutive days	7.85	10.10
2 consecutive days	9.35	11.90
1 day	10.90	13.85

2 LINE MINIMUM	Weekday	Sunday
4 or more consecutive days	6.85	9.00
3 consecutive days	8.45	11.10
2 consecutive days	10.00	12.70
1 day	11.55	14.65

Note: To qualify for the lower 3-line additional ad(s) rate, the additional ad(s) and the rateholder ad must run 3 lines or larger daily. If an additional ad is only 2 lines this order will receive the 2-line minimum rate.

OPEN RATES	Weekday	Sunday
7 to 29 consecutive days	7.25	9.45
4 to 6 consecutive days	7.70	10.11
3 consecutive days	9.60	12.40
2 consecutive days	11.05	14.20
1 day	12.50	16.00

Add 20¢ per line to the straight classified rates listed above for classified display and logo advertisements.

SAMPLE MARKET CHART

Quarter ______________

Business Recap

Community	# of sellers	# of buyers	% of total
Fairhaven			
Arlington			
Seaview			
Shorewood			
Royal Hill			
Totals			

Sources of Leads

Medium	# of sellers	# of buyers	% of total
The Daily News			
Fairhaven Tribune			
Radio KXR			
"Home Picture" Magazine			
For Sale and Sold Signs			
Direct Mailings			
Yellow Pages			
Referrals			
Personal Contacts			
Other			
Totals			

Another element to bear in mind when planning your advertising program is **budgetary considerations**. On the average, real estate offices devote 8%-12% of their overall budget to advertising, but how much you allocate will depend on your individual objectives. There are many methods for allocating money to advertising, some good and some bad. The following is a list of some of these methods, presented in the order of worst to best:

1. "**Leftovers**" — this means that whatever is left over after paying all other expenses will be devoted to advertising.
2. "**Arbitrary allocation**" — the person in charge of the budget will allocate resources to advertising as he or she feels is necessary.
3. "**Industry average**" — the office will spend the same amount on advertising that other offices do.
4. "**Meet the competition**" — the office will spend the same amount on advertising that the biggest competitor spends.
5. "**Objectives approach**" — the amount allocated is what is necessary to achieve the objectives you've set, consistent with available resources.

The last method, the **objectives approach**, is the most favored method. It is certainly the one that will best enable you to meet your advertising and marketing goals. An example of this method would be deciding that you want to hire 15 new associates this year. You know from previous experience that one out of every four candidates is hired, so you need a pool of 60 candidates. You also know that each advertisement you place for new associates brings in eight candidates. Thus you will need to run an ad eight times to bring in at least 60 candidates. Using the advertising rates for the medium you choose, you can budget a specific amount for obtaining new associates.

Not only does an entire amount need to be budgeted for the year's advertising, but a **month-to-month** budget must also be drawn up. There are four general approaches to timing advertisements:

- **placing ads in a steady pattern all year.** This works best for products/services that are used on a steady basis throughout the year (e.g., household goods);

- **advertising according to season.** This method is used for products/services that are used on a seasonal basis. For example, suntan lotion would be advertised in the summer and snow tires would be advertised in the winter;
- **advertising on an alternate basis**, e.g., advertising intensively every other month. This method helps increase the impact of the advertising by concentrating it into smaller time periods instead of spreading it out;
- **advertising during selected periods of time.** This method is usually the most effective for real estate offices. Each office should do a percentage breakdown of past sales to determine when their most active times are and then allocate the year's budget accordingly. If your primary selling season is spring, place the most advertisements in the spring. Take each month, and depending on the amount of business historically generated during that month, allocate a certain portion of the year's budget to it.

SAMPLE MONTHLY BUDGET

Month	Percent of Sales	Budget Allocation
January	5%	$ 2,250
February	6%	2,700
March	9%	4,050
April	11%	4,950
May	13%	5,850
June	15%	6,750
July	10%	4,500
August	9%	4,050
September	6%	2,700
October	6%	2,700
November	5%	2,250
December	5%	2,250
	100%	$45,000

The Advertising Process

An effective advertising campaign requires more than just designing an effective ad. It requires knowing what the advertising process is and following through with each step. An ad will not be effective no matter how creative it is if the wrong medium is used, the wrong audience is addressed, or the ad itself is designed to meet an inappropriate objective. For example, an ad designed to reach prospective sellers in one socioeconomic level will probably fail miserably, no matter how eye-catching, if the main objective is to attract sellers in a radically different socioeconomic level.

Creating an advertising strategy that will work for you is a four-step process. If any one of these steps is overlooked, your advertising will not be as effective as it could be. These four steps are:

1. determining your objectives
2. targeting your audience
3. selecting the appropriate media
4. designing the ad

Advertising Objectives

Real estate advertising has many different purposes and functions. You may want to accomplish all of them, or you may want to focus on the purpose that best suits your present needs. Real estate advertising:

- advises potential buyers of properties for sale, attracts their interest, and motivates them to seek out more information;
- informs both buyers and sellers of how your company can be of service to them;
- encourages sellers to list with your company;
- increases your company's name recognition and improves your company's image;

- educates and corrects any misconceptions held by the public regarding buying, selling and owning real estate;
- recruits new sales associates;
- shows the seller that you are doing everything in your power to sell the listed property; and
- helps keep staff morale high.

As you discover what your goals are, be sure to put them in concrete terms. Merely stating that you wish to increase your market share does little to inspire you to meet that goal nor does it provide you with a way to measure your performance. Set specific goals and set time limits. Some examples of concrete goals would be:

- increase sales by 25% this year
- recruit four new associates this quarter
- increase market share from 10% to 15% this year
- get 20 more listings this quarter
- increase profits by 10% this year

It is only when you know what you want to accomplish with your advertising that you can create ads designed to achieve your goals.

Target Audience

Many advertisers make the common mistake of placing ads designed to reach the largest number of people. This mistake is caused by the so-called **majority fallacy** which holds that success is best achieved by offering a product that will appeal to the broadest possible market. However, no product has just one mass market, but rather many submarkets, each with its own characteristics and requirements. A product or service should be made to appeal to **specific segments of the market**, rather than the generalized whole. Any product designed to appeal to the public in general will not have enough specific appeal to motivate any one segment to purchase it. Think about a particular house — to make it appeal to everyone, you would have to refrain from mentioning the specific attributes that would motivate a particular person to buy it.

The first step in targeting a market is to segment the market according to **relevant characteristics**. Some useful criteria include age, income, family size, marital status, and homebuyer's attitudes. Once this is done, draw up a profile of the typical prospect in each segment. For example, a young working couple with two children under the age of five will probably be concerned with convenient access to work, shopping and daycare facilities, good schools, proximity to parks and other family recreation, etc. By developing a profile, you will become familiar with the thoughts, feelings, concerns and needs of the members of each particular group.

Once you have segmented the market and drawn up a profile for each segment, you can determine which segment to target with your advertising. Your decision should be based on several factors:

- your **business strengths** (e.g., your name may already be familiar to retired people, you may be located in an area predominantly populated by professional couples, etc.);
- the **competition** in each segment (you may wish to pick a segment where there is less established competition);
- **statistical information** relevant to each group (e.g., which group is growing in numbers, which group is more likely to buy a home, etc.);
- **projections of profit potential** and the **costs** involved with reaching each segment;
- **your own judgment** based on personal knowledge of the market area.

Some questions you should be asking yourself as you decide which segment to target include the following:

- where does 75% of my business come from? (This can be determined from data obtained from a filled-in market chart similar to the one shown earlier.)

- should I concentrate more effort in this prime market area?
- do less profitable areas show signs of increased activity?
- is your market geographically larger for sellers than for buyers (or vice versa)? Do you need to target a different market for sellers than for buyers?

After choosing the most beneficial market segment, you must choose the media which will reach your segment the most efficiently.

Selecting the Media

There are several different media available to the advertiser. Which ones are chosen depends on the type of company doing the advertising, the type of advertisement, and the type of market to be reached. While many real estate offices rely exclusively on newspaper advertising, it is helpful to develop a multi-media approach. Media other than newspapers should at least be considered because different media are better able to fulfill different objectives. It is easier to attract attention with less-used media and using a different medium can help distinguish your company from all the other real estate companies. Also, by using more than one medium, you may get a greater overall effect as each medium will enhance the effect of the other. For example, if readers have already seen your billboard advertisement, they may be more likely to read your classified ads.

When choosing a medium, remember that the goal is not to reach the greatest number of people, but to reach the greatest number of potential prospects at the lowest possible cost. Ask yourself the following questions:

- what is my marketing objective?
    - to increase name recognition?
    - to increase market share?
    - to attract new associates?
    - to get more listings?
    - to sell listed properties?

- which medium is best able to achieve my objective? (For example, a billboard will not be the best medium to sell listed properties, but it may work very well to increase name recognition.)
- which specific media will best reach my target market? (A regional "country living" magazine may be an effective place to advertise a small horse ranch.)
- how can I avoid duplication?
- what is my advertising budget? (Choosing to spend your entire advertising budget on one television commercial would obviously be poor planning.)

The following is a brief summary of the various media and their characteristics:

Newspapers: the widest read local medium. Newspapers target a specific geographic area, cut across all income and class levels and are good for timely promotions as the lead time is very short. Newspapers usually offer discount rates for volume advertising. Some disadvantages to newspaper advertising include poor reader selectivity (reaching people who are not interested in your product), a short life (newspapers are read quickly and then thrown away), and poor color reproduction.

Weekly newspapers: including community newspapers, shopper's guides and special interest publications. Circulation and readership of these newspapers can vary wildly, so it is best to investigate their cost-effectiveness before choosing one. Weekly newspapers target specific audiences well and advertising rates are cheaper. Special interest papers may be especially useful for specialized properties.

Magazines: regional editions have a higher degree of customer selectivity. Many regional and metropolitan magazines have a real estate section that is useful for advertising distinctive, expensive properties. Magazines have a long life and are likely to be read in relaxed moments. Color reproduces very well in magazines. Disadvantages include a longer lead time and higher cost.

Television: ads in regular programming are generally too expensive to be worthwile even for a large brokerage (although national firms use television ads to build an image). However, most metropolitan areas now have at least one home show on cable TV, and these can be a very effective marketing method. The main drawback is that only a few homes make it onto the program; but the shows increase a broker's name recognition and bring in buyers for other properties. A few cities have a special cable channel completely devoted to real estate. For a flat weekly fee, a 30-second spot on each home is shown dozens of times.

Radio: the "accompaniment" medium (the audience listens to it while doing something else, e.g., driving). Radio offers a relatively high customer selectivity because different radio stations are tailored to appeal to different market segments. Radio also has a short lead time. To be effective, the radio advertisement must be simple (otherwise it may be difficult for the listener to follow). Radio is best suited to name identification or providing general information. Real estate brokers rarely use radio advertising so it may be an effective way to increase name recognition.

Direct Mail: gives the reader a message and then encourages the reader to seek more information by returning a response device (this results in additional names for mailing lists, phone calls and other sales promotion). With the proper mailing list, direct mail has a very high degree of customer selectivity, although the cost per prospect is relatively high. The results of direct mail advertising can be accurately measured through the returned response cards. Direct mail has a variety of uses: advising prospects of services offered, distributing "meet-your-neighbor" cards, and promoting listed properties. To get worthwhile results, it is imperative that the direct mailing be done properly. The envelope must be designed so that the prospect will open it (instead of immediately throwing it in the garbage); the cover letter must be personal, well-written and convince the reader to respond; any brochures or other enclosures must be attractive and professional looking; and a response card must be enclosed, preferably one that is pre-addressed and postage-paid.

Outdoor advertising: including billboards and transit advertising (on and in buses, subways, terminals and tops of cabs). Outdoor advertising offers the opportunity to create large, colorful ads that increase name recognition. It is important to keep the message short, however, as it will often be read while traveling at high speeds. This medium offers high geographic selectivity. Outdoor advertising is only effective as a secondary medium.

Design the Ad

After you determine what your objectives are and decide what market you are going to target and which media you are going to use, you can then begin designing your ad.

Designing the Ad

An effective ad convinces the prospect of the benefits of your products or services and motivates him or her to make use of them. An effective ad:

- attracts attention
- stimulates interest
- creates desire
- generates action

These principles of advertising are often referred to as AIDA (attention, interest, desire, action). For example, the headline of the ad should attract the attention of the reader. Then, as the reader goes on to read the copy of the ad, he or she becomes more interested in the property and begins to feel a desire for it. By the time the reader has finished reading the ad, he or she is ready to call the real estate broker and make an appointment to see the property.

Emotional and rational appeals. An advertisement attracts attention by speaking directly to prospects, by going right to "where they really live." It must address real needs, real desires, real fears. Some of these needs, desires, and fears are met by rational appeals, some by emotional appeals. **Rational appeals** are based on logic, are fairly straightforward, and are common to large segments of the population. Some rational appeals to buying/selling property include:

price	low interest rate	security
economy of ownership	comfort	good investment
solitude, privacy	convenience	

Emotional appeals are more subjective, more individualized. They are based on the fact that a product or service makes a statement to others and acts as a symbol. Some emotional appeals include:

happiness	pride of ownership	elegance
love	success, affluence	independence
guilt	fear	escape

Ads can (and sometimes should) combine both rational and emotional appeals. However, it is best to use just one primary appeal and then support it with a few secondary appeals. Too many appeals can simply overwhelm a prospect. Before you begin to design a particular ad, determine which appeal you will use and then develop an ad concept around that appeal.

Address the prospect's motives and fears. While different people have different motives for buying or selling a home, the advertiser must tell the prospect that his or her particular motives are both understood and met by the advertiser. Tell prospects just what you can do for them. If you're not sure, ask yourself why a seller should use an agent instead of selling the home him or herself. For example, the benefits of using your services to sell property include: your advertisements, your sign in the lawn, your ability to effectively show the property, your ability to help a prospective buyer obtain financing, etc. Telling the prospect what services you offer will encourage him or her to use those services.

Ask yourself what the biggest fear is that a person feels when thinking about buying a home. If a buyer's biggest fear is meeting the mortgage payments, address this fear in your advertisement, explaining the financial benefits of owning over renting and the currently available finance terms. The prospect will see that you have his or her concerns at heart and are willing to address them.

Finally, when designing your ad, remember that an ad does not have to be unusual or extremely attractive to get good results. Attractive ads in and of themselves are not successful. Successful ads are those that motivate prospects to act by appealing to their needs.

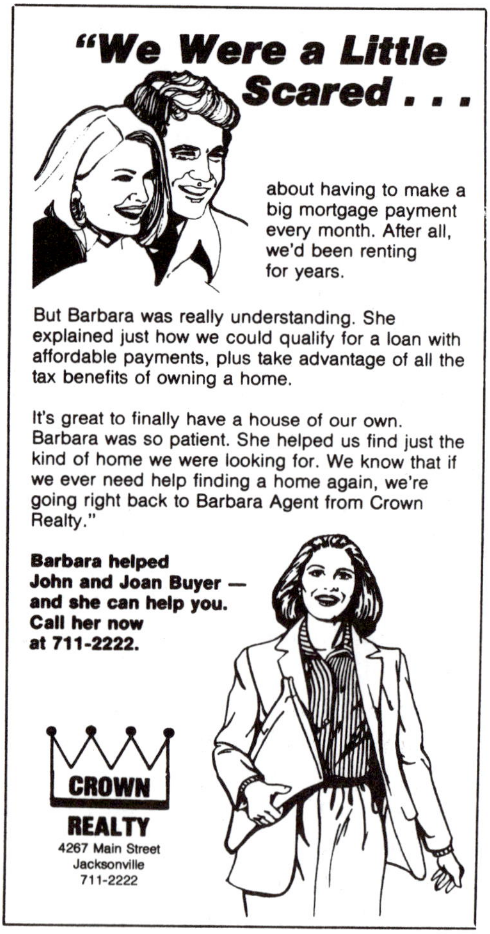

Image Advertising

Before discussing the nuts and bolts of designing classified and display ads, a few words should be said about image, or institutional advertising.

Name recognition is important to business — people would rather deal with someone they are familiar with than a stranger. This is true even if the familiarity is through name and image rather than personal contact. When people are considering making a major purchase (such as a home), they want to deal with a company they know, trust and feel comfortable with.

Of course, the public's perception of your company depends on more than just your advertising. It also depends on the services you provide, the appearance and demeanor of your associates, the interior of your office, publicity, and your company's general attitude towards the public. However, without customers, these company qualities will never be noticed. Institutional advertising can improve your image and increase your name recognition so customers will come in and see for themselves.

The public often readily accepts the stereotype that salespersons (especially insurance, car and real estate salespersons) are pushy, self-serving, and perhaps even dishonest. Your advertising should stress just the opposite. Emphasize the courtesy that your company's personnel exhibit towards the public, their friendliness and competence. Assure prospects that they will not be made to feel stupid because they don't know everything there is to know about real estate. Tell prospects their questions are welcomed, their patronage is valued and that everything possible will be done to earn their trust. To get ideas for **"welcome mat" ads**, ask your non-real estate friends why they would hesitate to come into a real estate office. Use the answers as themes for image advertisements.

Confidence in the quality of your service can also be built with the use of legitimate, candid **testimonials**. People feel more comfortable doing business with someone who has given good service to others. While testimonials are seldom used, they can be effective if they are believable and sincere. Satisfied customers will often be willing to comment on the quality of service they received from your office. At the close of a transaction, simply ask your customer if he or she would be willing to make such a statement. Remember to get their permission to use their name, statement and photo in an advertisement.

The personal **profiles of sales associates** is another effective way to make prospects feel comfortable about coming into your office. Instead of merely listing the associate's experience or credentials, try including an honest, relaxed statement telling prospects how the associate feels about his or her work or how he or she was able to help a customer solve a real estate problem.

Another approach to increasing name recognition is to **create a significant difference** in your product or service and then communicate that difference through advertising. For example, you may specialize in one or more types of real estate, e.g., investment properties, farms and ranches, starter homes, vacation and retirement homes, etc. If you can show why your services are superior in some way to your competitors, you will be on your way to increasing your market share.

Use institutional advertising to improve your image and address prospects' fears of hard-sell tactics and pushy salespersons and you will increase their responsiveness to your product advertising.

Classified Advertising

The first step in developing classified advertising (or any type of advertising) is to become familiar with the advertising rules of the medium you're going to use. For example, many newspapers don't allow the use of borders in classified ads.

The next step is to know your product. You should be familiar with the address, location, style, price and physical characteristics of the property you're advertising as well as what makes it special. A good way to do this is to fill out an ad writing worksheet similar to the one shown on the following page.

If possible, fill in the worksheet while you are viewing the house during the listing, so your impressions can be fresh and accurate. Also, ask the sellers why *they* bought the house or what they will miss most about it. This information can provide valuable ad ideas.

The house you have chosen to advertise should be interesting — an unusual feature such as a stream, exceptional view or a prestigious neighborhood will arouse more interest. Then, when you're writing the ad, be sure to pick the features that will appeal to your target market. Remember, you have to generate enough interest to motivate the prospect to contact you. For example, if the property is likely to appeal to

AD WRITING WORKSHEET
(for residential property)

ADDRESS: ____________________
TOWN/LOCATION: ____________________
PRICE: ____________________
TAXES: ____________________

NEIGHBORHOOD

STYLE OF HOMES: ____________
AGE OF HOMES: ____________
PUBLIC TRANSPORTATION: ____________
SHOPPING AREAS: ____________
CHURCHES: ____________
OTHER: ____________

OUTSIDE FEATURES

STYLE: ____________
OUTSIDE SURFACE: ____________
APPEARANCE: ____________
LANDSCAPING: ____________
DRIVEWAY: ____________
PATIO/DECK: ____________
POOL: ____________
FENCE: ____________
OUTSIDE GRILL: ____________
GARDEN: ____________
OTHER: ____________

INTERIOR

Room	Size, Number	Level	Features
Living Room			
Dining Room			
Kitchen			
Bedrooms			
Family Room			
Recreation Room			
Bathroom			
Basement			
Garage			

COSTS

GAS ________ ELECTRIC ________ OIL ________
WATER ____________
SEWER/GARBAGE ____________
OTHER ____________

BEST SELLING FEATURES

____
____
____
____

BENEFITS BECAUSE OF FEATURES

____
____
____
____

POTENTIAL BUYERS

TYPE	INCOME	NUMBER IN HOUSEHOLD	LIFESTYLE

young professionals, highlight the easy access to downtown employment. However, you must be honest in your advertising. Exaggerations or misleading statements will only generate disappointment and a lack of trust. Don't be afraid to point out negative qualities, especially if they can be turned into an advantage (e.g., if a house is in poor condition, you can appeal to people's desire to get a good deal by emphasizing that the purchaser can save money by fixing up the house him or herself).

Headlines. The headline is the ad's attention-getter. It is the most important part of the ad. The headline should be strong, eye-catching, reflect the major benefit of the property, and motivate the prospect to read the rest of the ad. While many headlines are short, don't hesitate to write longer headlines when needed. In fact, long headlines are often more effective than short ones. Use the headline to create a visual image that will capture the reader's imagination. Use the headline to involve the reader — if the reader can begin to imagine owning the home being described, the headline has done its job. The Reader's Digest, which employs some of the best headline writers in the business, has three guiding principles for headlines: present a benefit to the reader, make the benefit quickly apparent, and make the benefit easy to get.

You can vary the standard look of classified headlines by varying their position in the ad (centered, placed to the left, placed to the right), highlighting them with stars or punctuation marks, and changing capitalization (all caps, all lower case, a mixture of lower and upper case; NOTE: a mixture of both upper and lower is easier to read unless the headline is very short), or using the headline to lead into the copy (e.g., "SCENIC VIEWS FROM YOUR BREAKFAST NOOK will greet you every morning . . .").

It is important that the reader does not feel tricked into reading the ad copy. Make the headline fit the body of the ad.

Examples of Headline Variety

(centered)

Country Haven
copy copy copy copy copy
copy copy copy copy copy

(flush left)

Prestigious
Neighborhood
copy copy copy copy copy
copy copy copy copy copy

(flush right)

Easy Terms:
copy copy copy copy copy
copy copy copy copy copy

(all lower case)

invest in your future
copy copy copy copy copy
copy copy copy copy copy

(upper and
lower case)

Magical Setting
copy copy copy copy copy
copy copy copy copy copy

(highlighted)

*** * * A Star! * * ***
copy copy copy copy copy
copy copy copy copy copy

(lead into copy)

CLASSIC DESIGN
in an affordable
price range . . .
copy copy copy copy copy
copy copy copy copy copy

CLASSIFIED MEASURE

Charges for single column straight classified advertising are based on computer-generated line counts. There are approximately 14 lines to the inch. Space taken by logos, white space and larger type is billed in equivalents of classified lines (a 10 point line is billed as 2 lines, a 14 point line as 3 lines, etc.)

CLASSIFIED LOWER CASE world's leader in classified	28 letters and spaces	1 line
CLASSIFIED CAPITALS & NEWSPAPER ADVERTISING!	24 letters and spaces	1 line
10-POINT LOWER CASE for better results than ever	28 letters and spaces	2 lines
10-POINT CAPITALS NOW MORE READERS-WITH A	23 letters and spaces	2 lines
14-POINT LOWER CASE lowest cost per reader	22 letters and spaces	3 lines
14-POINT CAPITALS RESULTS–LEADERSHIP	18 letters and spaces	3 lines
18-POINT LOWER CASE first in the world	18 letters and spaces	4 lines
18-POINT CAPITALS SELL IT FASTER	14 letters and spaces	4 lines
24-POINT LOWER CASE find it quicker	15 letters and spaces	5 lines
24-POINT CAPITALS IN THE TIMES	12 letters and spaces	5 lines
30-POINT LOWER CASE classified –	11 letters and spaces	6 lines
30-POINT CAPITALS A LEADING	9 letters and spaces	6 lines
36-POINT LOWER CASE circulation	11 letters and spaces	7 lines
36-POINT CAPITALS GETS MORE	9 letters and spaces	7 lines

TYPEFACES

Character counts shown are to be used as a guideline only. Letters vary in width and an exact count cannot always be determined in advance.

42-POINT LOWER CASE readership	10 letters and spaces	8 lines
42-POINT CAPITALS BEST BUY	8 letters and spaces	8 lines
48-POINT LOWER CASE results	7 letters and spaces	9 lines
48-POINT CAPITALS TODAY	5 letters and spaces	9 lines
60-POINT LOWER CASE place	5 letters and spaces	11 lines
60-POINT CAPITALS YOUR	4 letters and spaces	11 lines
72-POINT LOWER CASE copy	4 letters and spaces	14 lines
72-POINT CAPITALS NOW	3 letters and spaces	14 lines

Copy. The function of the ad copy (the body of the ad) is to take the attention generated by the headline and change it into desire for the property. The first statement of the copy should pertain to the benefit described in the heading. The copy must motivate the reader to call your office for more information on the property. Relay information that is pertinent to your target market. The ads with the most factual information of interest to the prospect will get the best results. According to advertising research (performed by the MacDonald Classified Service and Classified International Advertising Service, Inc.), prospects are most interested in the following items (listed in order of importance):

- location
- price and terms*
- number of bedrooms
- size of lot
- square footage
  convenience to schools
- convenience to churches
- number of closets
- garage

Include any other information you think a prospect would want to know about the property, especially any special features or benefits. Many real estate agents hesitate to include the price for fear of discouraging a prospect, but according to a New York Times attitudinal survey, ads that state the price are over four times as likely to be successful as ads that do not.

When you mention the characteristics of the property, be specific. For example, if there is an unusually large master bedroom, give the dimensions instead of merely saying "large master bedroom." "Enormous 20' x 30' master bedroom" would be much more effective.

While you want to give the reader enough information to arouse his or her interest, don't overexplain the property. You want the reader to call

---

*If you mention financing terms in your advertisements, be sure you comply with the requirements of the Truth-in-Lending Act. Refer to Chapter 9, Real Estate Finance Disclosures.

you for more information, not rule out the property from what is included in the ad. If, when calling for more details, the prospect determines that the property is not suitable, you can then help the caller find a property that is suitable.

The copy should be descriptive as well as factual. A grocery list of the property's features is unlikely to excite a prospect's imagination. The copy should add to the visual impression created by the headline. However, be careful not to use the same descriptive phrases over and over. Words such as nice, large, lovely, and gorgeous are tired and overused. After you've written the copy, reread it and see if you can't replace a worn out phrase with something refreshing. (Use a thesaurus to come up with original phrases.) Try to use words that fit in with the general concept of the ad. Different words convey different feelings. For example, "exquisite" has a sophisticated sound while "delightful" conveys a more homey impression.

Copy should be written in a face-to-face, conversational style. Avoid using words many readers won't understand or an overly stiff tone. Since the purpose of copy is to motivate the reader, use persuasive words. According to a Yale University study, the following are the most persuasive words in the English language:

discover	love	need
proven	easy	health
results	safety	guarantee
money	save	you

One caveat — don't use excessive abbreviations or real estate terminology. Especially avoid non-standardized abbreviations. For example, only one out of five people who see "WBFP" will know that it means "wood burning fireplace." Using financing terminology (e.g., "growth equity mortgage with buydown") is likely to get the same response. While you may use these terms and abbreviations on an everyday basis, your prospects don't. Any confusion in the prospect's mind will cause him or her to ignore the ad.

Closing. The function of the closing is to call the reader to action. Tell the reader what to do and put a time limit on it. Convey a sense of urgency ("This one will go fast! CALL NOW!"). Give the agent's full name and the real estate company's name, phone number, and address. (By law, any ad placed by a real estate agent must include the broker's name and indicate that he or she is a licensed broker.)

Layout. The layout should carry the reader's eye through the ad elements in the proper sequence: from headline to copy to closing. Keep the appearance of your ads consistent so that readers will easily identify them on the page.

The layout can be used to call attention to the ad. Make white space (blank spots in the layout) work for you. Allowing enough white space in the ad will give it a clean, crisp appearance and prevents the ad from getting lost on the page. Trying to squeeze too much copy into the ad only serves to make it look cramped and more difficult to read. Your company logo can be eye-catching — try varying the size or reversing it (white on black).

It is more efficient to advertise properties in groups rather than placing individual ads for each property. The cost per prospect is significantly less for multiple ads than for single ads (a multiple ad generates more calls than all the single ads put together). Multiple ads also allow you to advertise properties together that share certain characteristics, e.g., location, size, style, or type (for example, seaside vacation homes). Also, you don't have to repeatedly pay for your company name as you do with each individual ad.

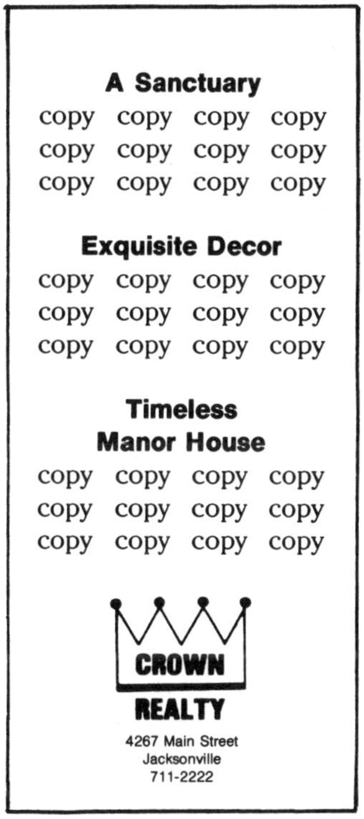

(Multiple Property Ad)

Starting Over? Take A Look!

Wedgewood
copy copy copy copy copy copy copy copy copy copy copy copy copy copy
$65,500

Loyal Heights
copy copy copy copy copy copy copy copy copy copy copy copy copy copy
$79,200

Ridgemont
copy copy copy copy copy copy copy copy copy copy copy copy copy copy
$98,000

Cherry Hill
copy copy copy copy copy copy copy copy copy copy copy copy copy copy
$112,400

Sarasota
copy copy copy copy copy copy copy copy copy copy copy copy copy copy
$129,700

CROWN REALTY

(This ad illustrates effective use of an inset and white-space. The multiple property format is organized by location.)

Working Mother?
Come home to a house planned just for you. Modern, well-equipped kitchen puts dishwasher, micro at your fingertips. Two baths means no morning congestion. This spacious, easy-to-clean 3-bedroom in Loyal Hill is just for you. $217,500. Call now! **Mike Gordon, Crown Realty, 711-2222**

(This ad is targeted to a specific segment of the market. The body of the ad follows through with the concept of the headline.)

ATTN. INVESTORS
Redmond 3 bdrm rmblr, 1¾ ba, fm rm, fplc w/ins, 2-cr gr, as is $153,500 contr terms. Call 711-2222.

Mike Gordon, Crown Realty

(This is an example of an ad with too many abbreviations.)

Display Advertising

A display advertisement is made up of five parts:

1. **the headline:** attention-getting print at the beginning of the ad;
2. **subheadline:** defines, reinforces or explains the headline; connects the headline to the ad copy (not all display ads have subheadlines);
3. **body copy:** describes the product and explains why the prospect should buy it using rational or emotional appeals;
4. **visualization:** photography, artwork or drawings that are designed to attract attention, create visual interest, and/or emphasize points made in the headline/copy;
5. **signature:** a symbolic reminder of the product or company (e.g., logo, trademark, trade name, etc.).

All of these elements should work together to convey the advertising message. The headline and visualization should attract the attention of the reader. The layout of the ad should help pull the reader through the ad. The copy should keep the reader interested and lead him or her to the closing call for action. The signature should serve to emphasize the product or company name.

Headline. As with classified ads, the headline is the most important part of the advertisement. The headline should grab the attention of the prospect and make him or her want to read the rest of the ad. The same principles that apply to classified headlines also apply to display headlines.

Visualization. The "visualization" refers to all the graphic elements of the ad, including photographs, drawings, borders, logo, typeface and any artwork. The graphic elements must blend in with and promote the ad's overall concept.

(Elements of a display ad.)

If a **photograph** of the property is used, it should show the property to its best advantage. Rectangular photos attract more attention than other shapes (especially irregular shapes). The photo should be sharp, clear and should not include any miscellaneous items (cars, telephone poles, wires, trees that hide the buildings, etc.). If you cannot get a good photo of the exterior, use an interior shot. Straight-on shots of homes tend to give them a flat, ordinary look; angle shots are more flattering and make the home appear larger.

If you want to include photographs of sales associates, make sure they convey a friendly, professional image. It is often effective to intersperse them throughout the ad next to property photos instead of placing them in single file. This will create a more pleasing visual impression and make each associate stand out as an individual.

Photos usually attract more attention than drawings and are considered to be more objective and believable. However, drawings should be used when the property is under construction. Drawings can also convey a feeling of rusticity or charm.

A display ad may have a **formal or informal balance.** Formal balance is where there is approximately equal weight on each side of the center of the ad. If there is more weight on one side, the balance is informal (this gives a pleasant effect and is different from being out of balance). Formally balanced ads generally flow from top to bottom. The eye must be led in informally balanced ads from the focal point (the beginning of the ad) to its conclusion. Focal points are slightly above the optical center. To find various focal points, draw the ad into thirds (both lengthwise and widthwise) — each intersecting line may be used as a focal point.

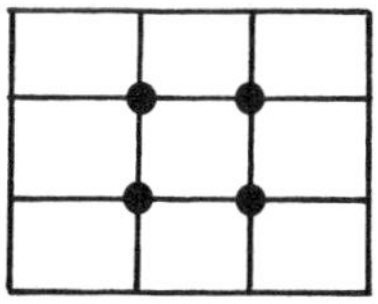

Many **layout formulas** create alphabetical or geometrical figures, for example: s, inverted-s, c, and reverse-c.

(This is an example of an inverted-s layout.)

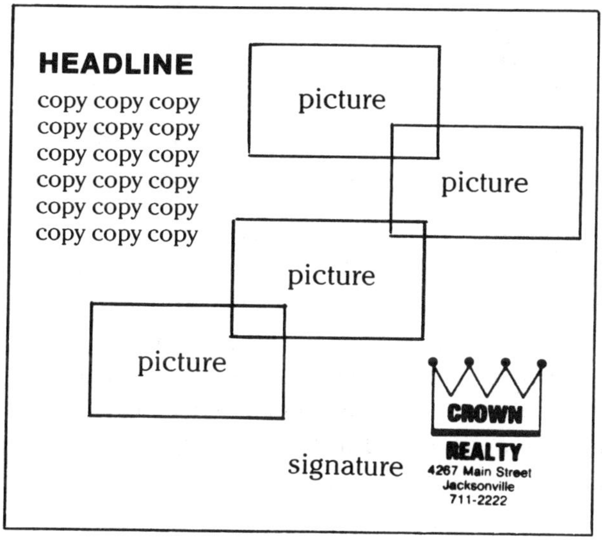

Several types of **graphic devices** are used to attract attention to display ads. The most commonly used (and most expensive) is size. While large ads do get more attention than small ads, additional attention is not attracted in direct proportion to the increase in size. For example, a full page ad will get more readers than a half-page ad, but not twice as many. If, because of budget constraints, you must choose between size and frequency, choose frequency. People remember better what they see more often.

Type styles, color and white space are also attention-getting devices. Different type styles can effectively alter the mood of an advertisement, but remember that readability is the most important consideration. Reverses (white on black), screens, patterns and textures may also be used. Reverses can be difficult to read and should be used in headlines only, never copy. Insets and borders draw attention, break up the copy and help keep the reader's attention. Distinctive borders can be used to convey the overall company theme or an impression of the individual properties. For example, stars may be used to border ads placed by Star Realty. Feature indicators (bold lines pointing to different parts of a photo or drawing) create reader involvement and direct attention to particular benefits of the property.

(This ad illustrates the use of reverses, highlights, and borders.)

Copy. As with classified ads, the copy of a display ad should be personal, direct, and focus on the benefits to the reader. The most important point (or benefit) should be made early in the copy, as most readers will not read the entire ad. Don't hesitate to use long copy if it's necessary. It will be read if it is interesting, relevant and well written. The sentence length should be varied (especially with long copy). This adds reading interest and a short sentence following a lengthy one will focus the reader on the point being made.

To make the copy look more inviting, try some of the following ideas:

- use a type style that is easy to read
- indent paragraphs
- use bold leads to draw attention to major points
- underline and use color, white space, italics, designs, and borders to break up copy
- the line length should be between 30 and 60 characters
- use photographs or drawings throughout the ad
- use numbers or bullets (•) to introduce points
- use insets to highlight major points

At the end of the copy, you should return to the main point and call for action from the reader. Including a coupon that the reader can send in for more information (for example, brochures that may interest the reader, e.g., "Financing a Condominium") often motivates the reader to act.

Review and revise. After you have written your ad (both classified and display), look for the following and revise if necessary:

- will the headline attract attention?
- have you included all relevant facts?
- does the ad read well? is it relaxed and flowing?
- have you created a visual image?
- have you used any excess or meaningless words? (superfluous words cost money)
- is your company name emphasized?

Sample Display Ad

SELLING YOUR HOME?

Let Crown Realty Make a Difference.

Six Ways a Crown Realty Agent Makes Selling Your Home Easier.

You want to sell your home for the best price in the shortest time. Crown Realty can help you do just that. Our agents are professional, well-trained and experienced. They know just what to do to market, promote and sell your home.

- **Competitive Market Analysis.** We study current market conditions, comparable home prices and the benefits your home has to offer to help you select the best listing price.

- **Preparing Your Home.** We can give you tips on what buyers want to see in a home, what you can do to prepare your home for showing and what minor improvements you can make to make your house more marketable.

- **Advertising.** Our agents are experts at creating the ads that will sell your house.

- **Showing Your Home.** We at Crown Realty have the training and skill to show your home to its best advantage. We know what's important to the buyer and can emphasize the best selling points of your home.

- **Negotiation.** We are experts at negotiating the sale. We know when to compromise and when to be firm.

- **Financing.** We can help the buyer get the financing that will be necessary for the sale to close.

At Crown Realty, you will find professional agents who are both experienced at selling homes and concerned about your needs. We know that selling your home can be a tough experience. Let us make a difference.

CROWN
REALTY

4267 Main Street Jacksonville 711-2222

Evaluation

Is your advertising program getting the results you want? If you don't set up a system for evaluating your advertising, you will never know. One of the most effective ways to gauge ad success is to fill in a traffic sheet when answering calls. A sample traffic sheet form is shown below.

This traffic sheet should be filled out every time a salesperson answers a call or gets a lead on a prospect. This way you can tabulate where your leads come from, which advertising medium generates the most responses, and which property types your prospects are most interested in. This information should be reviewed every month. If you don't feel that your advertising is bringing in enough responses, try varying the size, copy or design of your ads. Also try varying the media you use. For instance, you may find yourself getting significantly more responses if you start advertising in your community newspaper as well as the daily newspaper. Any low-yielding advertising should be cut.

If you change any element in your advertising program (e.g., different medium), be sure you measure the results. Compare the before-and-after statistics to see if it was an effective change. You may have to try several different combinations of media and ad designs until you find the one that works best for you.

TRAFFIC SHEET

Office *Magnolia Branch*
Salesperson *S. Jones*

Date *March 17,*

Date	Name	Phone #	Appt.	Property Address	Property Type	Times	Herald	Source Sign	Walk-In	Other	Comments
3-17	*Margie Smith*	*276-7070*	*2:00 3/18*	*217 Cherry*	*single family*		✓				
3-17	*Bruce Twining*	*289-1134*	*none*	*8276 Madison*	*single family*	✓					
3-17	*Lenore Savage*	*823-9725*	*4:30*	*21724 Olive*	*condo.*		✓				

## Chapter Seven

Property Management

Aside from assisting in the buying and selling of real property, real estate agents may also engage in property management. In fact, many brokerage offices do engage in property management to some degree, so it is wise for all licensees to have a basic knowledge of its principles.

"Property management" refers to a situation where a person other than the owner supervises the operation of income property in exchange for a fee. Property managers must have a real estate license because under California law, a real estate license is required when a person "leases or rents or offers to lease or rent, or places for rent, or solicits listings of places for rent, or solicits for prospective tenants, or negotiates the sale, purchase or exchanges of leases on real property . . . or collects rents from real property . . ." (*Business and Professions Code*)

History of Property Management

Property management is a relatively new field. Prior to the 1930's, real estate owners usually managed their own properties. At the most, "property managers" were used to collect rents. Then, during the depression there were massive mortgage defaults and many properties fell into the hands of the lenders. These lenders were saddled with management responsibilities for extensive property holdings but had little property management experience. Of necessity, they came to depend on the real estate industry to provide the necessary expertise or formed their own property management departments. It was during this time that a few real estate practitioners formed the Institute of Real Estate Management

(IREM). Originally, the organization focused on ethical standards of practice (e.g., no commingling of funds) but then diverted energy to improving the competence of its members. Through IREM, individuals could (and still can) become Certified Property Managers® after completing coursework and gaining the requisite amount of experience.

Although the lenders eventually resold the properties they acquired during the depression, the value of efficient property management had been discovered and more owners came to depend on property managers to operate their properties rather than doing it themselves.

In the years following World War II, property management became even more important. Both apartment and office buildings became ever larger as elevators and steel frames allowed the construction of multistory structures. Shopping centers replaced the corner store and flourishing commercial activity led to the creation of industrial parks. As it became increasingly difficult for property owners to manage all of their holdings, professional, efficient and effective outside management became a necessity rather than a luxury.

The Real Estate Market

To effectively manage property, the property manager must utilize a wide variety of knowledge and skills. For instance, the property manager frequently engages in negotiations between the landlord and tenants and diplomacy is essential. Knowledge of advertising and business promotion is important. It is also vital that the property manager be familiar with the real estate market and the factors that influence that market. Before going into greater detail about the specific functions of a property manager, we will briefly discuss a few principles about the real estate market that the property manager must know.

The student of property management may question the value of learning about the real estate market. After all, a property manager is not involved in the purchase or sale of property, only in the management of that property. On closer reflection, however, it is easy to see that the property manager is indeed marketing property. The property manager sells the

use of property. The property manager is constantly marketing the use of space and because that same space must be resold time and time again, the property manager often must know more about the real estate market than the real estate broker.

The primary function of the property manager is to preserve the value of the property while maximizing income for the owner. Of course, the source of that income is tenants paying for the use of the property. A property's income is derived from the user, therefore the value of the property depends on the economic conditions of the user — the number of potential users, their purchasing power, social status, location, and lifestyle. It is easy to see the importance of the user on the value of real estate if you take a moment to imagine what a 500-unit apartment building would be worth on a snow-covered mountain peak. Of course, it would have virtually no value. It would have slightly more value in a small farming village and a very significant value in a bustling urban community.

When determining the value of property (i.e., setting rental rates), there are several factors the property manager should consider, including the supply and value of money, trends in occupancy rates, market rental rates, general employment levels, and family size and lifestyles (for residential property).

Supply and value of money. How much the dollar is worth and how available it is for use in real estate transactions has an obvious impact on the value of property. If few people are willing to invest their money in real estate, the value of real estate will decline.

Occupancy. The total number of units available for occupancy in the area and the total number of potential tenants able to pay the rent for those units also affects the real estate market. This is simply the rule of supply and demand. The greater the supply and the less the demand, the less the value; the less the supply and the greater the demand, the greater the value. There may be a **technical oversupply**, where there are more units than consumers, or there may be an **economic oversupply**, where there are enough consumers, but they are unable to pay the current rent. Likewise, there can be a **technical shortage** (there are more consumers than units) or an **economic shortage** (there are more able-to-buy consumers than units).

Since the real estate market is affected by the number of comparable units available, the property manager will want to determine the occupancy trend for the locale. If the trend is towards rising occupancy levels, the value of the units will increase because space becomes more scarce and thus more valuable. It is during these times that managers raise rents and reduce services. On the other hand, if there is a growing vacancy rate, the units' value will decrease. In periods of high vacancy, the public is likely to resist rent increases and/or make more demands for services or repairs at renewal time.

Occupancy levels are constantly fluctuating. The direction and speed in which they are moving will have a significant impact on the property manager's operating and merchandising policies.

Rental level. Current rental rates are evidence of the economic strength of the existing real estate market. Rental rates move up and down in response to supply and demand (occupancy). A residential property manager can discover rental trends by using the Bureau of Labor statistics on rents paid for residential housing. A property manager may also survey the properties that he or she is managing to determine the average monthly rent per unit or square foot. Statistics kept by individual property managers can also be combined with those of other managers in the area to get a broader perspective. Rental rates given in classified ads can also be examined. These methods, while not statistically accurate, can give a manager a basic idea of rental trends.

Employment levels. The property manager should be aware of local employment trends. The basic questions the property manager will want to answer are: (1) how many consumers are in the able-to-buy category, (2) what is the trend of their earnings (up or down?), and (3) how do they feel about spending versus saving? Obviously, if a potential customer cannot afford the product or would rather save than spend, the product is not going to be sold. Gross purchasing power can be estimated from statistics on net income.

Family size and lifestyles. Family size has a great deal to do with the value of particular residential units. Assume for a moment that the average family size is three (two parents and one child). In these circumstances, five-bedroom units will have little appeal and two-bedroom units will be very attractive. Therefore, the two-bedroom units will command a higher price per square foot than the five-bedroom units. It is important that the property manager be aware of the nationwide trend toward smaller and even single person households and also any peculiarities in local family size trends.

MANAGEMENT TECHNIQUES

Types of Properties

The property manager will find him or herself managing one or more of the five basic types of income-producing properties. These include apartment buildings, cooperatives and condominiums, office buildings, retail property and industrial property. Each type of property has its own unique set of characteristics and management needs. Because each type of property demands a different kind of expertise, property managers often specialize in the management of one particular type of property. The following are a few examples of the differences between property types.

Apartment buildings will have a much higher turnover rate than industrial property (where leases may be for 5-10 year periods), so the residential property manager will spend more time marketing and leasing out space. The residential property manager will also have to be concerned with the legal responsibilities imposed by Landlord-Tenant laws which are designed to protect the health and well-being of residential tenants.

Office buildings have very different housekeeping requirements than residential buildings: they endure much heavier foot traffic, have facilities that get continuous use (e.g., washrooms, elevators) and thus need frequent cleanings, and the management is often responsible for cleaning the tenants' space as well as the common areas. Lease terms are also very different for office buildings than for residential space: rent is based on a price per square foot (rather than per unit), the leases are for longer periods of time and usually include some type of escalation clause (to provide for automatic increases in rent), and lease negotiations often include major concessions (e.g., free rent, remodeling , etc.).

Leasing space to the appropriate tenant assumes a much greater significance in managing a **shopping center** than, for instance, an industrial property. The success of each tenant depends on the customers generated by each of the other tenants, so it is vital to lease to quality tenants. Also, a portion of the rent is often dependent on the tenant's income from the business, so the owner has a vested interest in the financial success of each tenant. The tenant mix must appeal to the widest variety of potential shoppers while avoiding direct competition within the shopping center itself.

These are only a few of the ways in which property types differ, but even from such a small sampling it is easy to see that different management plans are required for each type. The benefits of specializing in one or two property types is evident.

The Management Agreement

The first step in the management process is entering into a management agreement. This is the document which establishes the working relationship between the property manager and the property owner. In the same way the listing agreement creates an agency relationship between a broker and a seller, the management agreement creates an agency relationship between the manager and owner.

The management agreement should be in writing and signed by both parties. A sample agreement is shown on the following pages. It is very important that the written document contain all the terms and conditions of the agreement and it should be as comprehensive as possible. It is especially important that the exact duties and powers of the manager be explicitly stated. What kinds of decisions can the manager freely

Between

OWNER____

and

AGENT____

for Property located at__________________________________

Beginning________________________________ 19________

Ending__________________________________ 19________

MANAGEMENT AGREEMENT

In consideration of the covenants herein contained,________________

______________________________________(hereinafter called "OWNER"), and______________________(hereinafter called "AGENT"), agree as follows:

1. The OWNER hereby employs the AGENT exclusively to rent and manage the property (hereinafter called the "Premises") known as________

____

____

upon the terms hereinafter set forth, for a period of________years beginning on the______day of__________________, 19______, and ending on the__________day of__________________, 19______, and thereafter for yearly periods from time to time, unless on or before _______ days prior to the date last above mentioned or on or before _______ days prior to the expiration of any such renewal period, either party hereto shall notify the other in writing that it elects to terminate this Agreement, in which case this Agreement shall be thereby terminated on said last mentioned date. (See also Paragraph 6(c) below.)

MANAGEMENT AGREEMENT—Cont.

2. THE AGENT AGREES:

(a) To accept the management of the Premises, to the extent, for the period, and upon the terms herein provided and agrees to furnish the services of its organization for the rental operation and management of the Premises.

(b) To render a monthly statement of receipts, disbursements and charges to the following person at the address shown:

Name	Address
____________________	____________________
____________________	____________________

and to remit each month the net proceeds (provided Agent is not required to make any mortgage, escrow or tax payment on the first day of the following month). Agent will remit the net proceeds or the balance thereof after making allowance for such payments to the following persons, in the percentages specified and at the addresses shown:

Name	Percentage	Address
____________________	________	____________________
____________________	________	____________________
____________________	________	____________________

In case the disbursements and charges shall be in excess of the receipts, the OWNER agrees to pay such excess promptly, but nothing herein contained shall obligate the AGENT to advance its own funds on behalf of the OWNER.

(c) To cause all employees of the AGENT who handle or are responsible for the safekeeping of any monies of the OWNER to be covered by a fidelity bond in an amount and with a company determined by the AGENT at no cost to the OWNER.

3. THE OWNER AGREES:

To give the AGENT the following authority and powers (all or any of which may be exercised in the name of the OWNER) and agrees to assume all expenses in connection therewith:

(a) To advertise the Premises or any part thereof, to display signs thereon and to rent the same; to cause references of prospective tenants to be investigated; to sign leases for terms not in excess of__________years and to renew and or cancel the existing leases and prepare and execute the new lease without additional charge to the OWNER; provided, however, that the AGENT may collect from tenants all or any of the following: a late rent administrative charge, a non-negotiable check charge, credit report fee, a subleasing administrative charge and/or broker's commission and need not account for such charges and/or commission to the OWNER; to terminate tenancies and to sign and serve such notices as are deemed needful by the AGENT; to institute and prosecute actions to oust tenants and to recover possession of the Premises; to sue for and recover rent: and, when expedient, to settle, compromise and release such actions or suits, or reinstate such tenancies.

MANAGEMENT AGREEMENT—Cont.

(b) To hire, discharge and pay all engineers, janitors and other employees; to make or cause to be made all ordinary repairs and replacements necessary to preserve the Premises in its present condition and for the operating efficiency thereof and all alterations required to comply with lease requirements, and to do decorating on the Premises; to negotiate contracts for non-recurring items not exceeding $_____________________________and to enter into agreements for all necessary repairs, maintenance, minor alterations and utility services; and to purchase supplies and pay all bills.

(c) To collect rents and/or assessments and other items due or to become due and give receipts therefor and to deposit all funds collected hereunder in the Agent's custodial account.

(d) To refund tenants' security deposits at the expiration of leases and, only if required to do so by law, to pay interest upon such security deposits.

(e) To execute and file all returns and other instruments and do and perform all acts required of the OWNER as an employer with respect to the Premises under the Federal Insurance Contributions Acts, the Federal Unemployment Tax Act and Subtitle C of the Internal Revenue Code of 1954 with respect to wages paid by the AGENT on behalf of the OWNER and under any similar Federal or State law now or hereafter in force (and in connection therewith the OWNER agrees upon request to promptly execute and deliver to the AGENT all necessary powers of attorney, notices of appointment and the like)

4. THE OWNER FURTHER AGREES:

(a) To indemnify, defend and save the AGENT harmless from all suits in connection with the Premises and from liability for damage to property and injuries to or death of any employee or other person whomsoever, and to carry at his (its) own expense public liability, elevator liability (if elevators are part of the equipment of the Premises), and workmen's compensation insurance naming the OWNER and the AGENT and adequate to protect their interests and in form, substance and amounts reasonably satisfactory to the AGENT, and to furnish to the AGENT certificates evidencing the existence of such insurance. Unless the OWNER shall provide such insurance and furnish such certificate within ________ days from the date of this Agreement, the AGENT may, but shall not be obligated to, place said insurance and charge the cost thereof to the account of the OWNER.

(b) To pay all expenses incurred by the AGENT, including, without limitation, attorney's fees for counsel employed to represent the AGENT or the OWNER in any proceeding or suit involving an alleged violation by the AGENT or the OWNER, or both, of any constitutional provision, statute, ordinance, law or regulation of any governmental body pertaining to fair employment, Federal Fair Credit Reporting Act, environmental protection, or fair housing, including, without limitation, those prohibiting or making illegal discrimination on the basis of race, creed, color, religion or national origin in the sale, rental or other disposition of housing or any services rendered in connection therewith (unless the AGENT is finally adjudicated to have personally and not in a representative capacity violated such constitutional provision, statute, ordinance, law or regulation), but nothing herein contained shall require the AGENT to employ counsel to represent the OWNER in any such proceeding or suit.

(c) To indemnify, defend and save the AGENT harmless from all claims, investigations and suits with respect to any alleged or actual violation of state or federal labor laws, it being expressly agreed and understood that as between the OWNER and the AGENT, all persons employed in connection

MANAGEMENT AGREEMENT—Cont.

with the Premises are employees of the OWNER not the AGENT. The OWNER's obligation under this paragraph 4(c) shall include the payment of all settlements, judgments, damages, liquidated damages, penalties, forfeitures, back pay awards, court costs, litigation expense and attorneys' fees.

(d) To give adequate advance written notice to the AGENT if payment of mortgage indebtedness, general taxes or special assessments or the placing of fire, steam boiler or any other insurance is desired.

5. TO PAY THE AGENT EACH MONTH:

(a) FOR MANAGEMENT: ________________ per month or ________

percent (________%) of the monthly gross receipts from the operation of the Premises during the period this Agreement remains in full force and effect, whichever is the greater amount.

(b) APARTMENT LEASING ________________________________

____

____

(c) FOR MODERNIZATION (REHABILITATION/CONSTRUCTION)

____

____

(d) FIRE RESTORATION ________________________________

____

____

____

(e) OTHER ITEMS OF MUTUAL AGREEMENT ________________

____

____

____

____

6. IT IS MUTUALLY AGREED THAT:

(a) The OWNER expressly withholds from the AGENT any power or authority to make any structural changes in any building or to make any other major alterations or additions in or to any such building or equipment therein, or to incur any expense chargeable to the OWNER other than expenses related to exercising the express powers above vested in the AGENT without the prior written direction of the following person:

Name	Address
________________________	________________________

MANAGEMENT AGREEMENT—Cont.

except such emergency repairs as may be required because of danger to life or property or which are immediately necessary for the preservation and safety of the Premises or the safety of the tenants and occupants thereof or are required to avoid the suspension of any necessary service to the Premises.

(b) The AGENT does not assume and is given no responsibility for compliance of any building on the Premises or any equipment therein with the requirements of any statute, ordinance, law or regulation of any governmental body or of any public authority or official thereof having jurisdiction, except to notify the OWNER promptly or forward to the OWNER promptly any complaints, warnings, notices or summonses received by it relating to such matters. The OWNER represents that to the best of his (its) knowledge the Premises and such equipment comply with all such requirements and authorizes the AGENT to disclose the ownership of the Premises to any such officials and agrees to indemnify and hold harmless the AGENT, its representatives, servants and employees, of and from all loss, cost, expense and liability whatsoever which may be imposed on them or any of them by reason of any present or future violation or alleged violation of such laws, ordinances, statutes or regulations.

(c) In the event it is alleged or charged that any building on the Premises or any equipment therein or any act or failure to act by the OWNER with respect to the Premises or the sale, rental or other disposition thereof fails to comply with, or is in violation of, any of the requirements of any consititutional provision, statute, ordinance, law or regulation of any governmental body or any order or ruling of any public authority or official thereof having or claiming to have jurisdiction thereover, and the AGENT, in its sole and absolute discretion, considers that the action or position of the OWNER or registered managing agent with respect thereto may result in damage or liability to the AGENT, the AGENT shall have the right to cancel this Agreement at any time by written notice to the OWNER of its election so to do, which cancellation shall be effective upon the service of such notice. Such notice may be served personally or by registered mail, on or to the person named to receive the AGENT's monthly statement at the address designated for such person as provided in Paragraph 2(b) above, and if served by mail shall be deemed to have been served when deposited in the mails. Such cancellation shall not release the indemnities of the OWNER set forth in Paragraphs 4 and 6(b) above and shall not terminate any liability or obligation of the OWNER to the AGENT for any payment, reimbursement or other sum of money then due and payable to the AGENT hereunder.

7. This Agreement may be cancelled by OWNER before the termination date specified in paragraph 1 on not less than __ days prior written notice to the AGENT, provided that such notice is accompanied by payment to the AGENT of a cancellation fee in an amount equal to __% of the management fee that would accrue over the remainder of the stated term of the Agreement. For this purpose the monthly management fee for the remainder of the stated term shall be presumed to be the same as that of the last month prior to service of the notice of cancellation.

This Agreement shall be binding upon the successors and assigns of the AGENT and their heirs, administrators, executors, successors and assigns of the OWNER.

MANAGEMENT AGREEMENT—Cont.

IN WITNESS WHEREOF, the parties hereto have affixed or caused to be affixed their respective signatures this________ day of ____________________, 19______.

WITNESSES:

____

____

____

OWNER:

____

____

____

____

AGENT:

Firm ______________________________

By ______________________________

____
Submitted by

POWER OF ATTORNEY

KNOW ALL MEN BY THESE PRESENTS, THAT

____
(Name)

____located at
(State whether individual, partnership or corporation, etc.)

____has made,
(Address)

constituted and appointed, and, by these presents does hereby make, constitute and appoint, ____________________________, a resident of the United States, whose address is____________________________, (its) true and lawful attorney for (it) (me) in (its) (my) name, place and stead to

execute and to file any Tax Returns due on and after ____________________

____

under the provisions of the Social Security Act, now in force or future amendments thereto.

Dated at _______________ this _____day of__________________, 19_____

____
Signature of Taxpayer

____
Title

Executed in presence of:

____
Signature of Taxpayer

____
Title

____
Witness

____
Signature of Taxpayer

____
Witness

____
Title

Acknowledged before me this______day of____________________, 19____
NOTARIAL
SEAL

make and what kinds must be referred to the owner? For example, suppose several units in an apartment building needed new carpets. Could the manager replace the carpets without consulting the owner, or is this a decision the owner wants to make? Other areas in which questions might arise would be the authority to execute leases, make major repairs, choose the insurance company and policy and embark on major advertising campaigns. At a minimum, the following points should be included in the management agreement:

- a description of the property
- the time period of the agreement
- a definition of management's responsibilities (duties should be stated, exceptions noted)
- a statement of the owner's purpose (e.g., to maximize income or to increase the capital value of the property)
- the extent of the manager's authority (e.g., fixing rental rates, hiring and firing, authorizing repairs, etc.)
- provisions for reporting back to owner (frequency and detail of reports on operation and financial condition of the property)
- the management fee (a percentage of gross income, a commission on new rentals, a fixed fee, or a combination of all of these)
- allocation of costs (which expenses the manager will pay and which expenses the owner will pay, e.g., office help, advertising, telephone expenses, etc.)

The property manager must bear in mind that after signing the management agreement, an agency relationship exists between the manager and the owner and thus the manager is bound to all the duties and responsibilities of an agent, e.g., good faith, loyalty, obeying instructions, etc.

The Management Plan

Once the manager has entered into a management agreement, the actual business of managing begins. The first, and often most important step in managing a property is drawing up a management plan. The management plan is an outline of a strategy of property management (both physical upkeep and repair and financial management) and focuses on achieving the owner's goals.

It is important to remember that there are many different reasons for investing in income property and that different property owners have different management goals. For instance, one property owner may simply wish a steady, reliable stream of income. Another owner may want a tax shelter. Others may wish to increase the capital value so as to be able to reap a bigger profit in later years. The owner's goals may also change over the period of ownership. In the beginning, when the owner has other sources of income, he or she may be most interested in the tax shelter aspects of real estate ownership. However, as retirement age approaches, the owner may want a steady cash flow.

The management plan should implement the owner's goals in the most effective manner possible. The plan can only be created after a comprehensive study of all the facets of the property, including its location, its physical characteristics, its financial status, and its policies of operation.

Regional analysis. The first step to take when preparing a management plan is to study the region (city or metropolitan area) in which the property is located. The manager should analyze the general economic conditions, physical attributes and population growth and distribution. The manager can gather data (often published by the federal government or trade associations) on the growth of business, industry, tourism and recreation. Other factors include public facilities, public transportation and traffic conditions, educational opportunities and economic stability.

Neighborhood analysis. Once the region has been studied, the manager then analyzes the specific neighborhood where the property is located. The student should note that what comprises a neighborhood will vary considerably from region to region. In rural areas, a neighborhood may consist of many square miles, while in an urban area it may be only a few square blocks. The qualities of the neighborhood have a significant bearing on the value and usage of the property. Some important neighborhood characteristics include the level of maintenance (are the buildings and grounds well cared for or in poor condition?), the growth or decline in population, and the economic level of the population. The reason behind any trends in the neighborhood should also be considered. Is the population of the neighborhood growing because single-family homes are changing to rooming-house tenancy, or because of further development? Is the level of maintenance declining because owner-occupant housing is changing to rentals or because the economic status of the residents has shifted? Why is the trend in average rental or purchase prices increasing or decreasing?

The purpose of the neighborhood analysis is to determine whether the location can be considered a desirable one or whether neighborhood conditions will be a detriment to the operation of the property. No matter how effectively a property is operated, its profitability will be determined (at least to a certain degree) by its location. Once the characteristics of that location are determined, realistic management goals can be set.

Property analysis. Of course, the manager will want to become intimately familiar with the physical characteristics of the property itself. The manager will personally inspect the property, noting its architectural design, physical condition, facilities and general layout. The following is a list of the characteristics to be noted:

- the number and size of the living units or number of rentable square feet
- the visual impression of the property and the rental space (age, layout, style, view, fixtures, etc.)
- the physical condition of the building (conditions of roofs, elevators, windows, trim, etc.)

- the physical condition of the rentable space (floor covering, stairways, shades or blinds, walls, entryways)
- the kinds of amenities provided (laundries, janitorial services, etc.)
- the relationship of the land to the building (is there adequate parking? is the land used efficiently?)
- the current occupancy rate and tenant composition
- the current staff size and efficiency

Market analysis. Before the property manager can perform a market analysis, he or she must first decide what the pertinent market is. The major subcategories of the real estate market are commercial, retail, industrial and residential. Each of these can be broken down even further. For instance, the residential market can be divided into single-family residences, the duplex, the garden apartment, the walk-up apartment and the multi-story apartment building. Once the market is identified, there are several characteristics that must be examined:

- the number of units available in the area
- the average age and character of the buildings in which the units are located
- the quality of the average unit in the market (e.g., size, equipment, layout)
- trend (increase or decrease?) in the number of potential customers in the area
- the current price for the average unit
- the trend of the occupancy level for the type of unit

Once the property manager has gathered the pertinent information about comparable properties in the neighborhood, they can be compared to the subject property. Thus the manager can correctly evaluate what the property has to offer, and what its disadvantages are. Armed with this information, the manager can begin to set up an effective management strategy.

The management proposal. The course of action proposed by the property manager is written up in the management plan. The manager's strategy includes such items as rental schedules, income and expense projections, day-to-day operations and any changes in the building itself that the manager might find advisable. For instance, after a thorough examination of the property, the customer base and the market, the manager may decide the building should be rehabilitated, modernized or altered. Suppose that an older building is made up of four- and five-bedroom units in a neighborhood predominantly made up of one- and two-person households. If the apartments were converted to smaller units, the owner's profit would probably increase significantly.

The **rental schedule** is based on the data discovered during the information gathering stage. Based on the regional, neighborhood, property and market analysis, the manager should be able to determine the optimum rent that can be charged while maintaining the optimum occupancy level. The market rental rate for the average unit in the neighborhood can be adjusted up or down to reflect the individual differences in the units being managed. Because this method of setting rates depends on market conditions, the rental schedule should constantly be reexamined to verify that it is current and the rates are valid. An unusually high vacancy rate or an unusually low vacancy rate can both be indications that the rental rates are out of line with the community. (If the vacancy rate is too high, the rent may be too expensive; if the vacancy rate is unusually low, the rent may be below the norm.)

The property manager also sets up a budget of **income and operating** expenses (see page 174 for an operating budget form). The manager will list the total value of all rentable space at the scheduled rent and subtract from that a figure for vacancy and delinquent rental payments. Any other income sources should also be listed (e.g., laundry facilities, parking, etc.). The yearly operation expenses will then be listed, both the fixed expenses and the variable expenses. Fixed expenses include such items as property taxes, insurance premiums and salaries. Variable expenses include utilities, maintenance and repairs. Once the estimated costs of operation are determined, they can be deducted from estimated revenues to arrive at a cash flow figure.

The property manager also has responsibility for the day-to-day operations of the property. This means that the manager will have to decide how much (if any) staff will be required and what the employment policies and procedures will be. The manager will have to decide what work must be done, outline the skills necessary to complete the work, estimate the number of people required and perform the necessary supervision.

Once the management proposal is completed, the manager should be able to present the owner with a comprehensive management plan aimed at accomplishing the owner's goals. When the plan is approved by the owner, the manager will have a basic blueprint to the management of the property.

OPERATING BUDGET

Property ______________________ For Year ______________________

	Jan	Feb	Mar	Apr	May	June	July	Aug	Sept	Oct	Nov	Dec	Annual
Income													
Scheduled Rents (Incl. Empl. Unit)													
Less:													
Vacancies													
Rent Loss													
Effective Rent													
Miscellaneous Income													
Total Income													
Expenses													
Administrative													
Management Costs													
Other Administrative Costs													
Operating													
Payroll													
Supplies													
Heating													
Electricity													
Water and Sewer													
Gas													

OPERATING BUDGET (cont.'d)

	Jan	Feb	Mar	Apr	May	June	July	Aug	Sept	Oct	Nov	Dec	Annual
Maintenance													
Grounds Maintenance													
Maintenance and Repairs													
Painting and Decorating, Interior													
Taxes and Insurance													
Real Estate Taxes													
Other Taxes, Fees, Etc.													
Insurance													
Contract Service													
Total Expenses													
Net Operating Income													
Less Reserves													
Net Income													
Less Debt Service													
Cash Flow													

Prepared by ____________________ Approved by ____________________

Date ____________ Date ______

Record-keeping and Manager/Owner Relations

As the manager supervises the operation of the property, he or she must account to the owner for the money received and expended. It is up to the owner to decide how detailed and frequent operating reports should be. The frequency and detail will depend on how involved the owner wants to be in the management of the property. For example, an owner with extensive property holdings who is also engaged in a full-time occupation will probably prefer that the property manager assume the bulk of the decision-making and will not want to be bothered with time-consuming detailed reports. On the other hand, a retired person with only one or two income-producing properties may want to be more intimately involved with the management of the property.

The property manager must also be sure to keep accurate trust account records. According to California license law, the property manager must keep a separate record for each property managed and must post entries of cash receipts and disbursements on a daily basis.

SEPARATE RECORD FOR EACH PROPERTY MANAGED

Owner ______________________ Deposit ______________________
Address ______________________ Monthly Rent ______________________
Property ______________________ Commission: ______________________
Tenant's Name ______________________ Leases ______________________
Units ______________________ Collection ______________________
Remarks ______________________ Management ______________________

Date	Rec. From or Paid To	Descrip.	Receipt or Check Number	Amt. Rec.	Dep. Date	Int.	Amt. Disb.	Balance

Statement of operations. One of the most important documents prepared by the property manager is the statement of operations. This is a periodic (usually monthly) report showing the money received and the money paid out, including collections (statements of income, occupancy, uncollected balances, evictions), disbursements (payroll, maintenance, repairs, purchasing), and the overall condition of the property.

The **summary of operations**, the key portion of the statement of operations, is a brief description of income and expenses which can be quickly read and understood. The summary allows both the manager and the owner to evaluate monthly performance and the information in the summary is supported by accompanying information.

The **rent roll** is a report on the collection of rent. Both occupied and vacant space is listed in the rent roll, and the total of rental income earned (both collected and uncollected) plus the rental value of the vacant space should equal the total rental value of the building. The rent roll breaks down the rental amounts into previous balance, current rent, total received and balance due. The information used in the rent roll is obtained from the individual ledger sheets kept on each tenant/rental space. The ledger sheet typically shows the tenant's name, phone number, unit, regular rent and recurring charges, security deposit information, move-in date, lease term, and payments and balances.

RENT ROLL

Property *Magnolia Heights* Period *April*

Owner *S. T. Jones* Prepared by *M. Smith*

Unit		Previous	Current	Date	Other Collections		Total	Balance
Number	Occupant	Balance	Rent	Received	Amount	Description	Received	Due
1	*G. Rhodes*	*0*	*$800*	*4-1*		—	*$800*	*0*
2	*F. Brown*	*0*	*$800*	*4-1*	*$80*	*parking*	*$880*	*0*
3	*C. Johnson*	*0*	*$700*	*4-4*		—	*$700*	*0*
4	*C. Flynn*	*0*	*$800*	*4-2*	*$80*	*parking*	*$880*	*0*

RENTAL LEDGER

Unit Number *2* Property *Magnolia Heights*

Monthly Rent Unit *2* $ *$800*

parking *$80*

Total $ *$880*

Date	Occupant	Rent Period Mo./Yr.		Payment Credited To				Total Amount Received	Remarks
		From	To	Rent	Security Deposit	Miscellaneous Amount	Miscellaneous Description		
4-90	*F. Brown*	*4-89*	*3-91*	*$800*	*$500*	*$80*	*parking*	*$1,380*	

The **statement of disbursements** lists all the expenses paid during that time period. Written orders should be prepared for every purchase and payment so that an accurate account can be made of all expenditures and their purpose. The disbursements are usually classified according to type, which makes their presentation easier to understand. For example, all maintenance expenses should be listed together, all tax and insurance expenses, and all administrative expenses, etc.

STATEMENT OF DISBURSEMENTS

Property *Magnolia Heights* Period *April*
Owner *S. T. Jones* Prepared by *M. Smith*

Check Number	Date	Description	Amount: Operating	Amount: Non-operating
20712	*April 1*	*electricity*	*$1,967*	
20713	*April 1*	*cleaning supplies*	*$189*	
		Totals		

In addition to the numerical accounts given to the owner, it is often helpful to include a **narrative report of operations**. This is simply a letter explaining the various elements of the statement of operations. The narrative report adds a personal touch and it is especially important if the income was lower or the expenses were higher than expected. If there is a deviation in the normal cash flow, the owner will want a clear and convincing explanation. If the reason for a drop in cash flow is not explained, the owner may doubt the competence or integrity of the property manager.

In addition to the various reports and statements sent to the owner, the manager may wish to contact the owner in person. A telephone call or personal visit to explain a particular proposal or problem or ask a question is much more effective than a letter. An interview is often advised if the monthly statement significantly differs from the norm.

Leasing and Tenant Relations

A primary function of the property manager is leasing out, or merchandising, the rental space and maintaining harmonious tenant relations. The property manager should be familiar with the various types and benefits of advertising, renting techniques, types of leases and lease documents and renewal techniques.

Marketing.

Obviously, the more people who view the rental space, the more likely it is to be rented out. Therefore, the property manager must somehow bring potential customers to the property. This is mainly done through advertising. As the property manager wants to reach the greatest number of potential tenants for the least possible cost, he or she must be aware of the various types of advertising and their ability to reach the market for the particular property.

Signs. Small and tasteful signs are often used, whether there is a vacancy or not, to inform passers-by of the name of the manager and how to acquire rental information. The use of signs is most successful for office buildings, large apartment complexes and shopping centers.

Newspaper advertising. Newspaper advertising reaches more people than any other type of advertising. **Classified** advertising (inexpensive advertising which appears in the "classified" section of the newspaper) is the most popular way of advertising rental space, especially residential units. **Display** advertising is larger, more expensive, and can appear in any section of the newspaper. This is often the most effective way of advertising space in a new office building, industrial park or shopping center.

Radio and television. Television advertising is usually too expensive to be effective for anything but a large commercial or residential property and generally, there are few potential renters in a radio audience. For these reasons, broadcast advertising is rarely used.

Direct mail. In order to be effective, direct mail advertising must be aimed at potential renters. Because brochures sent to the general public are not likely to get good results, a mailing list must be compiled (a time-consuming and expensive process). If a mailing list can be made up from local and/or private information and the format of the advertising is directly aimed at the socio-economic status of the recipient, direct mail can be an effective means of advertising. Also, the same type of brochure that is mailed out can also be handed out to those who visit the property.

Different types of properties will require different types and amounts of advertising. Generally, advertising is only necessary when there is a vacancy to fill; if the property is in a desirable location and attractive to potential renters, it may not be necessary at all. On the other hand, if the property is in an isolated location, advertising may be a requisite to filling a vacancy. The type of advertising chosen should bring in the most prospects in the least amount of time for the lowest cost. A general rule of thumb is that the cost of advertising should not exceed $10.00 to $20.00 per prospect. For example, newspaper advertising that costs $200.00 should bring 10 to 20 prospective tenants to the property.

Renting techniques and leases.

Once the prospect is on the premises, it is the manager's job to convince him or her that the unit is desirable. This is done by taking the prospect on an inspection tour and noting all the qualities of the property and the amenities offered. During the inspection of the property, the manager will want to point out traffic patterns and access to public transportation, the character of the other tenants, the exterior and interior condition of the property and its overall cleanliness. It is also the manager's responsibility to make sure that the prospect is qualified to lease the property, i.e., has the financial strength and willingness to pay the rent, take care of the premises, etc.

Once the prospect and manager decide that renting the space would be mutually beneficial, a rental agreement is entered into. The rental agreement, or lease, is a contract between the landlord and tenant that gives the tenant use or possession of the property for a certain amount of time in exchange for a specified payment. A written lease is beneficial to both parties. The lease assures the landlord of occupancy and rental payments for a certain period of time; it also assures the tenant of use or possession of the premises for the same period of time.

Types of leases. Different types of leases are used for different types of properties. A **fixed lease** (sometimes called a "gross lease") provides for a fixed rental amount. The tenant pays the fixed amount and the landlord pays all the utilities, maintenance costs, taxes and insurance (which may vary from period to period). This is the type of lease typically used for residential apartment units. The **graduated lease** is similar to a fixed lease, but includes periodic increases in the rental amount. These increases are usually set at specific future dates and are typically based on the cost-of-living index. A **percentage lease** is most often used for a commercial lease, particularly in shopping centers. The rental payment is based on a percentage of the tenant's income from the business operated on the premises. The lease will usually provide for a minimum rental amount plus a percentage of the tenant's income above the stated minimum. The percentage varies depending on the type of business and amount of overhead. For example, a tenant who operates a parking lot or garage will pay a higher percentage than a tenant who operates a grocery store. Under a **net lease**, the tenant pays the landlord a fixed rental amount plus some or all of the operating expenses. Net leases are most often used for office rentals.

Characteristics of a valid lease. All types of leases must have certain characteristics in order to be valid. While no particular language is necessary to create a lease, the intention to rent the property must be clear. The lease must include the names of all the parties, a description of the property, the amount of the rental payments and the length of time the lease will continue. All leases for terms of over a year must be in writing. The lease must be signed by the lessor (landlord). The lessor's signature shows his or her acceptance of the lease terms; the lessee's (tenant's) acceptance is shown by taking possession of the property. (It is always best to have both parties sign the lease.) Furthermore, both parties must be legally competent to enter into the agreement (e.g., mentally competent, of legal age).

The lease must have a legal purpose. For example, if parties enter into a lease in order to run an illegal gambling casino, the lease would not be enforceable. Unless otherwise stated, a tenant may use property for any legal purpose. Because "any legal purpose" covers a broad range of activities, many landlords include a provision in the lease which restricts the allowable uses of the property. For example, the owner of a shopping center may enter a lease with a major grocery store, promising that no other grocery store will be given space in the center. So in the leases with the other tenants, the landlord will provide that none of them may operate a grocery store on the premises.

Most property managers require a **security deposit** from the tenant when the tenant signs the lease, especially for residential properties. This deposit protects the owner from any tenant default — either a failure to pay the rent, or damage caused to the premises. At the end of the lease term, if the tenant has fulfilled all of the lease obligations, the deposit must be returned within 14 days of the termination of the lease. If a portion of the deposit is kept (e.g., to pay for damages), the reasons for its retention must be itemized and given to the tenant. State law limits the amount a residential landlord can demand as a security deposit.

Lease renewal. The property manager would much rather renew an existing lease than make a new one. Renewal eliminates vacancy between the time one tenant moves out and another moves in. A building has greater stability with long-term tenants and it is usually easier and less expensive to satisfy an existing tenant than improve the space for the new tenant.

The property manager should always be aware of which tenants are nearing the end of their lease term. These tenants should be notified that their leases are about to expire and then the manager should follow up on the notices, by phone or in person, to inquire whether the tenant wants to renew. If the tenant is going to renew the lease, the terms of the new lease must be negotiated, e.g., whether there is to be an increase in rent or repairs performed. Some leases contain **automatic renewal** clauses, which provide that the lease will be automatically renewed unless one party notifies the other of the wish to terminate the lease.

Rental collection. Obviously, the property will not be profitable unless the rents are collected when due. Careful selection of tenants in the first place is one of the most effective ways of avoiding delinquent rents. The property manager should not let pressure for a high occupancy rate take precedence over the wisdom of accepting only those tenants who are likely to meet their financial obligations. A careful property manager investigates the tenant's references and, if possible, contacts his or her former landlord.

The amount, time and place of payment and any penalties imposed for late payment should be clearly stated in the lease document. The manager should consistently follow a collection plan that includes adequate recordkeeping and immediate notification of late payments. When all collection attempts fail, the manager must be prepared to take legal action (e.g., a suit for eviction) in accordance with the owner's policies.

Maintenance.

Another important function of the property manager is the supervision of property maintenance. There are four basic categories of maintenance activities:

1. **preventive maintenance:** preserves the physical integrity of the premises and eliminates corrective maintenance costs (e.g., cleaning the gutters);
2. **corrective maintenance:** actual repairs that keep equipment, utilities and amenities functioning in a proper manner (e.g., fixing a leaking faucet);
3. **routine cleaning:** cleaning the common areas and grounds on a regular basis (e.g., vacuuming hallways and cleaning elevators); and

4. **new construction:** this includes tenant alterations made at the beginning of the tenancy and when the lease is renewed and cosmetic changes designed to make the building more attractive (e.g., remodeling the lobby). When managing commercial or industrial property, a property manager is often required to alter the interior of the building to meet the needs of a new tenant. These alterations can range from a simple repainting job to completely redesigning and rebuilding the space. If a new building is involved, designing the interior space is especially common as the interior is often left incomplete so that it can be built to fit the needs of the individual tenants.

Property managers are not required to know how to fix the building's plumbing or electrical wiring themselves. However, they are required to know the maintenance needs of the property and whom to call on to perform the necessary maintenance chores. Most maintenance activities are handled by building maintenance employees or by outside businesses that contract with the manager to provide these services.

The property manager should direct the activities of the maintenance staff or independent contractors with a schedule of inspection and maintenance. First, the manager should inventory the building's equipment and physical elements (e.g., plumbing, furnace, roof, walls, etc.) Then a schedule should be drawn up of when regular inspections, cleaning and repairs are to take place. For instance, walls and roofs should be scheduled for periodic inspection, painting and repairs. Elevators should be serviced on a regular basis. The property manager should keep accurate and up-to-date records on when the various elements were inspected, serviced, replaced or repaired. These routine inspections and maintenance activities will help preserve the capital value of the building and prevent major repair expenses.

PROPERTY MAINTENANCE RECORD

Property *Magnolia Heights*

Date	Action	Location	by Whom	Time	Cost
4/14	*inspect elevator*	*lobby*	*Top Repair*	*1 hr.*	*contract*

Summary

To briefly summarize, property management refers to the management of income-producing property by someone other than the owner. It is the property manager's responsibility to maintain the value of the property while producing the largest income possible for the owner. The various functions of the property manager include analyzing the property and its market to come up with an effective management plan, keeping the owner informed of the management operations, marketing and leasing the property, collecting rents, and supervising property upkeep and maintenance.

Section Two

Financing Practices

## Chapter Eight

Introduction to Finance

Immediately after choosing the house he or she wishes to purchase, the typical buyer will begin the search for financing. The knowledgeable real estate agent will be of tremendous help to such a buyer, who is likely to be mystified by the loan process. Of course, before the agent can help the buyer obtain financing, the agent must first know something about it him or herself.

While the world of real estate finance may seem complex, it is actually based on very straightforward principles. The following chapters in this text will attempt to explain these principles. First, however, we will take a brief look at the process of obtaining a real estate loan.

Application Process.

As might be expected, the first step in obtaining a real estate loan is to fill out the **loan application**. The buyer (or the real estate agent on behalf of the buyer) will set up an appointment with the lender. The buyer will attend this appointment armed with a good deal of personal and financial data which will be the basis of the lender's decision whether or not to make the loan. The types of information the buyer should take to this interview will be discussed shortly. It should be noted that if the buyer does not have all the necessary data at the interview, it will be necessary to provide the missing information at a later date which will cause a delay in the loan application process.

During the initial interview, the buyer will learn of the various types of **financing programs** offered by the lender. These will probably include

30-year fixed-rate mortgages, 15-year fixed-rate mortgages and several different versions of an adjustable-rate mortgage. Based on the information given by the lender and the buyer's own personal circumstances, the buyer will decide which program best suits his or her needs.

The lender will also require a **deposit** to cover the expenses that must be paid up front. These include the costs of the credit report, property appraisal and preliminary title report. This deposit will assure the lender that these fees will be paid, even if the loan does not close.

The **deposit receipt** will be examined at this interview as well. This is so the lender can be sure that the terms of the agreement are in keeping with the terms of the loan the lender can offer (e.g., interest rate and length of the term of the loan). Of particular concern is the agreed-upon closing date. Often, the deposit receipt will provide for a closing date which is far too early to be realistic. If it is impossible for the lender to meet the closing date, a more feasible one can be agreed on and later frustration avoided.

Once the application has been properly filled out, the lender can begin gathering other pertinent information on the buyer. **Verification** forms will be sent out to the buyer's employer, banks or other financial institutions, and any previous mortgage lender. The lender will order a **credit report** and have a **preliminary title report** prepared. An approved appraiser will be asked to **appraise** the property. After examining the application, the lender may also require the buyer to submit further information, including:

- a copy of any divorce decree (to verify any child support or alimony obligations and any settlement agreement that may be the source of the downpayment);
- investment account records;
- pension plan documentation;
- tax returns (if the buyer is self-employed or retired and living on investment income);
- any other documentation that may have an effect on the buyer's income or credit status.

The lender will be very concerned with the source of the buyer's **down-payment**. Savings, the sale of a previous home, or gifts are all acceptable sources of the downpayment. However, it is not permitted to use borrowed funds for the downpayment.

When the credit report, verification forms, preliminary title report and appraisal have all been received by the lender, a **loan package** is put together and submitted to the underwriting department. The loan underwriter thoroughly examines the loan package and then makes the decision to approve it, reject it, or approve it under certain conditions. A conditional approval usually requires the submission of additional information, such as:

- the closing statement from the sale of the buyer's previous home;
- pay stubs to verify income;
- a final inspection report;
- a commitment for **private mortgage insurance** (which is always a condition for the approval of a conventional loan with a less than 20% downpayment).

After the conditions are met, all the necessary documents are prepared for **closing**. The closing process ordinarily takes about one week if everything goes smoothly. If there are no unforeseen problems (e.g., the seller does not have title to the property), the loan papers will be signed and sent to the **funding** department. This department makes one final check to be sure that everything is in order and that it has the necessary instructions for the release of the funds. The loan funds are then released to the proper parties.

The Loan Application.

As mentioned earlier, the buyer fills out a loan application at the initial interview with the lender. A standard loan application which can be used for a conventional, FHA or VA loan is shown on the following pages.

Residential Loan Application

MGIC

MORTGAGE APPLIED FOR	Amount	Interest Rate	No. of Months	Monthly Payment Principal & Interest	Escrow/Impounds (to be collected monthly)
[X] Conventional [ ] FHA [ ] VA [ ] ______	$76,500.	10¼ %	360	$ 635.52	[X] Taxes [X] Hazard Ins. [X] Mtg. Ins. [ ] ______

Prepayment Option

Subject Property

Property Street Address	City	County	State	Zip	No. Units
712 N. 1st	Seaside	Ocean	CA	00012	1

Legal Description (Attach description if necessary): SEE ATTACHMENT — Year Built: 1971

Purpose of Loan: [X] Purchase [ ] Construction-Permanent [ ] Construction [ ] Refinance [ ] Other (Explain)

Complete this line if Construction-Permanent or Construction Loan: Lot Value Data — Year Acquired ____ ; Original Cost $ ____ ; Present Value (a) $ ____ ; Cost of Imps. (b) $ ____ ; Total (a + b) $ ____ ; ENTER TOTAL AS PURCHASE PRICE IN DETAILS OF PURCHASE.

Complete this line if a Refinance Loan: Year Acquired ; Original Cost $; Amt. Existing Liens $; Purpose of Refinance ; Describe Improvements [ ] made [ ] to be made ; Cost: $ ____

Title Will Be Held In What Name(s): James Turner, Sarah Turner, husband and wife

Manner In Which Title Will Be Held: community property

Source of Down Payment and Settlement Charges: savings

This application is designed to be completed by the borrower(s) with the lender's assistance. The Co-Borrower Section and all other Co-Borrower questions must be completed and the appropriate box(es) checked if [ ] another person will be jointly obligated with the Borrower on the loan, or [ ] the Borrower is relying on income from alimony, child support or separate maintenance or on the income or assets of another person as a basis for repayment of the loan, or [X] the Borrower is married and resides, or the property is located, in a community property state.

	Borrower	Co-Borrower
Name	James Turner	Sarah Turner
Age	35	36
School	Yrs 16	Yrs 16
Present Address — No. Years	2 [ ] Own [X] Rent	2 [ ] Own [X] Rent
Street	7280 Cherry Avenue	7280 Cherry Avenue
City/State/Zip	Seaside, California 00012	Seaside, California 00012
Former address if less than 2 years at present address — Street		
City/State/Zip		
Years at former address	[ ] Own [ ] Rent	[ ] Own [ ] Rent
Marital Status	[X] Married [ ] Separated [ ] Unmarried (incl. single, divorced, widowed)	[X] Married [ ] Separated [ ] Unmarried (incl. single, divorced, widowed)
Dependents other than listed by co-borrower / by borrower — No. / Ages		
Name and Address of Employer	Qwik Copy, 722 - 6th Avenue, Seaside, California 00012	Oceanview Community College, Seaside, California 00012
Years employed in this line of work or profession?	2 years	5 years
Years on this job	1	3
Self Employed*	[ ]	[ ]

Position/Title	Type of Business	Position/Title	Type of Business
Print Shop Asst. Mgr.	Printing	Minority Affairs Counselor/Student Counseling	

Social Security Number ***	Home Phone	Business Phone	Social Security Number ***	Home Phone	Business Phone
333-22-111	423-7890	221-7070	111-22-333	423-7890	435-2666

Gross Monthly Income

Item	Borrower	Co-Borrower	Total
Base Empl. Income	$ 1,558	$ 1,800	$ 3,358
Overtime	–	–	–
Bonuses	50	–	50
Commissions	–	–	–
Dividends/Interest	–	25	25
Net Rental Income	–	–	–
Other† (Before completing, see notice under Describe Other Income below.)	–	–	–
	–	–	–
	–	–	–
Total	$ 1,608	$ 1,825	$ 3,433

Monthly Housing Expense**

	Present	Proposed
Rent	$ 550	
First Mortgage (P&I)	–	$ 685.52
Other Financing (P&I)	–	–
Hazard Insurance	–	20
Real Estate Taxes	–	50
Mortgage Insurance	–	23
Homeowner Assn. Dues	–	–
Other:	–	–
Total Monthly Pmt.	$ 550	$ 751.52
Utilities	55	75
Total	$ 605	$ 826.52

Details of Purchase

Do Not Complete If Refinance	
a. Purchase Price	$85,000
b. Total Closing Costs (Est.)	11,050
c. Prepaid Escrows (Est.)	300
d. Total (a + b + c)	$96,350
e. Amount This Mortgage	(76,500)
f. Other Financing	(0)
g. Other Equity	(0)
h. Amount of Cash Deposit	(1,000)
i. Closing Costs Paid by Seller	(7,650)
j. Cash Reqd. For Closing (Est.)	$11,200

Describe Other Income

B–Borrower C–Co-Borrower	NOTICE: † Alimony, child support, or separate maintenance income need not be revealed if the Borrower or Co-Borrower does not choose to have it considered as a basis for repaying this loan.	Monthly Amount
		$

If Employed In Current Position For Less Than Two Years, Complete the Following

B/C	Previous Employer/School	City/State	Type of Business	Position/Title	Dates From/To	Monthly Income
B	Copy King	Seaside, CA	Print Shop	Clerk	8/1/87-10/15/89	$ 1,350

These Questions Apply To Both Borrower and Co-Borrower

If a "yes" answer is given to a question in this column, please explain on an attached sheet.	Borrower Yes or No	Co-Borrower Yes or No
Are there any outstanding judgments against you?	no	no
Have you been declared bankrupt within the past 7 years?	no	no
Have you had property foreclosed upon or given title or deed in lieu thereof in the last 7 years?	no	no
Are you a party to a law suit?	no	no
Are you obligated to pay alimony, child support, or separate maintenance?	no	no
Is any part of the down payment borrowed?	no	no
Are you a co-maker or endorser on a note?	no	no

	Borrower Yes or No	Co-Borrower Yes or No
Are you a U.S. citizen?	yes	yes
If "no," are you a resident alien?		
If "no," are you a non-resident alien?		

Explain Other Financing or Other Equity (if any). ____

*FHLMC/FNMA require business credit report, signed Federal Income Tax returns for last two years; and, if available, audited Profit and Loss Statement plus balance sheet for same period.
**All Present Monthly Housing Expenses of Borrower and Co-Borrower should be listed on a combined basis.
***Optional for FHLMC
FHLMC 65 Rev. 10/86

Fannie Mae Form 1003 Rev. 10/86

Statement of Assets and Liabilities

This Statement and any applicable supporting schedules may be completed jointly by both married and unmarried co-borrowers if their assets and liabilities are sufficiently joined so that the Statement can be meaningfully and fairly presented on a combined basis; otherwise separate Statements and Schedules are required (FHLMC 65A/FNMA 1003A). If the co-borrower section was completed about a spouse, this statement and supporting schedules must be completed about that spouse also.

☒ Completed Jointly ☐ Not Completed Jointly

Indicate by (*) those liabilities or pledged assets which will be satisfied upon sale of real estate owned or upon refinancing of subject property

Assets

Description	Cash or Market Value
Cash Deposit Toward Purchase Held By: Stella George, Broker	$ 1,000
Checking and Savings Accounts (Show Names of Institutions (Account Numbers)) Bank, S & L or Credit Union: Seaside Credit Union	8,023
Addr. 712 Main Street	
City Seaside, CA 00012	
Acct. No. 932157	
Bank, S & L or Credit Union: First National Bank	4,098
Addr. 2203 Market Street	
City Seaside, CA 00012	
Acct. No. 2172-813	
Bank, S & L or Credit Union: First National Bank	574
Addr. 2203 Market Street	
City Seaside, CA 00012	
Acct. No. 5769-813	
Stocks and Bonds (No./Description)	
Life Insurance Net Cash Value Face Amount $	
Subtotal Liquid Assets	13,695
Real Estate Owned (Enter Market Value from Schedule of Real Estate Owned)	
Vested Interest in Retirement Fund	
Net worth of Business Owned (ATTACH FINANCIAL STATEMENT)	
Automobiles Owned (Make and Year) Ford 1988	8,750
Toyota 1984	3,000

Liabilities and Pledged Assets

Creditors' Name, Address and Account Number	Acct. No.	Acct. Name if Not Borrower's	Mo. Pmt. and Mos. Left to Pay ($ Pmt/Mos.)	Unpaid Balance ($)
Installment Debts (include "revolving" charge accounts) Co. World Bank VISA Addr. 71258 - 132nd Ave. City Saratoga, NY	4567 82 9271		$ 25/15	$ 375
Co. Sears & Roebuck Addr. 512 Main St. City Seaside, CA 00012	4956 213 72		$ 15/10	$ 150
Co. Addr. City			/	
Co. Addr. City			/	
Co. Addr. City			/	
Other Debts including Stock Pledges			/	
Real Estate Loans Co. Addr. City			X	
Co. Addr. City			X	
Automobile Loans Co. Seaside Credit Union Addr. 712 Main Street City Seaside, CA 00012	72160 C		$210/27	$5,670
Co. City			/	

Furniture and Personal Property	15,000	Alimony/Child Support/Separate Maintenance Payments Owed to			
Other Assets (Itemize)		Total Monthly Payments		$ 250	
Total Assets	A $40,445	Net Worth (A minus B) $	$34,250	Total Liabilities	B $ $6,195

SCHEDULE OF REAL ESTATE OWNED (If Additional Properties Owned Attach Separate Schedule)

Address of Property (Indicate S if Sold, PS if Pending Sale or R if Rental being held for income)	⇩	Type of Property	Present Market Value	Amount of Mortgages & Liens	Gross Rental Income	Mortgage Payments	Taxes, Ins. Maintenance and Misc.	Net Rental Income
			$	$	$	$	$	$
		TOTALS →	$	$	$	$	$	$

List Previous Credit References

⇩ B–Borrower C–Co-Borrower	Creditor's Name and Address	Account Number	Purpose	Highest Balance	Date Paid
B/C	Atlas Savings & Loan, 352 Cherry, Seaside, CA/	71116-3	Personal-furn.	$ 8,000	1/2/88
C	Seaside Credit Union, 712 Main, Seaside, CA/	56052 D	Auto loan	5,600	3/7/87
B	First Bank Mastercard, 87632-189th N.E., Portland, ME	8926-438-92-41	1/Revolv.Credit	1,375	7/30/89

List any additional names under which credit has previously been received ____________

AGREEMENT: The undersigned applies for the loan indicated in this application to be secured by a first mortgage or deed of trust on the property described herein, and represents that the property will not be used for any illegal or restricted purpose, and that all statements made in this application are true and are made for the purpose of obtaining the loan. Verification may be obtained from any source named in this application. The original or a copy of this application will be retained by the lender, even if the loan is not granted. The undersigned ☐ intend or ☐ do not intend to occupy the property as their primary residence.

I/we fully understand that it is a federal crime punishable by fine or imprisonment, or both, to knowingly make any false statements concerning any of the above facts as applicable under the provisions of Title 18, United States Code, Section 1014.

James Turner (signature) Date 12/10/90 — Sarah Turner (signature) Date 12/10/90

Borrower's Signature — Co-Borrower's Signature

Information for Government Monitoring Purposes

The following information is requested by the Federal Government for certain types of loans related to a dwelling, in order to monitor the lender's compliance with equal credit opportunity and fair housing laws. You are not required to furnish this information, but are encouraged to do so. The law provides that a lender may neither discriminate on the basis of this information, nor on whether you choose to furnish it. However, if you choose not to furnish it, under Federal regulations this lender is required to note race and sex on the basis of visual observation or surname. If you do not wish to furnish the above information, please check the box below. (Lender must review the above material to assure that the disclosures satisfy all requirements to which the Lender is subject under applicable state law for the particular type of loan applied for.)

Borrower: ☒ I do not wish to furnish this information
Race/National Origin:
☐ American Indian, Alaskan Native ☐ Asian, Pacific Islander
☐ Black ☐ Hispanic ☐ White
☐ Other (specify) ____________
Sex: ☐ Female ☐ Male

Co-Borrower: ☒ I do not wish to furnish this information
Race/National Origin:
☐ American Indian, Alaskan Native ☐ Asian, Pacific Islander
☐ Black ☐ Hispanic ☐ White
☐ Other (specify) ____________
Sex: ☐ Female ☐ Male

To Be Completed by Interviewer

This application was taken by:
☐ face to face interview
☐ by mail
☐ by telephone

Interviewer ____________ Name of Interviewer's Employer ____________

Interviewer's Phone Number ____________ Address of Interviewer's Employer ____________

FHLMC Form 65 Rev 10 86 **REVERSE** Fannie Mae Form 1003 Rev 10 86

Form #71-3973 (10/86)

Property information. The application begins with a section on the property. Questions as to the type of loan sought, the terms of the loan, location and legal description of the property, the property's value, and the manner of taking title must be completed.

Borrower information. The next section of the application requests the borrower's name, address, phone number, social security number, marital status and employer. There is a parallel section requesting the same information on any co-borrower (e.g., spouse).

Income. The section regarding income provides spaces for primary employment income, overtime, bonuses, commissions, dividends and interest, net rental income and income from any other sources.

Monthly housing expense. The monthly housing expense is made up of such items as rent, principal and interest payments, any secondary financing payments, hazard insurance premiums, real estate taxes, mortgage insurance premiums, homeowner's association dues and utilities.

Details of purchase. The next section asks for information on the real estate transaction itself. The buyer is to fill in the purchase price, closing costs, prepaid escrow expenses, mortgage amount, any secondary financing amounts, other equity, amount of cash deposit, closing costs to be paid by the seller and an estimate of the cash amount that will be required for closing.

Employment history. If the borrower has been at his or her present job for less than two years, the name, address and type of business of previous employers must be included, along with the borrower's position, income and the dates of employment.

Credit history. This section is for information on the buyer's credit history, e.g., any outstanding judgments, bankruptcies, foreclosures, etc.

Assets and liabilities. In the next section of the application, the buyer is to list all assets and liabilities. Assets include cash deposits, checking and savings accounts, stocks and bonds, life insurance policies, real estate, retirement funds, automobiles and personal property. Liabilities would include any installment debts, automobile loans, real estate loans, and alimony and/or child support payments.

Credit references. In this segment, the buyer is to list other credit references, such as personal loans or revolving credit debts which have been paid off.

Borrower's signature. Finally, there is a space for the buyer to date and sign the application.

Loan Application Checklist.

In order to properly fill out the loan application, the buyer will need to know a variety of information which may not be easily recalled from memory. To ensure that all necessary data is at the buyer's fingertips, it would be wise for him or her to take the following information to the initial interview:

The **deposit receipt** or sales contract

A **residence history**:

- where the buyer has lived for the past two years
  - if the buyer is currently renting, the landlord or rental agency's name, address and phone number
  - if the buyer owns his or her present home, the name, address and phone number of the lender and the type of loan (e.g., FHA or conventional)

Employment history:

- names, addresses and zip codes of where the buyer has been employed for the last two years; the position held; whether the employment was full time, part time or temporary; and the income earned upon departure
- if self-employed or fully commissioned, the tax returns for the past two calendar years, plus a year-to-date income and expense statement
- if a major stockholder in a corporation (owns 25% or more of the stock), three years of corporate tax returns

Income:

- the amount and sources of income, including regular salary and secondary sources, such as:
  - military retirement
  - company pensions
  - social security benefits
  - disability benefits
  - child support or alimony
- the lender will need a statement of benefits from the corresponding sources of income listed above; child support or alimony will require a copy of the divorce decree

A list of **assets**:

- names, addresses, and account numbers for all bank accounts
- the value of household goods and personal property
- the make, model, year and market value of automobiles
- the cash and face value of insurance policies
- the address, description, and value of any other real estate owned; income properties should have a spread sheet showing relevant data (similar to the one shown below)

SCHEDULE OF REAL ESTATE

ADDRESS	MARKET VALUE	MORTGAGE BALANCE	EQUITY	GROSS RENT	MORTGAGE PAYMENT	INCOME	MORTGAGEE NAME, LOAN NUMBER & MAILING ADDRESS	SUBDIVISION NAME & COMMENTS

A copy of the **gift letter**:

- if a gift is the source of the downpayment or closing costs
- the letter must be signed by the donor (a close relative) and state that the funds are not to be repaid

A **list of liabilities**:

- the name, address and phone number for each creditor and the balance, monthly payment and account number
- a copy of the divorce decree if there is any child support or alimony obligation

A **Certificate of Eligibility** for VA loans

If there is to be the **sale of a present home**:

- the net dollar amount from the sale after deducting the sales commission and any expenses
- if the buyer is being relocated by an employer who is paying all or part of the closing costs, a letter from the employer stating exactly what costs will be paid by the company

Chapter Nine

Real Estate Finance Disclosures

The real estate agent should be aware of the various disclosure requirements in the field of finance. Some disclosures must be made by the agent, some must be made by the lender, and some must be made by the principal parties to the transaction. The source of the duty to disclose varies according to which disclosures are involved. Some disclosures are imposed by the licensee's status as an agent, some are imposed by federal law, some are imposed by state statute. We will first address the disclosures which must be made because of the licensee's status as an agent.

Disclosure by the Agent

The real estate agent is a **fiduciary** of the principal. This means that the agent owes certain duties to the principal, such as acting in the principal's best interest, obeying the principal's instructions, refraining from taking unfair advantage of the principal, etc. One of these duties is the duty of **full disclosure**. In addition to the principles of agency, the California License Law also imposes on the real estate agent the duty to refrain from engaging in fraudulent or dishonest dealings or making misrepresentations.

Agency principles combined with statutory duties require the real estate agent to make full disclosure regarding any transaction and to act in the utmost good faith. The real estate agent may well ask, "Just what must be disclosed?" Courts have interpreted the disclosure requirement to mean that the real estate agent must make a full disclosure to the principal of **all material facts that might affect the principal's decision**. A full disclosure includes all material facts that have or are likely to have a bearing on the desirability of the transaction from the point of view of the principal. A material fact is that which the agent should realize would be likely to affect the judgment of the principal in giving his or her consent to the transaction.

Obviously, this standard is rather vague. Just what is a material fact in any given situation? How is the agent to know what will or will not affect a principal's decision? Practically speaking, what constitutes full disclosure is likely to vary from situation to situation. In fact, courts have stated that the question of whether an agent has made full disclosure is one that is to be determined on a case by case basis. What is material to one person may not be material to another. Likewise, what will affect one person's decision may not affect another's.

To help get a feel for what may or may not be material in a particular set of circumstances, some true factual situations are presented below. Hopefully, these will give the agent a general idea of what types of factual information must be disclosed.

When deciding what should be disclosed, the agent should bear in mind that the courts feel that real estate licensees, by virtue of their semi-professional status and generous compensation, hold themselves out as experts on real estate financing and are justifiably relied upon as such by lenders and borrowers alike. Therefore, courts hold that agents have an affirmative duty to give expert advice to their clients as to the economic sense of a transaction.

Examples of full disclosure.

Three factual situations are presented below which, it is hoped, will give the real estate agent a better understanding of the meaning of "full disclosure" and "fiduciary duty."

Security and assets of purchaser. A property owner, named Alhino, owned property improved with an income producing building (apartment and commercial units). A real estate agent, Senjo, learned from his broker that the property was for sale and discussed the price and other terms of the sale with the owner. Shortly thereafter, Senjo showed the property to a previous customer, Ranker, to whom Senjo had sold other properties. Ranker told Senjo that he would buy the property only if Alhino (the owner) agreed to carry back the loan on an unsecured promissory note. Ranker told Senjo that he, Ranker, wanted to finance the property this way so that he could be late in making the payments without risking losing the property. Senjo presented Ranker's offer to the owner who accepted it after a brief discussion. Senjo told Alhino that Ranker was a very wealthy man with extensive property holdings, some of which Senjo was personally familiar with. He also told Alhino that he was better off taking an unsecured promissory note than a mortgage as in event of default, he could get a money judgment against Ranker instead of the property, which might be in a state of disrepair by then. Before the transaction closed, Ranker asked Senjo if he could pay his commission in the form of a promissory note and that he needed to borrow the amount of the downpayment. Senjo did not inform Alhino of Ranker's need to borrow these funds nor of Ranker's desire to be able to make late payments safely.

Ranker soon defaulted on the purchase money promissory note and, two years after the close of escrow, committed suicide. Alhino sued Ranker's estate, which was insolvent. Alhino then sued Senjo and the broker Senjo worked for at the time of the transaction for fraud and misrepresentation. The court ruled in favor of Alhino. The court listed the following misrepresentations or failures to disclose as supporting the claim of breach of fiduciary duties: the representation that Ranker was a wealthy man and claims of personal knowledge as to some of his holdings (which Senjo did not have); failure to disclose Ranker's need to borrow the downpayment and amount of the commission; and failure to disclose the fact that Ranker wanted to finance the property as he did so that he could default with impunity. (*Alhino v. Starr*)

Escrow instructions. A real estate agent, Kateen, negotiated the sale of a parcel of property. The purchase price was to be $165,000. The buyer was to assume an existing loan of $140,000 (secured by a first deed of trust) and execute a note for $25,000 (secured by a second deed of trust). Thus, there was to be no downpayment. Kateen, without the knowledge of the buyer or seller, directed that escrow instructions be prepared that reflected a sales price of $206,250 and a cash downpayment of $41,250. This was done to encourage the mortgage company to purchase the note secured by the second deed of trust. In fact, relying on the escrow instructions, the mortgage company did approve the loan package and sell the note to two investors. The company would not have done so if it had known there was to be no downpayment. Shortly after the close of escrow, the purchaser defaulted on both loans. Accusations were filed against Kateen with the Department of Real Estate, charging substantial misrepresentations and fraudulent and dishonest dealings. The Department revoked Kateen's license. Her actions in causing false escrow instructions to be prepared constituted sufficient grounds for revocation of her license. (*Kateen v. Department of Real Estate*)

Inquiry as to ability to repay. Peirce was a 77-year old widow who owned four parcels of property. Her rental income was barely enough to subsist on, so she contacted Hom, a real estate agent, to arrange a loan on her properties. Hom's real estate office was around the corner from where Peirce lived and they had known each other for many years on a nonbusiness basis. Hom arranged for two different loans on Peirce's properties, charging commissions of over 13% for each loan. Each loan also provided for a substantial balloon payment at the end of its term. Both loans violated the Mortgage Loan Broker Law, which is discussed later in this chapter. Hom prepared and presented to Peirce a "Broker's Loan Statement" which stated that the loans were in compliance with the Loan Broker Law. Peirce later testified that the loan terms were never fully explained to her, but she trusted Hom and believed the terms were legal.

Hom did not inquire as to Peirce's ability to repay the loans. He assumed she would use the proceeds to pay for living expenses, but in fact she had other debts to pay, including other mortgage loans. Eventually, Peirce was unable to keep up with all of her loan payments and all of her lenders foreclosed. Peirce sued Hom, partly on the basis of breach of fiduciary duty. The court stated that there was no doubt that

Hom stood in a fiduciary relationship to Peirce (he was her agent) and that Hom breached his fiduciary duty when he failed to inquire into Peirce's ability to repay the loans. As she came to him because of his expertise in real estate financial matters, he should at least have determined whether there was a reasonable likelihood of her repaying the loans. He also should have advised her as to a more prudent means of raising money on her property. He should have discussed the possibility of default and the consequent loss of her property and suggested the alternative of selling one of her properties instead of further borrowing. (*Peirce v. Hom*)

These examples are, for the most part, rather blatant instances of breaches of fiduciary duties. Other situations may not seem so obvious. The wisest thing for the real estate agent to do is to err on the side of caution, always acting with the utmost good faith and disclosing to the fullest extent possible.

Federal Disclosure Requirements

A second type of disclosure that the real estate agent should be familiar with is the disclosure requirements of various federal regulations. The two most pertinent are **Regulation "Z" of the Truth-in-Lending Act** and the **Real Estate Settlement Procedures Act**. These Acts require institutional lenders to make disclosures to borrowers during the time of loan application and prior to the close of escrow. The agent should understand these disclosures and what they mean so as to be able to explain them to the borrower.

In the next segment of this chapter, we will discuss the Truth-in-Lending Act. Refer to Chapter 19, Escrow, for a discussion of the Real Estate Settlement Procedures Act.

Truth-in-Lending Act.

The purpose of the Truth-in-Lending Act, enacted in 1969, is to promote the informed use of consumer credit. The disclosures are required so the consumer will know exactly what he or she is paying for credit. It is hoped that this knowledge enables the consumer to compare credit costs and shop around for the best credit terms. The Act is implemented by **Regulation Z**. While Regulation Z does not set limits on interest rates or other finance charges, it does regulate the disclosure of these items. Disclosures are required in two general areas - when lenders offer credit/funds to borrowers, and when credit terms are advertised to potential customers.

Coverage of the Act. The provisions of the Act and Regulation Z apply to each lender that offers or extends credit to **consumers** (if the consumer is a natural person) in the **ordinary course of business**, primarily for **personal, family or household purposes**. The credit offered must be subject to a **finance charge** or payable in **more than four installments**. One exemption from coverage of the Act is credit of over $25,000 which is NOT secured by real property or a dwelling.

Under the Act, the definition of credit includes all real estate loans made to consumers, no matter what the amount, if the purpose is for other than business or commercial reasons.

Disclosures. Lenders who offer the above described types of credit are responsible for making certain disclosures to the consumer. These disclosures must be made before the credit transaction is consummated. Lenders engaging in a residential mortgage transaction must make a good faith estimate of the required disclosures no later than **three business days** after the lender receives the buyer's written application. Most lenders give the applicant a disclosure statement at the same time the buyer applies for a real estate loan. If any of the estimated figures change over the course of the transaction, new disclosures must be made before settlement.

For residential mortgage transactions, the most important disclosure required is the **annual percentage rate (APR)**. The APR tells the borrower the cost of the loan in percentage terms. The APR is the relationship of the total finance charges to the total amount financed. Finance charges include interest, any points required by the lender, loan fees, etc. If the buyer must pay points and a loan fee, the APR will be higher than the interest rate. For example, the loan may bear an interest rate of 11%, but the APR may be 11¼%. Many borrowers are confused by this apparent contradiction. They thought they were getting a loan at one interest rate, but it appears as if they are being charged another. It would be helpful at this point for the real estate agent to explain that the APR includes not just the interest rate, but the total costs of the loan, including all other finance charges spread out over the life of the loan.

The APR and other required disclosures are made to the borrower in the form of a **disclosure statement**. Copies of two standard disclosure statement forms are shown on the following pages. The first form is the type of form a bank or savings and loan association would use; the second form is the type a real estate broker would use if he or she were the one arranging the credit.

The disclosure statement includes the following items:

1. the **identity** of the creditor;
2. the **amount** financed;
3. **notice** of a right to receive an itemization of the amount financed;
4. the **finance charge** — the interest rate plus the costs of obtaining the funds, e.g., an origination or loan fee, a commitment fee, prepaid interest, an assumption fee, prepaid mortgage insurance, prepaid creditor life insurance, etc.;
5. the finance charge expressed as an **annual percentage rate** (the APR is labeled with a phrase such as, "The cost of your credit as a yearly rate.");
6. the **number**, **amount** and **due dates** of the payments;
7. **new payment**, **late payment**, and **prepayment provisions**;
8. a **description and identification of the security** (e.g., "There is a security interest in the property purchased."); and
9. whether or not the loan can be **assumed** by a subsequent purchaser.

A number of additional disclosures are required for adjustable-rate loans.

DISCLOSURE STATEMENT FIXED RATE MORTGAGE

Loan Number ______________

Type of Loan

☐ Conventional

☐ F.H.A.

☐ V.A.

An Equal Housing Lender

______________ Borrower(s)

______________ Address

____

☐ Initial Disclosure

☐ Final Disclosure

ANNUAL PERCENTAGE RATE The cost of your credit as a yearly rate. %	FINANCE CHARGE The dollar amount the credit will cost you. $	AMOUNT FINANCED The amount of credit provided to you or on your behalf. $	TOTAL OF PAYMENTS The amount you will have paid after you have made all payments as scheduled. $

YOUR PAYMENT SCHEDULE WILL BE:

NO. OF PAYMENTS	AMOUNT OF PAYMENTS	WHEN PAYMENTS ARE DUE

_____ Private/FHA Mortgage Insurance Payments.		Monthly beginning Monthly beginning	which will decrease to which is the Last Payment Due

Security: You are giving a security interest in the real property located at: ______________________________

Insurance: You may obtain Property Insurance from any insurer you want that is acceptable to Puget Sound Savings Bank.

FEDERAL FLOOD INSURANCE will be required at the time the loan is closed if the property securing the loan is located in an area already designated by HUD as a special flood hazard area or if it is so designated by the time of closing.

Prepayment: If you pay off your loan before it is due, you:
May ☐ Will Not ☐ have to pay a penalty.
May be entitled to a refund of part of the Private Mortgage Insurance portion of the Finance Charge.

Late Charge: If a payment is __________ days late, you will be charged __________% of the payment amount.

Assumption:

☐ Someone buying your home may be allowed to assume the remainder of the mortgage, subject to conditions and a possible change in terms.

☐ Someone buying your home may assume the remainder of the mortgage on the original terms.

☐ This loan is not assumable.

This Obligation ☐ Does ☐ Does Not have a demand feature.

SEE YOUR NOTE AND DEED OF TRUST FOR ANY ADDITIONAL INFORMATION ABOUT NONPAYMENT, DEFAULT, ANY REQUIRED REPAYMENT IN FULL BEFORE THE SCHEDULED DATE, AND PREPAYMENT REFUNDS AND PENALTIES.

Borrower ______________________ Borrower ______________________ Date __________

51-716 (R 7/87)

CALIFORNIA ASSOCIATION OF REALTORS

REAL ESTATE CREDIT SALE DISCLOSURE STATEMENT

(For use when Broker/Arranger or Creditor sells property on credit.)

CALIFORNIA ASSOCIATION OF REALTORS® STANDARD FORM

BROKER/ARRANGER OF CREDIT

____
(name)

____
(address)

CREDITOR:

____
(name)

____
(address)

SELLER (Same as either Broker or Creditor):

____
(name)

I. SALE OF PROPERTY

A. Cash Price $ ________
Less: Cash Downpayment (Include proceeds of any separate loan) $ ________

B. Unpaid Balance of Cash Price $ ________

C. Charges not part of Finance Charge:

1. Appraisal .... $ ________
2. Credit Report .... $ ________
3. Notary .... $ ________
4. Recording .... $ ________
5. Title Insurance .... $ ________
6. Document preparation .... $ ________
7. Property insurance .... $ ________
8. Termite inspection .... $ ________
9. Sale escrow fee .... $ ________
10. Other ________ (describe) $ ________

Total Charges $ ________

D. Unpaid Balance (B + C) $ ________
Less: Prepaid Finance Charge (Item II. A. below) $ ________

E. AMOUNT FINANCED $ ________

II. FINANCE CHARGE:

A. Prepaid FINANCE CHARGE

Loan Broker's commission .... $ ________
Loan escrow fee .... $ ________
Other ________ $ ________
________ (describe) $ ________

(Total of A) $ ________

B. Interest for period of loan .... $ ________

FINANCE CHARGE (A + B) $ ________

Finance Charge accrues from ________, 19 ____.

III. ANNUAL PERCENTAGE RATE: _______ %

IV. INSURANCE:

Property insurance may be obtained by Buyer through any person of his choice. If it is to be purchased through the Broker or Creditor, the cost appears at Item I. C. 7. above.

Credit life and disability insurance are not required to obtain this loan.

V. SECURITY:

Payment of the Unpaid Balance plus interest (Finance Charge Item II. B.) is to be secured by a note and Deed of Trust in favor of the Creditor on the property purchased in this transaction, which is located at ____

____,

and is ☐ is not ☐ expected to be the location of the Buyer's principal residence. (NOTE: If it is, a Rescission Statement must be provided unless this transaction involves a first lien for the purchase or initial construction of a dwelling.)

The Deed of Trust may secure additional advances and may cover after-acquired property. This credit may also be secured by an assignment of proceeds from any required insurance protecting the property.

VI. PAYMENT TERMS:

Payable in _______ payments of principal and interest as follows: _______ monthly installments of $ __________ each, beginning _____________ , 19 _____ , and a final/balloon payment of $ __________ due on ____________ , 19 _____ .

TOTAL OF PAYMENTS (Item I. D. + Item II. B.) $ __________

There are no arrangements for refinancing balloon payments.

If any payment is not made within _____ days after it is due, a late charge must be paid by Buyer as follows: ____

____,

In addition, Creditor has the option to accelerate the indebtedness and to declare all payments immediately due and payable.

In the event of acceleration or other prepayment in full, unaccrued interest is cancelled and a default or prepayment charge will be computed as follows: _____________

____

VII. DEFERRED PAYMENT PRICE (Items I. A. + I. C. + II.: cash price plus all charges and the Finance Charge) $ __________

I HAVE READ AND RECEIVED A COMPLETED COPY OF THIS STATEMENT.

Date: ___________________________ , 19 _____ .

BUYER: ______________________________

BUYER: ______________________________

* IMPORTANT NOTE:
Asterisk denotes an estimate.

To order, contact — California Association of Realtors®
525 S. Virgil Ave., Los Angeles, California 90020

FORM CSD-14

EQUAL HOUSING OPPORTUNITY
MB-E6-MB/1

Right to rescind. Under the Act, the consumer has the right to rescind any credit transaction in which a security interest (e.g., mortgage) is given in his or her principal residence. The right to rescind extends until midnight of the third business day after the close of the transaction. A major exception to this right is a residential mortgage transaction which is used to finance the purchase or construction of the residence. The exception covers the "typical" mortgage transaction. However, the consumer would still have the right to rescind a home equity loan agreement—where the loan is for remodeling, education, or other consumer purposes.

The lender must always inform the consumer of the right to rescind. The notice of the right to rescind must be in a separate document from the sale and/or credit document and must describe the acquisition of the security interest, how the right to rescind is to be exercised, the effects of rescission and the date the period of rescission expires.

Advertisement. The Truth-in-Lending Act also contains provisions which apply to advertising. Prior to the passage of the Act, an advertiser might have disclosed only the most attractive credit terms, thus distorting the true costs of the financing. For example, the advertisement could have included the low monthly payments (e.g., $75.00 a month) without indicating the large downpayment necessary to qualify for that payment level. Advertisers did not have to disclose the APR or whether the transaction was a credit sale or lease. The Act now requires the advertiser to tell "the whole story."

If an advertisement contains any one of the terms specified in the Act, then that advertisement must also include the required disclosures. The specified terms "trigger" the disclosures. In other words, if the advertiser uses a "trigger" in the advertisement, the disclosures must be made; if the advertisement does not contain a "trigger," no disclosures must be made.

Anyone placing a consumer credit or lease advertisement must comply with the provisions of the Act. This includes real estate agents who advertise private homes for sale.

The "triggering" terms for real estate advertisement include:

1. The **amount of the downpayment** (e.g., "20% down").
2. The **amount of any payment** (e.g., "Pay less than $700 per month").
3. The **number of payments** (e.g., "only 360 monthly payments").
4. The **period of repayment** (e.g., "30-year financing available").
5. The **amount of any finance charge** (e.g., "1% finance charge").

Some examples of terms which do NOT trigger the required disclosures are:

"No downpayment"
"12% Annual Percentage Rate loan available here"
"Easy monthly payments"
"Graduated payment mortgages available"
"VA and FHA financing available"
"Terms to fit your budget"
"100% VA financing available"

If any of the listed triggering terms are used in the advertisement, ALL of the following disclosures must be made:

1. the amount or percentage of the downpayment;
2. the terms of repayment; and
3. the annual percentage rate, using that term spelled out in full. If the APR may increase (e.g., for adjustable-rate mortgages), that fact must also be disclosed.

If an advertisement discloses only the APR, the additional disclosures are not required. For example, an advertisement may simply state, "Assume an 11% annual percentage rate mortgage." If an adjustable-rate mortgage is being advertised, it should be described as "11% annual percentage rate, subject to increase after settlement." Fixed-rate buydowns are not adjustable-rate mortgages and must not be so described. The buydown involves different interest rates in effect during the life of the loan, but all the rates are known at the time of settlement.

When more than one simple interest rate is to be applied to the transaction, these rates may be advertised if all the interest rates and the terms during which the rates apply are disclosed and the annual percentage rate is stated. For example, assume a buydown plan where the interest rate the first year is 9%, 10% the second year, 11% the third year, and 12% for the remainder of the term. The following would be an acceptable method of disclosure:

9%	1st year
10%	2nd year
11%	3rd year
12%	remainder of loan
11¾%	annual percentage rate

Even though different interest rates may apply during the loan term, the loan only has one annual percentage rate.

If a mortgage in which the monthly payments vary (e.g., due to a graduated payment feature) is being advertised, it is not necessary to disclose all of the different payments that will apply over the life of the loan. However, the advertisement must state the number and timing of the payments, the largest and smallest payments, and that other payments will vary between these amounts. An example of an advertisement of a $200,000 house with a temporary buydown could be as follows:

Downpayment — $10,000
Annual Percentage Rate — 9%
360 monthly payments
The first 36 payments vary from $1,230.26 to $1,447.00.
The remaining 324 payments are $1,538.68

On the following pages are illustrations of typical real estate advertisements. Any violations of the Truth-in-Lending Act appearing in the illustrations are pointed out, along with advice on how they should be changed to meet the Act's requirements.*

---

*Illustrations obtained from "How to Advertise Consumer Credit," published by the Federal Trade Commission. Copies of this publication can be obtained from regional Federal Trade Commission offices.

WRONG

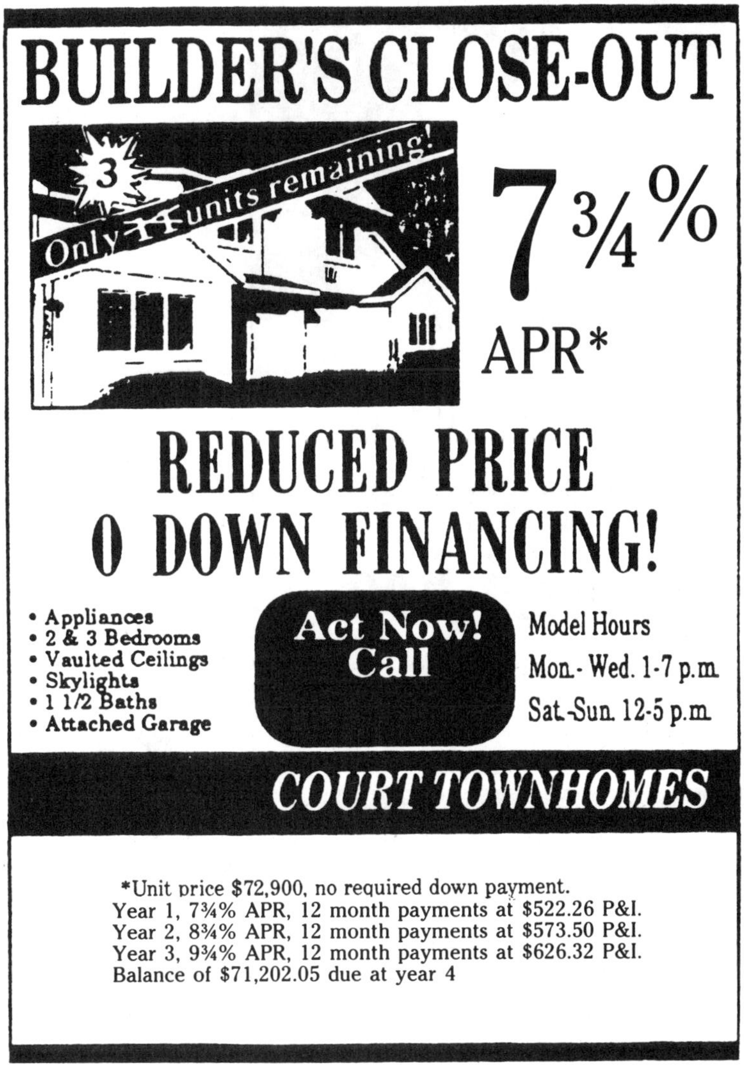

Improper Rate Disclosure

Improper Payment Disclosure

WRONG

Triggering Terms

Required Disclosures Needed

RIGHT

Triggering Terms

Required Disclosures

RIGHT

Proper Rate Disclosure

Seller Financing Disclosures

Federal regulations and general agency principles are not the only sources of disclosure requirements. In addition, California statutes provide for certain disclosures to be made when all or a portion of residential financing is provided by the seller.

The specified disclosures are required to be made when:

1. the transaction is for the purchase of a dwelling of one to four units;
2. credit is extended by the seller;
3. the credit involved is subject to a finance charge or is payable in more than four installments (not including the downpayment); and
4. there is an **arranger of credit**.

An arranger of credit is either:

1. a person who is NOT a party to the transaction who is involved in negotiating the credit terms, participates in the completion of the credit documents, and directly or indirectly receives compensation for arranging the credit or for the transfer of the real property which is facilitated by the extension of credit. This does not include an attorney or escrow officer involved in the transaction; or
2. a real estate licensee or an attorney who is a party to the transaction if neither party is represented by a real estate licensee.

Disclosures are not required for those transactions which fall under the provisions of the Truth-in Lending Act or the Real Estate Settlement Procedures Act. If disclosures are required, they must be made as soon as practicable, but in any case before the execution of any promissory note or security document (i.e., mortgage or deed of trust). The disclosure statement is to be signed by the arranger of credit and delivered to both the buyer and the seller. The seller and the arranger of credit are required to keep a copy of the statement for three years.

CALIFORNIA ASSOCIATION OF REALTORS

☐

SELLER FINANCING DISCLOSURE STATEMENT

(California Civil Code 2956-2967)
CALIFORNIA ASSOCIATION OF REALTORS® (CAR) STANDARD FORM

This two page disclosure statement from the Purchaser (Buyer) and Vendor (Seller) is prepared by an arranger of credit [defined in Civil Code 2957 (a)] and provided to **both** the Purchaser (Buyer) and Vendor (Seller) in a residential real estate transaction involving four or fewer units whenever the Seller has agreed to extend credit to the Buyer as part of the purchase price.

Buyer: ______________________________

Seller: ______________________________

Arranger of Credit: ______________________________

Real Property: ______________________________

A. **Credit Documents:** This extension of credit by the Seller is evidenced by ☐ note and deed of trust, ☐ all-inclusive note and deed of trust, ☐ installment land sale contract, ☐ lease/option (when parties intend transfer of equitable title), ☐ other (specify) ______________________________ .

B. **Credit Terms:**

1. ☐ See attached copy of credit documents referred to in Section A above for description of credit terms; **or**
2. ☐ The terms of the credit documents referred to in Section A above are: Principal amount $__________ interest at ______% per annum payable at $__________ per ________ (month/year/etc.) with the entire unpaid principal and accrued interest of approximately $__________ due ______________ 19_____ (maturity date).

Late Charge: If any payment is not made within _____ days after it is due, a late charge of $__________ or _____% of the installment due may be charged to the Buyer.

Prepayment: If all or part of this loan is paid early, the Buyer ☐ will, ☐ will **not**, have to pay a prepayment penalty as follows: ______________________________ .

Due on Sale: If any interest in the property securing this obligation is sold or otherwise transferred, the Seller ☐ has, ☐ does **not** have, the option to require immediate payment of the entire unpaid balance and accrued interest.

Other Terms: ______________________________ .

C. Available information on loans/encumbrances * that will be **senior** to the Seller's extension of credit:

	1st	2nd	3rd
1. Original Balance	$ ________	$ ________	$ ________
2. Current Balance	$ ________	$ ________	$ ________
3. Periodic Payment (e.g. $100/month)	$ ____ / ____	$ ____ / ____	$ ____ / ____
4. Amt. of Balloon Payment	$ ________	$ ________	$ ________
5. Date of Balloon Payment	________	________	________

6. Maturity Date	________	________	________
7. Due On Sale ('Yes' or 'No')	________	________	________
8. Interest Rate (per annum)	________%	________%	________%
9. Fixed or Variable Rate:	________	________	________
If Variable Rate:	☐ a copy of note attached ☐ variable provisions are explained on attached separate sheet	☐ a copy of note attached ☐ variable provisions are explained on attached separate sheet	☐ a copy of note attached ☐ variable provisions are explained on attached separate sheet
10. Is Payment Current?	________	________	________

☐ SEPARATE SHEET WITH INFORMATION REGARDING OTHER SENIOR LOANS/ENCUMBRANCES IS ATTACHED.

***IMPORTANT NOTE:** Asterisk (*) denotes an estimate.

D. Caution: If any of the obligations secured by the property calls for a balloon payment, then Seller and Buyer are aware that refinancing of the balloon payment at maturity may be difficult or impossible depending on the conditions in the mortgage marketplace at that time. There are no assurances that new financing or a loan extension will be available when the balloon payment is due.

E. Deferred Interest:

"Deferred interest" results when the Buyer's periodic payments are less than the amount of interest earned on the obligation, or when the obligation does not require periodic payments. This accrued interest will have to be paid by the Buyer at a later time and may result in the Buyer owing more on the obligation than at origination.

☐ The credit being extended to the Buyer by the Seller does **not** provide for "deferred interest," **or**

☐ The credit being extended to the Buyer by the Seller does provide for "deferred interest."

The credit documents provide the following regarding deferred interest:

☐ All deferred interest shall be due and payable along with the principal at maturity (simple interest); **or**

☐ The deferred interest shall be added to the principal ________ (e.g., annually, monthly, etc.) and thereafter shall bear interest at the rate specified in the credit documents (compound interest); **or**

☐ Other (specify) ________________

F. All-Inclusive Deed of Trust or Installment Land Sale Contract:

☐ This transaction does **not** involve the use of an all-inclusive (or wraparound) deed of trust or an installment land sale contract; **or**

☐ This transaction **does** involve the use of either an all-inclusive (or wraparound) deed of trust or an installment land sale contract which provides as follows:

1) In the event of an acceleration of any senior encumbrance, the responsibility for payment or for legal defense is:

☐ **Not** specified in the credit or security documents; **or**

☐ Specified in the credit or security documents as follows:

____

____

Buyer and Seller acknowledge receipt of copy of this page, which constitutes Page 1 of 2 Pages.

Buyer's Initials (________) (________) Seller's Initials ________) (________)

OFFICE USE ONLY

Reviewed by Broker or Designee ________

Date ________

EQUAL HOUSING OPPORTUNITY

SELLER FINANCING DISCLOSURE STATEMENT (SFD-14 PAGE 1 OF 2)

2) In the event of the prepayment of a senior encumbrance, the responsibilities and rights of Seller and Buyer regarding refinancing, prepayment penalties, and any prepayment discounts are:

☐ **Not** specified in the credit or security documents; **or**

☐ Specified in the credit or security documents as follows:

____

____

3) The financing provided that the Buyer will make periodic payments to ____________________ [e.g., a collection agent (such as a bank or savings and loan); Seller; etc.] and that ____________________ will be responsible for disbursing payments to the payee(s) on the senior encumbrance(s) and to the Seller.

CAUTION: The parties are advised to consider designating a neutral third party as the collection agent for receiving Buyer's payments and disbursing them to the payee(s) on the senior encumbrance(s) and to the Seller.

G. Buyer's Creditworthiness: Section 580(b) of the California Code of Civil Procedure generally limits a Seller's rights in the event of a default by the Buyer in the financing extended by the Seller, to a foreclosure of the property.

☐ No disclosure concerning the Buyer's creditworthiness has been made to the Seller; **or**

☐ The following representations concerning the Buyer's creditworthiness have been made by the Buyer(s) to the Seller:

1. Occupation: __________	1. Occupation: __________
2. Employer: __________	2. Employer: __________
3. Length of Employment: __________	3. Length of Employment: __________
4. Monthly Gross Income: __________	4. Monthly Gross Income: __________
5. Buyer ☐ has, ☐ has **not**, provided Seller a current credit report issued by: __________	5. Buyer ☐ has, ☐ has **not**, provided Seller a current credit report issued by: __________
6. Buyer ☐ has, ☐ has **not**, provided Seller a completed loan application.	6. Buyer ☐ has, ☐ has **not**, provided Seller a completed loan application.
7. Other (specify): __________	7. Other (specify): __________

H. Insurance:

☐ The parties' escrow holder or insurance carrier has been or will be directed to add a loss payee clause to the property insurance protecting the Seller; **or**

☐ No provision has been made for adding a loss payee clause to the property insurance protecting the Seller. Seller is advised to secure such clauses or acquire a separate insurance policy.

I. Request for Notice:

☐ A Request for Notice of Default under Section 2924(b) of the California Civil Code has been or will be recorded; **or**

☐ No provision for recording a Request for Notice of Default has been made. Seller is advised to consider recording a Request for Notice of Default.

J. Title Insurance:

☐ Title insurance coverage will be provided to **both** Seller and Buyer insuring their respective interests in the property; **or**

☐ No provision for title insurance coverage of **both** Seller and Buyer has been made. Seller and Buyer are advised to consider securing such title insurance coverage.

K. Tax Service:

☐ A tax service has been arranged to report to Seller whether property taxes have been paid on the property. __________ (e.g., Seller, Buyer, etc.) will be responsible for the continued retention and payment of such tax service; **or**

☐ No provision has been made for a tax service. Seller should consider retaining a tax service or otherwise determine that the property taxes are paid.

L. Recording:

☐ The security documents (e.g., deed of trust, installment land contract, etc.) will be recorded with the county recorder where the property is located; **or**

☐ The security documents will **not** be recorded with the county recorder. Seller and Buyer are advised that their respective interests in the property may be jeopardized by intervening liens, judgments or subsequent transfers which **are** recorded.

M. Proceeds to Buyer:

☐ Buyer will **NOT** receive any cash proceeds at the close of the sale transaction; **or**

☐ Buyer will receive approximately $__________ from __________ (indicate source from the sale transaction proceeds of such funds). Buyer represents that the purpose of such disbursement is as follows: __________

____

N. Notice of Delinquency:

☐ A Request for Notice of Delinquency under Section 2924(e) of the California Civil Code has been or will be made to the Senior lienholder(s); **or**

☐ No provision for making a Request for Notice of Delinquency has been made. Seller should consider making a Request for Notice of Delinquency.

The above information has been provided to: (a) the Buyer, by the arranger of credit and the Seller (with respect to information within the knowledge of the Seller); (b) the Seller, by the arranger of credit and the Buyer (with respect to information within the knowledge of the Buyer).

Date __________, 19____ Arranger of Credit __________

By __________

Buyer and Seller acknowledge that the information each has provided to the arranger of credit for inclusion in this disclosure form is accurate to the best of their knowledge.

Buyer and Seller hereby acknowledge receipt of a completed copy of this disclosure form.

Date __________, 19____ Date __________, 19____

Buyer __________ Seller __________

Buyer __________ Seller __________

OFFICE USE ONLY
Reviewed by Broker or Designee __________
Date __________

EQUAL HOUSING OPPORTUNITY

Page 2 of ______ Pages.

SELLER FINANCING DISCLOSURE STATEMENT (SFD-14 PAGE 2 OF 2)

A standard disclosure form is shown on the previous pages. Some of the required disclosures are as follows:

1. identification and description of the **terms of the note** and/or security documents and **the property** which is to be the security for the transaction;
2. the terms and conditions of any **senior liens** on the property (e.g., a first mortgage), including the original balance, the current balance, the periodic payment, any balloon payment, the interest rate, the maturity date, and whether or not there is any current default in the payments;
3. a warning that, if **refinancing** is required because the note is not fully amortized, such refinancing might be difficult or impossible in the conventional mortgage marketplace;
4. if **negative amortization** is a possibility, a clear statement of this fact and an explanation of its potential effect;
5. if the financing is a **wrap-around**, or all-inclusive mortgage, information regarding the person responsible for making payments to the prior lienholders, who the person to be paid is, and information relating to balloon payments or prepayment penalties on any prior encumbrances;
6. the **identity, occupation, employment, income and credit data** of the buyer;
7. a statement that a **request for a notice of default** has been (or should be) recorded;
8. a statement that a policy of **title insurance** has been obtained; and
9. if the buyer is to receive **cash from the proceeds** of the transaction, a statement of that fact, plus the amount, source of the funds and purpose of the disbursement.

If the financing transaction includes a **balloon payment**, the following requirements must be met:

1. the holder of the note must give the borrower **written notice,** not less than 90 nor more than 150 days before the balloon payment is due, and the notice must include:

a. the **name and address** of the person to whom the balloon payment is to be made;
b. the **due date** of the payment;
c. the **amount of the payment**; and
d. a description of the borrower's **right**, if any , **to refinance the debt**.

2. if proper notice is not given, the **due date of the balloon payment is extended** to 90 days from the date the notice is given. During the interim, the borrower is obligated to make payments according to the regular payment schedule.

Mortgage Loan Broker Law

Real estate agents often help buyers obtain financing. This assistance may go beyond simply helping the buyer apply to one institutional lender. In some cases, it's necessary to get loans from two or more lenders to raise enough cash to close the transaction.

California's Mortgage Loan Broker Law (also known as the Necessitous Borrowers Act or the Real Property Loan Law) regulates real estate agents who act as loan brokers. The law requires a loan broker to give the borrower a disclosure statement. And for some loans secured by residential property, the law places restrictions on the fees and commissions paid by the borrower or received by the loan broker, and regulates other aspects of the loan terms. Only an overview of some of the law's key provisions is presented here.

Disclosure Statement. The disclosure statement required by the Mortgage Loan Broker Law must be on a form approved by the Real Estate Commissioner. It discloses all the costs involved in obtaining the loan, and the actual amount the borrower will receive after all costs and fees are deducted. The borrower must receive the statement before signing the note and security agreement.

A disclosure statement is generally required whenever a real estate agent negotiates a loan or performs services for borrowers or lenders in connection with a loan. There is an important exception, however: the disclosure statement is not required if the lender is an institutional lender and the commission paid by the borrower is 2% of the loan amount or less.

Commissions, Costs, and Terms. For certain loans secured by residential property with one to four units, the Mortgage Loan Broker Law limits the commissions and costs that a real estate agent may charge the borrower for arranging the loan. Specifically, these restrictions apply when the loan involves a first deed of trust for less than $30,000 or a junior deed of trust for less than $20,000.

For these loans, the maximum commissions the loan broker can charge are:

- for a first deed of trust,
  - 5% of the principal if the loan term is less than three years, and
  - 10% of the principal if the loan term is three years or more.
- for a junior deed of trust,
  - 5% of the principal if the term is less than two years,
  - 10% of the principal if the term is at least two years, but less than three years, and
  - 15% of the principal if the term is three years or more.

Also, the costs of making these loans (such as the appraisal and escrow fees) cannot exceed 5% of the loan amount, or $390, whichever is greater. In any case, the costs charged to the borrower must never exceed $700, and must not exceed the actual costs.

The Mortgage Loan Broker Law also prohibits balloon payments in these loans if the loan term is short. When the security property is an owner-occupied home, balloon payments are prohibited if the term is less than six years. Otherwise, balloon payments are prohibited if the term is less than three years. (These rules don't apply to seller financing, however.) For the purposes of this law, a balloon payment is one that is more than twice as large as the smallest payment required by the loan agreement.

Chapter Ten

Finance Programs

There are a variety of financing programs available to the homebuyer. These can be categorized into three basic types: **conventional**, **FHA-insured** and **VA-guaranteed**. Each of these categories will be discussed in detail in the following pages. In addition, there are "alternate" methods of financing. However, rather than being a fourth category, these alternate methods are all found within the conventional, FHA-insured and VA-guaranteed programs.

Before plunging into the three major types of loans, a few words should be said about the "**traditional**" real estate loan.

Until the late 1970's, most real estate loans of any type (i.e., conventional, FHA or VA) were **long-term**, **fixed-rate**, **fully amortized** loans. The loan was repaid over a long period of time, typically 30 years, at an unchanging rate of interest. At the end of the loan term, both the principal and the interest were fully paid off by means of equal monthly payments over the life of the loan. This is the type of loan borrowers are most familiar with and the one they usually prefer when financing a home.

With the advent of rising interest rates and inflation, new types of financing were created. These include the **adjustable-rate loan** and the **15-year fixed-rate loan**. The adjustable-rate loan will be discussed in detail in the section on alternate financing.

The 15-year mortgage has become more popular in recent years for three major reasons:

- lenders offer lower interest rates on the shorter term loan because shorter terms mean less risk (they will be paid back sooner and thus be able to loan out the funds again at current market rates);
- the 15-year mortgage makes free and clear home ownership possible in half the time; and
- thousands of dollars can be saved because of lower total loan payments (the shorter term means less interest will be paid over the life of the loan).

The disadvantages of the 15-year loan include higher monthly payments, larger required downpayments, and loss of the tax exemption on the interest payments sooner.

Even with the advent of these new types of financing, the "traditional" mortgage remains popular and, for the most part, will be the type discussed in the following pages.

The Conventional Loan

A conventional loan is any loan not insured or guaranteed by a government agency. The details of the conventional loan programs discussed in this chapter reflect the criteria established by the national secondary market investors, primarily the Federal National Mortgage Association (FNMA) and the Federal Home Loan Mortgage Association (FHLMC). Lenders must make their loans in compliance with these criteria to be able to sell the loans on the secondary market.

The 80% Conventional Loan.

The **80% loan** has been the standard conventional loan for many years. The "80%" refers to the **loan-to-value ratio** (**LTV**) of the loan. The LTV is the relationship the amount of the loan bears to the total purchase price (or appraised value, whichever is less) of the property. For example, if the value and selling price of a home is $100,000 and the loan amount is $80,000, the LTV is 80%. In this case, the buyer would make a $20,000 or 20% downpayment and obtain a thirty-year, fixed-rate conventional loan for $80,000, the balance of the purchase price.

If a buyer cannot make a 20% downpayment, he or she may try to obtain:

1. a 90% conventional loan with a 10% downpayment;
2. a 95% conventional loan with a 5% downpayment;
3. a conventional loan of 75% or less with a 10% downpayment, with the seller carrying a second mortgage for the rest of the purchase price.

EXAMPLE: $120,000 sales price

$90,000	75% loan
12,000	10% downpayment
+ 18,000	15% 2nd mortgage (seller's)
$120,000	

Secondary financing. When a purchaser borrows money to pay for part of the downpayment or closing costs, it is called secondary financing. The buyer may obtain secondary financing from an institutional lender (the lender making the primary loan or another lender) or from the seller (the seller extends credit by taking back a promissory note from the buyer).

Conventional lenders allow secondary financing as long as the following requirements are met:

1. **Total financing may not exceed 90%.** The first mortgage may not exceed 75% of appraised value or sales price and the total first and second mortgage may not exceed 90%.

2. **Term not to exceed thirty years or be less than five years.** The "term," or payment period of the secondary financing cannot be longer than thirty years. It is believed that it should take

no longer to pay off the second mortgage than it does to pay off the first mortgage.

3. **No prepayment penalty permitted.** The second mortgage must be payable in part or in full at any time without penalty.
4. **Scheduled payments must be due on a regular basis.** Payments on the second must be regularly scheduled (e.g., monthly) and can be designed to fully amortize the debt, to partially amortize the debt (with a balloon payment at the end of the term) or to pay interest only with a balloon payment at the end of the term.
5. **No negative amortization.** The payment on the second mortgage must at least equal the interest on the loan. No negative amortization is allowed.

Loan origination fee. The lender always charges a **loan origination fee** (or **loan fee** or **loan service fee**) to cover the administrative costs of making the loan. The loan fee is a **percentage of the loan amount** and generally ranges from 1.5% to 3%. The buyer usually pays the loan fee.

Private Mortgage Insurance.

Private mortgage insurance is a mystery to the typical buyer. The buyer often does not understand what it is, why it is required and why private mortgage insurers often do their own underwriting. An informed real estate agent can solve the riddle of private mortgage insurance and make the process of obtaining financing that much smoother for the buyer.

80% conventional loans are considered "safe" by lenders because the substantial amount of equity the borrower has in the property (20% of the purchase price) is incentive to keep mortgage payments current. Furthermore, if there is a default, proceeds from a foreclosure sale are likely to cover at least 80% of the original sales price. However, once borrowers begin investing less than 20% of the purchase price into the property, lenders regard the loan as more risky. Under these circumstances, as assurance against loss, lenders require the borrower to obtain and pay for private mortgage insurance. The added safety provided by the mortgage insurance makes up for the risks of reduced borrower equity. Both FNMA and FHLMC require private mortgage insurance on loans with less than 20% downpayments.

How mortgage insurance works. The mortgage insurer assumes the primary element of the risk of the loan. Instead of insuring the entire loan amount, the insurer only insures the upper portion of the loan. The amount of coverage is typically 20% to 25% of the loan amount.

EXAMPLE: **20% coverage**

$200,000	sales price
× .90	LTV
$180,000	90% loan
× .20	amount of coverage
$36,000	amount of policy

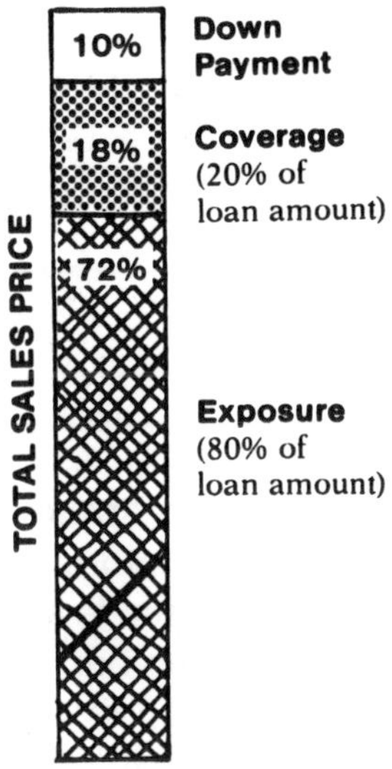

20% COVERAGE ON A 90% LOAN

In the above example, if the lender foreclosed the mortgage at a loss of $36,700, the mortgage insurer would pay the first $36,000 of loss and the lender would suffer the additional $700 of loss.

If the mortgage is foreclosed, the lender will either sell the property and make a claim for actual losses, if any, up to the policy amount or give the property to the insurer and claim actual losses up to the policy amount. Losses typically incurred by the lender take the form of unpaid interest, property taxes and hazard insurance, attorney's fees, the costs of preserving the property during the period of foreclosure and resale, and the expense of selling the property.

Example: Using figures from the previous example, the lender forecloses and resells the property for $184,500.

1.	$6,750	unpaid interest
	1,010	unpaid taxes and insurance
	1,100	attorney's fees
	7,150	resale costs
	+ 155	miscellaneous expenses
	$16,165	total cost of foreclosure and resale
2.	$184,500	resale price
	– 178,200	loan balance
	$6,300	gross profit on resale
3.	$6,300	
	– 16,165	foreclosure and resale costs
	[$9,865]	net loss — amount of claim

Private mortgage insurance premium (PMI). For the insurance protection, the mortgage insurance company charges a one time fee when the loan is made and a recurring fee, called a **renewal premium**, that is added to the borrower's mortgage payment. These charges are referred to as **PMI** (private mortgage insurance). Rates will vary somewhat between companies for different types and amounts of coverage. A portion of a rate schedule published by one national private mortgage insurer is shown on the opposite page.

Underwriting. Mortgage insurance companies experienced unprecedented losses in the mid-'80s due to rising mortgage defaults. As a result of these losses, mortgage insurance companies took a more active role in mortgage underwriting and significantly tightened their standards. Many times mortgage insurance companies will reject a loan package already approved by the lender. When this happens, the buyer can always try another mortgage insurance company, but may have to increase the size of the downpayment. Lenders will not make a conventional loan with an LTV of more than 80% without a commitment for private mortgage insurance.

FIXED-PAYMENT MORTGAGES

		SINGLE		*ANNUAL*	*RENEWAL PREMIUMS*		
		Term to 80% (8)				Constant (4)	
	LTV	No Refund	Refund (9)	1st-Year Premiums	Declining(3)	Yrs. 2-10	Yrs. 11-Term
25%	90.01 - 95%	3.60%	4.40%	1.10%	.50%	.49%	.25%
	85.01 - 90%	2.50	3.10	.65	.35	.34	.25
	85% & under	2.15	2.45	.50	.35	.34	.25
22%	90.01 - 95%	3.25	4.30	1.00	.50	.49	.25
	85.01 - 90%	2.35	3.00	.55	.35	.34	.25
	85% & under	2.05	2.40	.45	.35	.34	.25
20%	90.01 - 95%	3.05	4.15	.90	.50	.49	.25
	85.01 - 90%	2.20	2.95	.50	.35	.34	.25
	85% & under	1.95	2.35	.40	.35	.34	.25
17%	85.01 - 90%	2.00	2.85	.40	.35	.34	.25
	85% & under	1.75	2.30	.35	.35	.34	.25
12%	85.01 - 90%	1.70	2.80	.35	.35	.34	.25
	85% & under (5)	1.50	2.00	.30	.30	.29	.25

The 90% Conventional Loan.

Once private mortgage insurance became available, 90% loans became increasingly popular. However, even with mortgage insurance, the qualifying standards for 90% loans are more stringent. Lenders will adhere more closely to their underwriting criteria and marginal buyers and properties are more likely to be rejected.

10% downpayment; 5% from buyer. The buyer must make at least a 5% downpayment out of his or her own funds. The other 5% may come from a family member or equity in other property.

Loan fee and interest higher. The loan origination fees and interest rates are higher for 90% loans. A buyer trying to obtain 90% financing should expect a more expensive loan.

The 95% Conventional Loan.

The increasing popularity of the 90% loan led lenders and private mortgage insurers to offer a loan with an even higher LTV — the 95% loan.

Made primarily by savings and loans and mortgage companies, the 95% loan makes it possible to obtain conventional financing with as little as 5% cash down.

More expensive than 80% and 90% loans. Because of the increased risk of a loan with as little as 5% down, the 95% loan is the most expensive of all. Both interest rates and loan fees are higher for 95% loans than for either 80% or 90% loans. Private mortgage insurance fees are also substantially higher.

No secondary financing. The buyer must make the downpayment out of his or her own funds, without resorting to secondary financing or gift.

More stringent underwriting requirements. 95% loans are becoming more and more difficult to obtain. The underwriting criteria are very stringent and are closely followed. Lenders are much more careful today when making 95% loans than they have been in the past due to the increased foreclosure rate of high loan-to-value loans.

Alternate Financing

While conventional lenders are the predominant users of creative financing methods, some methods of alternate financing are also available within both the FHA and VA programs. For example, the FHA offers an adjustable rate mortgage and the VA offers a growth equity mortgage. As you read the following pages, keep in mind that it is not necessary to go through a conventional lender to take advantage of some of the types of loans that will be discussed.

In the last decade, rising interest rates and high levels of inflation made it difficult for lenders to reconcile their need for high rates of return with the borrower's need for affordable loans. In an effort to solve this dilemma, new methods of financing were created, such as buydowns, adjustable rate mortgages (ARMs), graduated payment mortgages (GPMs), growing equity mortgages (GEMs), and shared appreciation mortgages (SAMs). Due to the recent decline in interest rates, the popularity of most of these alternate financing plans quickly evaporated. Once again, the long-term, fixed-rate mortgage is affordable for the average homebuyer. However, today's lower interest rates may not continue and future rate increases may well revive an interest in alternate finance.

In this section, we will examine the more successful alternate financing methods: buydowns, ARMs and GEMs. Although these plans have less appeal in today's low interest market, they may become more popular in the future if interest rates begin to increase again.

Buydown Plans.

A common way to make a home loan more affordable is the "buydown." A buydown lowers the purchaser's monthly mortgage payments, thus helping him or her qualify for the loan. A buydown works as follows: the seller, buyer, or a third party (e.g., builder) makes a lump sum payment to the lender at the time the loan is made. The money paid to the lender reduces the interest rate and the borrower's payments either early in or throughout the life of the loan.

Example:

$200,000	30-year, 13% loan
$12,000	buydown
$2,212	quoted 13% loan payment
−2,057	buyer's payment at 12%
$155	savings resulting from buydown

In the above example, the quoted rate is 13%, but the borrower's interest rate has been bought down by 1%, reducing the interest rate to 12% for a $155/month savings. It is easier to sell property if the interest rate paid by the buyer is relatively low and affordable.

Discounts and Points. A buydown is effected through the use of **discount points**, or just "**points**." Points add to the lender's yield (profit) on the loan. If a lender can "discount" a loan, the lender will be earning a higher rate of return than the interest rate stated in the promissory note (the nominal rate). Depending upon the circumstances, the discount may be paid by the buyer, seller or a third party, but is most often paid by the seller. While points have traditionally been associated with FHA and VA financing, payment of points is increasingly common in conventional loans.

The term "point" is a contraction of the larger term "percentage point." A point is one percentage point or one percent of a loan amount. On a $100,000 loan, one point would be $1000; six points would be $6,000. The amount of the discount is computed on the loan amount, not the sales price.

Example:

$192,000	sales price
$163,200	loan amount
6%	discount

$163,200	loan amount
× .06	discount
$9,792	discount amount

Points are paid at closing by deducting the amount of the discount from the amount of the loan proceeds. For instance, if four points were paid on a $175,000 loan to get a lower interest rate, four percent of the loan amount ($7,000) would be deducted from the loan amount given to the borrower. Though the borrower would only receive $168,000 ($175,000 − 7,000), he or she would agree to repay the entire $175,000. Thus, the lender would advance only $168,000 but would be repaid $175,000. The buyer would transfer the amount of the loan proceeds received ($168,000) to the seller without making up the difference. In effect, the seller would end up paying the lender $7,000 to induce the lender to make a loan with a lower interest rate.

How many points? The number of points needed to increase the lender's yield by one percent is affected by many factors, including money market conditions, interest rates, and the average time it takes a loan to be paid off. Currently, it is assumed that it takes six points to increase the lender's yield on a thirty year loan by one percent. This is only a rough approach to computing discounts and should always be confirmed with the lender.

Two advantages to a buydown. There are two advantages to a buydown plan:

1. The buyer's monthly payment is lower than normal.
2. The lender evaluates the buyer on the basis of the reduced payment thereby making it easier to qualify for the loan.

Permanent buydowns. A buydown can be permanent or temporary. If a portion of the buyer's interest rate is permanently bought down (e.g., for thirty years), the lender's nominal rate (the rate stated in the promissory note) will be reduced accordingly.

For example, the lender quotes 13% for a $165,000 30-year loan. The seller agrees to buydown the nominal rate to 12%. To do so, the lender requires a lump sum payment of $9,900. By making this payment, the seller buys down the interest rate by 1%.

Temporary buydowns. Temporary buydowns are used to reduce the buyer's payment, sometimes substantially, in the early months or years of the loan. The buyer may feel that he or she could afford a larger payment later, but needs time to get established. There are two types of temporary buydowns:

Level payment. This plan calls for an interest reduction that is constant throughout the buydown period.

Graduated payment. A graduated buydown plan calls for the largest subsidies in the first year or two of the loan, with progressively smaller subsidies in each of the remaining years of the buydown period.

Adjustable Rate Mortgage.

A widely used type of alternate financing is the adjustable rate mortgage, or **ARM**. Because the ARM shifts the risk of rising interest rates to the borrower, lenders will normally charge a lower rate for an ARM than they will for a fixed-rate loan. Although most borrowers prefer a fixed-rate loan (if the rate is not too high), ARMs continue to attract a significant portion of borrowers, especially during times of rising interest rates. For example, in the last half of 1987, when mortgage rates rose significantly, ARMs made up almost 60% of all home loan mortgages. Even in times of lower interest rates, most lenders still offer ARMs at very competitive interest rates.

The adjustable rate mortgage permits the lender to periodically adjust the interest rate to reflect fluctuations in the cost of money. With an ARM, the borrower is affected by interest rate changes, not the lender. If rates climb, the borrower's payments go up; if they decline, his or her payments go down.

How does an ARM work? The interest rate of an ARM is initially determined by the cost of money at the time the loan is made. The rate is then tied to one of several widely accepted indexes, such as the monthly average yield on three year Treasury securities or the monthly average of weekly auction rates on Treasury bills. The interest rate adjustments are based on the upward and downward movements of the index. Since the index is a reflection of the cost of money, lenders add a **margin** to the index rate to provide for administrative expenses and profit. Margins usually range from 2% to 3%. **The index plus the margin equals the adjustable interest rate.**

Example:

7%	index rate
+ 2%	lender's margin
9%	adjustable interest rate

Elements of an ARM loan. An ARM contains several elements, including:

1. the index
2. the margin
3. the rate adjustment period
4. the interest rate cap (if any)
5. the mortgage payment adjustment period

6. the mortgage payment cap (if any)
7. the negative amortization cap (if any)

Index. Most lenders use one of the Treasury security indexes. Lenders generally use an index that is highly responsive to economic fluctuations.

Margin. The margin is the difference between the index rate and the interest rate charged to the borrower.

Rate adjustment period. This refers to the intervals at which a borrower's interest rate is adjusted, e.g., six months, one year, three years, etc. After checking the index, the lender will notify the borrower in writing of any rate increase or decrease. Annual rate adjustments are most common.

Interest rate cap. Two mechanisms are used to limit the size of the monthly payment increases that occur because of interest rate adjustments: **interest rate caps** and **payment caps**. An interest rate is "capped" when there is a limit on the number of percentage points the interest rate can increase during the term of a loan. Today, almost all ARMs have interest rate caps of some kind.

Mortgage payment cap. Extreme increases in mortgage payments can lead to **payment shock**, defaults due to inability to meet large payment increases. To avoid this danger, many lenders incorporate payment caps into their ARMs. A 5% annual cap is common. Other lenders only impose annual interest rate caps that also effectively limit payment increases. Still other lenders impose both rate and payment caps. Regardless of which policy a lender embraces, the objective is the same: to keep payment adjustments within a manageable range for the borrower.

Teaser rates. As ARMs grew more popular, lenders began competing vigorously for ARM customers. First year interest rates were lowered and borrowers were introduced to discounts and buydowns. These low initial rates were dubbed "**teaser rates**." The use of teaser rates in addition to normal market increases in interest rates can lead to greater payment shock and thus secondary agencies have imposed restrictions on discounts and buydowns. In fact, FHLMC requires lenders to qualify borrowers at the initial rate plus 2% (the maximum second year mortgage rate) to assure FHLMC that borrowers can afford the possible payment increase inherent in ARMs. This tightening of standards means it is more difficult for borrowers to qualify for ARMs as they have to qualify for a significantly higher monthly payment due to the higher qualifying interest rate.

Mortgage payment adjustment period. This defines the intervals at which a borrower's payments are changed. Depending on the terms of the loan, the payment changes may not coincide with the interest rate adjustments. There are two ways that rate and payment adjustments can be handled:

1. The lender may adjust the rate and then adjust the mortgage payment to reflect the rate change. Increases in mortgage payments can be made only after **30 days written notice** to the borrower.
2. The lender may adjust the rate more often than it adjusts the mortgage payment. For example, the loan agreement may call for interest rate adjustments every six months but changes in mortgage payments every three years. If a borrower's payments remain constant over the three year period but the interest rate has steadily increased, too little interest will have been paid during that time. The unpaid interest is then added to the loan balance; this is called **negative amortization**.

Avoid negative amortization. Mortgage plans that provide for a possibility of negative amortization are not as attractive to borrowers as those that do not permit negative amortization. Where negative amortization occurs, the monthly payment must be adjusted (with no cap) at least once every five years so that the new payments fully amortize the loan balance over the remaining term. This periodic **reamortization** reduces what would otherwise be a large increase in the borrower's debt which would have to be paid when the house was sold or the loan became due.

ARM Loan-to-value ratios. The potential for payment shock due to increasing ARM payments has led FNMA and FHLMC to place greater restrictions on them. ARM loan-to-value ratios may not be over 90% and FNMA and FHLMC require owner-occupancy for all ARMs they purchase. Owner-occupants are considered better risks than owners who live elsewhere.

Appraisals on properties secured by ARMS. Because ARMs are seen as being more risky, lenders are following underwriting guidelines much more strictly. This is especially so in regards to the validity of the appraisal. Lenders require the appraisal report to give an accurate estimate of the true value of the property, uninfluenced by discount rates, subsidy buydowns or other financing concessions.

Convertible. One very popular type of adjustable-rate mortgage is the convertible ARM. Convertibles are 30-year ARMs that give the borrower the right to convert to a fixed-rate loan during a specified period (usually the first five years of the loan term). Thus, borrowers get the advantages of an ARM as well as the ability to convert to a fixed-rate loan if interest rates decrease significantly.

Growth Equity Mortgage (GEM)

The growth equity mortgage (GEM) is a fixed-rate loan amortized over a long term. However, while the interest rate remains the same over the life of the loan, the monthly payments increase. The amount of the payment increase is applied directly to the principal balance, which means the loan amount will be paid off in a much shorter period than would occur without the payment increases.

All GEMs share the following characteristics:

1. the **interest rate is fixed** over the life of the loan;
2. first year payments of principal and interest are **based on a 30-year term**;

3. the borrower's payments are increased at specified intervals (**usually annually**) for all or a portion of the life of the loan. The payment is generally increased by a fixed percentage, typically 3% or 5%;
4. since the interest rate is fixed, **100% of the annual payment increases are used to reduce the principal balance**.

Because the payment increases reduce the mortgage debt, the GEM is paid off much sooner than a 30-year fixed rate mortgage. For example, if payments are increased 3% per year on a 15% loan, the entire debt will be retired in 13 years and seven months; with 5% annual increases, the same loan will pay off in just 11 years and four months. **Most GEMs pay off in 11 to 17 years**.

The major drawback to a GEM is that over the life of the loan, mortgage payments become substantially higher than level fixed-rate payments. In the past, this annual rate of increase was well below the rate of inflation and the payments did not increase as fast as the borrower's income. At current low rates of inflation, the GEM payment increases do not look so attractive.

GEM advantages for borrowers. The major advantage to a GEM is the accelerated equity buildup. Other advantages include:

Payments are predictable. The borrower's payments will increase annually, but (as opposed to ARMs) the amount of the annual increase is known at the outset of the loan.

No negative amortization. Instead, there is accelerated positive amortization.

Reduced interest costs. A GEM borrower will pay less than half the interest he or she would pay with a traditional 30-year, fixed-rate mortgage.

Simplicity of loan. In contrast to ARMs, the GEM is easy to understand and explain. Buyers are reluctant to commit to a major debt if they do not understand it.

Lower than market interest rate. Lenders are often willing to make GEM loans at lower than market rates because they will recapture the principal so quickly. Recaptured principal can be reinvested at competitive market rates. The lower than market rates make it easier to qualify for the loan.

FHA Programs

An "FHA loan" is a loan insured by the Federal Housing Administration (FHA). The FHA was given the authority to insure residential loans (the FHA does not make loans) by the National Housing Act of 1934 in a Congressional effort to meet the housing needs of the public. An FHA loan is a practical, affordable alternative to a conventional loan.

The FHA program is implemented through a government insurance program. In effect, the FHA insures lenders who make FHA loans against losses incurred from loan default and foreclosure. In order to fund this insurance program, the Mutual Mortgage Insurance Plan, all borrowers are required to pay an insurance premium, called the **MIP** (Mortgage Insurance Premium). The amount of the premium depends on the amount of the loan.

Because the FHA bears the risk of any loss caused by the default of an FHA-insured loan, it has set certain conditions which must be met before it will insure a loan. These conditions include underwriting standards (see Chapter 11, Qualifying Standards), eligibility requirements and other restrictions.

Loan Process.

The process for obtaining an FHA-insured loan is similar to that for obtaining a conventional loan. The following are steps the buyer must take in order to acquire FHA financing:

- The buyer selects a home for purchase;
- The buyer executes a deposit receipt with the seller;
- The buyer applies to an FHA-approved lending institution. The purchaser is expected to have the costs of the appraisal in cash

when applying. The interest rate of the loan is negotiated with the lender;
- An FHA appraisal, called a Conditional Commitment, is completed;
- An effective VA Certificate of Reasonable Value (CRV) may sometimes be used, if available, instead of an FHA appraisal;
- The lender presents all the paperwork to the FHA and FHA does the loan processing and underwriting;
- Alternatively, many lenders participate in HUD's direct endorsement program which allows them to do all the loan processing themselves (e.g., obtaining the appraisal, reviewing all necessary documents) and gives them the authority to approve and close the loan on their own. Lenders authorized to fully underwrite their own loan applications are called direct endorsers. Recently, more and more lenders are being qualified as direct endorsers in an effort to relieve FHA of the bulk of the underwriting burden.

Benefits to borrowers.

FHA-insured loans benefit the borrower in many ways. The following characteristics of an FHA-insured loan make it easier to obtain, more affordable and contribute to the resale value of the home:

Easier to obtain. Smaller downpayments are required and the loan underwriting standards are less restrictive than for conventional mortgages. This means FHA loans are more affordable, especially for first-time homebuyers who might not otherwise qualify for a home loan.

No prepayment penalty. There is no prepayment penalty on FHA loans; the borrower can prepay a part or all of the loan amount at any time without penalty (which for conventional loans is usually a percentage of the loan amount). However, the lender can require the borrower to make the prepayment on the regularly scheduled monthly due date. For loans issued prior to August 2, 1985, the borrower must give 30 days written notice when pre-paying in full or there will be a 30-day interest charge. Lenders can no longer require borrowers to give notice of intent to prepay.

Lower interest rate. While there is no longer a maximum interest rate, the lender's risk on an FHA loan is still less and the interest rate is generally below market rates.

Fixed interest rates. Most FHA-insured mortgages have interest rates which are fixed over the life of the loan (except for the FHA adjustable-rate mortgage).

Long term. The term for most FHA loans is 30 years, although many FHA programs allow for terms as short as 15 years at the borrower's option.

Quicker application time. For borrowers who use direct endorsement lenders, the loan application process is usually quicker.

Eligibility.

FHA programs are generally open to all borrowers who intend to occupy the property being financed. (The FHA used to insure loans for investment property as well as owner-occupied property, but investor loans were eliminated from nearly all FHA programs in 1989.)

Usually, any existing one- to four-family property in an accepted neighborhood is eligible. Properties on an individual water and/or sewer system will require local health authority approval. If utilities or other services (roads, water, sewers, etc.) are not provided/maintained by local public authorities, the FHA must approve the private supplier. If the house is new construction (less than a year old) and is not warranted by an approved construction insurance program, or is not VA- or FHA-approved, the loan amount will be less than the normal loan amount. Mobile homes permanently placed on individual lots will generally qualify.

Costs of the loan.

As with conventional loans, FHA-insured loans require certain up-front expenditures of the borrower. These include a portion of the closing costs and a downpayment towards the purchase price. (Maximum loan amounts are discussed later in this section.) The seller may pay all or some of the closing costs, but the loan amount will be reduced by the amount of the costs paid by the seller or a third party.

Lenders charge **discount points** (a certain percentage of the loan amount which is paid to the lender at closing) as compensation for providing a loan at lower than market interest rates. The amount of discount points is not set by the FHA, but negotiated with the lender. The buyer, the seller, or a third party may pay the points.

Source of the downpayment. The borrower is restricted to certain sources of funds for the downpayment and closing costs. The allowable sources of funds are:

- Verified **checking**, **investment**, and/or **savings accounts**.
- A **gift** from a family member: the borrower must submit a gift letter from the family member which states that the funds are a gift and not to be repaid. The gift funds must be deposited in the borrower's account at the time of application.
- "**Sweat equity**": the borrower may complete any work required by the FHA appraisal and receive credit towards the downpayment from the seller. The amount of credit that will be allowed is determined by the FHA estimate of the repair cost. For example, if the house needs to have the roof repaired and the estimated repair cost is $700, $700 is the maximum amount of credit that could be applied towards the downpayment by having the borrower do the work. The borrower must demonstrate that he or she has the time, money, and ability to make the repairs and the deposit receipt must itemize the work to be done and the amount of credit to be given.
- The borrower may sometimes have a **non-occupant co-borrower** assist in qualifying for the loan. The co-borrower's assets, income and debts are considered along with the borrower's to determine eligibility for the loan. The co-borrower is named on the mortgage note, is fully responsible for the loan repayment, and shares title to the property.
- The borrower can trade **personal property** (e.g., a car) to the seller to meet the downpayment requirements. The value of the property must be appraised in writing by a qualified third party and only the amount of the borrower's equity in the property can be applied towards the downpayment.
- The borrower's **equity** in the land upon which a new home is being built may be applied towards the downpayment requirement.

Secondary financing. The use of secondary financing is permitted only under certain circumstances:

a) The first and second mortgages together do not exceed the maximum loan amount for the particular FHA program. The rule is based on the theory that the buyer should be paying the minimum downpayment (which is generally less than that required for a conventional loan) out of his or her own funds. If the borrower has not invested any of his or her own resources in the property, there is an increased likelihood of default in times of financial difficulty.
b) The payments under both the first and second mortgage do not exceed the borrower's reasonable ability to pay.
c) The payments due on the second mortgage are collected on a monthly basis and are substantially the same amount from month to month.
d) The second mortgage does not provide for a balloon payment due in less than ten years and it permits prepayment without penalty.

Except as described above, there can be no other encumbrances besides the FHA-insured loan on the security property. However, the seller can carry back a second mortgage on other property owned by the borrower, if:

a) it is stated in the deposit receipt that the seller will take back a second mortgage on the other property;
b) the total indebtedness on the other property does not exceed 80% of the value of that property;
c) the buyer can afford the payments on the second mortgage.

The FHA payment.

An important feature that distinguishes FHA mortgage payments from conventional and VA mortgage payments is inclusion of the mutual mortgage insurance premium, more commonly know as the MIP (Mortgage Insurance Premium).

The MIP is a one-time premium that may be paid in cash at closing or financed over the term of the loan. The amount of the premium is currently 3.8% of the loan amount.

Example:

$67,000	loan amount
× .038	MIP premium
$2,546	amount of premium

If the premium is paid in cash at closing, it may be paid by either the borrower or the seller.

If the MIP is financed, the amount actually borrowed is the sum of the loan amount and the premium amount. Monthly payments are then calculated to pay off the total amount financed, including the MIP. When the MIP is financed, the total amount financed can exceed the FHA maximum loan amount by the amount of the MIP.

Example:

$67,000	loan amount
× .038	MIP premium
$ 2,546	amount of premium

$67,000	maximum loan amount
+ 2,546	MIP premium
$69,546	total amount financed

The borrower's loan fee is based on the actual loan amount only, not including the MIP. Discount points, however, are based on the total amount financed, including the MIP premium.

In addition to the one-time MIP, FHA borrowers also have to pay an **annual renewal premium**. This annual premium is 0.5% of the loan balance. The number of years the borrower has to pay this premium depends on the loan-to-value ratio. For loans closing in 1991 and 1992, borrowers will have to pay the annual premium for the following number of years:

LTV greater than 95%: ten years
LTV 90% to 95%: eight years
LTV under 90%: five years

Loan Programs.

The FHA has several different programs. Here is a brief list of the ones most likely to interest typical homebuyers:

Section 203b. Insures loans for the purchase or refinancing of single-family homes and residential duplexes, triplexes, and fourplexes. This is the standard FHA-insured loan, accounting for almost 75% of all FHA loans. This program is discussed in more detail below.

Section 203b(2). Insures loans for the purchase of single-family homes by veterans. (Not the same as a VA-guaranteed loan.)

Section 221d(2). Insures loans for the purchase or rehabilitation of low-income housing.

Section 234c. Insures loans for the purchase or refinancing of condominium units.

Section 245. Insurance for graduated payment mortgages (GPMs) and growth equity mortgages (GEMs).

Section 251. Insurance for adjustable-rate mortgages (ARMs), used in conjunction with the 203b program or 234c program. The loan term must be 30 years.

Section 203b.

Loan-to-value ratios. Effective February 17, 1991, the FHA has changed its loan-to-value ratio rules. To determine the maximum loan amount for a particular transaction, it is now necessary to perform two steps. After doing the calculations required for step one, you set that result aside and do the calculations for step two. Then compare the results: the lesser of the two results is the maximum loan amount.

Step One.

1. Subtract the amount of the closing costs to be paid by the seller from the sales price.
2. Compare this figure to the appraised value. Take the lesser figure and add 57% of the total closing costs.
3. Subtract $25,000 from that figure.
4. Multiply the answer by .95 (95%).
5. Add $24,250 (97% of the first $25,000: $25,000 × .97 = $24,250) to get the result of step one.

Step Two.

Multiply the appraised value by .9775 (97.75%) to get the result of step two.

Compare the results of step one and step two. The smaller of the two figures is the maximum loan amount for the transaction.

Example:

$90,000	Sales price and appraised value
$3,000	Closing costs, $1,000 to be paid by seller

Step one:

$90,000	Sales price
− 1,000	Seller-paid closing costs
$89,000	(Less than appraised value)

$89,000	Lesser figure from Calculation #1
+ 1,710	57% of total closing costs ($3,000 × .57)
$90,710	

$90,710	
− 25,000	Calculation #3
$65,710	
× .95	Calculation #4
$62,424	
+ 24,250	Calculation #5
$86,674	Result of step one

Step two:

$90,000	Appraised value
× .9775	Maximum LTV
$87,975	Result of step two

Maximum loan amount: $86,674 (the lesser of the two results)

Less expensive homes. The FHA applies a different loan-to-value formula to less expensive homes. If either the adjusted price (the sales price, minus the seller's contribution, plus 57% of the closing costs) or the appraised value plus 57% of the closing costs is $50,000 or less, simply multiply the lesser of those two figures by .97 (97%) to get the result of step one. And for step two, if the appraised value is $50,000 or less, multiply it by .9875 (98.75%), instead of the 97.75% figure used for more expensive homes.

New construction. The loan amount for new construction (less than one year old) that is not FHA-approved or warranted by an approved construction insurance program is limited to **90%** of the total FHA value or actual acquisition cost, whichever is less, including allowable closing costs.

Secondary residences. When a borrower buys a home as a secondary residence, the FHA loan is limited to 85% of the appraised value or purchase price (including closing costs). A borrower is only eligible for one secondary residence loan. The property must be a single-unit dwelling, and cannot be in the same area as the borrower's other home.

Refinancing. If the borrower will receive cash from the refinancing loan, the loan cannot exceed 85% of the appraised value (including closing costs). But if all the loan proceeds are used to pay off the existing mortgage and to pay for closing costs and FHA-required repairs, the loan-to-value ratio can be higher. The limit will be calculated in the same way as for a purchase loan: 97% of the first $25,000, 95% of the balance.

Maximum loan amounts. Aside from the limitations on the loan amount imposed by the loan-to-value ratios, there is a maximum possible loan amount which is set by HUD. This maximum loan amount is based on the medium range housing costs for the community and thus the maximum amount may vary from region to region. Allowable loan amounts are higher in areas of higher cost housing.

The basic maximum loan amount for single-family residences is $67,500. In high cost areas, this amount may be increased up to $124,875 or 95% of the median house price in the area (whichever is less). An area is determined to be "high cost" based on an application made by area lenders or other interested parties which shows that recent median sales prices of homes in the area significantly exceeded the maximum allowable loan amount. The maximum loan amount limitation directs FHA programs to persons who are in the low- to medium-priced housing market.

There are different loan ceilings for single family dwellings, duplexes, triplexes and fourplexes. Check with a local lender for the current maximum mortgage amounts in your community.

Section 245.

FHA-insured Graduated Payment Mortgages (GPMs) were authorized under the Housing and Community Development Act of 1974. As with other alternative financing plans, the popularity of FHA-GPMs has decreased significantly in the current lower interest rate environment.

The FHA GPM programs are only for those with a strong likelihood of increased income in future years. Payments during the early years of the loan are lower than those for a standard level-payment amortization schedule. The payments increase each year for the first five or ten years, depending on the plan, and then are level for the remainder of the loan term.

FHA ARM.

The popularity of adjustable rate mortgages (ARMs) in the early 1980s led HUD to initiate federal mortgage insurance for ARM loans. Adjustments are made each year based on the weekly average of U.S. Treasury Bills and cannot exceed 1% per year or 5% over the life of the loan.

The FHA also has growth equity mortgage programs that enable the borrower to pay off the loan approximately twice as fast as a fixed-rate loan. FHA GPMs and GEMs are only available for purchase loans, not refinancing.

VA Programs

A "VA loan" is a home loan, the repayment of which is guaranteed by the Veterans Administration. The main purpose of the VA loan program is to help veterans purchase homes with affordable, low interest financing. The VA-guaranteed loan program was established in 1944 with the passage of what is commonly known as the "GI Bill of Rights."

Advantages of VA loans.

There are several advantages to a VA loan over most conventional loans. The major advantage is that, in many circumstances, **no downpayment** is required. (The lender will require a downpayment if the purchase price is more than the reasonable value of the property.) The VA loan is more affordable as the **interest rate** (set by the Veterans Administration) is almost always lower than conventional mortgage interest rates, there are limitations on what **closing costs** the buyer can pay, and there are **no mortgage insurance** requirements. The loans are **long term** (30 years), and there is **no prepayment penalty.** The **VA appraisal** informs the buyer of the estimated reasonable value of the property. For construction loans, the VA examines the plans and specifications to ensure VA **minimum property requirements** are met and inspects the construction to ensure compliance with the approved plans. The VA will also show **leniency** to worthy VA homeowners who are experiencing temporary financial difficulty.

What the VA will NOT do is guarantee that the house is free of defects, give legal advice if the buyer runs into trouble buying or constructing the home, compel the builder to remedy defects in construction, nor guarantee that the buyer will be completely satisfied with the property or that he or she is making a good investment.

Requirements for VA loan approval.

As with conventional mortgages, a VA loan has certain requirements for approval. These include the VA underwriting standards which must be met (see Chapter 11, Qualifying Standards). In addition, the buyer must be an **eligible veteran** with **available home loan entitlement**, the loan must be for an **eligible purpose**, and the buyer must occupy or intend to **occupy the property** as his or her primary residence within a reasonable time after closing.

Eligible loan purposes.

A veteran may obtain a VA loan for a variety of purposes. These include the following:

- **To buy or build a home.** The VA loan may be used to buy or construct a one- to four-unit residential property. If more than one veteran is buying, one family unit is added to the initial four for each veteran who participates. For example, two veterans could buy five units, and three veterans, six units.

- **To buy a townhouse or condominium unit** in a project approved by the VA.
- **To repair, alter or improve** a home (including the installation of a solar heating or cooling system).
- To simultaneously **purchase and improve** a home.
- **To refinance an existing home.** Mortgage and/or other liens on an existing house may be paid off with the proceeds of a VA loan. The loan amount may include additional funds for any other acceptable purpose (e.g., improvements), plus closing costs, discount points, and the VA funding fee. The veteran must have unused home loan entitlement in order to get such a loan.
- **To refinance an existing VA loan to reduce the interest rate.** The property securing an existing VA loan may be refinanced to take advantage of lower interest rates. Loan entitlement is not required. The loan amount is limited to the balance of the old loan plus the closing costs, discount points, and funding fee.
- **To buy a mobile home and/or lot.**
- **To buy and improve a lot** on which to place a mobile home already owned and occupied.
- **To refinance a mobile home** in order to acquire a lot on which to place the mobile home.

The loan guaranty.

VA loans are not made by the Veterans Administration, but are made by private lenders such as banks, savings and loan associations, or mortgage companies. The eligible veteran applies for a loan with the lender and if the loan is approved, the VA **guarantees** the loan when it is closed. The guaranty protects the lender against loss if the buyer or a later owner fails to repay the loan. If the veteran defaults and the lender suffers a loss when the loan is foreclosed, the VA pays for that loss up to the guaranty amount. The amount paid by the VA in these circumstances must be repaid (to the VA) by the veteran.

The VA does not guarantee the full loan amount. The guaranty amount varies according to the loan amount obtained. The various guaranty amounts are as follows:

Loan Amount	Guaranty Amount
up to $45,000	50% of loan amount
$45,000 - $56,250	$22,500
$56,251 - $90,000	40% of loan amount
$90,001 - $144,000	$36,000
over $144,000	$36,000 plus 25% of the amount above $144,000, up to a maximum of $46,000

For example, if a veteran applies for a $75,000 loan, the maximum guaranty will be $30,000. For a $150,000 loan, the maximum guaranty will be $37,500. The maximum guaranty amount is referred to as the veteran's "entitlement."

There is no maximum VA loan amount (except that the loan may not exceed the property's appraised value or the purchase price, whichever is less), but the amount of the guaranty effectively places a limit on the amount a lender will be willing to lend. The general rule of thumb is that a lender will require the guaranty amount to equal at least 25% of the loan amount. (This is because lenders want a 25% safety margin. The lender has to bear any losses from default in excess of the guaranty amount, and those losses are rarely more than 25% of the loan amount.) This means that with the highest guaranty amount ($46,000), a veteran will find it difficult to obtain a VA loan greater than $184,000.

Eligibility

Eligibility for a VA loan is based on **active military service**. A veteran is eligible for a VA loan if his or her service falls into any of the following categories:

90 days continuous active duty, any part of which occurred:

1. September 16, 1940 through July 25, 1947 (WWII)
2. June 27, 1950 through January 31, 1955 (Korea)
3. August 5, 1964 through May 7, 1975 (Vietnam)

181 days continuous active duty, any part of which occurred:

1. July 26, 1947 through June 26, 1950
2. February 1, 1955 through August 4, 1964
3. May 8, 1975 through September 7, 1980

24 months continuous active duty for veterans who enlisted after September 7, 1980, **except**:

1. individuals discharged for disability;
2. individuals discharged for hardship;
3. any case in which it is established that the person is suffering from a service-connected disability not the result of willful misconduct and not incurred during a period of unauthorized absence.

Veterans who are discharged for hardship or for a nonservice-connected disability are eligible only if they have served a minimum of 181 days. There is no minimum active duty service requirement for veterans discharged for a service-connected disability.

Persons who have served six months active duty for training only are not eligible. There is also no eligibility for persons who received a dishonorable discharge.

A veteran's spouse may be eligible for a VA loan if:

1. the vet was killed in action or is a possible prisoner of war because of service during the Vietnam era;
2. the vet died of service-related injuries and the spouse has not remarried.

The VA determines the eligibility of the veteran, and if he or she is qualified, will issue a **Certificate of Eligibility**. Most eligible veterans who have been recently discharged are automatically issued a Certificate of Eligibility for VA home loan benefits shortly after discharge.

Any veteran who needs to obtain a Certificate must complete the VA form, Determination of Eligibility and Available Loan Guaranty Entitlement (shown on pages 262-263), and submit it with either the originals or legible copies of his or her most recent discharge or separation papers covering active military duty. These papers show active duty dates and the type of discharge. If separated from the service after January 1, 1950, the veteran must also submit the Report of Separation From Active Duty.

If the veteran is currently on active duty and has not been previously discharged from active duty service, he or she must submit a "statement of service" on military letterhead, signed by the appropriate service personnel. The statement must include date of entry to active duty and the duration of any time lost.

If a veteran has lost his or her original discharge papers and does not have a legible copy, the veteran should obtain a Certificate in Lieu of Lost or Destroyed Discharge.

Entitlement

Restoration of entitlement. Once a veteran uses his or her entitlement (the guaranty amount) to obtain a VA loan, the veteran is no longer eligible for another VA loan unless the initial entitlement is "restored." Entitlement is restored if the following conditions are met:

- the property securing the original loan has been sold and the loan has been paid in full; or
- a qualified veteran buyer must agree to assume the outstanding balance on the loan and agree to "substitute" his or her entitlement for the same amount of entitlement originally used to obtain the loan. The buyer must also meet the occupancy, income and credit requirements of the VA.

Even if these conditions are met, restoration of entitlement is not automatic. The veteran must apply for it by completing and returning the appropriate VA forms to any regional office or center. Application forms for substitution of entitlement may be requested from the VA office that guaranteed the loan.

Remaining entitlements. Even if the entitlement cannot be restored, the veteran may still have "remaining entitlement" that can be used to obtain another VA loan. The amount of the entitlement used to be much lower and has been increased over time by changes in the law. For example, a veteran who obtained a $25,000 loan in 1974 would have used only $12,500 in guaranty entitlement, the maximum then available. Assume that the veteran is seeking a $92,000 loan. The current guaranty amount is $36,000. Even if the first loan is not paid off, the veteran could use the remaining $23,500 entitlement ($36,000 - $12,500) for the new VA-guaranteed loan. With $23,500 in entitlement, the veteran could obtain a $92,000 loan with no downpayment and still meet the lender's 25% requirement. The veteran could also combine a downpayment with the remaining entitlement for a larger loan amount. The veteran may use secondary financing for the downpayment costs.

Applying for the VA loan.

VA-guaranteed loans are obtained by making application to private lending institutions. The local VA regional office will often provide a list of lenders who are active in the program. Most mortgage lenders will have all the necessary forms to apply for the loan, including the paperwork necessary to obtain a certificate of eligibility.

If the veteran already has a certificate of eligibility, he or she should present it to the lender when making the loan application as the lender will want to be sure the veteran is eligible before accepting the application. However, a lender will discuss the possibility of making a VA loan without seeing the certificate and may even assist the veteran in applying for it.

Form Approved
OMB No. 2900-0086

Veterans Administration

REQUEST FOR DETERMINATION OF ELIGIBILITY AND AVAILABLE LOAN GUARANTY ENTITLEMENT

TO: VETERANS ADMINISTRATION
ATTN: LOAN GUARANTY DIVISION

NOTE: Please read instructions on reverse before completing this form. If additional space is required attach separate sheet.

1. FIRST - MIDDLE - LAST NAME OF VETERAN

2A. ADDRESS OF VETERAN *(No., Street or rural route, City or P.O., State and ZIP Code)*

2B. VETERAN'S DAYTIME TELEPHONE NO. *(Include Area Code)*

3. DATE OF BIRTH

4. MILITARY SERVICE DATA (ATTACH PROOF OF SERVICE -- SEE INSTRUCTIONS ON REVERSE (Paragraphs F and G.1))

PERIOD OF ACTIVE SERVICE		NAME *(Show your name exactly as it appears on your separation papers (DD214) or Statement of Service)*	SERVICE NUMBER *(Enter Social Security No., if appropriate)*	BRANCH OF SERVICE
DATE FROM	DATE TO			
A.				
B.				
C.				
D.				

5A. WERE YOU DISCHARGED, RETIRED OR SEPARATED FROM SERVICE BECAUSE OF DISABILITY OR DO YOU NOW HAVE ANY SERVICE-CONNECTED DISABILITIES?

☐ YES ☐ NO *(If "Yes," Complete Item 5B)*

5B. VA CLAIM FILE NUMBER

C-

6. IS A CERTIFICATE OF ELIGIBILITY FOR LOAN GUARANTY PURPOSES ENCLOSED?

☐ YES ☐ NO *(If "No," Complete Items 7A and 7B)*

7A. HAVE YOU PREVIOUSLY APPLIED FOR A CERTIFICATE OF ELIGIBILITY FOR VA LOAN PURPOSES?

☐ YES ☐ NO *(If "Yes," give location of VA office(s))*

7B. HAVE YOU PREVIOUSLY RECEIVED SUCH A CERTIFICATE?

☐ YES ☐ NO *(If "Yes," give location of VA office(s))*

7C. COMPLETE THE FOLLOWING CERTIFICATION IF YOU HAVE PREVIOUSLY RECEIVED A CERTIFICATE OF ELIGIBILITY WHICH IS NOT ENCLOSED AND THIS IS A REQUEST FOR A DUPLICATE CERTIFICATE.

☐ THE CERTIFICATE OF ELIGIBILITY PREVIOUSLY ISSUED TO ME HAS BEEN LOST OR STOLEN. IF RECOVERED, IT WILL BE RETURNED TO THE VA.

8. HAVE YOU PREVIOUSLY ACQUIRED PROPERTY WITH THE ASSISTANCE OF A GI LOAN?

☐ YES ☐ NO *(If "Yes," complete Items 9 through 18. Please attach a separate sheet if more than one loan is involved. If "No," skip to Items 19 through 22.)*

9. ADDRESS OF REGIONAL OFFICE(S) WHERE LOAN WAS OBTAINED *(City and State)*

10. STATE TYPE(S) AND NUMBER OF LOAN(S) *(Home, Manufactured Home, Condominium, Direct, Farm, Business, etc.)*

11. ADDRESS(ES) OF PROPERTY PREVIOUSLY PURCHASED WITH GUARANTY ENTITLEMENT

12. DATE YOU PURCHASED THE PROPERTY(IES)

13. DO YOU NOW OWN THE PROPERTY DESCRIBED IN ITEM 11? ☐ YES ☐ NO *(If "Yes," do not complete Items 14 and 15)*	14. DATE(S) THE PROPERTY WAS SOLD	15. IS THERE ANY UNDERSTANDING OR AGREEMENT WRITTEN OR ORAL, BETWEEN YOU AND THE PURCHASERS THAT THEY WILL RECONVEY THE PROPERTY TO YOU? ☐ YES ☐ NO

NOTE: It will speed processing if you can complete Items 16, 17, and 18.

16. NAME AND ADDRESS OF LENDER(S) TO WHOM LOAN PAYMENTS WERE MADE	17. LENDER'S LOAN OR ACCOUNT NUMBER 18. VA LOAN NUMBER(S)

I certify that the statements herein are true to the best of my knowledge and belief.

19. SIGNATURE OF VETERAN	20. DATE SIGNED

FEDERAL STATUTES PROVIDE SEVERE PENALTIES FOR FRAUD, INTENTIONAL MISREPRESENTATION, CRIMINAL CONNIVANCE OR CONSPIRACY PURPOSED TO INFLUENCE THE ISSUANCE OF ANY GUARANTY OR INSURANCE BY THE ADMINISTRATOR.

21. THIS SECTION FOR VA USE ONLY

21A. DATE CERTIFICATE ISSUED AND DISCHARGE OR SEPARATION PAPERS AND VA PAMPHLETS GIVEN TO VETERAN OR MAILED TO ADDRESS SHOWN BELOW	21B. TYPE OF DISCHARGE OR SEPARATION PAPERS RETURNED	21C. INITIALS OF VA AGENT	21D. NAME AND ADDRESS TO WHOM CERTIFICATE MAILED

VA FORM 26-1880, MAR 1984

DO NOT DETACH

IMPORTANT - You must complete Item 22 since the Certificate of Eligibility along with all discharge and separation papers will be mailed to the address shown in Item 22 below. If they are to be sent to you, your current mailing address should be indicated, or if they are to be sent elsewhere, the name and address of such person or firm should be shown in Item 22.

The amount of loan guaranty entitlement available for use is endorsed on the reverse of the enclosed Certificate of Eligibility. This certificate must be returned to the VA at the time a loan application or loan report is submitted.

NOTE - PLEASE DELIVER THE ENCLOSED PAMPHLETS AND DISCHARGE OR SEPARATION PAPERS TO THE VETERAN PROMPTLY

NOTE - PLEASE DELIVER THE ENCLOSED PAMPHLETS AND DISCHARGE OR SEPARATION PAPERS TO THE VETERAN PROMPTLY

VA FORM MAR 1984 **26-1880**

EXISTING STOCKS OF VA FORM 26-1880, JUN 1982, WILL BE USED.

DO NOT DETACH

There are two ways a lender may process VA home loans — on a "prior approval" basis or an "automatic" basis.

When the loan is processed on a **prior approval** basis, the lender takes the application, sends a request to the VA to appraise the property, and verifies the applicant's income and credit record. All this information is put together in a loan package which is sent to the VA for review. If the VA approves the loan, a commitment to guarantee the loan is sent to the lender. The lender then closes the loan and sends a report of the closing to the VA. If the loan complies with VA requirements, the VA issues a certificate of guaranty to the lender.

In **automatic** processing, the lender still orders the appraisal from the VA, but has the authority to make the credit decision on the loan without the VA's approval. The biggest difference between prior approval and automatic processing is the time saved by not having to wait for the VA's approval before the loan is closed. Lenders must be specifically authorized by the VA before they can process loans on the automatic basis.

Closing costs.

The veteran may not be charged any commission or brokerage fees for obtaining the VA loan. However, the veteran can pay reasonable closing costs, including the costs of the VA appraisal, credit report, survey, title report, recording fees, and a funding fee of up to 1.875%. The closing costs (except the funding fee) may not be included in the loan amount, except when refinancing a VA loan.

Discount points. Generally, veterans are not permitted to pay discounts or "points" in connection with VA financing. Lenders require discount points when they consider the maximum VA interest rate to be too low to produce an acceptable yield. Any discount points charged by the lender must be paid by the seller or a third party. The amount of the discount is a matter of negotiation between the seller and the lender; the VA has no direct control over the charging of discounts.

Transfer of the property.

The veteran may transfer or sell the property purchased with a VA loan to another person, either veteran or nonveteran. The VA loan does not have to be paid in full in order to do so; the buyer may purchase the property by assuming the existing VA loan. However, when the veteran transfers the property and allows the transferee to assume the loan, the veteran is NOT automatically released from personal liability for repayment of the loan. The veteran continues to be liable for repayment unless he or she obtains a release of liability from the VA. The release is obtained by having the buyer assume all of the veteran's liabilities on the VA loan and by having the VA approve the buyer and the assumption agreement. (NOTE: a release of liability is not the same as a restoration of entitlement. The buyer must be a veteran willing and able to use his or her own entitlement before the seller's entitlement will be restored.)

Cal-Vet Loans

There is one additional type of financing available to California residents. This is the **Cal-Vet Loan** sponsored by the State of California.

In 1921, the California legislature enacted the California Veteran Farm and Home Purchase Program which enabled the California Department of Veterans Affairs to provide eligible veterans with affordable financing to purchase home or farm property. The Department originates, processes, funds and services the loan until it is fully repaid.

Source of funds.

The funds for the loan program are raised through the issuance and sale of General Obligation Bonds and Revenue Bonds. These bonds are repaid by the veterans who are participating in the loan program so there is no direct cost to California taxpayers. By federal regulation, the majority of the Revenue Bond funds are awarded to first-time homebuyers (those who have not owned a principal residence within the past three years). If a veteran does qualify as a first-time homebuyer, he or she should so inform the Cal-Vet representative when applying for the loan.

When funds for Cal-Vet loans are in short supply, there is a statutory **order of preference** for granting the loan funds. The loans are given in the order of the following categories:

1) Veterans who were wounded or disabled from war services. Disability must be rated at 10% by the United States Veterans Administration.
2) Former prisoners of war, unremarried spouses of veterans killed in the line of duty and unremarried spouses of veterans designated as missing in action.
3) Veterans who served during the Vietnam period (August 5, 1964 through May 7, 1975) and Indian veterans applying for loans on reservation or trust land.
4) All other qualified veterans.

Application/refinance.

Under state law, the application for the loan must be made within **30 years** from the date of release from active duty. However, that time limit does not apply to veterans who were wounded in action, prisoners of war, or disabled as a result of their service.

The applicant must follow certain steps in applying for a Cal-Vet loan:

1. Pay a fee of $25.00 at the time of filing the application.
2. Answer all questions on the loan application form completely.
3. Submit a certified copy of his or her military separation documents showing date of entry and release.
4. Submit two legible copies of a current preliminary title report with a plat map covering the property.
5. Submit a copy of the deposit receipt for the proposed transaction and a copy of current escrow instructions.
6. Complete the applicant's portion of the Verification of Employment forms and have his or her employer complete them and

return them to the Cal-Vet office.

7. If the applicant is self-employed, he or she must include a current profit and loss statement.
8. Sign and return a notice on federal laws prohibiting discrimination and credit information authorization forms.

The submission of all the required documents at the same time will facilitate the processing of the application.

The completed Cal-Vet application must be received by the Department of Veterans Affairs **before the purchase is completed** or an interest in the property is acquired. An exception to this rule is if the veteran has an interest in a building site, the structure has not been completed and a certificate of occupancy has not yet been issued. Cal-Vet loans may only be used to refinance construction loans or interim loans with a **term of 24 months or less**. The Department does not make construction loans itself and will only refinance a construction loan when the property is completed and ready for occupancy. If a veteran is building a home, he or she should apply for approval of the building site and a determination of eligibility before construction begins. Once the veteran is found qualified and the building site has been approved, the Department will issue a loan commitment, allowing 12 months for the construction to be completed.

Secondary financing may be used, but only with the Department's consent. The total amount of financing, both secondary and the Cal-Vet loan, cannot exceed 90% of the Department's appraised value of the property and a subordination agreement must be obtained from the secondary lender.

Occupation of premises.

The veteran or a member of the Veteran's immediate family must occupy the property within **60 days** of signing the Cal-Vet loan papers and must continue to use the property as the principal place of residence for the life of the loan. An exception is made for farm properties as long as the veteran personally cultivates the property (harvesting crops and/or tending livestock).

State of California
DEPARTMENT OF VETERANS AFFAIRS
DIVISION OF FARM AND HOME PURCHASES

LOAN APPLICATION (HOME)

Office use only (Date received)

SUBJECT TO AVAILABILITY OF FUNDS AND PREFERENCE CATEGORIES

APPLICANT

1. Veteran's Name (Last) (First) (MI)
2. Date of Birth (Mo.) (Day) (Yr.)
3. Social Security Number — —
4. Spouse's Name (Last) (First) (MI)
5. Date of Birth (Mo.) (Day) (Yr.)
6. Date Married (Mo.) (Day) (Yr.)
7. Home Address (Number & Street) City State Zip Code
7a. Place of Birth
8. Telephone Number
9. Years at Present Address
10. Ethnic Background (Optional)
11. No. & Age of Dependents living at Home

YOU MUST NOTIFY THE CAL-VET OFFICE OF ANY CHANGE IN YOUR ADDRESS

ELIGIBILITY

Date of Enlistment	State of Residence at Time of Enlistment	Date of Release

12. Were you wounded or disabled as a result of military service? If yes, check box and submit verification. ☐ Wounded ☐ Disabled
13. Were you ever a prisoner of war? ☐ Yes ☐ No
13a. Have you and/or your spouse owned an interest in the last 3 years in a home used as your principal residence? ☐ Yes ☐ No
14. Are you an unmarried spouse of a veteran missing in action or killed in the line of duty while on active duty. ☐ Yes ☐ No
15. Have you ever had a Cal-Vet Loan ☐ Yes ☐ No
15a. Date Paid in full (Mo.) (Day) (Yr.)
15b. Location
16. Have you ever requested or received a bonus or benefit from any other state for any military service? ☐ Yes ☐ No
16a. If yes, what state
16b. Period of service (Mo.) (Day) (Yr.)
17. Have you ever acquired an interest of record in the property being submitted? ☐ Yes ☐ No
17a. If yes, when? (Mo.) (Day) (Yr.)
17b. Guaranteed or insured by the Federal Government ☐ Yes ☐ No

SUBJECT PROPERTY

18. I REQUEST A CAL-VET LOAN OF $ ____________ TO PURCHASE SUBJECT PROPERTY AT PRICE $ ____________
19. Street Address City County Zip
20. ☐ Existing Home ☐ Unimproved Home Site ☐ Under Construction
20a. ☐ Single Family Home ☐ Condominium/PUD Mobilehome ☐ New ☐ Used ☐ Land ☐ Mobilehome Park
21. Under Construction
Cost of Unimproved Lot $ ____________
21a. Estimated Completion Date (Mo.) (Day) (Yr.)
21b. Balance Owed $ ____________
21c. Proposed Construction Cost $ ____________
21d. Date Lot Acquired (Mo.) (Day) (Yr.)
22. Current F.H.A. case number (if any)
23. Solar Heating Device ☐ Yes ☐ No
24. Property is: ☐ Vacant ☐ Occupied by: Name of occupant Phone Number

25. Access to property may be obtained by calling:
Name: Address: Phone:

PLEASE NOTIFY THE CAL-VET OFFICE OF ANY CHANGE IN PROPERTY ACCESS INFORMATION

EMPLOYMENT AND INCOME

26. Veteran's Present Employer	26a. Address of Employment		Gross Monthly Salary	Office Use Only
27. Occupation	27a. How long	27b. Telephone	$	
28. Spouse's present employer	28a. Address of Employment		Gross Monthly Salary	
29. Occupation	29a. How long	29b. Telephone	$	
30. Retirement Income: ☐ Military $ ______ ☐ Other $ ______			$	
31. V.A. Compensation			$	
32. Social Security ☐ Veteran $ ______ ☐ Spouse $ ______			$	
33. Child Support Received			$	
34. Interest/Dividends ☐ Savings ☐ Stocks/Bonds ☐ Notes/Trust Deeds ☐ Others			$	
35. Income from Real Estate: List each property. Attach additional sheet if necessary.			$	

Address of Property Indicate S if sold PS if pending sale	Status	Type of Property	Value	Gross Income	Loan Payment	Taxes & Expense	Net Monthly Income	
1		Personal Residence	$		$	$		
2			$	$	$	$	$	
3			$	$	$	$	$	

36. TOTAL MONTHLY INCOME FROM ALL SOURCES $

37. If not on current job for more than 1 year, list previous employment. Attach additional sheet if necessary.
V – Veterans S – Spouse

V/S	Previous Employment/School	City	Occupation	Gross Monthly Salary	Date From	Date To
				$		

A–1 (9/84) LOAN APPLICATION (HOME)

ASSETS:	SUB-TOTALS	OFFICE USE ONLY
38. Cash on hand (Funds under personal possession and not bank accounts)	$	
39. Checking Account(s) @ ______ Branch		
40. Savings Account @ ______ Branch		
Account @ ______ Branch		
41. Stocks and Bonds (Describe) ______		
42. Total Equity in Real Estate: Market Value $ ______ Less Loan Balance ______		
43. Trust Deed(s) owned (Current Value) ______		
44. Earnest Money or Deposit on this Property (Not included in other listed assets) ______		
45. Other Liquid Assets ______		
46. Additional Funds to complete this purchase ☐ Gift ☐ Personal Loan ☐ Secondary Financing		
SUB-TOTAL	$	
47. Automobiles: Year ______ Make ______		
Year ______ Make ______		
48. Household Furnishing and Personal Properties ______		
49. Other Assets: ______		
TOTAL	$	

LIABILITIES: PLEASE FURNISH NAMES, ADDRESS, AND ACCOUNT NUMBERS ON ALL LOANS AND ACCOUNTS.

	ACCOUNT NUMBER	MONTHLY PAYMENT	BALANCE OWED	OFFICE USE ONLY
50. Loans on Real Estate				
1. ______		$	$	
2. ______				
3. ______				
51. Automobile ______				
______				
52. Furniture ______				
53. Money Owed to Relatives ______				

54. Notes Payable (Unsecured) ____________

55. Personal Loans ____________

56. Alimony—Child Support ____________

57. Other (Including credit cards) ____________

TOTAL

58. Present Monthly Housing Expense for Residence:

Rent/Payment $ ________ Utilities $ ________ Taxes & Insurance $ ________ Total $ ________

59. Are there suits or judgments against you? (If yes, attach explanation) ☐ Yes ☐ No

60. Have you ever filed for bankruptcy? (If yes, submit schedule of debts or discharge of bankruptcy and attach explanation) ☐ Yes ☐ No

61. Names and Addresses of credit references (List accounts other than above) Account Number Open/Closed

1. ____________

2. ____________

3. ____________

PLEASE READ CAREFULLY AND SIGN

I hereby certify under penalty of perjury that all information contained in this application is given for the purpose of obtaining a Cal-Vet loan and is true, correct, and complete. I authorize the Department of Veterans Affairs and its agents, employees and officers to conduct credit investigations and to obtain information from and provide information to credit agencies and others pertaining to my credit and financial condition, except that information contained in this application may not be provided to credit agencies and others more than 120 days after the date this application is filed. I also understand and acknowledge that the Cal-Vet loan contract will provide for a flexible interest rate, which may result in periodic decreases or increases in the monthly installment.

________________ Date

________________ Signature of Veteran Applicant

________________ Signature of Spouse

DEPARTMENT OF VETERANS AFFAIRS
OF THE STATE OF CALIFORNIA

PURCHASER'S AFFIDAVIT
(Cal-Vet Loan Contract)

—As applicant(s) for a Cal-Vet loan, you must read this Affidavit carefully, including the Instructions printed on the reverse side, fill it in (print in ink or type), and sign it under oath before a Notary Public. By doing so, you promise that all the statements in it are true.

State of California)
) ss.
County of ______________)

YOU PROMISE THAT:

1. You intend to use the home you are purchasing as your principal residence within 60 days after the Cal-Vet loan is made.

2. You intend to use the home as your principal residence until the Cal-Vet loan is paid in full.

3. You haven't rented or sold the home to someone else and you don't intend to do so.

4. You won't allow the Cal-Vet loan to be assumed by someone else without the prior written consent of the Department of Veterans Affairs.

5. You won't use the home in a business or trade, or for any other commercial purpose.

6. You won't use the home as an investment property.

7. You won't use the home as a recreational property, or as a vacation or "weekend" home.

8. You don't have (and haven't had) existing financing for the home (whether paid in full or not), except for a construction loan or other temporary initial financing with a term of 24 months or less.

9. You haven't made and won't make an agreement to purchase the Department's bonds, directly or indirectly, in an amount related to the amount of the Cal-Vet loan.

10. The lot being purchased reasonably maintains the basic liveability of the home, and will not provide a source of income to you.

11. The home is ____ is not ____ permanently attached to the lot.

12. You have ____ haven't ____ had a present ownership interest in a home used as your principal residence during the three years before the Cal-Vet loan is made. (See Instructions.)

13. You have filed ____ have not filed and were not required to file ____ federal income tax returns for the last three years. (See Instructions.)

14. Your name is ______________________________. Your spouse's name is ______________________________. The home is located at ______________________________ ______________________________.

15. The "acquisition cost" of the home is $ ____________________. (See Instructions.)

16. Your "annualized gross income" is $ ____________________. (See Instructions.)

Signed: ______________________________

Signed: ______________________________

Subscribed and sworn to before me
this ____ day of __________,

(SEAL)

____
Notary Public in and for said
State and County

AP–2 (10/85)

INSTRUCTIONS FOR PURCHASER'S AFFIDAVIT

1. You need to determine whether you and/or your spouse had a ''present ownership interest'' in any home used as your principal residence during the three years before the Cal-Vet loan is made.[1]

''Present ownership interest'' includes outright ownership by you, and the following types of interests:

a. Joint tenancy, tenancy in common, tenancy by the entirety, or community property.

b. Interest of a tenant-shareholder in a stock cooperative or similar interest.

c. A Life Estate.

d. Interest under an installment land contract granting current possession of the home, with legal title to follow at a later date.

e. A lease with an option to purchase for a nominal amount.

f. Any of the above interests, including outright ownership, held in trust for you.

''Present ownership interest'' does not include the following types of interests:

a. A remainder interest (an interest you would have only upon the termination of an interest granted by someone else to another person).

b. A lease without an option to purchase, or a lease with an option to purchase at fair market value.

c. A mere expectancy to inherit an interest.

d. The interest of a purchaser under a ''marketing'' contract (any interest you might have had upon the signing of a real estate deposit receipt or similar contract, where you did not complete the purchase).

e. An interest in other than a principal residence during the previous three years.

2. You need to calculate and state the "acquisition cost" of the home to you.

"Acquisition cost" includes the following types of costs:

a. All amounts paid, in cash or in any other way, as the purchase price of the home.

b. If the home is incomplete, "acquisition cost" also includes the reasonable cost of completing the home.

c. Any additional amounts paid for fixtures, such as light fixtures, curtain rods, wall-to-wall carpeting and similar items.

"Acquisition cost" does not include these types of costs:

a. Settlement costs, such as title and transfer costs, title insurance premiums, and survey fees.

b. Financing costs, such as credit reference fees, legal fees, appraisal expenses and "points" which are paid by you.

c. The value of work done by you or your family in completing the home.

d. The cost of the lot upon which you are building your home, if you have owned the lot for at least two years before construction begins.

3. You need to calculate and state your "annualized gross income," which is your "gross monthly income" multiplied by 12. Gross monthly income includes:

a. Gross pay, overtime pay, bonuses, and income from part-time employment.

b. Pension checks and Veterans Administration compensation.

c. Dividends, interest, net rental income, and any additional income from investments.

d. Other income (such as alimony and child support if you choose to disclose such income).

[1]If you haven't had a present ownership interest in a home in the last three years, you must provide copies of your federal income tax returns for each of those years, or you must state that you haven't filed and were not required to file such returns.

DEPARTMENT OF VETERANS AFFAIRS
OF THE STATE OF CALIFORNIA

SELLER'S AFFIDAVIT

(Cal-Vet Loan Contract)

–As the seller(s) of a home to be financed with a Cal-Vet loan, you must read this Affidavit carefully, including the Instructions printed on the reverse side, fill it in (print in ink or type), and sign it under oath before a Notary Public. By doing so, you promise that all the statements in it are true.

State of California)
) ss.
County of ______________________)

YOU PROMISE THAT:

1. You are the seller(s) of the home located at ______________________ (Address), which is being purchased with Cal-Vet financing.

2. You are selling the home to ______________________ (Veteran's Name) and ______________________ (Veteran's Spouse)

3. The "acquisition cost" of the home is $ ______________. (See Instructions.)

Signed: ______________________________

Signed: ______________________________

Subscribed and sworn to before me
this ______ day of ____________,
19 ______.

(SEAL)

____
Notary Public in and for said
State and County

AP–3 (10/85)

INSTRUCTIONS FOR SELLER'S AFFIDAVIT

1. You need to calculate and state the "acquisition cost" of the home to the veteran.

"Acquisition cost" includes the following types of costs:

a. All amounts paid, in cash or in any other way, as the purchase price of the home.

b. If the home is incomplete, "acquisition cost" also includes the reasonable cost of completing the home.

c. Any additional amounts paid for fixtures, such as light fixtures, curtain rods, wall-to-wall carpeting and similar items.

"Acquisition cost" does not include these types of costs:

a. Settlement costs, such as title and transfer costs, title insurance premiums, and survey fees.

b. Financing costs, such as credit reference fees, legal fees, appraisal expenses and "points" which are paid by the veteran.

c. The value of work done by the veteran and family in completing the home.

d. The cost of the lot upon which the veteran is building the home, if the veteran and/or spouse owned the lot at least two years before construction.

The property may be rented out if the Department determines there is good cause. In no case may the property be rented for more than a total of four years during the life of the loan. Transfer, assignment, encumbrance or rental of the property requires the consent of the Department.

If a veteran must move out of the property, he or she may qualify to have the loan transferred to another property. There are established criteria which must be met and the veteran should contact a Cal-Vet representative to be sure of proper procedures.

Eligibility.

Both state and federal laws determine eligibility for Cal-Vet loans. The following are the requirements for eligibility:

1) the veteran must have been born in California or be able to prove bona fide residency at the time of entry into active duty;
2) the veteran must have been released from active duty under honorable conditions;
3) the veteran must have served at least 90 days on active duty (unless discharged because of a service-connected disability). At least one day of active duty must have been during one of the following wartime periods:

   - Vietnam period: August 5, 1964 - May 7, 1975
   - Korean hostilities: June 27, 1950 - January 31, 1955
   - World War II: December 7, 1941 - December 31, 1946
   - World War I: April 6, 1917 - November 11, 1918

   A veteran who was awarded a qualifying Campaign Medal or Armed Forces Expeditionary Medal for services during a peacetime period may also be eligible. Military service solely for the purpose of processing, physical examination or training does not qualify.
4) the veteran must not have accepted a bonus or benefit from another state for the qualifying period of military service.

Loan fees.

There is a **loan origination fee** charged on all Cal-Vet loans. At the time of this writing, the amount of the fee is $430, $25 to be paid at the time of application and the remainder to be collected at the close of escrow. Property taxes and insurance are also collected at closing.

Loan terms.

Qualifying properties, the **maximum loan amounts** and **loan-to-value ratios** are as follows:

Qualifying Properties	Maximum Loan Amount
Single-family home, including condos and townhouses	$125,000
Mobile homes on land owned by the borrower	90,000
Mobile homes in approved parks	70,000
Working farms	200,000

Homes equipped with solar energy heating devices may be approved for up to an additional $5,000 loan amount.

When the purchase price is $35,000 or less, the loan may be **97%** of the appraised value or purchase price, whichever is less. Where the purchase price is greater than $35,000, the loan may be **95%** of the appraised value or purchase price, whichever is less. For farm properties, the loan amount cannot be more than **95%** of the Department's appraised value which is based on net income from agricultural production.

The **interest rate** on a Cal-Vet loan used to vary over the life of the loan. This is no longer true. Now a straight 8% interest rate is charged on all types of Cal-Vet loans.

If the loan is prepaid (in whole or in part) within five years of its origination date, the borrower will have to pay a **prepayment** penalty equal to six months interest on the amount prepaid in excess of 20% of the original loan amount.

Chapter Eleven

Qualifying Standards

Pre-qualifying the Buyer.

Pre-qualifying the buyer is one of the first steps the real estate agent should take when approached by a potential buyer. The pre-qualification process enables the agent to determine the type and amount of loan that the buyer can hope to qualify for. Armed with this information, the buyer can then choose housing that is affordable.

The pre-qualifying process is remarkably similar to the lender's underwriting procedure. The agent sits down with the buyer, gathers the necessary income and expense data and uses the lender's underwriting standards to calculate the loan amount. A sample of the kind of form that is useful for this process is shown on the following page.

Before the agent attempts to pre-qualify the buyer, he or she should have a firm grasp of the pertinent underwriting standards, where they come from and why they exist. If the buyer will be seeking a VA-guaranteed or FHA-insured loan, the underwriting standards will be those of the appropriate government agency. If the buyer wants conventional financing, the standards used will be those of the secondary market.

The Secondary Market.

In the past, when a lender made a loan to a borrower, that lender kept the loan "**in portfolio**." This meant that the loan served as the lender's own investment: the profit or loss created by the loan was the lender's. The lender could determine its own underwriting standards since the lender was the one who would suffer a loss if the loan was foreclosed.

MGIC

Prequalification Worksheet

(Does not constitute a loan application or loan approval)

I. MONTHLY INCOME AND OBLIGATIONS ANALYSIS

Gross Monthly Income Calculation

Borrower Gross Monthly Income		$__________	
Co-Borrower(s) Gross Monthly Income	+	$__________	
1. Total Gross Monthly Income	=	$__________	**(1)**

Monthly Installment Debts

Include all debts for which 10 or more payments are remaining (i.e., car loans, mortgage loans and credit cards).

Creditor		Monthly Payments	
____________________		$__________	
____________________	+	$__________	
____________________	+	$__________	
____________________	+	$__________	
____________________	+	$__________	
2. Total Monthly Installment Payments	=	$__________	**(2)**

Housing Debt Test

3. Estimated Monthly Housing Expense

- Multiply line 1, *Income* × housing debt ratio
- $__________ × __________% $__________ **(3)**

  Line (1) (Ratio)

Total Debt Test

4. Estimated Total Monthly Expenses

- Multiply line 1, *Income* × total monthly debt ratio
- $__________ × __________% $__________ **(4)**

  Line (1) (Ratio)

Available Income Test

5. Income Available for Monthly Housing Expense

- Subtract line 2, *Total Monthly Installment Payments* from line 4, *Estimated Total Monthly Expenses*
- $__________ – __________ $__________ **(5)**

  Line (4) (Line 2)

Maximum P&I Payment Calculation

Indicate the smaller of Line 3 or Line 5		$__________	
Subtract:			
Estimated Monthly Property Taxes	–	$__________	
Estimated Monthly Hazard Insurance	–	$__________	
Other* (________________)	–	$__________	
6. Maximum P&I Payment	=	$__________	**(6)**

*For example, homeowners association dues, but excluding mortgage insurance. Typical mortgage insurance premium is assumed in the affordability factors for 95% and 90% LTVs.

On the other hand, a real estate loan can be bought and sold, just like other investments (e.g., stocks and bonds). Presently, most lenders sell their residential real estate loans to other investors. In fact, very few residential loans are kept "in portfolio." The investors who buy these real estate loans are referred to as the **secondary market**. Since these investors are the ones who will be bearing the risks of mortgage default, they are also the ones who set the underwriting criteria. If a lender wants to make a loan it can sell to an investor, it must make that loan according to the investor's standards.

A major reason lenders sell their real estate loans is to keep their assets more liquid. By selling the loans that they have already made, lenders will once again have funds that can be used to make new loans to new customers at current interest rates. Thus, the secondary market serves a vital function: it **promotes investments** in real estate by making funds available for real estate loans. The secondary market also provides a measure of **stability** in the local (or primary) real estate market by moderating the adverse effects of real estate cycles. For example, if a local community is experiencing a scarcity of money, local lenders can sell their loans to investors in a money-surplus region. In this way, funds are shifted from the money-surplus area to the money-shortage area and the effects of the local cycle are minimized.

The secondary market is able to function in this manner because of **standard, nation-wide underwriting criteria**. Each mortgage issued by each individual lender must conform to the secondary market's underwriting standards or it will not be purchased on the secondary market.

The national secondary market consists of both private investors and government agencies. Private investors do not have nearly the same influence on real estate markets as do the government agencies. Because government agencies make up the bulk of the secondary market, we will concentrate our attention on them. These three agencies are the **Federal National Mortgage Association (FNMA)**, the **Government National Mortgage Association (GNMA)**, and the **Federal Home Loan Mortgage Association (FHLMC)**. Since the vast majority of the lenders sell most of their residential mortgages to one or more of these agencies, they strictly follow the underwriting guidelines of these agencies when making their loans.

Federal National Mortgage Association. The Federal National Mortgage Association (FNMA, or "Fannie Mae") was created in 1938 as the first government-sponsored secondary market institution. The specific purpose of FNMA was to provide a secondary market for FHA-insured and VA-guaranteed mortgages. In 1968, FNMA became a public corporation although it remains government sponsored. FNMA's role was expanded in 1970 when federal legislation permitted FNMA to purchase conventional mortgages as well as FHA and VA mortgages. FNMA funds its operations by selling securities (debt instruments) which are backed by its pool of mortgages to the public.

Government National Mortgage Association. The Government National Mortgage Association (GNMA, or "Ginnie Mae") was created in 1968. It is a government-owned corporation which was established to replace FNMA when FNMA became privately owned. GNMA operates under the Department of Housing and Urban Development. It issues guarantees of FHA, VA and FmHA mortgages through its mortgage-backed securities program. Because GNMA guarantees the timely payments of both interest and principal on these mortgages, it enables the lenders/investors to pledge the mortgages as collateral for securities. GNMA also helps with the financing of urban renewal and housing projects by providing below market rates to low-income families.

Federal Home Loan Mortgage Association. The Federal Home Loan Mortgage Association (FHLMC, or "Freddie Mac") was created in 1970 to aid savings and loan associations. It is a non-profit, federally chartered institution controlled by the Federal Home Loan Bank System. FHLMC helps S&L's acquire additional funds for mortgage lending by purchasing the mortgages they have already made. FHLMC is authorized to deal in FHA, VA and conventional mortgages. Unlike FNMA, which emphasizes the purchase of mortgage loans, FHLMC also actively sells mortgage loans from its portfolio. The funds which are generated by the sale of the loans are used to purchase more mortgages.

Qualifying Standards.

The underwriting standards of the secondary agencies include guidelines as to adequacy of the amount of income, the types of income that can be considered stable, and standards for acceptable employment and credit history. The agent must use these same criteria to prequalify his or her buyer, so it is important to be well versed with these standards.

The standards of FNMA tend to be slightly stricter than those of FHLMC, so most lenders use FNMA's standards. By so doing, they are free to sell their loan packages to either secondary agency. If a lender is making a government insured or guaranteed loan, it will use the appropriate government underwriting standards.*

Before turning our attention to these standards, it should be noted that underwriting is said to be an art, not a science. Underwriting is not cut and dried. While there are certain strict underwriting criteria, such as the maximum expense-to-income ratios (and even these are sometimes flexible), there are other standards which may be less fixed. To a large extent, lenders underwrite on a case-by-case basis within the basic framework given to them by the secondary agencies. Therefore, the agent should always let the lenders be the final judge of creditworthiness, as particular lenders may show leniency towards certain borrowers. It is also wise to be willing to present a marginal loan application to more than one lender, as different lenders will view the loan package in different ways.

---

*GNMA guarantees FHA and VA loans and the underwriting standards of these government agencies are automatically acceptable to GNMA.

Conventional Underwriting Guidelines*

We will address the underwriting standards for conventional loans before turning our attention to government loans.

Secondary market investors are only willing to buy mortgages that are reasonably likely to be repaid in a timely manner through regular monthly payments. No one wants to invest in a mortgage that is a poor risk or whose terms are so burdensome to the borrower that default and foreclosure are likely. Thus, the secondary market has uniform guidelines designed to ensure the purchase of **investment quality** loans, that is, loans to borrowers "from whom timely repayment of the debt can be expected and secured by real property which provides sufficient value to recover the lender's investment if a loan default occurs."

To determine whether a loan will be "investment quality," underwriters require extensive information on both the **borrower** and the **property**. Can the borrower be expected to make timely repayments on the loan? Does the borrower's income reflect an ability to make the payments and does the borrower's credit history reflect a desire to do so? The underwriter is also concerned about the property — will the property be worth enough so that a foreclosure sale would generate enough money to pay off the loan and selling expenses? In this section, we will examine the underwriting standards as they apply to the borrower. For a discussion of some of the standards that apply to the property, see Chapter 5, Competitive Market Analysis.

---

*NOTE: Underwriting guidelines are different for borrowers who intend to occupy the property as a primary residence as opposed to those who intend to use the property for investment or income purposes. In this discussion, we will focus on the guidelines applicable to those who intend to occupy the property. On the loan application there is a place for the borrower to indicate whether the property is for primary residence purposes or not. The borrower should note that improper disclosure is a federal crime punishable by fine or imprisonment or both.

Loan application. The loan application is designed to provide all the pertinent data on the borrower. A FHLMC/FNMA loan application form is shown on the following pages. The application should be completed in as much detail as possible.

Income, net worth, credit history. There are three elements the underwriter will examine in regards to the borrower: income, net worth and credit history. Each of these elements is important in gauging the creditworthiness of the borrower. For example, if the borrower has an excellent credit record and moderate net worth, but does not have enough income to make the monthly mortgage payment, the loan will be rejected. On the other hand, even though the borrower has more than sufficient income and a substantial net worth, if his or her credit report shows a long history of bankruptcies, suits for nonpayment of debts, or previous mortgage defaults, it is highly unlikely that any lender would agree to make the loan. All three elements interact to present a reasonably complete picture of the borrower's creditworthiness.

Income.

We will first take a look at the underwriting standards pertaining to the borrower's income.

The underwriter wants to be certain that the borrower's income is adequate to meet the monthly mortgage payments. However, before the underwriter can judge the adequacy of the income, he or she must decide which types of income should be included in the analysis. It would be self-defeating to take short-term or unreliable income into consideration when deciding whether the borrower's income is sufficient to meet a long-term mortgage obligation. The underwriter must inquire into whether a particular type of income is **dependable** and **likely to continue** for a significant period of time.

For example, suppose Hawthorne is applying for a 30-year mortgage. Currently, Hawthorne is receiving the following income: a salary from full-time employment, child support for a sixteen-year old son, payments from a trust fund set up by Hawthorne's mother which will continue for another year and a half, and monthly rental payments from a

Residential Loan Application

MGIC

MORTGAGE APPLIED FOR	☐ Conventional ☐ FHA ☐ VA ☐ ____	Amount $	Interest Rate %	No. of Months	Monthly Payment Principal & Interest $	Escrow/Impounds (to be collected monthly) ☐ Taxes ☐ Hazard Ins. ☐ Mtg. Ins. ☐ ____

Prepayment Option

Subject Property

Property Street Address	City	County	State	Zip	No. Units

Legal Description (Attach description if necessary)	Year Built

Purpose of Loan: ☐ Purchase ☐ Construction-Permanent ☐ Construction ☐ Refinance ☐ Other (Explain)

Complete this line if Construction-Permanent or Construction Loan	Lot Value Data / Year Acquired	Original Cost $	Present Value (a) $	Cost of Imps. (b) $	Total (a + b) $	ENTER TOTAL AS PURCHASE PRICE IN DETAILS OF PURCHASE.

Complete this line if a Refinance Loan			Purpose of Refinance	Describe Improvements [ ] made [ ] to be made
Year Acquired	Original Cost $	Amt. Existing Liens $		Cost: $

Title Will Be Held In What Name(s)	Manner In Which Title Will Be Held

Source of Down Payment and Settlement Charges

This application is designed to be completed by the borrower(s) with the lender's assistance. The Co-Borrower Section and all other Co-Borrower questions must be completed and the appropriate box(es) checked if ☐ another person will be jointly obligated with the Borrower on the loan, or ☐ the Borrower is relying on income from alimony, child support or separate maintenance or on the income or assets of another person as a basis for repayment of the loan, or ☐ the Borrower is married and resides, or the property is located, in a community property state.

Borrower	Co-Borrower
Name / Age / School Yrs ____	Name / Age / School Yrs ____
Present Address No. Years ____ ☐ Own ☐ Rent	Present Address No. Years ____ ☐ Own ☐ Rent
Street ____	Street ____
City/State/Zip ____	City/State/Zip ____
Former address if less than 2 years at present address	Former address if less than 2 years at present address
Street ____	Street ____
City/State/Zip ____	City/State/Zip ____
Years at former address ☐ Own ☐ Rent	Years at former address ☐ Own ☐ Rent
Marital Status ☐ Married ☐ Separated ☐ Unmarried (incl. single, divorced, widowed) — DEPENDENTS OTHER THAN LISTED BY CO-BORROWER: NO / AGES	Marital Status ☐ Married ☐ Separated ☐ Unmarried (incl. single, divorced, widowed) — DEPENDENTS OTHER THAN LISTED BY BORROWER: NO / AGES
Name and Address of Employer — Years employed in this line of work or profession? ____ years; Years on this job ____; ☐ Self Employed*	Name and Address of Employer — Years employed in this line of work or profession? ____ years; Years on this job ____; ☐ Self Employed*
Position/Title — Type of Business	Position/Title — Type of Business

Social Security Number ***	Home Phone	Business Phone	Social Security Number ***	Home Phone	Business Phone

Gross Monthly Income				Monthly Housing Expense**			Details of Purchase	
Item	Borrower	Co-Borrower	Total	Rent	$ PRESENT	PROPOSED	Do Not Complete If Refinance	
Base Empl. Income	$	$	$	First Mortgage (P&I)		$	a. Purchase Price	$
Overtime				Other Financing (P&I)			b. Total Closing Costs (Est.)	
Bonuses				Hazard Insurance			c. Prepaid Escrows (Est.)	
Commissions				Real Estate Taxes			d. Total (a + b + c)	$
Dividends/Interest				Mortgage Insurance			e. Amount This Mortgage	( )
Net Rental Income				Homeowner Assn. Dues			f. Other Financing	( )
Other† (Before completing, see notice under Describe Other Income below.)				Other:			g. Other Equity	( )
				Total Monthly Pmt.	$	$	h. Amount of Cash Deposit	( )
				Utilities			i. Closing Costs Paid by Seller	( )
Total	$	$	$	Total	$	$	j. Cash Reqd. For Closing (Est.)	$

Describe Other Income

B—Borrower C—Co-Borrower	NOTICE: † Alimony, child support, or separate maintenance income need not be revealed if the Borrower or Co-Borrower does not choose to have it considered as a basis for repaying this loan.	Monthly Amount
		$

If Employed In Current Position For Less Than Two Years, Complete the Following

B/C	Previous Employer/School	City/State	Type of Business	Position/Title	Dates From/To	Monthly Income
						$

These Questions Apply To Both Borrower and Co-Borrower

If a "yes" answer is given to a question in this column, please explain on an attached sheet.	Borrower Yes or No	Co-Borrower Yes or No
Are there any outstanding judgments against you?		
Have you been declared bankrupt within the past 7 years?		
Have you had property foreclosed upon or given title or deed in lieu thereof in the last 7 years?		
Are you a party to a law suit?		
Are you obligated to pay alimony, child support, or separate maintenance?		
Is any part of the down payment borrowed?		
Are you a co-maker or endorser on a note?		

	Borrower Yes or No	Co-Borrower Yes or No
Are you a U.S. citizen?		
If "no," are you a resident alien?		
If "no," are you a non-resident alien?		

Explain Other Financing or Other Equity (if any). ________

*FHLMC/FNMA require business credit report, signed Federal Income Tax returns for last two years; and, if available, audited Profit and Loss Statement plus balance sheet for same period.
**All Present Monthly Housing Expenses of Borrower and Co-Borrower should be listed on a combined basis.
***Optional for FHLMC
FHLMC 65 Rev. 10/86

Fannie Mae Form 1003 Rev. 10/86

Statement of Assets and Liabilities

This Statement and any applicable supporting schedules may be completed jointly by both married and unmarried co-borrowers if their assets and liabilities are sufficiently joined so that the Statement can be meaningfully and fairly presented on a combined basis; otherwise separate Statements and Schedules are required (FHLMC 65A/FNMA 1003A). If the co-borrower section was completed about a spouse, this statement and supporting schedules must be completed about that spouse also.

☐ Completed Jointly ☐ Not Completed Jointly

Assets

Description	Cash or Market Value
Cash Deposit Toward Purchase Held By	$
Checking and Savings Accounts (Show Names of Institutions/Account Numbers) Bank, S & L or Credit Union	
Addr.	
City	
Acct. No.	
Bank, S & L or Credit Union	
Addr.	
City	
Acct. No.	
Bank, S & L or Credit Union	
Addr.	
City	
Acct. No.	
Stocks and Bonds (No./Description)	
Life Insurance Net Cash Value Face Amount $	
Subtotal Liquid Assets	
Real Estate Owned (Enter Market Value from Schedule of Real Estate Owned)	
Vested Interest in Retirement Fund	
Net worth of Business Owned (ATTACH FINANCIAL STATEMENT)	
Automobiles Owned (Make and Year)	
Furniture and Personal Property	
Other Assets (Itemize)	

Liabilities and Pledged Assets

Indicate by (*) those liabilities or pledged assets which will be satisfied upon sale of real estate owned or upon refinancing of subject property

Creditors' Name, Address and Account Number		Acct. Name if Not Borrower's	Mo. Pmt. and Mos. Left to Pay	Unpaid Balance
Installment Debts (Include "revolving" charge accounts) Co.	Acct. No.		$ Pmt./Mos. /	$
Addr.				
City				
Co.	Acct. No.		/	
Addr.				
City				
Co.	Acct. No.		/	
Addr.				
City				
Co.	Acct. No.		/	
Addr.				
City				
Co.	Acct. No.		/	
Addr.				
City				
Other Debts including Stock Pledges			/	
Real Estate Loans Co.	Acct. No.		X	
Addr.				
City				
Co.	Acct. No.		X	
Addr.				
City				
Automobile Loans Co.	Acct. No.		/	
Addr.				
City				
Co.	Acct. No.		/	
City				
Alimony/Child Support/Separate Maintenance Payments Owed to			/	X

		Total Monthly Payments	$		
Total Assets	A $	Net Worth (A minus B) $		Total Liabilities	B $

SCHEDULE OF REAL ESTATE OWNED (If Additional Properties Owned Attach Separate Schedule)

Address of Property (Indicate S if Sold, PS if Pending Sale or R if Rental being held for income)	⇨	Type of Property	Present Market Value	Amount of Mortgages & Liens	Gross Rental Income	Mortgage Payments	Taxes, Ins. Maintenance and Misc.	Net Rental Income
			$	$	$	$	$	$
		TOTALS →	$	$	$	$	$	$

List Previous Credit References

⇨ B–Borrower C–Co-Borrower	Creditor's Name and Address	Account Number	Purpose	Highest Balance	Date Paid
				$	

List any additional names under which credit has previously been received ______

AGREEMENT: The undersigned applies for the loan indicated in this application to be secured by a first mortgage or deed of trust on the property described herein, and represents that the property will not be used for any illegal or restricted purpose, and that all statements made in this application are true and are made for the purpose of obtaining the loan. Verification may be obtained from any source named in this application. The original or a copy of this application will be retained by the lender, even if the loan is not granted. The undersigned ☐ intend or ☐ do not intend to occupy the property as their primary residence.

I/we fully understand that it is a federal crime punishable by fine or imprisonment, or both, to knowingly make any false statements concerning any of the above facts as applicable under the provisions of Title 18, United States Code, Section 1014.

______ Date ______ ______ Date ______
Borrower's Signature Co-Borrower's Signature

Information for Government Monitoring Purposes

The following information is requested by the Federal Government for certain types of loans related to a dwelling, in order to monitor the lender's compliance with equal credit opportunity and fair housing laws. You are not required to furnish this information, but are encouraged to do so. The law provides that a lender may neither discriminate on the basis of this information, nor on whether you choose to furnish it. However, if you choose not to furnish it, under Federal regulations this lender is required to note race and sex on the basis of visual observation or surname. If you do not wish to furnish the above information, please check the box below. (Lender must review the above material to assure that the disclosures satisfy all requirements to which the Lender is subject under applicable state law for the particular type of loan applied for.)

Borrower: ☐ I do not wish to furnish this information
Race/National Origin:
☐ American Indian, Alaskan Native ☐ Asian, Pacific Islander
☐ Black ☐ Hispanic ☐ White
☐ Other (specify): ______
Sex: ☐ Female ☐ Male

Co-Borrower: ☐ I do not wish to furnish this information
Race/National Origin:
☐ American Indian, Alaskan Native ☐ Asian, Pacific Islander
☐ Black ☐ Hispanic ☐ White
☐ Other (specify): ______
Sex: ☐ Female ☐ Male

To Be Completed by Interviewer

This application was taken by:
☐ face to face interview
☐ by mail
☐ by telephone

______ Interviewer
______ Name of Interviewer's Employer
______ Interviewer's Phone Number
______ Address of Interviewer's Employer

FHLMC Form 65 Rev. 10/86 **REVERSE** Fannie Mae Form 1003 Rev. 10/86

Form #71-3973 (10/86)

roommate. It is clear that, other things remaining the same, Hawthorne will have substantially less income in two years: the child support and trust income will both come to an end and continuation of the rental payments from the roommate is difficult to predict. As the underwriter wants to be sure the borrower will have enough income to make the mortgage payments over the entire life of the loan, not just for the next two years, only those stable, reliable sources of income will be taken into account. Therefore, the underwriter must discount the child support, trust payments and rental payments and take into consideration only the salary from the full-time employment.

Stable income and secondary income.

Stable monthly income is the borrower's gross monthly income from primary employment plus any secondary income from acceptable sources. Acceptable secondary income includes such items as bonuses, commissions, or part-time employment. The following are considered to be acceptable sources of secondary income:

Bonuses, commissions, part-time employment. These three items can be considered part of stable monthly income only if they are typical for the borrower's occupation and likely to continue. They must have been received for the past two years and must be evidenced by the borrower's previous two W-2 forms or federal income tax statements.

Overtime. Overtime may also be considered part of stable monthly income only if it has been a part of the borrower's overall earning pattern for the preceding two years. Overtime is considered to be less likely to continue on a regular basis than commissions, bonuses or part-time employment and is thus often given less weight.

Alimony, child-support or separate maintenance. Income from alimony, child support or separate maintenance does not have to be revealed unless the borrower wants it to be. However, if a borrower does choose to disclose these sources of income, the underwriter will only consider them if they are likely to continue. Some of the factors examined include whether the payments are received pursuant to a written agreement or court decree; the length of time the payments have been received; the regularity of receipt; the availability of procedures to compel payment; whether full or partial payments have been made in the past; the age of any children (for child support payments only); and the creditworthiness of the payor.

The underwriter will need a copy of the divorce decree to establish the amount and enforceability of the payments. Income from child support payments becomes less and less durable the closer the child is to the age of 18. Most underwriters will refuse to consider child support payments as part of stable monthly income when the child is between 16 and 17 years of age.

Self-employment income. To establish the stability of a borrower's own business, profit and loss statements, balance sheets, and the income statements of the business for the previous two fiscal years should be submitted. If the business is less than two years old, qualification based on income from self-employment becomes much more difficult. In these circumstances, a more subjective review is required, including consideration of the borrower's training and experience in the profession, the type of the business, the business' working capital, location, number of employees, etc.

In addition, the borrower must submit copies of his or her own Federal Income Tax Returns, including appropriate schedules, for the previous two years.

If the borrower is a major stockholder in a corporation (he or she owns 25% or more of the stock), then the lender will require three years of the corporation's tax returns to substantiate the quality of the income.

Retirement benefits, pension plans, social security benefits. These payments will be considered as stable income to the extent that they are likely to be consistently made.

Rental income. Income and debt on rental property owned by the borrower warrants special attention. The gross income, mortgage payments, taxes, and operating expenses of the property must be itemized and the net rental income determined. Then, before any net income is included in stable income, the underwriter considers the type of property involved. For example, if the property is multi-family or commercial, the underwriter will want to become familiar with the rental demand for that type of property in the area and the pattern of operating costs. Increasing vacancy rates, real estate taxes, and operating costs may eventually absorb any net income received from the property.

If the subject property of the loan application is rental property, the borrower's income must be adequate to carry all of the borrower's personal expenses (housing, installment debt and so forth) as well as the monthly housing expenses of the rental property. An underwriter will generally recognize 75% of the proposed gross monthly rental income on a one-unit property when determining whether income is adequate to meet these needs. On a 2-4 unit property, 75% of the gross monthly rental income from the unit(s) not occupied by the borrower will be recognized. A Rental Income and Expense Analysis form is shown on the next page.

Unacceptable Income.

The following are unacceptable sources of secondary income:

Unemployment, welfare. Unemployment and welfare payments are considered to be temporary only and may not be included as stable monthly income.

Income from other family members. Income from members of the family besides the head(s) of household (e.g., teenage children or elderly parents) is also considered to be temporary and unreliable. As such income could stop without notice, it may not be included in stable monthly income.

Car allowances. Car allowances received from employers may not be considered part of stable monthly income.

Rental of primary residence. Any income the borrower may receive from the rental of his or her personal residence (i.e., rental payments from a roommate) should not be considered as stable monthly income.

Freddie Mac

Federal
Home Loan
Mortgage
Corporation

Rental Income and Expense Analysis

For 1-4 family investment properties and all 2-4 family properties

Monthly Housing Expense for Subject Property

First Mortgage P&I	$ 1,250.00
Secondary Financing P&I	-0-
Hazard and or Flood Insurance Premium	45.00
Real Estate Taxes Special Assessments and DeMinimis PUD Assessments	110.00
Mortgage Insurance Premium	25.00
Dues (Homeowner Association charges)	-0-
Ground Rent or Other	-0-
Total of Proposed Monthly Housing Expense	$ 1,430.00

Insert the above items, as applicable, in completing the "Monthly Housing Expense" section of FHLMC Form 13SF

Monthly Rental Income

Gross Rental Income	$ 1,400.00
Adjustment Factor	75 %
Proposed Rental Income	$ 1,050.00

**Insert this figure in the "Describe Other Income" section of the Residential Loan Application (FHLMC Form 65) and include it in the "All Other Income" section of FHLMC Form 13SF*

Monthly Cash Flow

Proposed Rental Income	$ 1,050.00
Proposed Total Monthly Housing Expense	1,430.00
Difference (Indicate [–] if Negative Amount)	$ [380]

Identify source(s) of Monthly Rental Income Projection

☐ Economic Rent from Appraisal Report ☒ Signed Lease with Existing or New Tenant ☐ Other (specify)

Rental of second home. For those borrowers who are purchasing second homes, any income generated through rental of that property cannot be considered as part of stable monthly income. A second home is defined as "a one-family property usually owned by an individual and occupied by the borrower for some portion of the year and which is not subject to any time sharing ownership or agreement. The property must also be suitable for year-round occupancy, must be available for the borrower's exclusive use and enjoyment and . . . not (be) subject to any rental pools or agreements."

Employment history.

Another facet of the income analysis is the borrower's employment history. While earnings from primary employment are naturally accepted as part of stable monthly income, the underwriter will want to determine just how stable that income really is. Some questions an underwriter is likely to ask include how long has the borrower been at his or her present employment, what is the likelihood of that employment continuing, and what is the particular job skill of the borrower (i.e., how marketable is the borrower?).

A borrower who has a history of **job stability** or who has a job skill in continuous demand should receive favorable consideration. The same is true for those in positions where advancement is possible. Education or training that enhances job opportunities and earning capacity is also viewed in a positive light.

On the other hand, a borrower who changes jobs frequently should be prepared to explain the reasons for such changes. Job changes for advancement in the same profession will be viewed favorably if it can be shown that the borrower was successful in the job but outgrew the opportunities provided by that employer. Job changes are recognized as the norm in many lines of work. Frequent job changes without advancement or from one line of work to another are likely to cause the underwriter to view the borrower's income as unstable. However, there may be a reasonable explanation for this kind of job changing as well, such as racial or sexual discrimination, and if a consistent income pattern has been maintained, the borrower's income may still be considered stable. A consistent ability to meet financial obligations and unusual financial strength can also offset an unstable employment history.

Borrower's age. The age of the borrower may not be used as a criterion for rejection of a loan application as long as the applicant has reached the legal age of majority. If the borrower is close to retirement age or already retired, the underwriting will be based on the borrower's retirement income and any available financial reserves. In these circumstances, factors such as large downpayments and a demonstrated ability to manage financial affairs are given favorable consideration.

Verification of employment. Verifications of employment and income must be completed on the appropriate forms. A copy of a Verification of Employment form is shown on the following pages.

These verification forms must be signed by the borrower, mailed to the employer, completed, signed and returned by mail to the lender. It is important that these verification forms be properly filled out as the underwriter may recognize all, none, or a portion of the income depending upon the documentation provided. Inadequate documentation of employment is a basis for rejection of the loan application.

Since the latter half of 1987, lenders may allow borrowers to verify their own income. The borrower can substantiate his or her own employment and income by providing W-2 forms for the previous two years and payroll stubs or vouchers for the previous 30-day period. The pay stubs must identify the borrower, employer, and the borrower's gross earnings for both the current pay period and year to date. Lenders then confirm the employment and earnings with a phone call to the employer.

Income ratios.

Once the underwriter determines the amount of the borrower's stable monthly income (based on acceptable sources of income and the borrower's employment history), the underwriter determines whether that

INSTRUCTIONS TO LENDER:
1. FILL OUT PART I — REQUEST
2. HAVE APPLICANT(S) SIGN EACH COPY (No Carbon Signatures)
3. FORWARD 2 COPIES CARBON INTACT TO EMPLOYER

VMP MORTGAGE FORMS • (313)293-8100 • (800)521-7291

6432SE

VMP®-29 (8910)

Request for Verification of Employment

U.S. Department of Housing and Urban Development

Department of Veterans Affairs
USDA, Farmers Home Administration

HUD OMB Approval No. 2502-0059 (exp. 7/31/89)
VA OMB Approval No. 2900-0460
FmHA OMB Approval No. 0575-0009

Privacy Act Notice: This information is to be used by the agency collecting it in determining whether you qualify as a prospective mortgagor under its program. It will not be disclosed outside the agency except to your employer(s) for verification of employment and as required and permitted by law. You do not have to give us this information, but if you do not, your application for approval as a prospective mortgagor or borrower may be delayed or rejected. The information requested in this form is authorized by Title 38, USC, Chapter 37 (if VA); by 12 USC, Section 1701 et. seq. (if HUD/FHA); and Title 42 USC, 1471 et. seq., or 7 USC., 1921 et. seq. (if USDA, FmHA).

Public reporting burden for this collection of information is estimated to average **10 to 30 minutes** per response, including the time for reviewing instructions, searching existing data sources, gathering and maintaining the data needed, and completing and reviewing the collection of information.
Send comments regarding this burden estimate or any other aspect of this collection of information, including suggestions for reducing this burden, to the Reports Management Officer, Office of Information Policies and Systems, U.S. Department of Housing and Urban Development, Washington, D.C. 20410-3600 and to the Office of Management and Budget, Paperwork Reduction Project (2502-0059), Washington, D.C. 20503.

Lender or **Local Processing Agency (LPA):** Complete items 1 through 7. Have the applicant complete item 8. Forward the completed form directly to the employer named in item 1.

Employer: Complete either parts II and IV or parts III and IV. Return the form directly to the lender or local processing agency named in item 2 of part I.

Part I - Requested of:	Requested by:	
1. Name & Address of Employer	2. Name & Address of Lender or Local Processing Agent (LPA)	
3. Name & Address of Applicant	4. I certify that this verification has been sent directly to the employer and has not passed through the hands of the applicant or any other interested party. Signature of Lender, Official of LPA, or FmHA Loan Packager X	
I have applied for a mortgage loan or rehabilitation loan and stated that I am/was employed by you. My signature in the block below authorizes verification of my employment information.	5. Title	
8. Applicant's Signature & Employer Identification X	6. Date	7. HUD/FHA/CPD, VA or FmHA No.

Part II - Verification of Present Employment

10. Present Position	11. Date of Employment	12. Probability of Continued Employment	13a. Salaried ☐ Yes ☐ No Commission ☐ Yes ☐ No	13b. Is overtime/bonus likely to continue? Overtime: ☐ Yes ☐ No Bonus: ☐ Yes ☐ No

14. Current Base Pay ☐ Annual ☐ Monthly ☐ Weekly ☐ Hourly ☐ Other (specify):
$

15a. Base Earnings Year-to-Date $	Past Year $
b. Overtime Year-to-Date $	Past Year $
c. Commissions Year-to-Date $	Past Year $
d. Bonuses Year-to-Date $	Past Year $

16a. Monthly Taxable Pay (for Military Personnel Only)

Base Pay	Career C Pay	Pro Pay
$	$	$
Flight Pay $	Other (specify) $	

16b. Monthly Nontaxable Pay (for Military Personnel Only)

Quarters	VHA	Clothing
$	$	$
Rations $	Other (specify) $	

17. Remarks: If paid hourly, please indicate average hours worked each week during current and past year. AVERAGE HOURS WORKED PER WEEK: ________ HOURS

GROSS EARNINGS 19____, $________
GROSS EARNINGS 19____, $________
GROSS EARNINGS YTD 19____, $________

INDICATE FUTURE RAISES DUE:
DATE ________
AMOUNT ________
(Indicate per Year, Month Week, Hour ►) PER ________

IF THIS EMPLOYEE WAS OFF FOR ANY LENGTH OF TIME, PLEASE INDICATE DATES:
FROM ________
TO ________

Part III - Verification of Previous Employment

18. Salary/Wage at Termination: ☐ Yearly ☐ Monthly ☐ Weekly	Base Pay $	Overtime $	Commissions $	Bonus $

19. Dates of Employment
from: to:

20. Reasons for Leaving

21. Position Held

Part IV - Certification Federal statutes provide severe penalties for any fraud, intentional misrepresentation, or criminal connivance or conspiracy purposed to influence the issuance of any guaranty or insurance by the VA or USDA, FmHA Administrators, or the FHA Commissioner.

22. Signature	23. Title of Employer	24. Date
X		

Previous editions may be used until supply is exhausted

FmHA form **410-5** **VA** form **26-8497**

form **HUD-92004-G** (2/89)
ref. handbooks 4155.1, 4310.5

VMP-29 (8910) VMP MORTGAGE FORMS • (313)293-8100 • (800)521-7291

EMPLOYER - RETURN BOTH COMPLETED COPIES TO LENDER
LENDER-DETACH THIS COPY AND FILE FOR FOLLOW-UP

income is sufficient to meet the monthly mortgage payments. The underwriter does this through the use of ratios.

Two underwriting ratios are used to determine the adequacy of the borrower's income. The first is the ratio of the borrower's monthly housing expense to monthly income. The second is the ratio of the borrower's total monthly debt payments (including housing expenses) to monthly income. The borrower must qualify under both ratios.

Housing expense-to-income ratio. A conventional loan underwriter will consider the borrower's income adequate if the total monthly housing expense does not exceed **28%** of the borrower's stable monthly income.

"Monthly housing expense" is the sum of the monthly **principal** and **interest** payments on the mortgage, real property **taxes**, and the hazard **insurance** premium (these four items are often referred to as **PITI**), the **mortgage insurance** premium (if the loan amount is more than 80% of the property's value), and any **homeowners' association dues** (if applicable). Utility charges are not included in the housing expense because these charges vary considerably depending on utility rates, family size, and living style. However, the underwriter will consider the effect that utility charges have on the borrower's ability to meet monthly housing expenses and maintain the property.

EXAMPLE:

$3,100	stable monthly income
$837	proposed monthly mortgage payment*

$$\$3{,}100 \overline{)\ 837} = .27$$ housing expense-to-income ratio

In this example, $3,100 would be an adequate income to support a $837 monthly mortgage payment as the mortgage payment is only 27% of stable monthly income.

*This figure includes principal, interest, taxes, insurance, and private mortgage insurance.

If the borrower's monthly housing expense will increase significantly as the result of buying instead of renting, or substantially "trading-up" the price of the home, the analysis of the monthly housing expense becomes even more important. Underwriters are wary of too great an increase in the overall monthly housing expense. In comparing the previous housing expense to the new housing expense, the underwriter will carefully examine the borrower's ability to accumulate savings and maintain a favorable debt position.

Total monthly debt payments-to-income ratio. An underwriter will consider a borrower's income to be adequate if the total monthly debt payments do not exceed **36%** of the borrower's monthly income. Total monthly debt payments are the sum of the **monthly housing expense,** payment on any **installment debt that has more than six remaining payments,** and **alimony, child support,** or **maintenance payments.**

EXAMPLE:

$3,100	stable monthly income
$837	proposed monthly mortgage payment
265	auto payment (24 monthly installments remaining)
25	personal loan payments (14 monthly installments remaining)
$1,127	total monthly debt payments

$$\frac{1{,}127}{\$3{,}100} = .36$$

total monthly debt payments-to-income ratio

Investment property. If the property is being purchased as an investment property or second home, the borrower's personal housing expense will be included in the total monthly payment calculation. Generally, total monthly debt payments should not exceed 33% to 36% of the stable monthly income of a borrower purchasing a 1-2 unit property. A borrower purchasing a 3-4 unit property generally should not have a total debt-to-income ratio greater than 33%.

Mitigating factors. Although the secondary market encourages underwriters to exceed these ratios only in exceptional circumstances, the following is a list of the factors that might be taken into consideration when determining the adequacy of income:

- the borrower's proven ability to devote a larger than average portion of income to basic needs (e.g., housing expense);
- the borrower's proven ability to maintain good credit, accumulate savings, and remain debt-free;
- a large cash downpayment;
- the borrower's potential for increased income, indicated by education or job training;
- the borrower's net worth shows an ability to repay the mortgage;
- the amount, nature and duration of any child support obligations.

Ratios for 95% loans. For loans with a loan-to-value ratio higher than 90%, underwriters use more stringent expense-to-income ratios. The housing expense-to-income ratio cannot exceed **28%** and the total monthly debt payments-to-income ratio cannot exceed **33%**. The lower debt ratio is required to offset the greater perceived risks of the low equity loan. If the underwriter makes any exception to these ratios, the reasons for that exception must be fully documented in the loan file.

FNMA/FHLMC RATIOS

Loan-to-Value	Housing Expense	Total Debt Service/ Fixed Payments
90% or less (downpayment 10% or more	28%	36%
FNMA more than 90% (downpayment 5%)	28%	33%

Net Worth.

The second major factor examined by the loan underwriter is the borrower's net worth. A substantial net worth can overcome marginal income and debt service ratios. There are two major reasons for the weight given to net worth. The first is that the accumulation of net worth is a good indication of the borrower's creditworthiness. It shows an ability to manage financial affairs and accumulate assets over and above necessary expenses. The second reason is that if the net worth is liquid (i.e., capable of being quickly converted into cash), it can be used at a moment's notice to pay monthly expenses, any unusual obligations, and provide a hedge against short-term interruptions of income. It is for these reasons that substantial net worth is viewed very favorably by the underwriter.

The loan application includes an "Assets" section in which the borrower should itemize his or her assets (both liquid and otherwise). The liquid assets are those that would be available for use towards the cash downpayment, prepaid items, and closing costs.

Verification of deposit. Any cash in depository accounts which is to be used toward the downpayment and/or closing costs must be verified. A standard verification of deposit form is shown on the following pages.

This form is sent directly to the borrower's bank. Once the form is filled in by the bank and returned directly to the underwriter, it will be examined for the following:

- is the verified information the same as stated in the application?
- are there enough funds in the account to meet the expenses of the purchase?
- was the bank account opened recently (within the last few months)?
- is the present balance significantly higher than the average balance?

The deposit verification will generally provide the average balance for the last several months. The lender is likely to investigate the matter if the verification indicates that the account was recently opened, a large deposit was recently received, or the account balance averaged considerably less during the previous few months. Any of these might be an indication of borrowed funds. Borrowed funds may not be used to close a real estate transaction.

Lenders may also now allow borrowers to verify their own deposits: the borrower may submit the original bank statements for the previous three months to verify sufficient cash for closing.

INSTRUCTIONS TO LENDER:
1. Fill out Part 1- Request
2. Have Applicant(s) sign each copy (no carbon signatures)
3. Forward 2 copies to Depository

VMP MORTGAGE FORMS • (313)293-8100 • (800)521-7291

64325D

INSTRUCTIONS TO DEPOSITORY:
1. **Complete Part II - Verification**
2. **Return both completed copies to Lender**

VMP - 28 (8711)

OMB No. 2502-0059

VETERANS ADMINISTRATION AND U.S. DEPARTMENT OF HOUSING AND URBAN DEVELOPMENT
HUD COMMUNITY PLANNING AND DEVELOPMENT
HUD HOUSING - FEDERAL HOUSING COMMISSIONER

REQUEST FOR VERIFICATION OF DEPOSIT

PRIVACY ACT NOTICE STATEMENT - This information is to be used by the agency collecting it in determining whether you qualify as a prospective mortgagor for mortgage insurance or guaranty or as a borrower for a rehabilitation loan under the agency's program. It will not be disclosed outside the agency without your consent except to financial institutions for verification of your deposits and as required and permitted by law. You do not have to give us this information, but, if you do not, your application for approval as a prospective mortgagor for mortgage insurance or guaranty or as a borrower for a rehabilitation loan may be delayed or rejected. This information request is authorized by Title 38, U.S.C., Chapter 37 *(if VA)*; by 12 U.S.C., Section 1701 et seq., *(if HUD/FHA)*; and by 42 U.S.C., Section 1452b *(if HUD/CPD)*.

INSTRUCTIONS

LENDER OR LOCAL PROCESSING AGENCY: Complete Items 1 through 8. Have applicant(s) complete Item 9. Forward directly to the Depository named in Item 1. DEPOSITORY: Please complete Items 10 through 15 and return DIRECTLY to Lender or Local Processing agency named in Item 2.

PART I - REQUEST

1. TO *(Name and Address of Depository)*	2. FROM *(Name and Address of Lender or Local Processing Agency)*

I certify that this verification has been sent directly to the bank or depository and has not passed through the hands of the applicant or any other party.

3. Signature of Lender or Official of Local Processing Agency	4. Title	5. Date	6. Lender's Number *(Optional)*
	loan Processor		

7. INFORMATION TO BE VERIFIED:

Type of Account and/or Loan	Account/Loan in Name of	Account/Loan Number	Balance
			$
			$
			$
			$

TO DEPOSITORY: I have applied for mortgage insurance or guaranty or for a rehabilitation loan and stated that the balance on deposit and/or outstanding loans with you are as shown above. You are authorized to verify this information and to supply the lender or the local processing agency identified above with the information requested in Items 10 through 12. Your response is solely a matter of courtesy for which no responsibility is attached to your institution or any of your officers.

8. NAME AND ADDRESS OF APPLICANT(S)	9. SIGNATURE OF APPLICANT(S)
	X
	X

TO BE COMPLETED BY DEPOSITORY

PART II - VERIFICATION OF DEPOSITORY

10. DEPOSIT ACCOUNTS OF APPLICANT(S)

Type of Account	Account Number	Current Balance	Average Balance for Previous Two Months	Date Opened
		$	$	
		$	$	
		$	$	
		$	$	

11. LOANS OUTSTANDING TO APPLICANT(S)

Loan Number	Date of Loan	Original Amount	Current Balance	Installments (Monthly/Quarterly)	Secured by	Number of Late Payments within Last 12 Months
		$	$	$ per		
		$	$.	$ per		
		$	$	$ per		

12. ADDITIONAL INFORMATION WHICH MAY BE OF ASSISTANCE IN DETERMINATION OF CREDIT WORTHINESS: *Please include information on loans paid-in-full as in Item 11 above)*

13. Signature of Depository Official	14. Title	15. Date
X		

The confidentiality of the information you have furnished will be preserved except where disclosure of this information is required by applicable law. The completed form is to be transmitted directly to the lender or local processing agency and is not to be transmitted through the applicant or any other party.

DEPOSITORY-RETURN BOTH COPIES TO LENDER

VA-26-8497-a (7-80) HUD-92004-F (11-85) HB 4155 1

LENDER-DETACH THIS COPY AND FILE FOR FOLLOW UP

Financial statement. If the borrower has significant assets, it may be advantageous to submit a financial statement. A financial statement contains an itemized list of all the borrower's assets and liabilities which indicates total net worth. This may be the best way to illustrate the borrower's creditworthiness if his or her financial affairs are complex.

PERSONAL FINANCIAL STATEMENT
as of ____________(Date)

1		2	
Name of ☑ Individual as Borrower, or ☐ Partner, Officer or Stockholder of Borrowing Entity, or ☐ Guarantor	Samantha M. Smith	Name of Individual ☐ As Co-Borrower ☐ Not as Co-Borrower	n/a
Home Address	1213 Acorn Way, Anytown	Home Address	
Employer (name and address)	Continental Carriers 4004 Industrial Way Anytown, USA	Employer (name and address)	
Years with this Employer: 7	Current Position: comptroller	Years with this Employer	Current Position

STATEMENT OF ASSETS AND LIABILITIES

Indicate by (*) those liabilities or pledged assets which will be satisfied upon sale or real estate owned or upon refinancing of subject property.

ASSETS

Description	Cash or Market Value
Cash Deposit Toward Purchase Held By: Reliable Realty	$ 5,000
Checking and Savings Accounts (show names of institutions/acct. nos.)	
~~1st National Bank~~ checking Acct.# 001000	6,500
Big Savings & Loan savings Acct.# 22220	18,400
Stocks and Bonds (no./description) Series "E"	2,000
Life Insurance Net Cash Value Face Amount ($ 100,000)	2,500
SUBTOTAL LIQUID ASSETS	$ 34,400
Real Estate Owned (enter Market Value from Schedule of Real Estate Owned)	112,000
Vested Interest in Retirement Fund	18,500
Net Worth of Business Owned (ATTACH FINANCIAL STATEMENT)	n/a
Automobiles (make and year) 19 . Ford	4,000
Other personal property	12,000
TOTAL ASSETS	A $ 180,900

LIABILITIES AND PLEDGED ASSETS

Creditors' Names, Addresses and Acct. Nos.	Acct. Name if Not Borrower's	Mo. Pmt. and Mos. left to pay	Unpaid Balance
Installment Debts (include 'revolving' charge accts.) Sears		$ Pmt./Mos. 50/14	$ 700
Bank of Compton		35/6	190
Other Debts including stock pledges		/	
Real Estate Loans: Big Savings & Loan		$712	80,000
Automobile Loans: GMAC		140/11	1,310
Alimony, Child Support and Separate Maintenance Payments Owed To: n/a		/	
TOTAL MONTHLY PAYMENTS		$ 937	82,200
NET WORTH (A minus B) $ 98,700		TOTAL LIABILITIES	B $ 82,200

Samantha M Smith
Signature ____ Date ____   Signature ____ Date ____

Home Phone: 222-1111 Bus. Phone: 111-2222 Home Phone: ____ Bus. Phone ____

Gift letter. It is acceptable for a borrower to use a gift (evidenced by a gift letter) to pay the downpayment and closing costs but only if the gift is from an immediate relative and does not have to be repaid. Even with the gift, however, the borrower must still make the required 5% cash contribution.

Real estate for sale. If the borrower is selling one property in order to buy another, the borrower's equity in the property is an asset which may be included in the borrower's net worth. **Equity** is the difference between the present market value of the property and mortgages, liens and selling expenses of the property.

EXAMPLE:

$92,000	present market value
75,000	conventional mortgage
5,000	property tax lien
- 6,000	selling expenses
$6,000	borrower's equity

Other real estate. Any equity that the borrower might hold in other real estate may also be considered an asset. If the borrower owns properties that are income producing or which have solid equities, any debt obligations on the properties (e.g., mortgage payments) are treated more favorably than consumer debt or unsecured obligations. The borrower can always sell the property and be relieved of the financial obligation without jeopardizing his or her credit.

Credit History.

The third item examined by the underwriter is the borrower's credit history. Credit history is important because it reflects the borrower's attitude towards credit obligations. It makes little difference whether a borrower has the means to pay a mortgage obligation if he or she has no desire to do so. On the other hand, a history of prompt payments and a responsible attitude towards financial obligations augurs well for the borrower.

All lenders automatically order credit reports on all borrowers and underwriters examine these reports carefully.

STANDARD FACTUAL DATA REPORT

ACCOUNT NO. 8572F
ACCOUNT NAME
REPORT ORDERED BY
DATE ORDERED March 3, 19
DATE COMPLETED March 17, 19
INDIVIDUAL OR JOINT REPORT Joint
TYPE REPORT (CASE OR FILE NO.)
REPORT PREPARED BY
PRICE

BASE	NON-LOCAL	ADDITIONAL	TAX	TOTAL

REPOSITORY INFORMATION OBTAINED FROM: John J. Jones (BORROWER) Joan J. Jones (CO-BORROWER)

ALL INQUIRIES WITHIN THE LAST 6 MONTHS HAVE BEEN CHECKED AND ANY OPENED ACCOUNTS ARE REFLECTED BELOW.

This standard factual data report meets all underwriting requirements set by FHA, VA, FNMA and FHLMC.

GENERAL INFORMATION	
1. BORROWER'S NAME AND AGE / CO-BORROWER'S NAME AND AGE	John J. Jones, 37; Joan J. Jones, 35
2. CURRENT ADDRESS	101 1st Ave., Anytown, USA 00000
3. LENGTH OF TIME AT PRESENT ADDRESS / OWN?	6 months/No
4. PREVIOUS ADDRESS	275 - 14th Street, Anytown, USA 00000
5. BORROWER SS # / CO-BORROWER SS #	001-01-1111 ; 100-10-2222
6. MARITAL STATUS / YEARS / DEPENDENTS	Married/4/3
BORROWER'S EMPLOYMENT	
7. NAME OF EMPLOYER / ADDRESS	Lucky Larry's Used Auto; 121 Main St., Anytown
8. POSITION HELD / LENGTH OF EMPLOYMENT	Salesperson/ 8 months
9. EMPLOYMENT VERIFIED BY	Larry Jones
10. PREVIOUS EMPLOYMENT / LENGTH OF EMPLOYMENT	Totem Car Sales/18 months
CO-BORROWER'S EMPLOYMENT	
11. NAME OF EMPLOYER / ADDRESS	ABC Department Store; 421 Main St., Anytown
12. POSITION HELD / LENGTH OF EMPLOYMENT	Department Manager/8 years
13. EMPLOYMENT VERIFIED BY	C. Bellows
14. PREVIOUS EMPLOYMENT / LENGTH OF EMPLOYMENT	---

THE REPORTING BUREAU CERTIFIES THAT: Public records have been checked for judgments, garnishments, foreclosures, bankruptcies and other legal action involving the BORROWER [X] CO-BORROWER [X] (or equivalent results have been obtained through the use of qualified public records reporting services) with the following results:
PUBLIC RECORD ITEMS FOUND BORROWER Divorce 8/82 PUBLIC RECORD ITEMS FOUND CO-BORROWER N/A

THE REPORTING BUREAU CERTIFIES THAT: The credit record of the borrower (and co-borrower if any) has been checked as to payment of obligations: a. [X] through the credit accounts extended by designated credit grantors, if any; and, b. [X] through accumulated credit records of such credit grantors of the community in which the subject(s) resides, with the results indicated below.

CREDIT HISTORY

BUSINESS	DATE ACCOUNT OPENED	HIGHEST CREDIT	BALANCE OWING	MONTHLY PAYMENT	PAYMENT PATTERN	PAST DUE AMOUNT	TIMES PAST DUE 30	TIMES PAST DUE 60	TIMES PAST DUE 90+	DATE LAST PAST DUE
Boles Inc.	7/81	$200	-0-	$17	as agreed	-0-				--
Acme Drugs	9/81	$150	$90	revolv.	slow	$26	12	2		current
Penney's	8/86	$950	$900	$45	slow	$45	2	1		current
Mastercard	9/85	$500	$489	revolv.	as agreed	-0-				--
ABC Finance	4/87	$1,500	$1,500	$92	too soon to rate	-0-				--
HFC Finance	6/85	$4,800	$1,900	$185	slow	$185	4			current

Credit Report Authorization

As part of your loan package, a credit report will be prepared by a credit reporting service. Within the next few days, you should expect to receive a phone call from the reporting service. At that time, they will review with you the credit information you have already provided and seek additional details required to complete your report. This telephone interview will also provide you with an opportunity to inform them of any disputes and to locate and eliminate error.

By requesting that your mortgage credit report be prepared, you are authorizing charges for that report whether or not your mortgage loan is closed.

I authorize all creditors to release all information necessary to complete my credit report. I further understand that use of a photocopy of this form may be necessary to verify one or more of my credit references. I authorize that use and request that such a copy by honored fully.

Dated this __________ day of __________________________ 19 ________

Applicant ____

Co-Applicant ____

The credit report is based on up-to-date information and includes all information bearing on the borrower's ability and willingness to repay the mortgage. The credit report will verify current employment and salary and provide references on all debts, both those listed on the credit application and those which are not. If there are any significant debts not disclosed by the borrower on the application, the lender will require a written explanation from the borrower and will include the explanation in the mortgage file.

Derogatory credit information. Any indication of problems meeting credit obligations will cause the underwriter to carefully analyze the borrower's credit history. If there is a pattern of slow payments, suits for nonpayment of debts or judgments to creditors, convincing explanations will be required before the borrower will be given favorable consideration. The borrower should keep in mind that there are often satisfactory explanations, for example, death or illness in the family, prolonged unemployment, or divorce. Occurrences such as these are generally beyond the borrower's control and unlikely to occur on a regular basis. Thus, the borrower could show that exceptional circumstances led to the poor credit rating, rather than a propensity on the part of the borrower to neglect financial obligations. In such an instance, the borrower should also be able to show good credit ratings preceding and subsequent to the extenuating circumstances.

When explaining derogatory credit, the borrower should take care to accept responsibility for the poor credit rather than blaming the creditors. As a future creditor, the underwriter is unlikely to look very favorably on such denials of responsibility.

Refinancings and consolidations. Underwriters view borrowers who continually increase liabilities and then periodically bail out through refinancing and bill consolidations to be marginal credit risks. A regular pattern of refinancings is an indication to the underwriter that the borrower is living beyond his or her means. A debt amount which steadily increases over an extended period of time is considered a sign of credit weakness.

No credit history. The secondary market encourages underwriters to give favorable consideration to a borrower who has shown the ability to manage his or her financial affairs without resorting to credit.

Bankruptcy. Borrowers who have gone through bankruptcy proceedings or other legal actions (e.g., suits for nonpayment of debts) or who have given a deed in lieu of foreclosure will be held to a very strict standard of creditworthiness. While a borrower who has had temporary financial difficulty should not be unduly penalized, there must be a history of recovery and good financial standing before he or she will be given favorable consideration. If there is no valid reason for bankruptcy, liens, or judgments, there must be strong offsetting factors if the loan application is to be approved.

FHA Underwriting Guidelines

The underwriting guidelines for an FHA-insured loan are set by the Department of Housing and Urban Development. The secondary market has little effect on these standards, as GNMA buys FHA loans (and VA loans as well) without imposing any additional standards on them.

As with conventional loans, in order to qualify for an FHA-insured loan, the borrower must have sufficient income to support the proposed housing payments as well as other living expenses, a satisfactory credit rating, and enough verifiable cash assets to meet the closing requirements of the transaction. However, specific underwriting standards differ significantly between those for conventional loans and those for FHA loans. Generally speaking, the standards for obtaining an FHA-insured loan are substantially more lenient than those for obtaining a conventional loan.

The **credit history** and **net worth** requirements are much the same as for conventional loans; it is the **income** requirements that differ.

Income.

As previously discussed, stable monthly income is income from reliable sources which is likely to continue for a significant period of time. The

FHA standards for determining stable income are basically the same as the conventional standards. The amount of stable monthly income required to qualify for an FHA loan is determined by the expense-to-income ratios.

Expense-to-income ratios.

As with conventional underwriting standards, two expense-to-income ratios are used to qualify a borrower for an FHA loan.

Housing expense-to-income. The borrower's monthly housing expense is divided into his or her income to arrive at the housing expense-to-income ratio. The following are included in the monthly housing expense: principal and interest payments, monthly property taxes, property assessments, homeowner's insurance (the monthly premiums), an estimated monthly maintenance expense, estimated monthly utilities, and any homeowners' association fees. The maximum housing expense-to-income ratio for an FHA loan is **29%.**

EXAMPLE:

$3,020	monthly income
$628	principal and interest payment
35	property taxes
17	homeowners' insurance
35	maintenance expense
75	utilities
$790	total monthly housing expense

$$\$3{,}020 \overline{\smash{)}\,790\,} = .26$$

.26 housing expense-to-income ratio

Total monthly obligations-to-income. The sum of the borrower's total monthly obligations is divided into his or her income in order to arrive at the total monthly obligations-to-income ratio. Total monthly obligations include the monthly housing expenses (as computed above) plus all other recurring liabilites. Examples of these would be personal loans, department store and credit card debts, child support payments and automobile loan payments. Total monthly obligations should not exceed **41%** of the borrower's monthly income.

EXAMPLE:

$790	monthly housing expense
275	auto payment
45	revolving account
40	personal loan
$1,150	total monthly obligations

$$\begin{array}{r} .38 \\ \$3{,}020 \overline{)\ 1{,}150} \end{array}$$ total monthly obligations-to-income ratio

VA Underwriting Guidelines

We will now turn our attention to the underwriting guidelines of VA-guaranteed loans. These guidelines are set by the Veterans Administration and must be followed by all lenders who underwrite VA-guaranteed loans. Like FHA standards, VA underwriting standards are significantly less stringent than those for conventional loans. Those not eligible or only marginally eligible for a conventional loan will have an easier time qualifying for a VA-guaranteed loan. (Of course, VA loans are restricted to eligible veterans.)

In determining creditworthiness, the underwriter will keep in mind that an entitlement is involved. The law intends for the veteran to have the benefit of a VA-guaranteed loan as long as the requirements of the underwriting guidelines are met. However, the Veterans Administration is also aware that it serves no purpose to approve a loan if the veteran will be unable to meet the payment terms or is not a good credit risk. Underwriters who approve risky loans are only doing the veteran a disservice

Veterans Administration

LOAN ANALYSIS

LOAN NUMBER

SECTION A–LOAN DATA

1. NAME OF BORROWER	2. AMOUNT OF LOAN	3. CASH DOWN PAYMENT ON PURCHASE PRICE
	$	$

SECTION B–BORROWER'S PERSONAL AND FINANCIAL STATUS

4. APPLICANT'S AGE	5. OCCUPATION OF APPLICANT	6. NUMBER OF YEARS AT PRESENT EMPLOYMENT	7. LIQUID ASSETS (*Cash, savings, bonds, etc.*)	8. CURRENT MONTHLY HOUSING EXPENSE
			$	$
9. UTILITIES INCLUDED ☐ YES ☐ NO	10. SPOUSE'S AGE	11. OCCUPATION OF SPOUSE	12. NUMBER OF YEARS AT PRESENT EMPLOYMENT	13. AGE OF DEPENDENTS

NOTE: ROUND ALL DOLLAR AMOUNTS BELOW TO NEAREST WHOLE DOLLAR.

SECTION C – ESTIMATED MONTHLY SHELTER EXPENSES

(This Property)

SECTION D – DEBTS AND OBLIGATIONS

(Itemize and indicate by (√) which debts considered in Section E, Line 41)

	ITEMS	AMOUNT		ITEMS	(√)	MO. PAYMENT	UNPAID BAL.
14.	TERM OF LOAN: YEARS		23.			$	$
15.	MORTGAGE PAYMENT (*Principal and Interest*) @ ____ %	$	24.				
16.	REALTY TAXES		25.				
17.	HAZARD INSURANCE		26.				
18.	SPECIAL ASSESSMENTS		27.				
19.	MAINTENANCE		28.				
20.	UTILITIES (*Including heat*)		29.				
21.	OTHER (*HOA, Condo fees, etc.*)		30.	JOB RELATED EXPENSE (*e.g., child-care*)			
22.	TOTAL	$	31.	TOTAL		$	$

SECTION E – MONTHLY INCOME AND DEDUCTIONS

	ITEMS		SPOUSE	BORROWER	TOTAL
32.	GROSS SALARY OR EARNINGS FROM EMPLOYMENT		$	$	$
33.	DEDUCTIONS	FEDERAL INCOME TAX			
34.		STATE INCOME TAX			
35.		RETIREMENT OR SOCIAL SECURITY			

36.	OTHER *(Specify)*			
37.	TOTAL DEDUCTIONS	$	$	$
38.	NET TAKE-HOME PAY			
39.	PENSION, COMPENSATION OR OTHER NET INCOME *(Specify)*			
40.	TOTAL *(Sum of lines 38 and 39)*	$	$	$
41.	LESS THOSE OBLIGATIONS LISTED IN SECTION D WHICH SHOULD BE DEDUCTED FROM INCOME			
42.	TOTAL NET EFFECTIVE INCOME			$
43.	LESS ESTIMATED MONTHLY SHELTER EXPENSE *(Line 22)*			
44.	BALANCE AVAILABLE FOR FAMILY SUPPORT			$

45. PAST CREDIT RECORD

☐ SATISFACTORY ☐ UNSATISFACTORY

46. DOES LOAN MEET VA CREDIT STANDARDS? *(Give reasons for decision under "Remarks," if necessary, e.g., borderline case)*

☐ YES ☐ NO

47. REMARKS *(Use reverse, if necessary)*

SECTION F – DISPOSITION OF APPLICATION

☐ Recommend that the application be approved since it meets all requirements of Chapter 37, Title 38, U.S. Code and applicable VA Regulations and directives.

☐ Recommend that the application be disapproved for the reasons stated under "Remarks" above.

48. DATE	49. SIGNATURE OF EXAMINER

50. FINAL ACTION ☐ APPROVE APPLICATION ☐ REJECT APPLICATION	51. DATE	52. SIGNATURE AND TITLE OF APPROVING OFFICIAL

VA FORM 26-6393
SEP 1983

EXISTING STOCKS OF VA FORM 26-6393, MAY 1979, WILL BE USED.

as the loan approval could result in a mortgage foreclosure, the veteran owing a debt to the U.S. Government, and a poor credit rating for the veteran.

As with conventional loans, underwriters look at the borrower's income, assets and credit history. In order to qualify for a VA loan, the veteran must have enough income to meet the mortgage payments, cover the costs of owning a home, take care of other obligations and expenses, and still have enough income left over for family support. The veteran must also have a good credit record.

The Veterans Administration emphasizes that there is no one factor that is the final determinant in any borrower's qualification for a VA-guaranteed loan. The adequacy of the borrower's income for family support is important, but other factors are also examined. One consideration is the amount currently being paid for rental or housing expenses. If the proposed housing expense will be significantly more than what is currently being paid, the underwriter will scrutinize the application carefully. Other factors to be considered include the ability of the borrower to accumulate liquid assets and the amount of debts that were incurred while paying a lesser amount for housing. For example, if the borrower already has excessive obligations and little cash reserves, the underwriter may well conclude that a substantial increase in housing expenses cannot be absorbed. Another factor of prime importance is the applicant's manner of meeting his or her obligations. A poor credit history alone is a basis for disapproving a loan. As one might expect, when one aspect of the loan application is marginal, the remaining factors will be closely examined.

In reviewing a loan application, the Veterans Administration uses the loan analysis form shown on the preceding pages. From this form, the VA gets a concise overview of all the pertinent data.

Income.

Many of the VA guidelines regarding the borrower's income are the same as the conventional guidelines. However, there are some distinctions which are presented below.

Income reliability.

Income received by the borrower is only considered if it is likely to continue during the foreseeable future. Income from annuities, pensions or part-time employment may be considered if it is shown to be reliable. If overtime or second jobs can be shown to be continuous, they will also be considered. Income from overtime work and part-time employment which is not eligible for consideration (cannot be shown to be continuous) may still be used to offset payments due on short-term debts and obligations.

The amount of any pension or other income such as dividends from stocks, interest from bonds, savings accounts, or other deposits, rents, royalties, etc., will be considered as reliable income if it is likely that such income will continue in the future. Otherwise, it may only be used to offset short-term debt. Certain military allowances of uncertain duration (e.g., flight or hazard pay, overseas pay, or combat pay) will also only be used to offset short-term obligations. Such income will only be considered stable if it can be shown that it has continued for a prolonged period and can be expected to continue because of the nature of the recipient's assigned duties.

The contingent nature of a number of additional income sources precludes their being considered as part of stable income. Temporary income items such as VA educational allowances and unemployment compensation do not represent stable and reliable income and will not be taken into consideration. Income from public assistance programs may be used to qualify for a loan if it can be shown that the income will probably continue for a substantial fraction of the term of the loan, i.e., one-third or more. For instance, aid to dependent children being received for a five-year old child that will continue until the child achieves majority could be used to qualify for a 30-year loan.

Alimony, child support, maintenance payments. As for a conventional loan, income from alimony, child support or maintenance payments is considered stable income only to the extent that the payments are likely to be consistently made.

Commissions. It is necessary to establish the stability of commission income before it will be considered in the loan analysis. Written verification of the actual amount of commissions paid to date is required, as well as the basis for the payment of the commissions, and when the commissions are paid, i.e., monthly, quarterly, semi-annually, or annually. The length of time the veteran has been employed in this type of occupation is an important factor in assessing the stability of the income. If the veteran has been employed for a relatively short time, the income is normally not considered stable unless the product or service was the same or closely related to the product or service sold in an immediately prior position.

Self-employment. The same documentation is required for the self-employed veteran as for conventional loan applicants (e.g., tax returns, profit and loss statements, etc.). When the self-employment has been of short duration (less than two years), the applicant must show the training and experience necessary to be successful in the enterprise. If the business is of an unusual type and it is difficult to determine the probability of its continuation, explanations as to the function and purpose of the business may be needed from the borrower.

Recently discharged veterans. Loan applications received from recently discharged veterans with little or no job experience other than their military occupation or from veterans who have retired after 20 years of active military duty receive special attention. (The retirement income of the veterans in many cases is not sufficient to meet income requirements.) The facts related to these veteran's present employment and retirement income must be fully developed and each case is to be considered on its individual merits.

If a recently discharged or retired veteran has no prior employment history and the veteran has been at his or her present job for a short time, the underwriter may consider the duties the veteran performed in the military service. If these duties were similar to the duties of the veteran's present position, they add weight to the present employment experience. For example, an underwriter could use short-term employment to qualify a veteran with experience as an airplane mechanic in the military service when the veteran's employment after discharge is as an auto mechanic or machinist. On the other hand, the past experiences of an Air Force pilot recently employed as an insurance salesperson on commission would do little to improve his or her job status.

Rental income. When a veteran is applying for a loan on a multi-family dwelling, the prospective rental income is not considered unless:

- the veteran can demonstrate a reasonable likelihood of success as a landlord (based on prior experience), and
- the veteran has sufficient cash reserves to make the loan payments without assistance from the rental income for a period of at least six months.

The amount of rental income considered is based on the prior rental history of the units for existing structures or, for proposed construction, the appraiser's opinion of the property's fair monthly rental.

Adequacy of income.

Once the amount of the borrower's stable monthly income is determined, the adequacy of that income must be examined. The adequacy of the income is determined by using two methods: the residual income method and the expense-to-income ratio. The VA loan underwriter must compute both figures for use in the loan analysis, rather than using one or the other

The residual income method is based on the theory that there should be a minimum amount of income left after paying monthly obligations with which to meet the expenses of food, clothing, groceries, etc. Monthly obligations are the same as those calculated for the expense-to-income method. If a borrower meets the residual income requirements, it is assumed that he or she will have enough income left over after paying monthly obligations to meet day-to-day living expenses.

Residual income is what remains of net income after all monthly payments to "total monthly obligations" have been made. The required amounts of residual income according to family size are shown below. These figures may vary slightly from community to community.

Residual income. The residual income figures are based on data supplied by the Consumer Expenditure Survey which is published by the Department of Labor. There are different figures for each of the four Census Bureau regions: the West, South, Midwest and Northeast. The table below shows the figures for these regions. The veteran would have the requisite amount of income remaining after all monthly debt obligations have been paid.

RESIDUAL INCOMES BY REGION FOR
LOAN AMOUNTS OF $69,999 AND BELOW

Family Size*	North-East	Mid-West	South	West
1	$348	$340	$340	$379
2	583	570	570	635
3	702	687	687	765
4	791	773	773	861
5	821	803	803	894

*For families with more than five members, add $70 for each additional member up to a family of seven.

RESIDUAL INCOMES BY REGION FOR
LOAN AMOUNTS OF $70,000 AND ABOVE

Family Size*	North-East	Mid-West	South	West
1	$401	$393	$393	$437
2	673	658	658	733
3	810	792	792	882
4	913	893	893	995
5	946	925	925	1031

*For families with more than five members, add $75 for each additional member up to a family of seven.

"Monthly debt obligations" refers to all known recurring debts and obligations (including any alimony and/or child support payments). An automobile loan with seven monthly installments remaining would be included as a monthly debt obligation. Significant obligations which have relatively short terms will still be considered in the loan analysis. For example, monthly payments of $150 on an auto loan with a remaining balance of $750 would be included regardless of the fact that the account will be paid off in five months. Similarly, when credit information shows revolving or open accounts of several years' duration, their regualr monthly payments should also be considered long-term obligations.

Alimony, child support. Obligations for alimony and/or child support are included in the monthly debt obligation figure. Verification of these obligations will be required, usually by means of submitting a copy of the divorce decree. If the borrower fails to reveal these obligations, the underwriter will have to resolve the discrepancy before the application can be looked on favorably.

Job-related expenses. The borrower is to list all known job-related expenses as well. This includes costs for any dependent care, union dues, group hospitalization insurance, significant commuting costs, etc.

EXAMPLE:

$2,430	monthly income for a family of four
$675	monthly housing expense
190	auto payment
200	child support
$1,065	total monthly obligations
$1,031	residual income required for family of four
$2,430	monthly income
- 1,065	total monthly obligations
$1,365	residual income — more than the required minimum amount

Lenders underwriting VA-guaranteed loans must use these figures when underwriting a loan, but flexibility is encouraged. For example, the VA recognizes that the purchase of a new home may affect family expenditure levels differently in individual cases. While not considered in establishing the minimum residual incomes, this factor may be given consideration in the final analysis of a loan application. For instance, the purchase of a home in a more expensive neighborhood may cause the family to incur higher-than-average expenses to support a lifestyle comparable to that of the environment, while the purchase of a substantially lower-priced home would not.

It is to be emphasized that these figures are a guide only — whether the borrower's income does or does not meet these requirements is not the sole determinant for approving or rejecting the loan application.

Income ratio. The second figure considered is the ratio of the total monthly debt payments (housing expense, installment debts, etc.) to gross monthly income. Like the residual income, the ratio is used only as a guide when underwriting the loan application. The fact that a higher than recommended ratio exists does not automatically mean that the loan will be rejected.

The ratio is determined by taking the sum of PITI (principal, interest, taxes and insurance), homeowners' association fees, assessments and other monthly obligations (e.g., car payments, child support payments) and dividing this by gross income.

EXAMPLE:

$2,430	monthly income
$675	proposed monthly housing expense
190	auto payment
200	child support
$1,065	total monthly debt payments
.44	monthly debt payments-to-income ratio
$2,430 ⟌ 1,065	(over 41% maximum)

If the ratio is more than **41%**, the underwriter must provide a statement listing the reasons which justify approval, signed by the underwriter's supervisor. This statement lists compensating factors such as a substantial amount of income over and above the required minimum residual amount. The presence and size of any downpayment may also be a mitigating factor. However, the fact that a sizable downpayment is made will not of itself qualify a borrower for a loan if he or she does not have the ability to meet the monthly payments.

Credit History.

The creditworthiness of the borrower is based on a careful analysis of all the available credit data. Credit reports and verifications must be no more than 90 days old to be considered valid. The discussion of credit history under conventional underwriting guidelines is equally applicable here.

Prior VA loans. When the borrower has made previous use of a VA-guaranteed loan, the underwriter will consider the borrower's experience with that prior loan. The borrower's loan history may be so unfavorable that further credit is not warranted. Since lenders may not report experience with a VA loan to credit agencies, credit reports obtained to evaluate the history of a previous loan will be deficient. Underwriters must seek information on the prior loan from the originator or holder of that loan. The underwriter may also contact the VA regional office through which the loan was obtained.

Bankruptcy. Evidence that the borrower has been declared bankrupt does not in itself disqualify the loan application. However, in such cases it is necessary to develop complete information as to the facts and circumstances concerning the bankruptcy. Generally speaking, when the borrower has been regularly employed (not self-employed) and has been discharged in bankruptcy within the last two or three years, the borrower will not be considered a satisfactory credit risk unless both of the following requirements are satisfied:

- the borrower has obtained consumer items on credit after the

INCOME AND EXPENSE STANDARDS FOR CONVENTIONAL, FHA, AND VA LOANS.

	HOUSING EXPENSE	TOTAL DEBT SERVICE/ FIXED PAYMENTS	CASH FLOW ANALYSIS
FNMA/FHLMC (conventional) Loan-to-Value 90% or less	—principal, interest, taxes, insurance, and PMIP —not to exceed 28% of stable monthly income	—housing expense plus debts with more than ten payments remaining —not to exceed 36% of stable monthly income	
FNMA Loan-to-Value More Than 90%	—not to exceed 28% of stable monthly income	—not to exceed 33% of stable monthly income	
FHA	—principal, interest, taxes, insurance, maintenance and utilities —not to exceed 29% of income	—housing expense plus recurring debts —not to exceed 41% of income	
VA		—housing expenses plus recurring debts —should not exceed 41% of gross income	—cash flow should equal or exceed specified region figures for appropriate family size + loan amount

bankruptcy and has met the payments obligations in a satisfactory manner over a continued period of time, and

- the bankruptcy was caused by circumstances beyond the borrower's control (e.g., unemployment, prolonged strikes, medical bills not covered by insurance). The alleged circumstances must be verified. If a borrower is self-employed, has been adjudicated bankrupt, and subsequently obtains a permanent position, a finding as to satisfactory credit risk can still be made provided there is no derogatory credit information prior to self-employment, there is no evidence of derogatory credit information subsequent to the bankruptcy, and the failure of the business was not due to the borrower's misconduct. A bankruptcy discharged more than five years ago can be disregarded.

Chapter Twelve

Finance Documents

The typical homebuyer is often as unfamiliar with the documents of finance as he or she is with the process of obtaining financing. The terms "promissory note," "mortgage," and "deed of trust" seem yet further examples of legal jargon designed to confuse the average person.

In actuality, the principles behind these legal documents are very simple. Since the typical homebuyer does not have enough cash to pay for the home being purchased, he or she must borrow the money from another source. Of course, before the homebuyer can borrow money, he or she must promise to pay it back, with interest. This written promise to pay the money back is called a **promissory note**. The lender, however, may be wary of lending money without more assurance that it will be repaid than the borrower's promise. The lender will want a **security interest** in the property being purchased. In this way, if the borrower breaks his or her promise to pay, the lender will have an interest in the property which can be sold to recover the loan amount. This security interest is given to the lender by way of a **mortgage** or **deed of trust**.

Each of these documents has certain characteristics and required elements. In this chapter, we will examine those characteristics and elements. We will discuss the promissory note first.

Promissory Notes

When a homebuyer finances the purchase of his or her home by borrowing money, the debt is evidenced by a promissory note. At its most basic, a promissory note is a written promise to pay a certain amount of money to a certain person at a certain time. A promissory note is a **negotiable instrument**, which means the lender can sell or transfer it to another party. The legal requirements of a negotiable instrument are:

1. the note must contain an unconditional promise,
2. in writing,
3. made by one person to another,
4. signed by the maker,
5. promising to pay on demand or at a fixed or determinable future time,
6. a certain sum of money,
7. payable to order or to the bearer.

The standard form.

The elements listed above can be seen in the standard fixed-rate promissory note form shown on the following pages.

When examining the note form, pay particular attention to the first section which is the borrower's promise to pay. The borrower promises, in writing, to pay a certain amount (plus interest) to the lender. The third section sets forth the definite time of payment. At the end of the note are lines for the maker's signature. As you can see, these few clauses in the form cover all the necessary requisites to a valid promissory note. However, additional terms are also included in the form. Some simply clarify the basic promise to pay, some set forth rights of the borrower, and others set forth rights of the lender.

At the top of the form are blank lines for the date, city and state, and property address. In Section 2 the rate of interest charged is set forth. Section 3 includes terms as to the place of payment and the amount of monthly payments. Section 4 sets out the borrower's right to prepay the note amount. A section on borrower default is also included: late charges for overdue payments, an acceleration clause (the entire amount can be declared due and payable upon default), and payment of the note holder's costs and expenses in the event of default. Section 7 protects the borrower by requiring any necessary notice to be given by hand delivery or first-class mail. The last section provides that a security instrument (e.g., deed of trust) dated the same date as the note was executed in favor of the note holder and that the loan amount may be due and payable if the property is transferred (a due-on-sale clause).

If any of the listed necessary elements is missing from the promissory note, it may still be valid between the parties. For example, if A promised in writing to pay B the equivalent of the fair market value of one milk cow, A is legally bound to pay that amount to B, even though the promise does not have all the necessary requirements of a negotiable instrument (not a definite dollar amount). So, you might ask, what is the value of the listed elements if the promise to pay may still be binding without them? The value is in the **negotiability** of the promise to pay.

As discussed earlier, most real estate lenders immediately sell the real estate loans they make to the secondary market. Secondary market investors will only buy a promissory note that is negotiable. The investors are not concerned with whether the promise to pay is valid as between the borrower and lender, they are concerned with whether the promise to pay is valid as between the borrower and them. The secondary investor wants to be entitled to the maximum amount of rights possible under the note. The way to do this is to be a holder in due course of a negotiable instrument. A holder in due course of a negotiable instrument has certain rights above and beyond those of the payee of a promissory note.

Holder in due course. A holder in due course is a party who takes a negotiable instrument when:

1. the note is complete and regular on its face;
2. the party took it before the note was overdue and without notice of any previous refusal to honor the note;
3. the party took it in good faith and for valuable consideration;
4. the party took it with no knowledge of any infirmity or defect.

An example of a holder in due course would be FNMA, purchasing a promissory note from a lender for a fair price when there is no indication of any irregularity as to the note. On the other hand, if Smith gives a promissory note to her brother for his birthday, the brother is not a holder in due course as no valuable consideration was paid for the note.

NOTE

...., 19.........   ...., ...
[City]   [State]

....
[Property Address]

1. BORROWER'S PROMISE TO PAY

In return for a loan that I have received, I promise to pay U.S. $.................... (this amount is called "principal"), **plus interest, to the order of the Lender. The Lender is California Federal Savings and Loan Association** I understand that the Lender may transfer this Note. The Lender or anyone who takes this Note by transfer and who is entitled to receive payments under this Note is called the "Note Holder".

2. INTEREST

Interest will be charged on unpaid principal until the full amount of principal has been paid. I will pay interest at a yearly rate of ....%.

The interest rate required by this Section 2 is the rate I will pay both before and after any default described in Section 6(B) of this Note.

3. PAYMENTS

(A) Time and Place of Payments

I will pay principal and interest by making payments every month.

I will make my monthly payments on the 1st day of each month beginning on .... 19........ I will make these payments every month until I have paid all of the principal and interest and any other charges described below that I may owe under this Note. My monthly payments will be applied to interest before principal. If, on .... I still owe amounts under this Note, I will pay those amounts in full on that date, which is called the "maturity date".

I will make my monthly payments at .... or at a different place if required by the Note Holder.

(B) Amount of Monthly Payments

My monthly payment will be in the amount of U.S. $..

4. BORROWER'S RIGHT TO PREPAY

I have the right to make payments of principal at any time before they are due. A payment of principal only is known as a "prepayment." When I make a prepayment, I will tell the Note Holder in writing that I am doing so.

I may make a full prepayment or partial prepayments without paying any prepayment charge. The Note Holder will use all of my prepayments to reduce the amount of principal that I owe under this Note. If I make a partial prepayment, there will be no changes in the due date or in the amount of my monthly payment unless the Note Holder agrees in writing to those changes.

5. LOAN CHARGES

If a law, which applies to this loan and which sets maximum loan charges, is finally interpreted so that the interest or other loan charges collected or to be collected in connection with this loan exceed the permitted limits, then: (i) any such loan charge shall be reduced by the amount necessary to reduce the charge to the permitted limit; and (ii) any sums already collected from me which exceeded permitted limits will be refunded to me. The Note Holder may choose to make this refund by reducing the principal I owe under this Note or by making a direct payment to me. If a refund reduces principal, the reduction will be treated as a partial prepayment.

6. BORROWER'S FAILURE TO PAY AS REQUIRED

(A) Late Charge for Overdue Payments

If the Note Holder has not received full amount of any monthly payment by the end of the 16th calendar day after the date it is due, I will pay a late charge to the Note Holder. The amount of the charge will be 5% of my overdue payment of principal and interest. I will pay this late charge promptly but only once on each late payment.

(B) Default

If I do not pay the full amount of each monthly payment on the date it is due, I will be in default.

(C) Notice of Default

If I am in default, the Note Holder may send me a written notice telling me that if I do not pay the overdue amount by a certain date, the Note Holder may require me to pay immediately the full amount of principal which has not been paid and all the interest that I owe on that amount. That date must be at least 30 days after the date on which the notice is delivered or mailed to me.

(D) No Waiver By Note Holder

Even if, at a time when I am in default, the Note Holder does not require me to pay immediately in full as described above, the Note Holder will still have the right to do so if I am in default at a later time.

(E) Payment of Note Holder's Costs and Expenses

If the Note Holder has required me to pay immediately in full as described above, the Note Holder will have the right to be paid back by me for all of its costs and expenses in enforcing this Note to the extent not prohibited by applicable law. Those expenses include, for example, reasonable attorneys' fees.

7. GIVING OF NOTICES

Unless applicable law requires a different method, any notice that must be given to me under this Note will be given by delivering it or by mailing it by first class mail to me at the Property Address above or at a different address if I give the Note Holder a notice of my different address.

Any notice that must be given to the Note Holder under this Note will be given by mailing it by first class mail to the Note Holder at the address stated in Section 3(A) above or at a different address if I am given a notice of that different address.

MULTISTATE FIXED RATE NOTE—Single Family—**FNMA/FHLMC UNIFORM INSTRUMENT**

8. OBLIGATIONS OF PERSONS UNDER THIS NOTE

If more than one person signs this Note, each person is fully and personally obligated to keep all of the promises made in this Note, including the promise to pay the full amount owed. Any person who is a guarantor, surety or endorser of this Note is also obligated to do these things. Any person who takes over these obligations, including the obligations of a guarantor, surety or endorser of this Note, is also obligated to keep all of the promises made in this Note. The Note Holder may enforce its rights under this Note against each person individually or against all of us together. This means that any one of us may be required to pay all of the amounts owed under this Note.

9. WAIVERS

I and any other person who has obligations under this Note waive the rights of presentment and notice of dishonor. "Presentment" means the right to require the Note Holder to demand payment of amounts due. "Notice of dishonor" means the right to require the Note Holder to give notice to other persons that amounts due have not been paid.

10. UNIFORM SECURED NOTE

This Note is a uniform instrument with limited variations in some jurisdictions. In addition to the protections given to the Note Holder under this Note, a Mortgage, Deed of Trust or Security Deed (the "Security Instrument"), dated the same date as this Note, protects the Note Holder from possible losses which might result if I do not keep the promises which I make in this Note. That Security Instrument describes how and under what conditions I may be required to make immediate payment in full of all amounts I owe under this Note. Some of those conditions are described as follows:

> **Transfer of the Property or a Beneficial Interest in Borrower.** If all or any part of the Property or any interest in it is sold or transferred (or if a beneficial interest in Borrower is sold or transferred and Borrower is not a natural person) without Lender's prior written consent, Lender may, at its option, require immediate payment in full of all sums secured by this Security Instrument. However, this option shall not be exercised by Lender if exercise is prohibited by federal law as of the date of this Security Instrument.
>
> If Lender exercises this option, Lender shall give Borrower notice of acceleration. The notice shall provide a period of not less than 30 days from the date the notice is delivered or mailed within which Borrower must pay all sums secured by this Security Instrument. If Borrower fails to pay these sums prior to the expiration of this period, Lender may invoke any remedies permitted by this Security Instrument without further notice or demand on Borrower.

WITNESS THE HAND(S) AND SEAL(S) OF THE UNDERSIGNED.

....(Seal)
-Borrower

....(Seal)
-Borrower

....(Seal)
-Borrower

[Sign Original Only]

Holder in due course status confers on the transferee the benefit of **immunity from certain defenses**. This means that if the holder in due course tries to collect on the note, some defenses which may have been used by the maker against the original payee will not be valid. The holder in due course will get paid in circumstances where the original payee may not have. The following defenses are NOT valid against a holder in due course:

1. **fraud** in the inducement (when the original holder convinces the maker to sign the note by making false statements);
2. **failure of consideration** (when the maker never gets what the original holder promised to give in return for the note);
3. **prior payment** or **cancellation** (when the maker pays the note, but does not have the note returned and the original holder then sells it to someone else); and
4. a **set-off** (when the original holder owes the maker money which could be set-off against the amount the maker owes the original holder on the note).

For example, Smith purchases property from Brown and executes a promissory note for the purchase price. Two weeks after Smith moves into the house, Smith is informed that Brown never really had title to the property and Green is the true owner of the house. Since Smith did not get what Brown promised (title to the property), Smith does not have to pay off the promissory note. On the other hand, assume that the day after Smith signs the promissory note, Brown sells it to a secondary market investor (Mortgage, Inc.) under circumstances which made the investor a holder in due course. Even though Smith did not receive what Brown promised, Smith would still have to pay Mortgage, Inc. according to the terms of the note because failure of consideration is not a defense against a holder in due course. Smith would have to sue Brown to try to get the purchase price back.

Although the above enumerated defenses are not valid against a holder in due course, there are some defenses which are "good against the world," that is, good against both the original holder and any subsequent holder in due course. These defenses are:

1. **incapacity** (the maker was a minor or mentally incompetent when he or she signed the note);
2. **illegality** of the instrument (the instrument was entered into in connection with illegal activities, e.g., gambling);
3. **forgery**;
4. **material alteration** (when the original holder unilaterally changes the terms of the note).

For example, Brown forges Smith's name to a promissory note. Brown then sells the note to Mortgage, Inc., a holder in due course. Because the signature was forged, Smith does not have to pay either Brown or Mortgage, Inc.

Transferability. The major advantage to negotiable instruments is that they are so freely transferable. In fact, they are often treated as the equivalent of cash. If the note is made payable "to bearer," transfer of the note is as simple as delivering it to the other party. If the note is payable "to the order of" a named person, the person named must **endorse** the note over to the other party. There are several different types of endorsements. These include:

1. **blank endorsement**: the holder simply signs his or her name on the back of the note;
2. **special endorsement**: the holder writes "Pay to the order of ________________" and then signs the note;
3. **restrictive endorsement**: the holder restricts future negotiation by writing, for example, "Pay to Seaside Bank, for deposit only" and then signs the note:
4. **qualified endorsement**: the holder writes "Without recourse" when signing the note, which means that if the maker of the note refuses to pay, the holder will not be liable for the amount.

The negotiability of the note is not altered by adding certain clauses, such as a clause for the payment of court costs and reasonable attorney's fees in the event of litigation, or an acceleration clause (if the maker defaults on one payment, the entire sum will become immediately due and payable). These types of clauses are often routinely added to promissory notes and, if anything, make the note even more negotiable as they give further protection to the holder.

Types of notes. There are four types of notes that are commonly used in real estate transactions. These are:

1. a **straight note** which calls for the payment of interest only during the term of the note (a balloon payment will be required at the end of the loan term to pay off the principal amount of the loan);
2. an **installment note** which calls for periodic payments of the principal amount only (a balloon payment is also required);
3. a **fully amortized installment note** which calls for periodic payments of both principal and interest which are calculated to fully pay off the loan amount by the end of the loan term (the most common); and
4. an **adjustable rate** note which provides for an interest rate that varies up or down depending on the cost of money (as determined by an agreed on index).

Deed of Trust

In the next portion of this chapter, we will discuss the instrument which secures the promissory note. The two most common types of security instruments are the mortgage and the deed of trust. In California, virtually all lenders use the deed of trust. Mortgages are used only rarely. In fact, it was reported by California title insurance companies that deeds of trust are used in approximately 98% of all recorded real estate transactions. Because of its widespread usage, we will focus our attention on the deed of trust.

A deed of trust (or **trust deed**) places a **voluntary lien** on property. That is, the lien is created with the approval of the property owner. The act of giving an interest in real property (in this case, a lien) to secure a debt is called **hypothecation**.

[Space Above This Line For Recording Data]

DEED OF TRUST

THIS DEED OF TRUST ("Security Instrument") is made on ...., 19.......... The trustor is .... ("Borrower"). The trustee is .... ("Trustee"). The beneficiary is ...., which is organized and existing under the laws of ...., and whose address is .... ("Lender"). Borrower owes Lender the principal sum of .... Dollars (U.S. $..................................). This debt is evidenced by Borrower's note dated the same date as this Security Instrument ("Note"), which provides for monthly payments, with the full debt, if not paid earlier, due and payable on .... This Security Instrument secures to Lender: (a) the repayment of the debt evidenced by the Note, with interest, and all renewals, extensions and modifications; (b) the payment of all other sums, with interest, advanced under paragraph 7 to protect the security of this Security Instrument; and (c) the performance of Borrower's covenants and agreements under this Security Instrument and the Note. For this purpose, Borrower irrevocably grants and conveys to Trustee, in trust, with power of sale, the following described property located in .... County, California:

which has the address of ...., ...,
[Street] [City]

California .... ("Property Address");
[Zip Code]

TOGETHER WITH all the improvements now or hereafter erected on the property, and all easements, rights, appurtenances, rents, royalties, mineral, oil and gas rights and profits, water rights and stock and all fixtures now or hereafter a part of the property. All replacements and additions shall also be covered by this Security Instrument. All of the foregoing is referred to in this Security Instrument as the "Property."

BORROWER COVENANTS that Borrower is lawfully seised of the estate hereby conveyed and has the right to grant and convey the Property and that the Property is unencumbered, except for encumbrances of record. Borrower warrants and will defend generally the title to the Property against all claims and demands, subject to any encumbrances of record.

THIS SECURITY INSTRUMENT combines uniform covenants for national use and non-uniform covenants with limited variations by jurisdiction to constitute a uniform security instrument covering real property.

CALIFORNIA—Single Family—**FNMA/FHLMC UNIFORM INSTRUMENT** **Form 3005 12/83**

UNIFORM COVENANTS. Borrower and Lender covenant and agree as follows:

1. Payment of Principal and Interest; Prepayment and Late Charges. Borrower shall promptly pay when due the principal of and interest on the debt evidenced by the Note and any prepayment and late charges due under the Note.

2. Funds for Taxes and Insurance. Subject to applicable law or to a written waiver by Lender, Borrower shall pay to Lender on the day monthly payments are due under the Note, until the Note is paid in full, a sum ("Funds") equal to one-twelfth of: (a) yearly taxes and assessments which may attain priority over this Security Instrument; (b) yearly leasehold payments or ground rents on the Property, if any; (c) yearly hazard insurance premiums; and (d) yearly mortgage insurance premiums, if any. These items are called "escrow items." Lender may estimate the Funds due on the basis of current data and reasonable estimates of future escrow items.

The Funds shall be held in an institution the deposits or accounts of which are insured or guaranteed by a federal or state agency (including Lender if Lender is such an institution). Lender shall apply the Funds to pay the escrow items. Lender may not charge for holding and applying the Funds, analyzing the account or verifying the escrow items, unless Lender pays Borrower interest on the Funds and applicable law permits Lender to make such a charge. Borrower and Lender may agree in writing that interest shall be paid on the Funds. Unless an agreement is made or applicable law requires interest to be paid, Lender shall not be required to pay Borrower any interest or earnings on the Funds. Lender shall give to Borrower, without charge, an annual accounting of the Funds showing credits and debits to the Funds and the purpose for which each debit to the Funds was made. The Funds are pledged as additional security for the sums secured by this Security Instrument.

If the amount of the Funds held by Lender, together with the future monthly payments of Funds payable prior to the due dates of the escrow items, shall exceed the amount required to pay the escrow items when due, the excess shall be, at Borrower's option, either promptly repaid to Borrower or credited to Borrower on monthly payments of Funds. If the amount of the Funds held by Lender is not sufficient to pay the escrow items when due, Borrower shall pay to Lender any amount necessary to make up the deficiency in one or more payments as required by Lender.

Upon payment in full of all sums secured by this Security Instrument, Lender shall promptly refund to Borrower any Funds held by Lender. If under paragraph 19 the Property is sold or acquired by Lender, Lender shall apply, no later than immediately prior to the sale of the Property or its acquisition by Lender, any Funds held by Lender at the time of application as a credit against the sums secured by this Security Instrument.

3. Application of Payments. Unless applicable law provides otherwise, all payments received by Lender under paragraphs 1 and 2 shall be applied: first, to late charges due under the Note; second, to prepayment charges due under the Note; third, to amounts payable under paragraph 2; fourth, to interest due; and last, to principal due.

4. Charges; Liens. Borrower shall pay all taxes, assessments, charges, fines and impositions attributable to the Property which may attain priority over this Security Instrument, and leasehold payments or ground rents, if any. Borrower shall pay these obligations in the manner provided in paragraph 2, or if not paid in that manner, Borrower shall pay them on time directly to the person owed payment. Borrower shall promptly furnish to Lender all notices of amounts to be paid under this paragraph. If Borrower makes these payments directly, Borrower shall promptly furnish to Lender receipts evidencing the payments.

Borrower shall promptly discharge any lien which has priority over this Security Instrument unless Borrower: (a) agrees in writing to the payment of the obligation secured by the lien in a manner acceptable to Lender; (b) contests in good faith the lien by, or defends against enforcement of the lien in, legal proceedings which in the Lender's opinion operate to prevent the enforcement of the lien or forfeiture of any part of the Property; or (c) secures from the holder of the lien an agreement satisfactory to Lender subordinating the lien to this Security Instrument. If Lender determines that any part of the Property is subject to a lien which may attain priority over this Security Instrument, Lender may give Borrower a notice identifying the lien. Borrower shall satisfy the lien or take one or more of the actions set forth above within 10 days of the giving of notice.

5. Hazard Insurance. Borrower shall keep the improvements now existing or hereafter erected on the Property insured against loss by fire, hazards included within the term "extended coverage" and any other hazards for which Lender requires insurance. This insurance shall be maintained in the amounts and for the periods that Lender requires. The insurance carrier providing the insurance shall be chosen by Borrower subject to Lender's approval which shall not be unreasonably withheld.

All insurance policies and renewals shall be acceptable to Lender and shall include a standard mortgage clause. Lender shall have the right to hold the policies and renewals. If Lender requires, Borrower shall promptly give to Lender all receipts of paid premiums and renewal notices. In the event of loss, Borrower shall give prompt notice to the insurance carrier and Lender. Lender may make proof of loss if not made promptly by Borrower.

Unless Lender and Borrower otherwise agree in writing, insurance proceeds shall be applied to restoration or repair of the Property damaged, if the restoration or repair is economically feasible and Lender's security is not lessened. If the restoration or repair is not economically feasible or Lender's security would be lessened, the insurance proceeds shall be applied to the sums secured by this Security Instrument, whether or not then due, with any excess paid to Borrower. If Borrower abandons the Property, or does not answer within 30 days a notice from Lender that the insurance carrier has offered to settle a claim, then Lender may collect the insurance proceeds. Lender may use the proceeds to repair or restore the Property or to pay sums secured by this Security Instrument, whether or not then due. The 30-day period will begin when the notice is given.

Unless Lender and Borrower otherwise agree in writing, any application of proceeds to principal shall not extend or postpone the due date of the monthly payments referred to in paragraphs 1 and 2 or change the amount of the payments. If under paragraph 19 the Property is acquired by Lender, Borrower's right to any insurance policies and proceeds resulting from damage to the Property prior to the acquisition shall pass to Lender to the extent of the sums secured by this Security Instrument immediately prior to the acquisition.

6. Preservation and Maintenance of Property; Leaseholds. Borrower shall not destroy, damage or substantially change the Property, allow the Property to deteriorate or commit waste. If this Security Instrument is on a leasehold, Borrower shall comply with the provisions of the lease, and if Borrower acquires fee title to the Property, the leasehold and fee title shall not merge unless Lender agrees to the merger in writing.

7. Protection of Lender's Rights in the Property; Mortgage Insurance. If Borrower fails to perform the covenants and agreements contained in this Security Instrument, or there is a legal proceeding that may significantly affect Lender's rights in the Property (such as a proceeding in bankruptcy, probate, for condemnation or to enforce laws or regulations), then Lender may do and pay for whatever is necessary to protect the value of the Property and Lender's rights in the Property. Lender's actions may include paying any sums secured by a lien which has priority over this Security Instrument, appearing in court, paying reasonable attorneys' fees and entering on the Property to make repairs. Although Lender may take action under this paragraph 7, Lender does not have to do so.

Any amounts disbursed by Lender under this paragraph 7 shall become additional debt of Borrower secured by this Security Instrument. Unless Borrower and Lender agree to other terms of payment, these amounts shall bear interest from the date of disbursement at the Note rate and shall be payable, with interest, upon notice from Lender to Borrower requesting payment.

If Lender required mortgage insurance as a condition of making the loan secured by this Security Instrument, Borrower shall pay the premiums required to maintain the insurance in effect until such time as the requirement for the insurance terminates in accordance with Borrower's and Lender's written agreement or applicable law.

8. Inspection. Lender or its agent may make reasonable entries upon and inspections of the Property. Lender shall give Borrower notice at the time of or prior to an inspection specifying reasonable cause for the inspection.

9. Condemnation. The proceeds of any award or claim for damages, direct or consequential, in connection with any condemnation or other taking of any part of the Property, or for conveyance in lieu of condemnation, are hereby assigned and shall be paid to Lender.

In the event of a total taking of the Property, the proceeds shall be applied to the sums secured by this Security Instrument, whether or not then due, with any excess paid to Borrower. In the event of a partial taking of the Property, unless Borrower and Lender otherwise agree in writing, the sums secured by this Security Instrument shall be reduced by the amount of the proceeds multiplied by the following fraction: (a) the total amount of the sums secured immediately before the taking, divided by (b) the fair market value of the Property immediately before the taking. Any balance shall be paid to Borrower.

If the Property is abandoned by Borrower, or if, after notice by Lender to Borrower that the condemnor offers to make an award or settle a claim for damages, Borrower fails to respond to Lender within 30 days after the date the notice is given, Lender is authorized to collect and apply the proceeds, at its option, either to restoration or repair of the Property or to the sums secured by this Security Instrument, whether or not then due.

Unless Lender and Borrower otherwise agree in writing, any application of proceeds to principal shall not extend or postpone the due date of the monthly payments referred to in paragraphs 1 and 2 or change the amount of such payments.

10. Borrower Not Released; Forbearance By Lender Not a Waiver. Extension of the time for payment or modification of amortization of the sums secured by this Security Instrument granted by Lender to any successor in interest of Borrower shall not operate to release the liability of the original Borrower or Borrower's successors in interest. Lender shall not be required to commence proceedings against any successor in interest or refuse to extend time for payment or otherwise modify amortization of the sums secured by this Security Instrument by reason of any demand made by the original Borrower or Borrower's successors in interest. Any forbearance by Lender in exercising any right or remedy shall not be a waiver of or preclude the exercise of any right or remedy.

11. Successors and Assigns Bound; Joint and Several Liability; Co-signers. The covenants and agreements of this Security Instrument shall bind and benefit the successors and assigns of Lender and Borrower, subject to the provisions of paragraph 17. Borrower's covenants and agreements shall be joint and several. Any Borrower who co-signs this Security Instrument but does not execute the Note: (a) is co-signing this Security Instrument only to mortgage, grant and convey that Borrower's interest in the Property under the terms of this Security Instrument; (b) is not personally obligated to pay the sums secured by this Security Instrument; and (c) agrees that Lender and any other Borrower may agree to extend, modify, forbear or make any accommodations with regard to the terms of this Security Instrument or the Note without that Borrower's consent.

12. Loan Charges. If the loan secured by this Security Instrument is subject to a law which sets maximum loan charges, and that law is finally interpreted so that the interest or other loan charges collected or to be collected in connection with the loan exceed the permitted limits, then: (a) any such loan charge shall be reduced by the amount necessary to reduce the charge to the permitted limit; and (b) any sums already collected from Borrower which exceeded permitted limits will be refunded to Borrower. Lender may choose to make this refund by reducing the principal owed under the Note or by making a direct payment to Borrower. If a refund reduces principal, the reduction will be treated as a partial prepayment without any prepayment charge under the Note.

13. Legislation Affecting Lender's Rights. If enactment or expiration of applicable laws has the effect of rendering any provision of the Note or this Security Instrument unenforceable according to its terms, Lender, at its option, may require immediate payment in full of all sums secured by this Security Instrument and may invoke any remedies permitted by paragraph 19. If Lender exercises this option, Lender shall take the steps specified in the second paragraph of paragraph 17.

14. Notices. Any notice to Borrower provided for in this Security Instrument shall be given by delivering it or by mailing it by first class mail unless applicable law requires use of another method. The notice shall be directed to the Property Address or any other address Borrower designates by notice to Lender. Any notice to Lender shall be given by first class mail to Lender's address stated herein or any other address Lender designates by notice to Borrower. Any notice provided for in this Security Instrument shall be deemed to have been given to Borrower or Lender when given as provided in this paragraph.

15. Governing Law; Severability. This Security Instrument shall be governed by federal law and the law of the jurisdiction in which the Property is located. In the event that any provision or clause of this Security Instrument or the Note conflicts with applicable law, such conflict shall not affect other provisions of this Security Instrument or the Note which can be given effect without the conflicting provision. To this end the provisions of this Security Instrument and the Note are declared to be severable.

16. Borrower's Copy. Borrower shall be given one conformed copy of the Note and of this Security Instrument.

17. Transfer of the Property or a Beneficial Interest in Borrower. If all or any part of the Property or any interest in it is sold or transferred (or if a beneficial interest in Borrower is sold or transferred and Borrower is not a natural person) without Lender's prior written consent, Lender may, at its option, require immediate payment in full of all sums secured by this Security Instrument. However, this option shall not be exercised by Lender if exercise is prohibited by federal law as of the date of this Security Instrument.

If Lender exercises this option, Lender shall give Borrower notice of acceleration. The notice shall provide a period of not less than 30 days from the date the notice is delivered or mailed within which Borrower must pay all sums secured by this Security Instrument. If Borrower fails to pay these sums prior to the expiration of this period, Lender may invoke any remedies permitted by this Security Instrument without further notice or demand on Borrower.

18. Borrower's Right to Reinstate. If Borrower meets certain conditions, Borrower shall have the right to have enforcement of this Security Instrument discontinued at any time prior to the earlier of: (a) 5 days (or such other period as applicable law may specify for reinstatement) before sale of the Property pursuant to any power of sale contained in this Security Instrument; or (b) entry of a judgment enforcing this Security Instrument. Those conditions are that Borrower: (a) pays Lender all sums which then would be due under this Security Instrument and the Note had no acceleration occurred; (b) cures any default of any other covenants or agreements; (c) pays all expenses incurred in enforcing this Security Instrument, including, but not limited to, reasonable attorneys fees; and (d) takes such action as Lender may reasonably require to assure that the lien of this Security Instrument, Lender's rights in the Property and Borrower's obligation to pay the sums secured by this Security Instrument shall continue unchanged. Upon reinstatement by Borrower, this Security Instrument and the obligations secured hereby shall remain fully effective as if no acceleration had occurred. However, this right to reinstate shall not apply in the case of acceleration under paragraphs 13 or 17.

NON-UNIFORM COVENANTS. Borrower and Lender further covenant and agree as follows:

19. Acceleration; Remedies. Lender shall give notice to Borrower prior to acceleration following Borrower's breach of any covenant or agreement in this Security Instrument (but not prior to acceleration under paragraphs 13 and 17 unless applicable law provides otherwise). The notice shall specify: (a) the default; (b) the action required to cure the default; (c) a date, not less than 30 days from the date the notice is given to Borrower, by which the default must be cured; and (d) that failure to cure the default on or before the date specified in the notice may result in acceleration of the sums secured by this Security Instrument and sale of the Property. The notice shall further inform Borrower of the right to reinstate after acceleration and the right to bring a court action to assert the non-existence of a default or any other defense of Borrower to acceleration and sale. If the default is not cured on or before the date specified in the notice, Lender at its option may require immediate payment in full of all sums secured by this Security Instrument without further demand and may invoke the power of sale and any other remedies permitted by applicable law. Lender shall be entitled to collect all expenses incurred in pursuing the remedies provided in this paragraph 19, including, but not limited to, reasonable attorneys' fees and costs of title evidence.

If Lender invokes the power of sale, Lender shall execute or cause Trustee to execute a written notice of the occurrence of an event of default and of Lender's election to cause the Property to be sold. Trustee shall cause this notice to be recorded in each county in which any part of the Property is located. Lender or Trustee shall mail copies of the notice as prescribed by applicable law to Borrower and to the other persons prescribed by applicable law. Trustee shall give public notice of sale to the persons and in the manner prescribed by applicable law. After the time required by applicable law, Trustee, without demand on Borrower, shall sell the Property at public auction to the highest bidder at the time and place and under the terms designated in the notice of sale in one or more parcels and in any order Trustee determines. Trustee may postpone sale of all or any parcel of the Property by public announcement at the time and place of any previously scheduled sale. Lender or its designee may purchase the Property at any sale.

Trustee shall deliver to the purchaser Trustee's deed conveying the Property without any covenant or warranty, expressed or implied. The recitals in the Trustee's deed shall be prima facie evidence of the truth of the statements made therein. Trustee shall apply the proceeds of the sale in the following order: (a) to all expenses of the sale, including, but not limited to, reasonable Trustee's and attorneys' fees; (b) to all sums secured by this Security Instrument; and (c) any excess to the person or persons legally entitled to it.

20. Lender in Possession. Upon acceleration under paragraph 19 or abandonment of the Property, Lender (in person, by agent or by judicially appointed receiver) shall be entitled to enter upon, take possession of and manage the Property and to collect the rents of the Property including those past due. Any rents collected by Lender or the receiver shall be applied first to payment of the costs of management of the Property and collection of rents, including, but not limited to, receiver's fees, premiums on receiver's bonds and reasonable attorneys' fees, and then to the sums secured by this Security Instrument.

21. Reconveyance. Upon payment of all sums secured by this Security Instrument, Lender shall request Trustee to reconvey the Property and shall surrender this Security Instrument and all notes evidencing debt secured by this Security Instrument to Trustee. Trustee shall reconvey the Property without warranty and without charge to the person or persons legally entitled to it. Such person or persons shall pay any recordation costs.

22. Substitute Trustee. Lender, at its option, may from time to time appoint a successor trustee to any Trustee appointed hereunder by an instrument executed and acknowledged by Lender and recorded in the office of the Recorder of the county in which the Property is located. The instrument shall contain the name of the original Lender, Trustee and Borrower, the book and page where this Security Instrument is recorded and the name and address of the successor trustee. Without conveyance of the Property, the successor trustee shall succeed to all the title, powers and duties conferred upon the Trustee herein and by applicable law. This procedure for substitution of trustee shall govern to the exclusion of all other provisions for substitution.

23. Request for Notices. Borrower requests that copies of the notices of default and sale be sent to Borrower's address which is the Property Address.

24. Riders to this Security Instrument. If one or more riders are executed by Borrower and recorded together with this Security Instrument, the covenants and agreements of each such rider shall be incorporated into and shall amend and supplement the covenants and agreements of this Security Instrument as if the rider(s) were a part of this Security Instrument. [Check applicable box(es)]

☐ Adjustable Rate Rider ☐ Condominium Rider ☐ 2–4 Family Rider

☐ Graduated Payment Rider ☐ Planned Unit Development Rider

☐ Other(s) [specify]

BY SIGNING BELOW, Borrower accepts and agrees to the terms and covenants contained in this Security Instrument and in any rider(s) executed by Borrower and recorded with it.

....(Seal)
—Borrower

....(Seal)
—Borrower

[Space Below This Line For Acknowledgment]

Lien theory vs. title theory.

While the lender is given a security interest in the property, the lender does not obtain any rights to possess the property. When Smith goes to the local savings and loan association and takes out a loan on her property, she goes back home to that mortgaged property. The savings and loan association does not acquire possession of the property by virtue of the mortgage or deed of trust. The borrower retains both title to the property and all the attendant rights of ownership: the right to use, lease, sell, enjoy, etc. The deed of trust merely acts as a lien on the property. This principle is referred to as the lien theory and applies to all deeds of trust and mortgages used in California. Historically, security devices such as the mortgage and deed of trust conveyed actual legal title to the lender (**bare title**) while the borrower retained **equitable title** (the right to use and possess the property in the absence of legal title). The concept of a deed of trust conveying title to the lender is called the **title theory**.

How a trust deed works.

The deed of trust is a **three-party** device. The parties are the trustor (the borrower), the beneficiary (the lender) and the trustee (a neutral third party). The trust deed was designed to convey bare title to the trustee (thus the name trust *deed*) for the term of the loan. During this time, possession of the property remains with the trustor (borrower). When the loan is fully repaid, the trustee reconveys the title of the property back to the trustor. This is done with a **deed of reconveyance**. If the trustor defaults on the loan, the trustee has the power to sell the property for the benefit of the beneficiary (the lender). The **power of sale** clause in the deed of trust gives the trustee this power.

For a deed of trust to be valid, it must contain certain provisions. These include a statement pledging the property as collateral for a debt (a **granting clause**), a complete and unambiguous **property description**, the **amount of the debt**, the **maturity date** of the debt, a **defeasance clause** (the trust deed will be canceled when the debt is paid), and a **power of sale clause**.

A standard deed of trust form is shown on the previous pages. As you can see, this form includes all the necessary elements listed above. Most lenders use the standard FNMA/FHLMC trust deed form so the loan will be easily salable to these agencies. If FNMA or FHLMC had to carefully inspect the provisions of each individual deed of trust they purchased, it would be an impracticably time-consuming process. When all lenders use a standard form, secondary investors can be assured of receiving a deed of trust with acceptable provisions.

Trust deed foreclosure.

The **power of sale** clause is a statement authorizing the trustee to sell the property upon the default of the trustor. At the direction of the beneficiary, the trustee conducts an out-of-court sale, or auction, called a **trustee's sale**. The proceeds from the sale are used to pay off the trustor's debt. Any sale proceeds in excess of the debt amount belong to the trustor. For example, Smith bought a home with a loan from National Savings and Loan. The loan amount was $80,000. Smith executed a promissory note and deed of trust with National as the beneficiary. Homeowner's Title was named as the trustee in the deed of trust. Soon after closing, Smith defaults on the loan payments. The power of sale clause in the deed of trust allows Homeowner's to sell the property at a trustee's sale. The property is sold for $80,000. The funds from the sale go to National to pay off Smith's loan. Since there was nothing left over after paying off the debt, Smith does not get any money from the sale of the property.

Before there can be a foreclosure, the lender must first notify the trustee of the default. The trustee will then send a **notice of default** to the borrower. The trustee must also give notice of default to all other lienholders and anyone else who has recorded a request for notice of default and sale.

Reinstatement. The borrower can prevent the sale of the property by **reinstating** the loan. A loan is reinstated by paying all the delinquent amounts any time from the notice of default until five business days before the sales date. The amount the borrower must pay includes all the past due installments plus any late charges that may be imposed by the lender.

If the loan has not been reinstated three months after the notice of default was sent, the trustee will publish a weekly **notice of sale** in a newspaper of general circulation. The trustee also sends the notice to the borrower and posts it on the property. After **20 days** from the date of the first publication of the notice, the trustee can sell the property.

Five business days before the date set for the trustee's sale, the borrower can no longer reinstate the loan. At this point, the only way the borrower can prevent the trustee's sale is to pay the entire loan balance prior to the sale. If the borrower is unable to do this, he or she may avoid the foreclosure sale by giving the lender a **deed in lieu of foreclosure**. If the lender is willing to accept the deed, the costs of foreclosure can be avoided and the borrower may be able to protect his or her credit rating.

Trustee's deed. Once the sale takes place, the borrower loses all rights to the property. The borrower loses both the title to the property and all rights of possession and use. At the sale, the trustee issues a **trustee's deed** to the successful bidder. If the successful bidder is the lender, the amount due on the loan may be applied towards the bid price (this is called **credit bidding**). For example, Jones has defaulted on her loan payments to Mortgage, Inc. and the property is being sold at a trustee's sale. The amount due on the loan is $85,000. At the trustee's sale Mortgage, Inc. bids $85,000. This is the highest bid for the property. Mortgage, Inc. is the successful bidder, the trustee executes a trustee's deed to Mortgage, Inc., and Mortgage, Inc. applies the amount due on the loan towards the bid price. In this way, Mortgage, Inc. acquires title to the property without having to extend any cash towards the purchase price. After the sale, Jones no longer has any rights to the property and her debt to Mortgage, Inc. is extinguished.

Deficiency judgment. When the lender forecloses the property through a trustee's sale, the lender must be satisfied with only the proceeds from the sale. There can be **no deficiency judgment** against the borrower, even if the proceeds do not cover the full loan amount. This means that if the loan amount were $75,000 and the sale of the property brought $71,000, the lender could not take any further action against the borrower for the remaining $4,000. The $71,000 from the sale of the property is all the lender will ever be able to get to apply to the loan amount.

> **NOTE:** The mortgage differs from the deed of trust in several important ways. First, the mortgage must be foreclosed judicially (through the courts). A complaint must be filed, the judge must order the sale, and the sheriff then sells the property (this is called the "sheriff's sale"). Mortgage foreclosure takes significantly longer than a deed of trust foreclosure. A deed of trust may also be foreclosed judicially, but because of the time considerations, lenders rarely use this alternative. Another important distinction of a mortgage is that, after the sale of the property, the borrower has one year in which to redeem the property and may remain in possession for that period of time. A third distinction is that a deficiency judgment against the borrower is possible when the lender forecloses through a judicial sale. The lengthy foreclosure time and the period of redemption are the two major factors which cause lenders to prefer a deed of trust over a mortgage.

Junior lienholders. Sometimes, real estate agents have a difficult time convincing a seller to carry back a second loan. Property owners often believe that there is little security protecting a second loan. They often know little about foreclosure rights and hesitate to become involved in what they see as a complicated situation. In fact, the holder of a junior lien (i.e., second mortgage) has the same rights as the holder of the first lien. If the purchaser defaults on the second loan, the junior lienholder can go through the simple procedures outlined above in order to foreclose his or her interest in the property.

There are some disadvantages to being in the position of a junior lienholder, however. The major source of these disadvantages is the fact that if the borrower cannot make payments on the second loan, he or she generally cannot make payments on the first loan either. If the borrower is in default on the first loan and the first lienholder forecloses the property, the second lienholder could lose all of his or her interest in the property.

The second lienholder loses his or her interest in the property when the first lien foreclosure sale only raises enough money to pay off the first loan. Under these circumstances, the second lienholder would get nothing from the foreclosure sale (if the sale proceeds exceeded the amount of the first loan, the second lienholder would get the excess up to the second loan amount). If the second lienholder is not paid off at the foreclosure sale, he or she cannot sue the borrower for the loan amount since there can be no deficiency judgment in conjunction with a trustee's sale. Furthermore, once the property has been foreclosed and sold at the trustee's sale, the second lien no longer attaches to the property. The purchaser at the trustee's sale obtains title to the property free and clear of the second lien.

There is a way for the junior lienholder to protect his or her interest in the property. When the junior lien is first created, the junior lienholder can record a "request for notice of default." The trustee under the first deed of trust will then notify the junior lienholder of the borrower's default. Once notified of the default, the junior lienholder can reinstate the first loan by paying the amount owed and continue to make the monthly payments while beginning his or her own foreclosure proceedings. Once the first loan is reinstated, the first lienholder can no longer begin foreclosure proceedings. While making payments on the first loan may work a financial hardship on the junior lienholder, the payments usually only have to be made for the few months required to foreclose the property.

By foreclosing the second lien, the junior lienholder can try to recoup the amount of the second loan. It must be remembered, however, that the foreclosure of a second lien does not extinguish the first lien and any purchaser at the trustee's sale would take title to the property subject to the first lien.

Special Provisions

There are some provisions inserted in promissory notes or deeds of trust that the real estate agent should be familiar with. These provisions appear with such frequency that they are almost considered standard.

Alienation clause. An alienation, or **due-on-sale** clause provides that the entire loan balance must be paid immediately if the borrower transfers any interest in the property without the written consent of the lender. This clause is used to prevent the sale of the realty by means of an assumption or land contract. By virtue of federal legislation (the Garn-St. Germain Act) all alienation clauses are fully enforceable in California by any lender.

Assumption. Even if there is no due-on-sale clause, or the lender has consented to the transfer of the property, there will still often be some kind of condition imposed on the assumption of the loan. An assumption fee may be required or there may be an upward adjustment of the interest rate.

Late payment. Any penalty for late payment must be clearly set out in the agreement. Any charge that is considered excessive by a court will not be enforced.

Lock-in clauses. These clauses prohibit the early payment of the debt. A lock-in provision does not allow the borrower to prepay the debt, so the borrower is "locked-in" to the loan for the entire term. This is generally so the lender can take advantage of the interest rate that was in effect at the time the loan was made.

Prepayment provision. In the absence of a lock-in clause, the borrower is presumed to have the right to prepay a loan. Often, however, the lender will impose certain restrictions on prepayment. These may take the form of when the prepayments can be made (e.g., on the same date as the regular monthly payment), how much can be prepaid (e.g., up to 15% of the loan amount in any 12-month period), and what fees will be charged for prepayments made in excess of the stated amount (e.g., the equivalent of six months interest if the loan amount is paid in full within five years of the origination date).

Subordination clause. A subordination clause is used to give another lien higher priority. The clause is found in the first security document and provides that a subsequent lien will be given priority, even though the first lien was executed and recorded first. This is often found in deeds of trust securing raw land. The borrower will obtain a loan to purchase raw land, but a subsequent lender will not loan the money necessary to construct a building on the land unless that lender is assured a first lien position. Therefore, a subordination clause is put in the first deed of trust (securing the loan for the raw land), providing that it will take a subordinate position to any subsequent construction lien.

Section Three

Sales Practices

Chapter Thirteen

Overview of the Deposit Receipt

Why Deposit Receipts Are Used

Most transactions for the purchase and sale of real estate begin with a written contract between the buyer and seller. An initial question might be, "Why?"

If Mr. and Mrs. Buyer have decided they want to buy Mr. and Mrs. Seller's house and Mr. and Mrs. Seller are willing to sell at the price that the Buyers are willing to pay, why bother with writing up a long contract and getting everyone to sign it? Why not have the Buyers give the Sellers the money and the Sellers give the buyers the deed? The Sellers could then move out and the Buyers could move in, the sale would be accomplished and everyone would be happy. After all, when you buy most other things, such as groceries or even furniture, you generally just pay cash, write a check or give the seller your credit card, the merchandise is given to you and you leave.

Perhaps a short answer would be that buying real estate is quite a bit more involved than buying a watermelon at a fruit stand. In a typical watermelon transaction, the buyer pays by cash or personal check. The seller immediately delivers the watermelon to the buyer who leaves without a second thought as to rights of possession or ownership or concern as to whether the seller really had the right to sell the watermelon in the first place. In a real estate transaction, though, questions relating to financing, possession, the condition of title, the possibility that persons other than the seller might have liens or other interests in the property, and arrangements for conveying possession and title must be addressed.

In a typical home purchase, Mr. and Mrs. Buyer do not have the available cash to buy the house. They must either make arrangements to borrow the money somewhere else (from a savings and loan, bank, or other lender) or must convince the seller to finance the transaction through some type of delayed payment plan. If the buyers intend to borrow the money from an outside source, time will be required to obtain lender approval. This process, which may involve an appraisal and inspection of the property, a credit report on the borrowers, confirmation of the borrower's assets and employment information, and obtaining mortgage insurance can easily be a matter of weeks, not days. The buyers need some way to keep the sellers obligated to sell on the agreed terms during the time it takes them to arrange the financing. The buyers do not want to borrow the money unless they are sure they will be able to buy the house when they get the loan.

Also, in most cases the buyers do not want to be forced to buy the house (or lose their downpayment or other deposit) if they are unable to arrange the type of financing they want. This means that there must be some sort of agreement between the buyers and the sellers which releases the buyers from an obligation to buy and allows them a refund of their deposit if they cannot obtain the intended financing after a good faith effort.

Another concern for the buyers is that at the time they decide to buy the house they usually do not know whether the seller really owns it or not. Questions regarding title to land are anything but simple. Even if the seller has legal title to the property, there may be encumbrances on the property (such as easements across it which interfere with the buyer's use or judgment, tax or other liens against the property). This particular aspect of the transaction is handled in most states in one of two ways: an abstract of title or a title insurance policy. In California, it is customary to arrange to have a title insurance company conduct a title search, prepare a preliminary report and issue a policy of title insurance.

To avoid belaboring the point, maybe it would be sufficient to say that a real estate transaction is usually a pretty complicated affair in addition to the fact that, for most people, a large amount of money is involved.

Financing must be arranged, title searched, existing liens (such as the seller's mortgage or assessments for local improvements) must be paid off or an agreement reached for the buyer to assume them, fire insurance must be obtained, and there are often a number of other matters which must be handled prior to the time the buyer pays the price and the seller delivers title and possession. During the time that both parties are performing their respective tasks, they both want to keep the other side obligated to perform. The buyer does not want to spend several hundred dollars in appraisal, credit report and other financing-related fees only to find out that the seller no longer wants to sell the house. The seller does not want to take the house off the market and spend several hundred dollars to search title or provide a title insurance policy only to find out that the buyer no longer wants to buy the house.

It is therefore mutually advantageous that an enforceable contract to buy and sell the property be entered. These agreements are commonly known by a number of names in different states, such as "purchase and sale agreement," "earnest money agreement," "deposit receipt," "binder" and others. In California, "deposit receipt" is the most widely used term.

Although many buyers and sellers are under the mistaken impression that these forms are merely non-binding preliminary agreements, they are, in fact, binding contracts if properly filled out and signed. Most forms make some indication that a binding contract is intended. This notice is normally found near the top of the form on the first page. The phrase found directly below the heading of the California Association of Realtors form is typical. The parties are cautioned that the form is more than just a receipt for the buyer's deposit, it is intended to be a legally binding contract and both parties should, therefore, read it carefully before signing.

CALIFORNIA ASSOCIATION OF REALTORS

REAL ESTATE PURCHASE CONTRACT AND RECEIPT FOR DEPOSIT

THIS IS MORE THAN A RECEIPT FOR MONEY. IT IS INTENDED TO BE A LEGALLY BINDING CONTRACT. READ IT CAREFULLY.
CALIFORNIA ASSOCIATION OF REALTORS® (CAR) STANDARD FORM

The Importance of Proper Preparation.

Regardless of which particular form is used, once it has been signed by both parties (assuming it has been properly completed with the necessary information), **the agreement becomes a binding contract** which may be enforced by a court of law. Depending on the facts of the particular transaction and the terms of the contract form used, a party who has not breached the contract may be able to sue the party who did breach the contract for money damages or for specific performance (specific performance is a court order which directs the individual to perform his or her obligations under the contract according to its terms) or the seller may be able to keep the deposit made by a buyer who defaults.

The deposit receipt establishes the obligations of the parties regarding the sale of the property: the price to be paid; the terms of payment; identification of the property which is to be transferred; and the time for delivery of title and possession, among other matters. The subsequent closing or settlement follows the terms of the deposit receipt. It can be seen, then, that proper preparation of the deposit receipt is essential for a smooth and successful real estate transaction and for a smooth and successful real estate practice.

Necessary Elements.

Having covered why a contract is necessary and the importance of proper preparation, we will next cover, in a general fashion, what should be included in the agreement. In order to be an enforceable contract, the four essentials needed for any contract to be enforceable must be present: parties with **capacity**; an agreement or **mutuality**; **consideration**; and a **lawful object**. A contract for the sale of real estate must be in writing in order to comply with the Statute of Frauds, but what must be included in the writing?

The deposit receipt must include:

1) the identities of the buyer(s) and seller(s);

2) the total price;

3) the time and manner of payment; and,

4) a description of the property.

The above list is a pretty bare bones approach to a contract to buy and sell real estate. Although California courts have held that some other terms, such as opening of escrow, furnishing a deed, proration of taxes and payment of the title insurance premium may be determined based on local custom, it is by far the better practice to have a contract which spells out **all** the terms in order to avoid ambiguities which can lead to disputes and litigation.

Preparation of Form Documents.

For the purposes of this book it will be assumed that real estate brokers and salespersons will be preparing purchase and sale agreements by completing or filling in the blanks in a form, that the blank form has been developed by competent professionals who are familiar with applicable state law, and that such a form, if properly filled in and/or completed, will satisfy the requirements of state law for an enforceable real estate contract.

In this book, the REAL ESTATE PURCHASE CONTRACT AND RECEIPT FOR DEPOSIT forms published and distributed by the California Association of REALTORS® will be used for illustrations and examples.

The Role of the Agent.

The aim of a real estate broker or salesperson should be to prepare an agreement which clearly expresses the intentions and understandings of the parties so that each side understands its own obligations and the rights and obligations of the other party. The goal of the real estate agent is to avoid misunderstandings which can lead to disagreements and a refusal by one or both parties to proceed with the transaction. Such disagreements or refusals can result in delayed or failed transactions and lawsuits. Delayed or abandoned transactions caused by the broker's or salesperson's failure to properly complete a form are not only a poor service to the client and the public, they are unlikely to give rise to positive recommendations by the parties involved. They may also result in loss of the commission and, possibly, legal liability for damages on the part of the agent who negligently or improperly prepared the agreement.

Overview of Purchase and Sale Forms.

The following materials covering deposit receipts will focus on particular provisions and portions of the forms, but before getting into a detailed analysis of the individual parts, it would be helpful to first take an overview of a typical form. As has been mentioned, there is considerable variation from state to state in the laws applicable to real estate transactions, local customs and practices, and in the contract forms themselves. However, there is enough similarity in the basic content and form of deposit receipts designed to be completed by real estate agents to permit a general discussion of a typical contract.

The California Association of REALTORS® standard form REAL ESTATE PURCHASE CONTRACT AND RECEIPT FOR DEPOSIT, which will be used for illustrations and examples in the remainder of our coverage of deposit receipts, is reproduced on the following pages. As a quick scanning of the document will reveal, the contract form is comprised, for the most part, of preprinted clauses and provisions which are incomplete. There are blanks to be filled in or boxes to be checked by the agent to supply the information necessary to create a binding contract for a specific transaction.

We will now take a quick and somewhat general overview of the form. Materials later in the course will cover the individual clauses in much greater detail, along with suggestions and examples for completing the blanks. As we review each section of the California REALTORS® sample form, you should compare it to the form you use in your every day business, if you use a different form. A comparison of the similarities and differences between your form and the sample form will serve two purposes. First, it will help you become familiar with what is included in your form, and what is not included. Second, it should begin to raise questions in your mind as to why your form is written the way it is, whether you use the REALTORS® form illustrated in the text or some other form. These questions will be answered later in the text where we examine each section of the deposit receipt in detail.

Heading. As with most forms, the California REALTORS® form begins with a title which identifies the nature and purpose of the form. In this case, the form is identified as a real estate purchase contract and receipt for the buyer's deposit. There is then a caution that the form is more than a receipt for a deposit; it is intended to be a binding contract and the parties should read it carefully before signing.

In the first paragraph in the body of the contract form, below the heading, there are lines to indicate the date and place the offer is made, to identify the buyer(s), to acknowledge that a deposit has been received from the buyer and space for the property description. Lines for the street address of the property are located at the top of the other three pages of the form.

Paragraph 1. Paragraph 1, titled "FINANCING," states that the agreement is contingent on the buyer's obtaining the financing described. There are then clauses and blanks to set forth the deposit, the downpayment and various methods of paying the rest of the purchase price, including a new loan, assumption of the seller's existing loan and purchase money note and deed of trust to the seller. At the end of the paragraph, the numbers are summed up for the total purchase price.

Paragraphs 2 and 3. The next two short paragraphs have boxes and blanks to show whether the buyer intends to live in the property as his or her primary residence and to indicate any addenda which are attached to the form and which are to be considered as part of the contract.

CALIFORNIA ASSOCIATION OF REALTORS®

REAL ESTATE PURCHASE CONTRACT AND RECEIPT FOR DEPOSIT

THIS IS MORE THAN A RECEIPT FOR MONEY. IT IS INTENDED TO BE A LEGALLY BINDING CONTRACT. READ IT CAREFULLY
CALIFORNIA ASSOCIATION OF REALTORS® (CAR) STANDARD FORM

☐

_______________, California, _______________ 19___

Received from _______________

herein called Buyer, the sum of _______________ Dollars $ ______

evidenced by ☐ cash, ☐ cashier's check, ☐ personal check or ☐ _______________, payable to _______________

_______________, to be held uncashed until acceptance of this offer as deposit on account of purchase price of

_______________ Dollars $ ______

for the purchase of property, situated in _______________, County of _______________, California,

described as follows: _______________

1. **FINANCING:** The obtaining of Buyer's financing is a contingency of this agreement.

A. DEPOSIT upon acceptance, to be deposited into _______________ $ ______

B. INCREASED DEPOSIT within ______ days of acceptance to be deposited into _______________ $ ______

C. BALANCE OF DOWN PAYMENT to be deposited into _______________ on or before _______________ $ ______

D. Buyer to apply, qualify for and obtain a NEW FIRST LOAN in the amount of .... $ ______
payable monthly at approximately $______ including interest at origination not to exceed ______%,
☐ fixed rate, ☐ other _______________ all due ______ years from date of origination. Loan fee not to exceed ______. Seller agrees to pay a maximum of ______ FHA/VA discount points.
Additional terms _______________

E. Buyer ☐ to assume, ☐ to take title subject to an EXISTING FIRST LOAN with an approximate balance of .... $ ______
in favor of ______ payable monthly at $______ including interest at ______% ☐ fixed rate,
☐ other _______________. Fees not to exceed ______.
Disposition of impound account _______________
Additional terms _______________

F. Buyer to execute a NOTE SECURED BY a ☐ first, ☐ second, ☐ third DEED OF TRUST in the amount of .... $ ______
IN FAVOR OF SELLER payable monthly at $______ ☐ or more, including interest at ______% all due
______ years from date of origination, ☐ or upon sale or transfer of subject property. A late charge of ______
______ shall be due on any installment not paid within ______ days of the due date.
☐ Deed of Trust to contain a request for notice of default or sale for the benefit of Seller. Buyer ☐ will, ☐ will not execute a request for notice of delinquency. Additional terms _______________

G. Buyer ☐ to assume, ☐ to take title subject to an EXISTING SECOND LOAN with an approximate balance of .... $ ______
in favor of _______________ payable monthly at $______ including interest at ______%
☐ fixed rate, ☐ other _______________. Buyer fees not to exceed ______.
Additional terms _______________

H. Buyer to apply, qualify for and obtain a NEW SECOND LOAN in the amount of . . . . $ ________
payable monthly at approximately $________ including interest at origination not to exceed ______% ☐ fixed rate.
☐ other ________________, all due ______ years from date of origination.
Buyer's loan fee not to exceed ________. Additional terms ________

I. In the event Buyer assumes or takes title subject to an existing loan, Seller shall provide Buyer with copies of applicable notes and Deeds of Trust. A loan may contain a number of features which affect the loan, such as interest rate changes, monthly payment changes, balloon payments, etc. Buyer shall be allowed ______ calendar days after receipt of such copies to notify Seller in writing of disapproval. FAILURE TO NOTIFY SELLER IN WRITING SHALL CONCLUSIVELY BE CONSIDERED APPROVAL. Buyer's approval shall not be unreasonably withheld. Difference in existing loan balances shall be adjusted in ☐ Cash, ☐ Other ________

J. Buyer agrees to act diligently and in good faith to obtain all applicable financing. ________

K. ADDITIONAL FINANCING TERMS: ________

L. TOTAL PURCHASE PRICE . . . . $ ________

2. **OCCUPANCY:** Buyer ☐ does, ☐ does not intend to occupy subject property as Buyer's primary residence.

3. **SUPPLEMENTS:** The ATTACHED supplements are incorporated herein:
   - ☐ Interim Occupancy Agreement (CAR FORM IOA-11)
   - ☐ Residential Lease Agreement after Sale (CAR FORM RLAS-11)
   - ☐ VA and FHA Amendments (CAR FORM VA/FHA-11)
   - ☐ ________
   - ☐ ________
   - ☐ ________

4. **ESCROW:** Buyer and Seller shall deliver signed instructions to ________ the escrow holder, within ______ calendar days of acceptance of the offer which shall provide for closing within ______ calendar days of acceptance. Escrow fees to be paid as follows: ________

Buyer and Seller acknowledge receipt of copy of this page, which constitutes Page 1 of ______ Pages.

Buyer's Initials (______) (______) Seller's Initials (______) (______)

THIS STANDARDIZED DOCUMENT FOR USE IN SIMPLE TRANSACTIONS HAS BEEN APPROVED BY THE CALIFORNIA ASSOCIATION OF REALTORS® IN FORM ONLY. NO REPRESENTATION IS MADE AS TO THE APPROVAL OF THE FORM OF ANY SUPPLEMENTS NOT CURRENTLY PUBLISHED BY THE CALIFORNIA ASSOCIATION OF REALTORS® OR THE LEGAL VALIDITY OR ADEQUACY OF ANY PROVISION IN ANY SPECIFIC TRANSACTION. IT SHOULD NOT BE USED IN COMPLEX TRANSACTIONS OR WITH EXTENSIVE RIDERS OR ADDITIONS.

A REAL ESTATE BROKER IS THE PERSON QUALIFIED TO ADVISE ON REAL ESTATE TRANSACTIONS. IF YOU DESIRE LEGAL OR TAX ADVICE, CONSULT AN APPROPRIATE PROFESSIONAL.

OFFICE USE ONLY
Reviewed by Broker or Designee ______
Date ______

EQUAL HOUSING OPPORTUNITY

M-PM-MAR-91

BROKER'S COPY

REAL ESTATE PURCHASE CONTRACT AND RECEIPT FOR DEPOSIT (DLF-14 PAGE 1 OF 4)

Subject Property Address: ______________________________

5. **TITLE:** Title is to be free of liens, encumbrances, easements, restrictions, rights and conditions of record or known to Seller, other than the following: (a) Current property taxes, (b) covenants, conditions, restrictions, and public utility easements of record, if any, provided the same do not adversely affect the continued use of the property for the purposes for which it is presently being used, unless reasonably disapproved by Buyer in writing within __________ calendar days of receipt of a current preliminary report furnished at __________ expense, and (c) __________

____

Seller shall furnish Buyer at __________ expense a California Land Title Association policy issued by __________ Company, showing title vested in Buyer subject only to the above. If Seller is unwilling or unable to eliminate any title matter disapproved by Buyer as above, Buyer may terminate this agreement. If Seller fails to deliver title as above, Buyer may terminate this agreement; in either case, the deposit shall be returned to Buyer.

6. **VESTING:** Unless otherwise designated in the escrow instructions of Buyer, title shall vest as follows: __________

____

(The manner of taking title may have significant legal and tax consequences. Therefore, give this matter serious consideration.)

7. **PRORATIONS:** Property taxes, payments on bonds and assessments assumed by Buyer, interest, rents, association dues, premiums on insurance acceptable to Buyer, and __________ shall be paid current and prorated as of ☐ the day of recordation of the deed; or ☐ __________. Bonds or assessments now a lien shall be ☐ paid current by Seller, payments not yet due to be assumed by Buyer; or ☐ paid in full by Seller, including payments not yet due; or ☐ __________. County Transfer tax shall be paid by __________. The __________ transfer tax or transfer fee shall be paid by __________. **PROPERTY WILL BE REASSESSED UPON CHANGE OF OWNERSHIP. THIS WILL AFFECT THE TAXES TO BE PAID.** A Supplemental tax bill will be issued, which shall be paid as follows: (a) for periods after close of escrow, by Buyer (or by final acquiring party if part of an exchange), and (b) for periods prior to close of escrow, by Seller. TAX BILLS ISSUED AFTER CLOSE OF ESCROW SHALL BE HANDLED DIRECTLY BETWEEN BUYER AND SELLER.

8. **POSSESSION:** Possession and occupancy shall be delivered to Buyer, ☐ on close of escrow, or ☐ not later than __________ days after close of escrow, or ☐ __________

9. **KEYS:** Seller shall, when possession is available to Buyer, provide keys and/or means to operate all property locks, and alarms, if any.

10. **PERSONAL PROPERTY:** The following items of personal property, free of liens and without warranty of condition, are included: __________

____

11. **FIXTURES:** All permanently installed fixtures and fittings that are attached to the property or for which special openings have been made are included in the purchase price, including electrical, light, plumbing and heating fixtures, built-in appliances, screens, awnings, shutters, all window coverings, attached floor coverings, TV antennas, air cooler or conditioner, garage door openers and controls, attached fireplace equipment, mailbox, trees and shrubs, and __________ except __________

12. **SMOKE DETECTOR(S):** State law requires that residences be equipped with an operable smoke detector(s). Local law may have additional requirements. Seller shall deliver to Buyer a written statement of compliance in accordance with applicable state and local law prior to close of escrow.

13. **TRANSFER DISCLOSURE:** Unless exempt, Transferor (Seller), shall comply with Civil Code §§1102 et seq., by providing Transferee (Buyer) with a Real Estate Transfer Disclosure Statement: (a) ☐ Buyer has received and read a Real Estate Transfer Disclosure Statement; or (b) ☐ Seller shall provide Buyer with a Real Estate Transfer Disclosure Statement within __________ calendar days of acceptance of the offer after which Buyer shall have three (3) days after delivery to Buyer, in person, or five (5) days after delivery by deposit in the mail, to terminate this agreement by delivery of a written notice of termination to Seller or Seller's Agent.

14. **TAX WITHHOLDING:** (a) Under the Foreign Investment in Real Property Tax Act (FIRPTA), IRC §1445, every Buyer of U.S. real property must, unless an exemption applies, deduct and withhold from Seller's proceeds 10% of the gross sales price. The primary FIRPTA exemptions are: No withholding is required if (i) Seller provides Buyer with an affidavit under penalty of perjury, that Seller is not a "foreign person," or (ii) Seller provides Buyer with a "qualifying statement" issued by the Internal

Revenue Service, or (iii) Buyer purchases real property for use as a residence and the purchase price is $300,000 or less and Buyer or a member of Buyer's family has definite plans to reside at the property for at least 50% of the number of days it is in use during each of the first two 12-month periods after transfer. (b) In addition, under California Revenue and Taxation Code §§18805 and 26131, every Buyer must, unless an exemption applies, deduct and withhold from the Seller's proceeds 3⅓% of the gross sales price if the Seller has a last known street address outside of California, or if the Seller's proceeds will be paid to a financial intermediary of the Seller. The primary exemptions are: No withholding is required if (i) the Seller has a homeowner's exemption for the subject property, for local property taxes, for the year in which the title transfers, or (ii) the property is selling for $100,000 or less, or (iii) the Franchise Tax Board issues a certificate authorizing a lower amount or no withholding, or (iv) the Seller signs an affidavit stating that the Seller is a California resident or a corporation qualified to do business in California. (c) Seller and Buyer agree to execute and deliver as directed any instrument, affidavit, or statement reasonably necessary to carry out those statutes and regulations promulgated thereunder.

15. **MULTIPLE LISTING SERVICE:** If Broker is a Participant of an Association/Board multiple listing service ("MLS"), the Broker is authorized to report the sale, its price, terms, and financing for the publication, dissemination, information, and use of the authorized Board members, MLS Participants and Subscribers.

16. **ADDITIONAL TERMS AND CONDITIONS:**

ONLY THE FOLLOWING PARAGRAPHS 'A' THROUGH 'K' *WHEN INITIALLED BY BOTH BUYER AND SELLER* ARE INCORPORATED IN THIS AGREEMENT.

Buyer's Initials Seller's Initials

________ ________ **A. PHYSICAL AND GEOLOGICAL INSPECTION:** Buyer shall have the right, at Buyer's expense, to select a licensed contractor and/or other qualified professional(s), to make "Inspections" (including tests, surveys, other studies, inspections, and investigations) of the subject property, including but not limited to structural, plumbing, sewer/septic system, well, heating, electrical, built-in appliances, roof, soils, foundation, mechanical systems, pool, pool heater, pool filter, air conditioner, if any, possible environmental hazards such as asbestos, formaldehyde, radon gas and other substances/products, and geologic conditions. Buyer shall keep the subject property free and clear of any liens, indemnify and hold Seller harmless from all liability, claims, demands, damages, or costs, and repair all damages to the property arising from the "Inspections." All claimed defects concerning the condition of the property that adversely affect the continued use of the property for the purposes for which it is presently being used (☐ or as ________________) shall be in writing, supported by written reports, if any, and delivered to Seller within ______ calendar days FOR "INSPECTIONS" OTHER THAN GEOLOGICAL, and/or within ______ calendar days FOR GEOLOGICAL "INSPECTIONS," **of acceptance of the offer.** Buyer shall furnish Seller copies, at no cost, of all reports concerning the property obtained by Buyer. When such reports disclose conditions or information unsatisfactory to the Buyer, which the Seller is unwilling or unable to correct, Buyer may cancel this agreement. Seller shall make the premises available for all Inspections. BUYER'S FAILURE TO NOTIFY SELLER IN WRITING SHALL CONCLUSIVELY BE CONSIDERED APPROVAL.

Buyer's Initials Seller's Initials

________ ________ **B. CONDITION OF PROPERTY:** Seller warrants, through the date possession is made available to Buyer: (1) property and improvements, including landscaping, grounds and pool/spa, if any, shall be maintained in the same condition as upon the date of acceptance of the offer, and (2) the roof is free of all known leaks, and (3) built-in appliances, and water, sewer/septic, plumbing, heating, electrical, air conditioning, pool/spa systems, if any, are operative, and (4) Seller shall replace all broken and/or cracked glass; (5) ________________

Buyer's Initials Seller's Initials

________ ________ **C. SELLER REPRESENTATION:** Seller warrants that Seller has no knowledge of any notice of violations of City, County, State, Federal, Building, Zoning, Fire, Health Codes or ordinances, or other governmental regulation filed or issued against the property. This warranty shall be effective until the date of close of escrow.

Buyer and Seller acknowledge receipt of copy of this page, which constitutes Page 2 of _____ Pages.

Buyer's Initials (______) (______) Seller's Initials (______) (______)

OFFICE USE ONLY
Reviewed by Broker or Designee ______
Date ________

EQUAL HOUSING OPPORTUNITY

REAL ESTATE PURCHASE CONTRACT AND RECEIPT FOR DEPOSIT (DLF-14 PAGE 2 OF 4)

Subject Property Address ______________________________

Buyer's Initials **Seller's Initials**

_____/_____ _____/_____ **D. PEST CONTROL:** (1) Within __________ calendar days of acceptance of the offer, Seller shall furnish Buyer at the expense of ☐ Buyer, ☐ Seller, a current written report of an inspection by ______________________________, a licensed Structural Pest Control Operator, of the main building, ☐ detached garage(s) or carport(s), if any, and ☐ the following other structures on the property: ______________________________

(2) If requested by either Buyer or Seller, the report shall separately identify each recommendation for corrective measures as follows:

"Section 1": Infestation or infection which is evident.

"Section 2": Conditions that are present which are deemed likely to lead to infestation or infection.

(3) If no infestation or infection by wood destroying pests or organisms is found, the report shall include a written Certification as provided in Business and Professions Code § 8519(a) that on the date of inspection "no evidence of active infestation or infection was found."

(4) All work recommended to correct conditions described in "Section 1" shall be at the expense of ☐ Buyer, ☐ Seller.

(5) All work recommended to correct conditions described in "Section 2," if requested by Buyer, shall be at the expense of ☐ Buyer, ☐ Seller.

(6) The repairs shall be performed with good workmanship and materials of comparable quality and shall include repairs of leaking showers, replacement of tiles and other materials removed for repairs. It is understood that exact restoration of appearance or cosmetic items following all such repairs is not included.

(7) Funds for work agreed to be performed after close of escrow, shall be held in escrow and disbursed upon receipt of a written Certification as provided in Business and Professions Code § 8519(b) that the inspected property "is now free of evidence of active infestation or infection."

(8) Work to be performed at Seller's expense may be performed by Seller or through others, provided that (a) all required permits and final inspections are obtained, and (b) upon completion of repairs a written Certification is issued by a licensed Structural Pest Control Operator showing that the inspected property "is now free of evidence of active infestation or infection."

(9) If inspection of inaccessible areas is recommended by the report, Buyer has the option to accept and approve the report, or within __________ calendar days from receipt of the report to request in writing further inspection be made. BUYER'S FAILURE TO NOTIFY SELLER IN WRITING OF SUCH REQUEST SHALL CONCLUSIVELY BE CONSIDERED APPROVAL OF THE REPORT. If further inspection recommends "Section 1" and/or "Section 2" corrective measures, such work shall be at the expense of the party designated in subparagraph (4) and/or (5), respectively. If no infestation or infection is found, the cost of inspection, entry and closing of the inaccessible areas shall be at the expense of the Buyer.

(10) Other ______________________________

Buyer's Initials **Seller's Initials**

_____/_____ _____/_____ **E. FLOOD HAZARD AREA DISCLOSURE:** Buyer is informed that subject property is situated in a "Special Flood Hazard Area" as set forth on a Federal Emergency Management Agency (FEMA) "Flood Insurance Rate Map" (FIRM), or "Flood Hazard Boundary Map" (FHBM). The law provides that, as a condition of obtaining financing on most structures located in a "Special Flood Hazard Area," lenders require flood insurance where the property or its attachments are security for a loan.

The extent of coverage and the cost may vary. For further information consult the lender or insurance carrier. No representation or recommendation is made by the Seller and the Broker(s) in this transaction as to the legal effect or economic consequences of the National Flood Insurance Program and related legislation.

Buyer's Initials **Seller's Initials**

_____/_____ _____/_____ **F. SPECIAL STUDIES ZONE DISCLOSURE:** Buyer is informed that subject property is situated in a Special Studies Zone as designated under §§ 2621-2625, inclusive, of the California Public Resources Code; and, as such, the construction or development on this property of any structure for human occupancy may be subject to the findings of a geologic report prepared by a geologist registered in the State of California, unless such a report is waived by the City or County under the terms of that act.

Buyer is allowed ________ calendar days from acceptance of the offer to make further inquiries at appropriate governmental agencies concerning the use of the subject property under the terms of the Special Studies Zone Act and local building, zoning, fire, health, and safety codes. When such inquiries disclose conditions or information unsatisfactory to the Buyer, which the Seller is unwilling or unable to correct, Buyer may cancel this agreement. BUYER'S FAILURE TO NOTIFY SELLER IN WRITING SHALL CONCLUSIVELY BE CONSIDERED APPROVAL.

Buyer's Initials ____/____ Seller's Initials ____/____

G. ENERGY CONSERVATION RETROFIT: If local ordinance requires that the property be brought in compliance with minimum energy Conservation Standards as a condition of sale or transfer, ☐ Buyer, ☐ Seller shall comply with and pay for these requirements. Where permitted by law, Seller may, if obligated hereunder, satisfy the obligation by authorizing escrow to credit Buyer with sufficient funds to cover the cost of such retrofit.

Buyer's Initials ____/____ Seller's Initials ____/____

H. HOME PROTECTION PLAN: Buyer and Seller have been informed that Home Protection Plans are available. Such plans may provide additional protection and benefit to a Seller or Buyer. The CALIFORNIA ASSOCIATION OF REALTORS® and the Broker(s) in this transaction do not endorse or approve any particular company or program:

a) ☐ A Buyer's coverage Home Protection Plan to be issued by ______________________ Company, at a cost not to exceed $____________, to be paid by ☐ Buyer, ☐ Seller; or

b) ☐ Buyer and Seller elect not to purchase a Home Protection Plan.

Buyer's Initials ____/____ Seller's Initials ____/____

I. CONDOMINIUM/P.U.D.: The subject of this transaction is a condominium/planned unit development (P.U.D.) designated as unit ________ and ________ parking space(s) and an undivided interest in community areas, and ______________________ ______________________. The current monthly assessment charge by the homeowner's association or other governing body(s) is $____________. As soon as practicable, Seller shall provide Buyer with copies of covenants, conditions and restrictions, articles of incorporation, by-laws, current rules and regulations, most current financial statements, and any other documents as required by law. Seller shall disclose in writing any known pending special assessment, claims, or litigation to Buyer. Buyer shall be allowed ________ calendar days from receipt to review these documents. If such documents disclose conditions or information unsatisfactory to Buyer, Buyer may cancel this agreement. BUYER'S FAILURE TO NOTIFY SELLER IN WRITING SHALL CONCLUSIVELY BE CONSIDERED APPROVAL.

Buyer's Initials ____/____ Seller's Initials ____/____

J. LIQUIDATED DAMAGES: If Buyer fails to complete said purchase as herein provided by reason of any default of Buyer, Seller shall be released from obligation to sell the property to Buyer and may proceed against Buyer upon any claim or remedy which he/she may have in law or equity; provided, however, that by initialling this paragraph Buyer and Seller agree that Seller shall retain the deposit as liquidated damages. If the described property is a dwelling with no more than four units, one of which the Buyer intends to occupy as his/her residence, Seller shall retain as liquidated damages the deposit actually paid, or an amount therefrom, not more than 3% of the purchase price and promptly return any excess to Buyer. Buyer and Seller agree to execute a similar liquidated damages provision, such as CALIFORNIA ASSOCIATION OF REALTORS® Receipt for Increased Deposit (RID-11), for any increased deposits. (Funds deposited in trust accounts or in escrow are not released automatically in the event of a dispute. Release of funds requires written agreement of the parties, judicial decision or arbitration.)

Buyer and Seller acknowledge receipt of copy of this page, which constitutes Page 3 of ______ Pages.

Buyer's Initials (________) (________) Seller's Initials (________) (________)

OFFICE USE ONLY
Reviewed by Broker or Designee ________
Date ____________

EQUAL HOUSING OPPORTUNITY

REAL ESTATE PURCHASE CONTRACT AND RECEIPT FOR DEPOSIT (DLF-14 PAGE 3 OF 4)

Subject Property Address ______________________

K. ARBITRATION OF DISPUTES: Any dispute or claim in law or equity arising out of this contract or any resulting transaction shall be decided by neutral binding arbitration in accordance with the rules of the American Arbitration Association, and not by court action except as provided by California law for judicial review of arbitration proceedings. Judgment upon the award rendered by the arbitrator(s) may be entered in any court having jurisdiction thereof. The parties shall have the right to discovery in accordance with Code of Civil Procedure § 1283.05. The following matters are excluded from arbitration hereunder: (a) a judicial or non-judicial foreclosure or other action or proceeding to enforce a deed of trust, mortgage, or real property sales contract as defined in Civil Code § 2985, (b) an unlawful detainer action, (c) the filing or enforcement of a mechanic's lien, (d) any matter which is within the jurisdiction of a probate court, or (e) an action for bodily injury or wrongful death, or for latent or patent defects to which Code of Civil Procedure § 337.1 or § 337.15 applies. The filing of a judicial action to enable the recording of a notice of pending action, for order of attachment, receivership, injunction, or other provisional remedies, shall not constitute a waiver of the right to arbitrate under this provision.

Any dispute or claim by or against broker(s) and/or associate licensee(s) participating in this transaction shall be submitted to arbitration consistent with the provision above only if the broker(s) and/or associate licensee(s) making the claim or against whom the claim is made shall have agreed to submit it to arbitration consistent with this provision.

"NOTICE: BY INITIALLING IN THE SPACE BELOW YOU ARE AGREEING TO HAVE ANY DISPUTE ARISING OUT OF THE MATTERS INCLUDED IN THE 'ARBITRATION OF DISPUTES' PROVISION DECIDED BY NEUTRAL ARBITRATION AS PROVIDED BY CALIFORNIA LAW AND YOU ARE GIVING UP ANY RIGHTS YOU MIGHT POSSESS TO HAVE THE DISPUTE LITIGATED IN A COURT OR JURY TRIAL. BY INITIALLING IN THE SPACE BELOW YOU ARE GIVING UP YOUR JUDICIAL RIGHTS TO DISCOVERY AND APPEAL, UNLESS THOSE RIGHTS ARE SPECIFICALLY INCLUDED IN THE 'ARBITRATION OF DISPUTES' PROVISION. IF YOU REFUSE TO SUBMIT TO ARBITRATION AFTER AGREEING TO THIS PROVISION, YOU MAY BE COMPELLED TO ARBITRATE UNDER THE AUTHORITY OF THE CALIFORNIA CODE OF CIVIL PROCEDURE. YOUR AGREEMENT TO THIS ARBITRATION PROVISION IS VOLUNTARY."

"WE HAVE READ AND UNDERSTAND THE FOREGOING AND AGREE TO SUBMIT DISPUTES ARISING OUT OF THE MATTERS INCLUDED IN THE 'ARBITRATION OF DISPUTES' PROVISION TO NEUTRAL ARBITRATION."

Buyer's Initials ____/____ Seller's Initials ____/____

17. **OTHER TERMS AND CONDITIONS:** ______________________

18. **ATTORNEY'S FEES:** In any action, proceeding or arbitration arising out of this agreement, the prevailing party shall be entitled to reasonable attorney's fees and costs.
19. **ENTIRE CONTRACT:** Time is of the essence. All prior agreements between the parties are incorporated in this agreement which constitutes the entire contract. Its terms are intended by the parties as a final expression of their agreement with respect to such terms as are included herein and may not be contradicted by evidence of any prior agreement or contemporaneous oral agreement. The parties further intend that this agreement constitutes the complete and exclusive statement of its terms and that no extrinsic evidence whatsoever may be introduced in any judicial or arbitration proceeding, if any, involving this agreement.
20. **CAPTIONS:** The captions in this agreement are for convenience of reference only and are not intended as part of this agreement.
21. **AGENCY CONFIRMATION:** The following agency relationship(s) are hereby confirmed for this transaction:

LISTING AGENT: ____________________ is the agent of (check one):
(Print Firm Name)

☐ the Seller exclusively; or ☐ both the Buyer and Seller

SELLING AGENT: ____________________ (if not the same as Listing Agent) is the agent of (check one):
(Print Firm Name)

☐ the Buyer exclusively; or ☐ the Seller exclusively; or ☐ both the Buyer and Seller.

22. **AMENDMENTS: This agreement may not be amended, modified, altered or changed in any respect whatsoever except by a further agreement in writing executed by Buyer and Seller.**

23. **OFFER:** This constitutes an offer to purchase the described property. Unless acceptance is signed by Seller and a signed copy delivered in person, by mail, or facsimile, and received by Buyer at the address below, or by ____________________ who is authorized to receive it, on behalf of Buyer, within ________ calendar days of the date hereof, this offer shall be deemed revoked and the deposit shall be returned. Buyer has read and acknowledges receipt of a copy of this offer. This agreement and any supplement, addendum or modification relating hereto, including any photocopy or facsimile thereof, may be executed in two or more counterparts, all of which shall constitute one and the same writing.

REAL ESTATE BROKER ____________	BUYER ____________
By ____________	BUYER ____________
Address ____________	Address ____________
____________	____________
Telephone ____________	Telephone ____________

ACCEPTANCE

The undersigned Seller accepts and agrees to sell the property on the above terms and conditions and agrees to the above confirmation of agency relationships (☐ subject to attached counter offer).

Seller agrees to pay to Broker(s) ____________________

compensation for services as follows: ____________________.

Payable: (a) On recordation of the deed or other evidence of title, or (b) if completion of sale is prevented by default of Seller, upon Seller's default, or (c) if completion of sale is prevented by default of Buyer, only if and when Seller collects damages from Buyer, by suit or otherwise, and then in an amount not less than one-half of the damages recovered, but not to exceed the above fee, after first deducting title and escrow expenses and the expenses of collection, if any. Seller shall execute and deliver an escrow instruction irrevocably assigning the compensation for service in an amount equal to the compensation agreed to above. In any action, proceeding, or arbitration between Broker(s) and Seller arising out of this agreement, the prevailing party shall be entitled to reasonable attorney's fees and costs. The undersigned has read and acknowledges receipt of a copy of this agreement and authorizes Broker(s) to deliver a signed copy to Buyer.

Date ________ Telephone ________	SELLER ____________
Address ____________	
____________	SELLER ____________

Real Estate Broker(s) agree to the foregoing.

Broker ____________ By ____________ Date ____________

Broker ____________ By ____________ Date ____________

This form is available for use by the entire real estate industry. The use of this form is not intended to identify the user as a REALTOR®. REALTOR® is a registered collective membership mark which may be used only by real estate licensees who are members of the NATIONAL ASSOCIATION OF REALTORS® and who subscribe to its Code of Ethics.

Page 4 of ________ Pages.

OFFICE USE ONLY
Reviewed by Broker or Designee ________
Date ________

EQUAL HOUSING OPPORTUNITY

REAL ESTATE PURCHASE CONTRACT AND RECEIPT FOR DEPOSIT (DLF-14 PAGE 4 OF 4)

Paragraph 4. In the "ESCROW" Paragraph are blanks to name the escrow agent, to set the closing date and to allocate payment of the escrow fee.

At the bottom of the page is an acknowledgment and blanks for initials for the buyer and seller to acknowledge receiving a copy of page one of the agreement and a statement of the total number of pages in the contract. This clause is found at the bottom of each page of the form.

Below those lines is a paragraph which warns the parties that the form is intended for relatively simple real estate transactions and may not be suited for all transactions. The parties are advised that real estate agents are skilled in providing real estate advice, not tax or legal advice.

At the top of the second page, and also at the top of pages threé and four, is a line to write in the street address of the property.

Paragraph 5. Paragraph 5 contains representations of the seller as to the condition of title which will be transferred and an agreement by the seller to provide the buyer with a title insurance policy. If insurable title cannot be furnished as represented by the seller, the buyer may terminate the agreement.

Paragraph 6. The "VESTING" paragraph states how the buyer(s) will take title (for example, as community property or tenants in common).

Paragraph 7. The prorations paragraph sets out the agreement as to proration of property taxes and other expenses, payment of assessments and transfer taxes.

Paragraph 8. The next paragraph sets out the date that possession is to be delivered to the buyer.

Paragraphs 9, 10, and 11. The next three paragraphs all concern items to be delivered to the buyer. The buyer gets the keys when possession is delivered. Paragraph 10 and 11 list personal property and fixtures which are to be included in the sale or which are excepted from the sale.

Paragraph 12. The seller agrees to give the buyer a written statement of compliance with state and local smoke detector laws, before closing.

Paragraph 13. Paragraph 13 sets forth the seller's obligation to provide the buyer with a Real Estate Transfer Disclosure Statement and includes a blank to fill in stating when the statement shall be so provided.

Paragraph 14. The "TAX WITHHOLDING" provision sets out certain requirements of federal and state tax laws which apply to some real estate transactions.

Paragraph 15. The next paragraph authorizes the broker to report information concerning this transaction to his or her multiple listing service.

Paragraph 16. Paragraph 16 contains eleven separate provisions, lettered A through K. The parties may choose to make any of these provisions part of their agreement by initialing the blanks directly preceding each of the provisions. These provisions will all be analyzed individually later in the course. For now it is sufficient to note the general nature of the provisions and to recognize that some of the provisions would have wide applicability and be included in most home sales; other provisions would have more limited application and would be appropriate only in a minority of home sales.

The general subject matter of the additional terms and conditions in Paragraph 16 are as follows:

A. PHYSICAL AND GEOLOGICAL INSPECTION: the buyer's right to have the property inspected for problems with the structures, systems, and appliances, and for environmental and geological hazards;

B. CONDITION OF PROPERTY: certain guarantees of the seller regarding maintenance and physical condition of the property;

C. SELLER REPRESENTATION: seller's warranties that there are no known violations of building codes, zoning or other government regulations;

D. PEST CONTROL: agreements relating to having the property inspected by a professional for termite or pest infestation or damage and the duty to correct any damage found;

E. FLOOD HAZARD ZONE DISCLOSURE: notice regarding flood insurance for property located in a flood zone;

F. SPECIAL STUDIES ZONE DISCLOSURE: notice that special building restrictions may apply for property located within a Special Studies Zone;

G. ENERGY CONSERVATION RETROFIT: agreement to allocate costs of bringing property into compliance with energy conservation regulations;

H. HOME PROTECTION PLAN: notice and agreement relating to purchase of a home protection plan;

I. CONDOMINIUM/PUD: certain information and agreements relating to homeowner's association assessments, association bylaws and other matters which are relevant when the property is a condominium or planned unit development unit;

J. LIQUIDATED DAMAGES: in the event of default by the buyer, seller will retain the deposit as liquidated damages;

K. ARBITRATION OF DISPUTES: provides that any dispute between the parties will be decided by binding arbitration instead of a lawsuit.

Paragraph 17. The next paragraph contains several blank lines to fill in any other terms or conditions which the parties wish to have included and which are not part of the preprinted form.

Paragraph 18. The "ATTORNEY'S FEES" clause entitles the prevailing party to a reasonable attorney's fee if there is any legal action, proceeding, or arbitration arising out of the contract.

Paragraph 19. This is an "integration" clause which holds that the entire agreement of the parties is contained in this written contract and that there are no oral agreements or understandings.

Paragraph 20. This paragraph simply states that the captions at the beginning of each paragraph, such as "LIQUIDATED DAMAGES" or "ENTIRE CONTRACT" are intended simply to help the parties refer to particular provisions in the contract; the captions themselves are not part of the agreement.

Paragraph 21. In this provision, the parties confirm the particular agency relationships involved — whether the listing and/or selling agents represent the buyer, the seller, or both.

Paragraph 22. Finally, there is a bold print sentence that the written agreement may only be modified or changed by another written agreement between the parties.

Paragraph 23. Following the list of special conditions is Paragraph 23 which states that the preceding terms and provisions are the buyer's offer to buy the property. Time limits and procedures for accepting the offer are also set out in this paragraph.

There are then signature lines for the agent and buyer(s).

The last paragraph in the form contains the seller's acceptance of the buyer's offer and an agreement to pay the broker's commission. This commission arrangement in most cases would be merely a reaffirmation of the agreement in an earlier listing agreement. However, in some transactions, where the broker has been operating under an oral or implied listing agreement, this might be the only written promise to pay the broker a commission.

There are then signature lines for the agent(s) and seller(s).

Chapter Fourteen

Deposit Receipt: Parties, Signatures, Deposits and Property Description

Parties and Signatures

A **proper identification of the parties** is one of the necessary elements of an enforceable contract to buy and sell real estate. The contract should contain the full names of the parties, their signatures, and, if someone is signing for one of the parties, indicate his or her authority (such as a power of attorney). It is a general rule of law that the **signature of the person against whom the contract is to be enforced** must appear on the document. So, in order for the contract to be enforceable against the buyer, the buyer's signature must appear on the contract, and in order for the contract to be enforceable against the seller, the seller's signature must appear on the contract. Deposit receipt forms are normally worded so that the contract is not formed unless both parties sign. For an example, refer to Paragraph 23 of the CAR form, where it is stated that the buyer's offer will be deemed revoked unless the seller signs an acceptance and delivers a signed copy of the acceptance to the buyer.

Preprinted Forms.

Most purchase and sale forms used by real estate agents have signature lines at the bottom for the buyer and seller. There are also often blanks in the body of the contract for the names of the buyer and seller to be printed legibly. These blanks may be located together near the top of the document, or the buyer's name may appear in one place and the seller's in another (often as offer and acceptance). In the REALTORS' form we are using for illustration, there is a blank in the first paragraph to legibly print the buyer(s)' name(s). There are signature lines at the end of the contract form (bottom of page four) for the buyer(s) and seller(s) but no separate blank to print out the seller(s)' name(s). If the seller's signature is illegible, the agent should print the seller's name clearly on the document.

Necessary Parties and Signatures.

As a general approach, it is best to obtain the signatures of all persons presently holding an interest in the property (all of the sellers) or the signatures of their authorized agent(s), along with evidence of their authority. Similarly, it is best to obtain the signatures of all persons intending to acquire an interest in the property (all of the buyers) or the signatures of their authorized representatives, along with evidence of their authority. Some questions which the agent might address in considering whose signatures to seek might include the following:

1) Is the seller or buyer of age and mentally competent? (If not, a guardian or other representative may be needed; a minor who has married, is on active duty with the armed forces, or who has received a declaration of emancipation is an emancipated minor and does have the capacity to buy and sell real estate.);

2) Was the seller married when the property was acquired or is the seller now married? (In either event, the signature of the spouse will probably be needed, or a quitclaim deed or waiver from the spouse.);

3) Is the property homestead property?

4) Is the property held in joint tenancy or tenancy in common? (If the entire property is to be sold, the signatures of all owners should be obtained.);

5) If the property is or was held in joint tenancy, has a joint tenant died? [If so, certain formalities may be required to vest title in the survivor(s).]

6) Is title to the property held wholly or in part by the estate of a decedent? (If so, court approval is required for the executor or administrator to sell the property.);

7) Do any of the sellers have names which are now different from the names under which they acquired title to the property?

8) If the seller is a partnership, has a statement of partnership (for general partnerships) or certificate of partnership (for limited partnerships) been recorded and are the general partners available for signature?

9) If the buyer or seller is a corporation, are there particular formalities (such as a resolution of the board of directors) that must be followed and are the appropriate officers available for signature?

10) Is the buyer married?

Marital Status.

In the simplest situation, one unmarried individual is the buyer and another unmarried individual is the seller. Even in this kind of case, where neither party is married, it is better to indicate marital status on the form. This is because in California it is difficult, if not impossible, for a married person to sell (and in some cases to buy) real estate without obtaining the other spouse's consent to the transaction. This is particularly true if the property is, or is intended to be, the family home. Under California community property laws, both spouses must execute any document by which community real property will be sold, conveyed, encumbered or leased for longer than one year. So, to avoid potential delays, have the contract itself clearly show that the person is not married if that is the case.

Received from *"Mary R. Smith, an unmarried woman"*

If any of the parties are married, their spouses' names should be indicated and they should all sign the agreement.

Received from *"John J. Smith and Mary R. Smith, husband and wife"*

The fact that the seller or buyer is married may be shown by any phrase which clearly indicates the marital relationship, such as:

John J. Smith and Mary R. Smith, husband and wife;
John J. Smith and Mary R. Smith, a married couple;
John J. Smith and Mary R. Smith, his wife.

The simple fact that two buyers have the same last name does not, of course, mean that they are married to each other. They may be parent and child, or brother and sister, for example, or they may by some coincidence have the same surname. It is also increasingly common for husband and wife to have different surnames. It cannot be assumed that a man and woman buying or selling property are or are not married because their last names are or are not the same. Therefore, the **actual status should be indicated** on the form.

The marital status of the buyers may influence the form in which they take title. In some states, it is presumed that a married couple takes title as tenants by the entirety. In California and other community property states, the presumption is in favor of community property. Although a married couple may also take title as joint tenants, as tenants in common or as the separate property of one of the spouses, there is a strong presumption in favor of community property. If the instrument refers to the buyers as husband and wife and makes no specific mention of how they are to take title, they take title as community property.

Two or more buyers who are not married to each other are presumed to take title as tenants in common. If they intend to take title in some other manner (such as joint tenancy), that should be shown in the contract, so that the closing agent (broker, attorney or escrow agent) will know how to prepare the deed.

On the CAR deposit receipt form, the manner in which the buyers wish to take title is specifically indicated in the blank in Paragraph 6, which will be covered later in the materials.

It should be emphasized at this point, and will be mentioned again in the discussion of Paragraph 6 of the CAR form, that the manner in which the buyers take title may have significant legal, financial or tax consequences and that giving advice as to how to take title to property may be construed as rendering professional legal, financial or tax advice. **Therefore, real estate brokers and salespersons who are not licensed to practice law and/or are not professionally qualified to render financial or tax advice should avoid counseling potential buyers as to how they should take title to the property.** Buyers frequently fail to discuss with real estate agents all the information regarding their personal circumstances that would be important in making a decision as to holding title. If the buyers have questions concerning the advantages and disadvantages of particular forms of joint ownership for their particular circumstances, they should be told to seek legal, financial or tax counsel.

The main role to be played by the real estate agent here is to insure that the contract form correctly shows the names and marital status of the parties and to get the necessary signatures. Failure to indicate the marital status and to obtain the signature of a spouse may lead to delays in closing the transaction. Title insurance companies frequently refuse to insure title without an exception or exclusion from coverage for the potential interest in the property held by a possible spouse if the marital status is not clear. If there is a spouse and that spouse has not signed the agreement, the same problems are encountered. Failure of a title insurance company to insure title may well mean failure of the transaction. In other states where abstracts and attorneys' opinions are normally relied upon instead of title insurance, the same sort of difficulties may arise. Failure to indicate marital status and to obtain the spouse's signature may cause the attorney giving the opinion as to marketability of title to make an exception or give an opinion that the title is not marketable.

The reasons for these difficulties lie in the various state laws designed to protect spouses. In some states such laws may apply only to property which is the family home and in other states the laws may apply to all property which is acquired by the couple while married. In most states a husband or wife has an interest in real property which is acquired by the other during marriage. The nature and extent of this interest (usually called dower or curtesy in lieu of dower in the common law states and community property in the community property states) varies considerably from state to state, but the one common rule is that it may not be released by anyone else. This means simply that a husband or wife generally does not have complete and clear title to property acquired during marriage and, therefore, cannot transfer clear title. In community property states, there is a general presumption that all property acquired during marriage belongs to the husband and wife equally. Community property laws usually require the signatures of both spouses to convey community real property (as does California community property law mentioned above) and the laws in some community property states also require the signature of both spouses to buy community real property.

As long as you have a married couple buying the property and both sign the agreement, or as long as you have a married couple selling the property and both sign the agreement, things are relatively simple and straightforward. They can become very complicated very quickly when a married person is attempting to buy or sell property without the other spouse signing anything.

The quickest way of eliminating potential title problems is to have the other spouse either join in the transaction (agree to it and sign the contract and deed) or sign some other document which clearly indicates that the nonjoining spouse waives any objection to the transaction or releases any possible interest in the property. This may be done with a waiver, which might be attached to the deposit receipt, or a quitclaim deed. A waiver would prevent the spouse from later objecting to the sale (a spouse who does not sign the instrument conveying or encumbering community real property may otherwise void the transaction up to one year after the instrument is recorded). An example of a waiver clause is shown directly below. Title insurance companies, however, frequently require a quitclaim deed rather than a waiver before they will issue title insurance.

EXAMPLE:
Waiver by Spouse for Sale of Property Owned by Other Spouse

Mary R. Smith acknowledges that she is the spouse of John J.Smith who executed the attached purchase and sale agreement. She further acknowledges that the property described in the attached purchase and sale agreement is the seller's separate property and waives any requirement that she join in the execution of any document required for the purchase and sale described in the attached agreement. She agrees that she will execute a quitclaim deed to the property described in the attached agreement if necessary in order for the buyer to obtain title insurance.

Date ______________________

______________________________ *(signature)*

To sum up, the safest way to insure a closing without delay is get the signatures of both spouses.

Multiple Buyers and Sellers.

In cases whether either the seller or buyer consists of multiple parties, you should of course include the names of all the sellers and all the buyers on the form and get their signatures. If there are more than two, you will probably have to attach an addendum since most of the forms (including the CAR form illustrated in this course) have spaces for only two names for the seller and two for the buyer. Just as in cases where the buyer or seller is a married couple, failure to obtain the signatures of all the sellers or all the buyers may result in an unenforceable contract.

Although it is certainly more complicated, it is safest to indicate the marital status of each buyer and seller. If any are married, it is best to get the signature of his or her spouse.

If you are in doubt in a particular transaction as to whose signatures you are going to need in order to have a smooth processing through the title insurance stage of the transaction, you can sometimes obtain some assistance from the title company. They may be able to tell you which signatures will be necessary in order to avoid delays relating to title matters. The advice received from underwriters or other personnel at the title company (other than their staff attorneys) would not be legal advice as to which signatures would be sufficient or required for an enforceable contract, it would be advice relating to their insurance underwriting procedures and which signatures they would require in order to issue a title insurance policy. Questions relating to the signatures or other evidence of joinder which would be sufficient to establish an enforceable real estate contract in a particular set of facts would have to be referred to an attorney with expertise in the real estate field.

Receipt for Deposit

Although it is not necessary to have an earnest money deposit in order to have an enforceable purchase and sale contract, as a matter of practice almost all purchase and sale agreements for residential property entail a deposit made by the purchaser in connection with the written offer. The deposit is intended to provide evidence of the buyer's good faith (that he or she is making a bona fide offer to buy the property) and to serve as a source of liquidated damages for the seller if the buyer defaults. The amount of the deposit should be enough to provide an economic incentive to the buyer to complete the transaction and to adequately compensate the seller for the time and expense involved in taking the house off the market and having to place it back on the market if the buyer fails to consummate the purchase. California law places certain limits on the amount of liquidated damages permitted in residential transactions. These are referred to in Paragraph 16J. of the CAR deposit receipt form (not more than three percent of the purchase price).

Agency law and California license law require the broker to make a full disclosure to the seller of the amount and form of the deposit (Is the deposit in the form of cash, personal check, postdated check? Has the broker actually received the deposit or has the buyer merely promised to make a deposit "tomorrow?"). Failure to make a proper disclosure may subject the licensee to disciplinary action and may render the agent liable to the seller for any damages occasioned by failure to actually receive the deposit or for failure of the transaction. Blanks and boxes are provided on the form in the head paragraph to indicate the amount of the deposit and whether it is in the form of cash, cashier's check, personal check or some other form, such as a promissory note. The license law requires the broker to give the deposit to the principal or place it in a neutral escrow or in his or her trust account by the end of the next banking day after receipt unless directed to hold a check uncashed. The CAR form states that the broker is to hold the check uncashed pending acceptance of the offer. This is intended to avoid situations in which the seller may reject the offer after the broker has already placed the deposit check in the trust account. The buyer will likely ask for a refund of the deposit and the broker will likely be unwilling to write a check on his or her trust account for the refund before the buyer's check clears since a later dishonor of the buyer's check would result in a shortage in the broker's trust account. If the broker holds the check uncashed, he or she may simply give it back to the buyer if the seller rejects the offer.

There are additional blanks in Subparagraphs 1. A. and 1. B. to indicate the disposition of the deposit upon acceptance of the offer and to provide for the buyer's making an additional deposit within a specified number of days. Although the deposit may be given to the seller, placed in a neutral escrow or placed in the broker's trust account, by far the most common disposition of the deposit in residential transactions is to put it in the broker's trust account. The provision for increasing the deposit may be used in cases where for one reason or another the buyer is either unable or unwilling to make a large deposit now but will be willing to increase it after acceptance of the offer. This may be because the buyer simply does not want money tied up until the seller accepts the offer or it may be because the buyer does not have enough cash right now but will in a few more days (after arranging for a transfer of funds into his or her checking account or after a certificate of deposit matures or some other reason).

Property Description

Contracts for the purchase and sale of real estate must identify or describe the property which is to be sold. The standard which must be met in order to comply with the requirement for an adequate description varies considerably from state to state. In some states, only a full legal description (metes and bounds, government fractional survey or reference to lot and block on a recorded subdivision map) or reference to a document where such a description may be found, is sufficient. The law in such states will not allow oral testimony to be used to clarify an ambiguous property description, so the contract is not enforceable unless it contains a complete and proper description of the property.

Other states have more liberal policies regarding land descriptions. Some will allow use of a street address or commonly known name (such as "the Smith farm"). Others allow the parties to clarify their intent by oral testimony, or by referring to other evidence which is not actually a part of the contract itself. California follows this more liberal approach. The property description in the deposit receipt must be certain enough to satisfy the statute of frauds. A street address may be sufficient if it includes the entire property to be sold. However, an address alone is not sufficient if it does not include the entire property.

Regardless of the strict legal requirement, the safest and best course of action for a real estate agent completing a deposit receipt is to use the most accurate and unambiguous description available. It is far simpler (and less expensive) to use the correct property description in the first place than it is to have to resort to a court of law to settle a dispute over an improperly worded or ambiguous description.

Where to Find Legal Descriptions.

The safest way to avoid the possibility of a void or unenforceable contract and to avoid litigation regarding adequacy of the description is to obtain the full and correct legal description and incorporate it into the contract. If the seller is selling the same property which he or she acquired, the description may be obtained from the deed which conveyed the property to the seller or from the seller's title insurance policy, assuming that the seller is in fact selling all the property described in the deed and/or title insurance policy. The agent may resort to a title insurance company for the description as shown on its records. It is generally advisable to order a preliminary title report to see if record title is in harmony with what the seller believes to be the description of his or her property. If the seller is conveying something different than what he or she originally acquired (particularly if conveying only a portion of the parcel originally acquired), the agent should contact an attorney or have one of the parties contact an attorney to insure that there has been proper compliance with any applicable subdivision laws or ordinances. If the seller is conveying something different than what he or she acquired, it may be necessary to have a survey done and a new legal description prepared.

Using Standard Forms.

As can be seen in the figure below, the blanks on many agreement forms are not large enough for anything but the briefest legal descriptions.

for the purchase of property, situated in ______________, County of ____________ California,
described as follows: ____

The complete legal description may be attached to the form with a reference, such as "for complete legal description, see Addendum 'A'." For long and/or complicated descriptions, it is probably best to photocopy the description from a deed, title insurance policy or other document containing a full and accurate legal description. You may thereby easily avoid the dangers of copying errors which are inherent in trying to manually copy a long or complicated legal description.

for the purchase of property, situated in ______________, County of ____________ California,
described as follows: ____________ *"For complete description see Addendum 1, attached to and incorporated in this agreement."*

A photocopy of the complete legal description would then be labeled (e.g., "Addendum A" or "Exhibit A") and attached to the deposit receipt form. The **attachment** (and all other attachments) **should be dated and signed** by the seller(s) and buyer(s) to indicate that the attachment is part of the contract agreed to by the parties.

Often the selling agent does not have the complete description available at the time the offer to purchase is filled out. Some standard forms address this problem by inserting a clause which gives the real estate agent or closing agent the authority to insert the proper description later. For example, a clause of this nature might read something like this: "Buyer and seller authorize agent to insert over their signatures the legal description of the property and/or to correct any legal description entered." The California REALTORS®' form used as an example in this course has no such clause. If a clause of this type is part of the form you use in your practice and you rely on that clause and intend to insert a correct description after signature by one or more of the parties, you should make a diligent effort to obtain the proper description, attach it as soon as reasonably possible and have the parties initial the attachment.

Chapter Fifteen

Deposit Receipt: Third Party Financing

A deposit receipt must show the total purchase price and method of paying the purchase price. We will first cover payment by means of FHA, VA and conventional financing. Seller financing will be covered in the next chapter.

Price

First, state the total price, including all trust deeds, contracts or other liens to which the buyer agrees to take subject or which the buyer agrees to assume. This may seem pretty simple, but more than one lawsuit has been filed because of misunderstandings as to the total purchase price.

For example, does a purchase price of "... one hundred thousand dollars, subject to a mortgage of thirty thousand dollars ..." mean that the total purchase price is $100,000, which includes the $30,000 mortgage or does it mean that the total purchase price is $130,000 ($100,000 plus the $30,000 mortgage)? Probably most people would assume that the purchase price would include the mortgage, unless it was specified otherwise (a total price of $100,000), but the very fact that parties have initiated lawsuits over this question should show clearly that not all people would think so. Similar questions could arise on account of any other liens, such as tax liens, which the buyer agrees to assume or to which the buyer agrees to take subject. If the contract clearly spells out how the buyer is to pay the price, such misunderstandings can be avoided.

Purchase and sale forms used by real estate agents normally have separate blanks to be completed to show these two elements: the total purchase price and the method of payment. In the California REALTORS® form, the total purchase price is found in two places: in the heading paragraph, directly preceding the description blank and at the bottom of the FINANCING paragraph (Paragraph 1).

Payment Clauses

Some forms provide a large blank space for describing the method of payment. Other forms have pre-printed sections with blanks to be completed to indicate how the total price is to be paid (for example, how much is the buyer's deposit, how much will be paid in cash at closing and how much will be paid through deferred financing) and/or to describe some of the more common financing arrangements (such as, assumption of an existing mortgage or purchase money financing by the seller). The REALTORS® deposit receipt form comes in both versions. The difference between the two variations of the form is in the FINANCING paragraph located on the first page. In one version, Form DLF-14, there are pre-printed standard provisions for a number of the most common payment plans. In the other version, Form DL-14, the financing paragraph contains about one half page of blank lines for the agent to write out the method of payment for those transactions in which the payment plan does not directly correspond to one of the pre-printed standard plans on Form DLF-14. The two variations of the FINANCING paragraph are shown on the next two pages.

REAL ESTATE PURCHASE CONTRACT AND RECEIPT FOR DEPOSIT (DLF-14 PAGE 1)

1. **FINANCING:** The obtaining of Buyer's financing is a contingency of this agreement.

A. DEPOSIT upon acceptance, to be deposited into ______________________________ $ __________

B. INCREASED DEPOSIT within ________ days of acceptance to be deposited into ______________________ $ __________

C. BALANCE OF DOWN PAYMENT to be deposited into ____________________ on or before ____________________ $ __________

D. Buyer to apply, qualify for and obtain a NEW FIRST LOAN in the amount of . . . . $ __________
payable monthly at approximately $____________________ including interest at origination not to exceed ________%, ☐ fixed rate, ☐ other ____________________ all due ________ years from date of origination. Loan fee not to exceed ____________________. Seller agrees to pay a maximum of ____________________ FHA/VA discount points.
Additional terms ____
____.

E. Buyer ☐ to assume, ☐ to take title subject to an EXISTING FIRST LOAN with an approximate balance of . . . . $ __________
in favor of ____________________ payable monthly at $____________________ including interest at ________% ☐ fixed rate, ☐ other ____________________________________. Fees not to exceed ____________________.
Disposition of impound account ____.
Additional terms ____.

F. Buyer to execute a NOTE SECURED BY a ☐ first, ☐ second, ☐ third DEED OF TRUST in the amount of . . . . $ __________
IN FAVOR OF SELLER payable monthly at $________________ ☐ or more, including interest at ________________% all due ________ years from date of origination, ☐ or upon sale or transfer of subject property. A late charge of ____________________ shall be due on any installment not paid within ________________ days of the due date.
☐ Deed of Trust to contain a request for notice of default or sale for the benefit of Seller. Buyer ☐ will, ☐ will not execute a request for notice of delinquency. Additional terms ____
____.

G. Buyer ☐ to assume, ☐ to take title subject to an EXISTING SECOND LOAN with an approximate balance of . . . . $ __________
in favor of ______________________________ payable monthly at $____________ including interest at ________%
☐ fixed rate, ☐ other ____________________________. Buyer fees not to exceed ____________________________.
Additional terms ____
____.

H. Buyer to apply, qualify for and obtain a NEW SECOND LOAN in the amount of . . . . $ __________
payable monthly at approximately $________________ including interest at origination not to exceed ________% ☐ fixed rate, ☐ other ____, all due ________ years from date of origination.
Buyer's loan fee not to exceed ______________________________. Additional terms ____________________
____.

I. In the event Buyer assumes or takes title subject to an existing loan, Seller shall provide Buyer with copies of applicable notes and Deeds of Trust. A loan may contain a number of features which affect the loan, such as interest rate changes, monthly payment changes, balloon payments, etc. Buyer shall be allowed ________ calendar days after receipt of such copies to notify Seller in writing of disapproval. FAILURE TO NOTIFY SELLER IN WRITING SHALL CONCLUSIVELY BE CONSIDERED APPROVAL. Buyer's approval shall not be unreasonably withheld. Difference in existing loan balances shall be adjusted in ☐ Cash, ☐ Other ____________________
____.

J. Buyer agrees to act diligently and in good faith to obtain all applicable financing. ____________________
____
____.

K. ADDITIONAL FINANCING TERMS: ____
____
____
____.

L. TOTAL PURCHASE PRICE . . . . $ __________

REAL ESTATE PURCHASE CONTRACT AND RECEIPT FOR DEPOSIT

THIS IS MORE THAN A RECEIPT FOR MONEY. IT IS INTENDED TO BE A LEGALLY BINDING CONTRACT. READ IT CAREFULLY.
CALIFORNIA ASSOCIATION OF REALTORS® (CAR) STANDARD FORM

____________________, California, ____________________, 19____

Received from ____________________

herein called Buyer, the sum of ____________________ Dollars $____________

evidence by ☐ cash, ☐ cashier's check, ☐ personal check or ☐ ____________, payable to ____________

____________________, to be held uncashed until acceptance of this offer as deposit on account of purchase price of

____________________ Dollars$____________

for the purchase of property, situated in ____________________, County of ____________ California,

described as follows ____________________

1. **FINANCING:** The obtaining of Buyer's financing is a contingency of this agreement.

A. DEPOSIT upon acceptance, to be deposited into ____________________ $ ________

B. INCREASED DEPOSIT within ______days of acceptance to be deposited into ____________ $ ________

C. BALANCE OF DOWN PAYMENT to be deposited into ____________on or before ____________ $ ________

D. BALANCE OF PURCHASE PRICE AS FOLLOWS: ____________________ $ ________

E. In the event Buyer assumes or takes title subject to an existing loan, Seller shall provide Buyer with copies of applicable notes and Deeds of Trust. A loan may contain a number of features which affect the loan, such as interest rate changes, monthly payment changes, balloon payments, etc. Buyer shall be allowed ______calendar days after receipt of such copies to notify Seller in writing of disapproval. FAILURE TO NOTIFY SELLER SHALL CONCLUSIVELY BE CONSIDERED APPROVAL. Buyer's approval shall not be unreasonably withheld. Difference in existing loan balances shall be adjusted in ☐ Cash, ☐ Other ____________________

F. Buyer agrees to act diligently and in good faith to obtain all applicable financing.

G. OTHER FINANCING TERMS AND CONDITIONS: ____________________

2. **OCCUPANCY:** Buyer ☐ does, ☐ does not intend to occupy subject property as Buyer's primary residence.

REAL ESTATE PURCHASE CONTRACT AND RECEIPT FOR DEPOSIT (DL-14 PAGE 1)

In the first form illustrated (the form which contains financing clauses), there are pre-printed provisions with blanks to be completed to show that the buyer intends to pay the purchase price through: cash; a new first loan; assumption or taking subject to an existing first loan; a purchase money trust deed to the seller; assumption or taking subject to an existing second loan; obtaining a new second loan; or some combination of those methods. These are the most common ways of paying for a house. There are also a few blanks in Subparagraph 1. K. to write in some additional payment terms not provided for in the pre-printed clauses.

In the second form, the financing paragraph has pre-printed clauses only for the deposit and downpayment. Any deferred payment plan must be described in the blanks provided. This form would be used if the payment plan contemplated by the parties cannot be easily described by filling in the blanks and boxes in the form with the pre-printed financing clauses.

In the first form, the various amounts to be paid by cash, first and second trust deeds, assumptions and/or other methods are all summed up and entered in the blank for the total purchase price (Subparagraph 1. L.). Although Paragraph 1 in the second form does not include a blank for the total purchase price, it is a good idea to add that information. Of course, on either form, the total purchase price stated in the financing paragraph should match the amount shown in the heading paragraph at the top of the page.

Cash

Certainly the simplest method of payment is **all cash at closing**. Most transactions involve some sort of deposit made by the buyer, called earnest money, a good faith deposit, or simply a deposit. Forms used by real estate agents usually have blanks to be filled in by the agent receipting this deposit. The deposit is then normally held by the broker pending closing (although it is sometimes paid directly to a third party escrow agent and even sometimes paid directly to the seller).

_______________________________, California. _______________________, 19 ______

Received from ____

herein called Buyer, the sum of two thousand and no/100 ______________ Dollars $ 2,000.00

evidenced by ☐ cash, ☐ cashier's check, ☒ personal check or ☐ ______________, payable to Max Realty Trust Account ______________, to be held uncashed until acceptance of this offer as deposit on account of purchase price of

____ Dollars $ ______

In any event, if the buyer has made a deposit towards the purchase price, this should be reflected in describing the method of payment. For example, if the buyer intends to pay all cash at closing, the contract might read as follows:

1. **FINANCING:** The obtaining of Buyer's financing is a contingency of this agreement.

A. DEPOSIT upon acceptance, to be deposited into Max Realty Trust Account ______________ $ 2,000.00

B. INCREASED DEPOSIT within ________ days of acceptance to be deposited into ______________ $ ______

C. BALANCE OF XXXX PAYMENT to be deposited into Escrow ________ on or before October 15, 1990 $ ______

D. Buyer to apply, qualify for and obtain a NEW FIRST LOAN in the amount of .... $ 98,000.00
payable monthly at approximately $ ________ including interest at origination not to exceed ________%, ☐ fixed rate, ☐ other ______________ all due ________ years from date of origination. Loan fee not to exceed ______________. Seller agrees to pay a maximum of ______________ FHA/VA discount points.
Additional terms ____

E. Buyer ☐ to assume, ☐ to take title subject to an EXISTING FIRST LOAN with an approximate balance of .... $ ______
in favor of ______________ payable monthly at $ ________ including interest at ________% ☐ fixed rate, ☐ other ______________. Fees not to exceed ______________.
Disposition of impound account ____
Additional terms ____

F. Buyer to execute a NOTE SECURED BY a ☐ first, ☐ second, ☐ third DEED OF TRUST in the amount of .... $ ______
IN FAVOR OF SELLER payable monthly at $ ________ ☐ or more, including interest at ________% all due ________ years from date of origination, ☐ or upon sale or transfer of subject property. A late charge of ______________ shall be due on any installment not paid within ________ days of the due date.
☐ Deed of Trust to contain a request for notice of default or sale for the benefit of Seller. Buyer ☐ will, ☐ will not execute a request for notice of delinquency. Additional terms ____

G. Buyer ☐ to assume, ☐ to take title subject to an EXISTING SECOND LOAN with an approximate balance of .... $ ______
in favor of ______________ payable monthly at $ ________ including interest at ________% ☐ fixed rate, ☐ other ______________. Buyer fees not to exceed ______________.
Additional terms ____

H. Buyer to apply, qualify for and obtain a NEW SECOND LOAN in the amount of .... $ ______
payable monthly at approximately $ ________ including interest at origination not to exceed ________% ☐ fixed rate, ☐ other ______________, all due ________ years from date of origination.
Buyer's loan fee not to exceed ______________. Additional terms ______________________________

I. In the event Buyer assumes or takes title subject to an existing loan, Seller shall provide Buyer with copies of applicable notes and Deeds of Trust. A loan may contain a number of features which affect the loan, such as interest rate changes, monthly payment changes, balloon payments, etc. Buyer shall be allowed ________ calendar days after receipt of such copies to notify Seller in writing of disapproval. FAILURE TO NOTIFY SELLER IN WRITING SHALL CONCLUSIVELY BE CONSIDERED APPROVAL. Buyer's approval shall not be unreasonably withheld. Difference in existing loan balances shall be adjusted in ☐ Cash, ☐ Other ______________

J. Buyer agrees to act diligently and in good faith to obtain all applicable financing. ______________________________

K. ADDITIONAL FINANCING TERMS: ____

L. TOTAL PURCHASE PRICE .... $ 100,000.00

Conventional Loans

The lives of real estate brokers and salespersons would be much simpler if most of their transactions involved full cash payment by the buyer without the necessity of arranging a loan for the buyer to get the cash. However, all cash transactions without a contingency for obtaining the cash through third party financing are quite rare. Third party financing is financing through someone other than the seller, usually a savings and loan association, bank, mortgage company or other lending institution. In most cases, then, in which the buyer plans to borrow all or part of the purchase price from a savings and loan association or other third party lender, the agent filling in the deposit receipt form will be filling both the blanks relating to the method of payment and the blanks concerning the financing condition(s).

Financing conditions or contingencies and other types of contingencies will be covered later in the deposit receipt materials. At this point we will address completion of the financing (or method of payment) blanks to indicate that all or part of the purchase price will be paid from the proceeds of a loan to be obtained from a third party lender: conventional, FHA or VA. Although it is true that the buyer will be paying and the seller will be receiving all cash at closing, both the buyer and the seller usually prefer that the contract form show what portion of the purchase price the buyer expects to pay from his or her own cash resources (which may be savings and/or proceeds from the sale of property owned by the buyer, such as the buyer's current or previous home), and which part of the purchase price the buyer expects to borrow. As was just mentioned, in most cases, the buyer's offer to purchase will be expressly conditioned upon receiving such a loan.

Let us assume a transaction for the purchase of a single-family residence at a price of $100,000. The buyer intends to make a downpayment of twenty percent (20%) of the purchase price and obtain a conventional loan for the remainder. (A conventional loan is a loan which is not FHA-insured or VA-guaranteed.) For a transaction on those terms, the FINANCING PARAGRAPH might read as in the example below:

1. **FINANCING:** The obtaining of Buyer's financing is a contingency of this agreement.

A. DEPOSIT upon acceptance, to be deposited into Broker Trust Account .... $ 2,000.00

B. INCREASED DEPOSIT within ______ days of acceptance to be deposited into ______ $ ______

C. BALANCE OF DOWN PAYMENT to be deposited into Escrow on or before October 15, 1990 $ 18,000.00

D. Buyer to apply, qualify for and obtain a NEW FIRST LOAN in the amount of .... $ 80,000.00

payable monthly at approximately $ 762.00 including interest at origination not to exceed 11 %, [X] fixed rate, [ ] other ______ all due 30 years from date of origination. Loan fee not to exceed 1.5% . Seller agrees to pay a maximum of NO FHA/VA discount points.

Additional terms ______

Loan Application Expenses

It is the usual practice for the buyer (borrower) to pay the fees and costs associated with arranging the financing, such as appraisals, credit reports, and loan application fees required by the lender. Many contract forms have pre-printed clauses to that effect. If there is no such provision in your standard form, it is a good idea to include a clause to clearly indicate who has the obligation to pay the fees and costs associated with applying for and arranging the loan.

Example:

K. ADDITIONAL FINANCING TERMS: Purchaser agrees to pay all expenses in connection with loan application, including, but not limited to loan fee, appraisal fee and credit report fee.

These loan expenses would normally be paid by the buyer, although, as is discussed below, the seller may assist the buyer in paying some or all of the expenses connected with obtaining the loan. In a situation where the buyer has some doubt as to who should pay for the loan application, you probably will also want to make it clear to the buyer that if the loan application is denied, the money paid for the fees and expenses, such as appraisal and credit report, will not be refunded.

Discount Points

At this point, it might be useful to discuss the payment of points or discounts. Most real estate loans involve the payment of a **loan fee** (also called a loan origination fee, service fee, administrative charge or some similar name) which is usually between 1% and 3% of the loan amount. This loan fee is intended to cover the lender's **administrative costs** in processing the loan application. This charge is generally viewed as part of the loan application costs and almost always paid by the buyer.

In many loans, the lender charges some additional "points." A "point" is **1% of the loan amount**. This type of point, or discount point, is really interest paid in advance. The lender agrees to charge a lower interest rate on the loan in return for being paid a lump sum up front. Until a few years ago, points of this type were found primarily in connection with FHA and VA loans and were paid by the seller because FHA and VA rules which set maximum interest rates prohibited the buyer from paying discount points.

The purpose of charging the points was to **increase the lender's yield** on the FHA and VA loans, where the interest rates were normally lower than on conventional loans, to a level which was competitive with the return on conventional loans. In the current market, many conventional loans, particularly those with variable interest rates, involve the payment of points in order to reduce the borrower's interest rate for the first few years of the loan.

With the exception of VA loans (where the VA still sets a maximum interest rate and prohibits the buyer from paying points in excess of the 1% loan fee and 1.25% funding fee), these discount points may be paid by either the buyer or seller. In many cases, some or all of the points are paid by the seller as a way of subsidizing the buyer's financing in order to make the property more affordable and, therefore, easier to sell. This is called a "buydown." The payment of some points in advance results in a lower interest rate for the first three to five years of the loan (a "temporary buydown") or for the entire loan term (a "permanent buydown").

If the seller has agreed to assist the buyer in this way, it should be indicated on the agreement. The maximum amount that the seller is willing to pay in order to help the buyer obtain a lower interest rate loan should be shown either as a dollar amount or as a percentage of the loan. The REALTORS® form has a pre-printed clause and blank to set out the seller's willingness to pay points in connection with FHA and VA loans, but not in connection with conventional loans. For an FHA or VA loan, the agreement to pay points may be shown simply by filling in the appropriate blank.

Example:

D. Buyer to apply, qualify for and obtain a NEW FIRST LOAN in the amount of . . . . $ 80,000.00
payable monthly at approximately $ 765.00 including interest at origination not to exceed 11 %,
☒ fixed rate, ☐ other ________ all due 30 years from date of origination. Loan fee not to exceed 1% . Seller agrees to pay a maximum of Three FHA/VA discount points.
Additional terms ________

For conventional loan transactions, an agreement by the seller may be shown by writing it in the "Additional terms . . ." blank in Subparagraph 1. D. (the new loan clause) or farther down the FINANCING paragraph in Subparagraph 1. K., "ADDITIONAL FINANCING TERMS."

Example:

FHA/VA discount points. Additional terms Seller agrees to pay a discount in connection with purchaser's loan not to exceed three percent (3%) of the loan amount

FHA Loans

The buyer who intends to purchase by means of an FHA loan typically wishes to pay the absolute minimum downpayment. If that is the situation, the contract may be written to indicate the intention of the buyer to make the minimum cash downpayment required by the particular program for which the buyer expects to apply (for example, FHA 203b or 203b2) and to pay the rest of the purchase price with the loan proceeds.

Example:

K. ADDITIONAL FINANCING TERMS: Purchaser agrees to pay the purchase price by paying in cash at close of escrow the minimum down payment required for an FHA 203b loan, which cash down payment shall include the receipted deposit. The balance of the purchase price shall be paid by purchaser from the proceeds of an FHA 203b loan. Purchaser agrees to make written application for such a loan within three business days of seller's acceptance of this offer.

You may also refer to FHA loan tables or perform your own calculations to find the maximum FHA loan amount for a particular sales and enter the actual dollar amounts in blanks provided on the form.

Example:

1. FINANCING: The obtaining of Buyer's financing is a contingency of this agreement.
A. DEPOSIT upon acceptance, to be deposited into Broker Trust Account $ 2,000.00
B. INCREASED DEPOSIT within ______ days of acceptance to be deposited into ______ $ ______
C. BALANCE OF DOWN PAYMENT to be deposited into ______ on or before ______ $ ______
D. Buyer to apply, qualify for and obtain a NEW FIRST LOAN in the amount of .... $ 86,000.00
payable monthly at approximately $ 787.00 including interest at origination not to exceed 10.5 %,
☒ fixed rate, ☐ other ______ all due 30 years from date of origination. Loan fee not to exceed 1% . Seller agrees to pay a maximum of Three FHA/VA discount points.
Additional terms ______

Work Orders

In transactions financed with FHA loans, inspection of the property is required. Inspections often result in "work orders," specifying certain repairs, maintenance or improvements necessary to bring the property up to FHA standards. The required work may be relatively minor, such as replacing a couple of worn treads on back porch steps or replacing a cracked window. It can also be quite major, such as putting on a new roof.

Inspections (and work orders) are also found in connection with VA loan applications and, to a certain extent, with conventional loan applications. Regardless of the proposed type of financing, if the loan application process will entail an inspection of the property (which always carries with it the possibility of a requirement for some work to be done in order to meet whatever standards are applicable), it is advisable to discuss this with the seller. The seller should be informed as to the reason for the inspection(s) and the consequences of a bad report or "work order."

To avoid unpleasant surprises and to clarify the seller's obligation in the event of a work order or work orders, it may be a good idea to reach an agreement as to how much money the seller is willing to pay to make repairs or otherwise satisfy work orders necessary for approval of the buyer's loan application.

Example

K. ADDITIONAL FINANCING TERMS: To assist purchaser in obtaining FHA financing, seller agrees to pay for repairs or other work or improvements required by FHA work orders to the extent that the cost of complying with such work orders does not exceed five hundred dollars ($500.00).

FHA/VA Amendment

In both FHA and VA loan transactions, if the appraised value of the property does not at least equal the agreed upon sales price, the buyer may not be required to buy the property or suffer loss of the deposit or any other penalty for failure to complete the transaction. The buyer may elect to purchase the property even though the appraised value is less than he or she has agreed to pay. In such cases, the maximum loan amount is based upon the appraised value, not the sales price. The buyer would then have to pay the excess in cash out of his or her own resources; the property may not be encumbered by financing in excess of the appraised value of the property or the FHA maximum loan amount, whichever is less. It is also both an FHA and VA requirement that the purchase and sale agreement include a clause which advises the purchaser of his or her rights to cancel the transaction without penalty in event that the appraisal is below the agreed upon price. This clause may be included in the pre-printed form or attached as an addendum for FHA and VA transactions.

The CAR deposit receipt form has a box in Paragraph 3. SUPPLEMENTS to be checked to indicate that the transaction is an FHA or VA transaction and that the FHA/VA amendment is attached to and incorporated in the purchase and sale agreement. The FHA/VA Amendments form is reproduced on the next page.

The first paragraph in the VA AND FHA AMENDMENTS form serves to identify the transaction to which the amendment relates. There are blanks to indicate the pages and date of the deposit receipt and for the names of the buyer(s) and seller(s). There are then paragraphs setting forth the VA and FHA rules concerning the right of the buyer to withdraw from the transaction if the appraised value (reasonable value) is less than the agreed purchase price. The FHA paragraph also includes a disclaimer in which it is stated that the purpose of the FHA appraisal is to assist HUD in establishing the maximum insurable loan, not to inspect the property for the benefit of the buyer. No warranty is made to the buyer regarding the value or condition of the property and the buyer is cautioned to conduct his or her own inspection and analysis to reach a decision regarding value and condition.

The buyer(s) and seller(s) would sign in the blanks following the VA or FHA paragraph, as appropriate.

VA Loans

In VA loan transactions, the buyer/borrower often makes no downpayment. That's one of the features that makes VA loans particularly attractive. Also, in some VA transactions the seller will agree to pay most of the closing costs that would be paid by the buyer in a conventional loan transaction.

If the buyer will be paying the closing costs which VA regulations permit the buyer to pay (the usual "zero down" VA loan), the payment clause might read as follows:

CALIFORNIA ASSOCIATION OF REALTORS

VA AND FHA AMENDMENTS

CALIFORNIA ASSOCIATION OF REALTORS® STANDARD FORM

This addendum is attached as Page ________ of ____________ Pages to the Real Estate Purchase Contract and Receipt for Deposit dated ________________ 19 ______ in which ____

____

is referred to as Buyer and ____

____ is referred to as Seller.

VA LOAN

It is expressly agreed that, notwithstanding any other provisions of this contract, the purchaser shall not incur any penalty by forfeiture of earnest money or otherwise or be obligated to complete the purchase of the property described herein, if the contract purchase price or cost exceeds the reasonable value of the property established by the Veterans Administration. The purchaser shall, however, have the privilege and option of proceeding with the consummation of this contract without regard to the amount of the reasonable value established by the Veterans Administration.

Receipt of a copy is hereby acknowledged.

DATED: ______________________________, 19 _____ BUYER: ______________________________

____

Receipt of a copy is hereby acknowledged.

DATED: ______________________________, 19 _____ SELLER: ______________________________

____

FHA LOAN

It is expressly agreed that notwithstanding any other provisions of the contract, the buyer shall not be obligated to complete the purchase of the premises and shall not incur any penalty or loss of his deposit money or otherwise unless the seller has delivered to the buyer a written statement issued by the Federal Housing Commissioner setting forth the appraised value of the property for mortgage insurance purposes of not less than $ ______________________, which statement the seller shall deliver to the buyer promptly after such appraised value statement is made available to the seller.

The buyer shall, however, have the privilege and option of proceeding with the consummation of this contract without regard to the amount of the appraised valuation made by the Federal Housing Commission.

The appraised valuation is arrived at to determine the maximum mortgage the Department of Housing and Urban Development will insure, HUD does not warrant the value or the condition of the property. The purchaser should satisfy himself/herself that the price and condition of the property are acceptable.

Receipt of a copy is hereby acknowledged.

DATED: ______________________, 19____ ______________________

Receipt of a copy is hereby acknowledged.

DATED: ______________________, 19____ SELLER: ______________________

____

NO REPRESENTATION IS MADE AS TO THE LEGAL VALIDITY OF ANY PROVISION OR THE ADEQUACY OF ANY PROVISION IN ANY SPECIFIC TRANSACTION. A REAL ESTATE BROKER IS THE PERSON QUALIFIED TO ADVISE ON REAL ESTATE. IF YOU DESIRE LEGAL ADVICE CONSULT YOUR ATTORNEY.

For these forms, address—California Association of Realtors®
505 Shatto Place, Los Angeles, California 90020

VA-FHA-11

MB-E6-MB/1

1. **FINANCING:** The obtaining of Buyer's financing is a contingency of this agreement.
 A. DEPOSIT upon acceptance, to be deposited into Broker Trust Account $ 2,000.00
 B. INCREASED DEPOSIT within ______ days of acceptance to be deposited into ______ $ ______
 C. BALANCE OF DOWN PAYMENT to be deposited into ______ on or before ______ $ ______
 D. Buyer to apply, qualify for and obtain a NEW FIRST LOAN in the amount of . . . . . . $ 100,000.00
 payable monthly at approximately $ 915.00 including interest at origination not to exceed 10.5 %,
 ☒ fixed rate, ☐ other ______ all due 30 years from date of origination. Loan fee not to exceed 1% . Seller agrees to pay a maximum of Three FHA/VA discount points.
 Additional terms Purchaser agrees to pay 1.25% VA funding fee in addition to 1% lender's loan fee.

If the seller agrees to pay the buyer's closing costs, the method of payment clause will be written in much the same manner as illustrated above, except that it must also provide for return of the deposit money to the buyer at closing. This type of VA transaction is often called a "zero-zero" or "00" down VA loan, meaning that not only does the buyer pay no downpayment, the buyer also does not pay the normal closing costs or prepaid items. On the CAR deposit receipt form, the seller's agreement to pay the buyer's closing costs and prepaid items could be written in the "Additional terms" blank in Subparagraph 1.D. or in Subparagraph 1.K., ADDITIONAL FINANCING TERMS.

Example:

1. **FINANCING:** The obtaining of Buyer's financing is a contingency of this agreement.
 A. DEPOSIT upon acceptance, to be deposited into Broker Trust Account $ 2,000.00
 B. INCREASED DEPOSIT within ______ days of acceptance to be deposited into ______ $ ______
 C. BALANCE OF DOWN PAYMENT to be deposited into ______ on or before ______ $ ______
 D. Buyer to apply, qualify for and obtain a NEW FIRST LOAN in the amount of . . . . . . $ 100,000.00
 payable monthly at approximately $ 916.00 including interest at origination not to exceed 10.5%,
 ☒ fixed rate, ☐ other ______ all due 30 years from date of origination. Loan fee not to exceed 1% . Seller agrees to pay a maximum of Three FHA/VA discount points.
 Additional terms Purchaser agrees to pay 1.25% VA funding fee in addition to 1% lender's loan fee.
 E. Buyer ☐ to assume, ☐ to take title subject to an EXISTING FIRST LOAN with an approximate balance of . . . . . . $ ______
 in favor of ______ payable monthly at $______ including interest at ______% ☐ fixed rate,
 ☐ other ______ . Fees not to exceed ______ .
 Disposition of impound account ______ .
 Additional terms ______ .
 F. Buyer to execute a NOTE SECURED BY a ☐ first, ☐ second, ☐ third DEED OF TRUST in the amount of . . . . . . $ ______
 IN FAVOR OF SELLER payable monthly at $______ ☐ or more, including interest at ______% all due ______ years from date of origination, ☐ or upon sale or transfer of subject property. A late charge of ______ shall be due on any installment not paid within ______ days of the due date.
 ☐ Deed of Trust to contain a request for notice of default or sale for the benefit of Seller. Buyer ☐ will, ☐ will not execute a request for notice of delinquency. Additional terms ______ .
 G. Buyer ☐ to assume, ☐ to take title subject to an EXISTING SECOND LOAN with an approximate balance of . . . . . . $ ______
 in favor of ______ payable monthly at $______ including interest at ______%
 ☐ fixed rate, ☐ other ______ . Buyer fees not to exceed ______ .
 Additional terms ______

H. Buyer to apply, qualify for and obtain a NEW SECOND LOAN in the amount of .... $ ______________
payable monthly at approximately $______________ including interest at origination not to exceed ________% ☐ fixed rate,
☐ other ____, all due ________ years from date of origination.
Buyer's loan fee not to exceed ______________________________. Additional terms ______________________________
____.

I. In the event Buyer assumes or takes title subject to an existing loan, Seller shall provide Buyer with copies of applicable notes and Deeds of Trust. A loan may contain a number of features which affect the loan, such as interest rate changes, monthly payment changes, balloon payments, etc. Buyer shall be allowed ________ calendar days after receipt of such copies to notify Seller in writing of disapproval. FAILURE TO NOTIFY SELLER IN WRITING SHALL CONCLUSIVELY BE CONSIDERED APPROVAL. Buyer's approval shall not be unreasonably withheld. Difference in existing loan balances shall be adjusted in ☐ Cash, ☐ Other ______________________
____.

J. Buyer agrees to act diligently and in good faith to obtain all applicable financing. ______________________________
____
____.

K. ADDITIONAL FINANCING TERMS: Seller agrees to pay purchaser's closing costs and prepaid items.
Purchaser's deposit is to be returned to purchaser at close of escrow.

CAL-VET Financing

Low-interest rate loans are available to qualified veterans who were California residents at the time of their enlistment or induction into the armed services under the CAL-VET program. For a complete discussion of the program, conditions of and eligibility for CAL-VET financing, see the CAL-VET materials in the financing section of the text.

The CAR DLF-14 form has no specific printed clause for CAL-VET financing, so payment as proceeds of a CAL-VET loan would be shown in an addendum or by using the CAR DL-14 form, which provides a number of blank lines for indicating the method of payment. For example, if the purchase price were $75,000 and the veteran wanted to finance 95% of the purchase price through the CAL-VET program, the payment clause might read as follows:

> "The total purchase price of $75,000 is to be paid as follows:
>
> 1) $3,750 Downpayment, to be paid in cash at close of escrow, including the receipted for deposit;
> 2) $71,250 As proceeds of a CAL-VET loan.

This agreement is conditioned upon purchaser's ability to obtain a CAL-VET loan in the above amount for the subject property. Purchaser agrees to make written application for said loan within three days of seller's written acceptance of this offer and to obtain final approval for said loan within sixty days of seller's acceptance."

Checklist

Price

- Total purchase price, including all trust deeds, liens or encumbrances to be assumed or taken subject to by the buyer

Method of Payment

- Cash
  - Deposit to:
    - Broker
    - Escrow
    - Seller
  - Remainder of cash at close of escrow
- Conventional loan
  - Deposit
  - Portion of purchase price to be paid by loan (percentage or dollar amount)
  - Remainder of cash downpayment to be paid at close of escrow (percentage or dollar amount)
  - Type of loan applied for
  - Party to pay application expenses
  - Party(ies) to pay points in connection with loan

    - Loan fee points
    - "Interest in advance" discount or buydown points
    - Maximum cost of repairs necessary for loan approval to be paid by seller
- FHA loan
    - Deposit
    - Portion of purchase price to be paid by loan (percentage or dollar amount)
    - Type of FHA loan applied for
    - Party to pay loan application expenses
    - Party(ies) to pay points in connection with loan
    - Loan fee points
    - "Interest in advance" discount points
    - Maximum cost of repairs (work orders) necessary for loan approval to be paid by seller
- VA loan
    - Deposit
        - Disposition of deposit at close of escrow
    - Portion of purchase price to be paid by loan (percentage or dollar amount)
    - Remainder of cash downpayment, if any, to be paid at close of escrow
    - Type of VA loan applied for
    - Party to pay loan application expenses
    - Maximum points to be paid by seller
    - Maximum cost of repairs necessary for loan approval (work orders) to be paid by seller

Chapter Sixteen

Deposit Receipt: Seller Financing

A seller-financed (or owner-financed) transaction is a transaction in which the seller agrees to take all or part of the purchase price in deferred payments, rather than receiving the entire price at closing. This is often referred to as a "carry back" transaction because the seller "carries back" some of the purchase price in the form of paper from the buyer (e.g., promissory notes, trust deeds, installment contracts). In most cases the buyer makes a downpayment and then makes installment payments for the remainder. There are a large number of possible arrangements. Financing may be by means of a note and mortgage or deed of trust given to the seller, often called a "purchase money trust deed," or by some sort of installment contract. In California, the most frequently used documents are promissory notes and trust deeds. The buyer may take subject to or assume the seller's existing loan. The arrangement may involve some sort of combination, such as a downpayment for part of the purchase price, assumption of the seller's loan for part of the purchase price, and a second trust deed to the seller for the remainder of the price.

Probably the main reason for most seller-financed transactions is the unavailability or high cost of traditional financing through savings and loans or other institutional lenders. During periods of high interest rates, many potential buyers find it impossible to qualify for institutional loans. In such environments, sellers often find it necessary to carry some or all of the financing in order to sell their property.

Another reason for some seller-financed transactions is that some properties do not meet lender standards for home loans. For example, some lenders will not make home loans for property where the value of the land exceeds 30% of the total value of the property or if the property is not accessible by an all-weather secondary road. Both of these circumstances often exist in rural areas. There may be other reasons for a particular piece of property not meeting the standards required by local lenders.

In situations where the property, the buyer, or both fail to meet qualifying standards the parties will have to resort to owner financing. In some cases, the parties prefer owner financing even though the property and the buyer would qualify for institutional financing. The seller may be willing to offer a lower interest rate than is available from institutional lenders and/or the seller may want an installment sale in order to defer the taxable gain over a number of years and lower his or her overall income tax liability. Both parties may desire the relatively quicker closing which is possible with seller financing, since there is no need for the time-consuming steps of loan application and approval.

Advantages and Disadvantages of Seller Financing

Deferred payment of equity. Seller financing has some advantages and disadvantages for both buyers and sellers when compared to financing from institutional lenders. One of the main disadvantages for the sellers is that they do not receive full payment for their equity at closing, but must wait for some future payment or payments.

The seller's equity in the property is the seller's interest in the property. It is generally defined as the difference between the value of the property and the liens against it. For example, if the property is worth $100,000 and there is an existing $40,000 trust deed and no other liens against the property, the seller's equity would be $60,000 (the difference between the value and the liens: $100,000 – 40,000 = $60,000). In a traditional home purchase transaction where the buyer makes a downpayment (20%, for example) and borrows the rest from a bank or savings and loan, the seller would receive this entire $60,000 at closing. Of course, there would be a number of deductions for costs, such as the real estate broker's commission, title insurance, and other closing costs, but the seller would be paid the entire (net) equity at closing.

In a seller-financed transaction, this is usually not true. For instance, the buyer might make a 20% downpayment to the seller and give the seller a second trust deed for the remainder of the seller's equity. The seller, then, would receive only the downpayment at closing, in this example, $20,000, minus costs of closing, such as the commission. The seller would be paid for the rest of his or her equity ($40,000) sometime in the future in one or more installment payments. These payments may be scheduled over a long period, such as 20 or 30 years, or a much shorter period, such as one to three years.

Resale of purchase money securities. There may be, of course, situations where the seller prefers to defer the gain from the sale of the property, for tax planning or for some other purpose, but probably in most cases, the seller of an owner-occupied residence would rather get all the money at closing. Many of the instruments used in seller financing (contracts or notes and trust deeds) may be sold to third party investors if the seller needs immediate cash. However, such sales are usually at a discount, sometimes a pretty large discount.

When a note or contract is sold at a discount, it means the seller does not receive the full face value of the note or contract. The amount of the discount varies depending upon the term and interest rate of the paper being sold (e.g., a five-year note at 14% or a 20-year note at 10%), the amount of equity in the property, the condition of the property, market rates of interest, and other factors. Discount rates, though, are often in the neighborhood of 20-30%. In the example, if the seller took a note and second trust deed for the $40,000 remaining equity and sold that note at a 30% discount, the seller would receive only $28,000 (30% of $40,000 is $12,000; $40,000 – $12,000 = $28,000).

Rate of return. As was mentioned earlier, though, the deferral of the income from the sale would be considered an advantage by some sellers. In many situations, income tax consequences can be reduced through an installment sale. Some sellers may desire a future income stream for retirement or other reasons. Also, in "wraparound" or "all-inclusive" trust deed financing, which will be discussed later, it is possible for the seller to substantially increase the rate of return on his or her equity. Even without wraparound financing, the seller usually receives a higher rate of return than if the money were in a savings account.

Defaults. Probably the greatest concern of sellers contemplating seller financing, other than the fact that they will not receive full payment at closing, is concern as to the consequences of buyer default. The question is usually phrased something like, "If they don't make their payments, how do I get my house back and how much will it cost me?" Unfortunately, there is no simple answer to this question. The time required and the total cost of a foreclosure or forfeiture may vary considerably from one case to another, but it is almost never quick or cheap.

Another potentially serious problem arises if the seller does not own the property free and clear, but instead, must make installment payments to a lender or seller. In those cases, if the buyer defaults, the seller will have to keep the first trust deed or contract current by making up the default and continuing to make the monthly payments while he or she is foreclosing the buyer. Otherwise, the seller's interest in the property may be foreclosed by the senior lienholder (the seller's lender). The necessity of continuing to make payments on the underlying loan or contract while not receiving any payments from the buyer can impose a severe financial strain on many sellers.

Sales price. Probably the primary advantage to the seller in most seller-financed transactions is that the property can usually be marketed more quickly and for a higher price. This is because sellers generally offer more attractive financing terms than do institutional lenders. The better financing terms, especially of owner-occupied residences, permit buyers to afford higher prices.

Qualification. The easier financing conditions and lower costs of seller financing are the primary advantage for the buyer. Qualification standards and procedures, if any are used at all, are usually less stringent and more flexible than those employed by institutional lenders. Some of the costs frequently incurred in institutional financing, such as appraisals, mortgage insurance, and loan fees, are normally not required in connection with seller financing. These costs can easily amount to thousands of dollars. Sellers do occasionally require that the buyer submit to a credit investigation, but this is a relatively minor expense in comparison to the other financing costs.

The time involved in applying for and obtaining a loan from a savings and loan, mortgage company or other lender is usually cause for the longest delay in closing a home sale. That delay is eliminated in seller-financed transactions so, in most cases, the sale can be closed more quickly. This is an advantage to both parties.

In any event, a considerable number of transactions do involve owner financing for at least part of the purchase price because it is often the only way, or at least the quickest and best way, to get the property sold. In owner-financed transactions, the buyer and the seller must agree upon the payment terms, so, as a general rule, these types of transactions are more complicated for the person preparing the deposit receipt form.

Pre-printed Forms

Many deposit receipt forms have provisions which are intended to be completed for seller-financed transactions and in some areas there are entire forms designed for seller-financed transactions. The REALTORS® form has several clauses within the FINANCING paragraph (clauses 1. E. through 1. I.) which may be completed to describe some of the most common forms of seller financing: assumption or taking subject to an existing loan and/or a purchase money note and trust deed to the seller.

E. Buyer ☐ to assume, ☐ to take title subject to an EXISTING FIRST LOAN with an approximate balance of $ ________
in favor of ________ payable monthly at $ ________ including interest
at ____ % ☐ fixed rate, ☐ other ________
Fees not to exceed ________. Disposition of impound account ________.
Additional Terms ________.

F. Buyer to execute a NOTE SECURED BY a ☐ first, ☐ second, ☐ third DEED OF TRUST in the amount of.. $ ________
IN FAVOR OF SELLER payable monthly at $ ________ ☐ or more, including interest at ____% all due
____ years from date of origination, ☐ or upon sale or transfer of subject property. A late charge of ____
shall be due on any installment not paid within ____ days of the due date. ☐ Deed of Trust to contain a request for notice of default or sale for the benefit of Seller. Buyer ☐ will, ☐ will not execute a request for notice of delinquency. Additional terms ________.

G. Buyer ☐ to assume, ☐ to take title subject to an EXISTING SECOND LOAN with an approximate balance of $ ________
in favor of ________ payable monthly at $ ________ including interest
at ____ % ☐ fixed rate, ☐ other ________. Buyer fees not to exceed ________.
Additional terms ________.

H. Buyer to apply, qualify for and obtain a NEW SECOND LOAN in the amount of .... $ ________
payable monthly at approximately $ ________ ☐ or more, including interest at origination not to exceed
____ % ☐ fixed rate, ☐ other, ________
____, all due ____ years from date of origination. Buyer's loan fee not to exceed ________.
Additional Terms ________.

I. In the event Buyer assumes or takes title subject to an existing loan, Seller shall provide Buyer with copies of applicable notes and Deeds of Trust. A loan may contain a number of features which affect the loan, such as interest rate changes, monthly payment changes, balloon payments, etc. Buyer shall be allowed ____ calendar days after receipt of such copies to notify seller in writing of disapproval. FAILURE TO SO NOTIFY SELLER SHALL CONCLUSIVELY BE CONSIDERED APPROVAL. Buyer's approval shall not be unreasonably withheld. Difference in existing loan balances shall be adjusted in ☐ Cash, ☐ Other ________.

Subparagraph 1. E. is to be filled in if the buyer is to take subject to or assume the seller's existing first lien trust deed. There are boxes to indicate whether the buyer will assume the loan or merely take subject to it. There are then blanks to describe some important features of the loan: the current balance, the lender, the monthly payments, interest rate, and whether the interest rate is fixed or variable. There is then a blank to indicate the maximum fee that the buyer is willing to pay to assume the loan. Assumption fees range from a modest administrative charge of approximately $100 up to pretty steep charges that are the equivalent of another loan fee (1-3% of the principal balance to be assumed). If the seller's existing loan has an impound account, as most home loans do, the buyer may assume the seller's account and pay the seller at closing an amount equal to the account at that time or the buyer may establish a new impound account at closing. In that case, the seller's existing impounds would be refunded to the seller at closing. Finally, there is a blank to fill in any additional terms or to refer to an addendum for additional terms.

In the following example, the buyer agrees to assume an existing $40,000 FHA first trust deed. The loan has monthly principal and interest payments of $420 and bears interest at a fixed rate of 9½%. The buyer agrees to pay an assumption fee of not over $150 and will assume the seller's impounds.

Example:

E. Buyer [X] to assume, [ ] to take title subject to an EXISTING FIRST LOAN with an approximate balance of .... $ 40,000.00
in favor of 1st National Bank payable monthly at $ 420.00 including interest at 9.5 % [X] fixed rate,
[ ] other ______ . Fees not to exceed $150.00 .
Disposition of impound account Buyer will assume Seller's impound account and
XXXXXXXXXX reimburse seller at close of escrow.

If the buyer is to assume or take subject to a second trust deed, then Subparagraph 1. G. would also be filled out. The blanks to be completed in that subparagraph are substantially identical to the ones in Subparagraph 1. E. discussed just above.

Subparagraph 1.F. is to be used if the buyer will execute a purchase money trust deed to the seller for any part of the purchase price. There may or may not be any existing loans which the buyer will take subject to or assume. If the buyer is to take subject to or assume one or more existing loans, Subparagraph 1. E. (existing first loan) or Subparagraph 1. G. (existing second loan) would also be filled out. The note and deed of trust executed by the buyer may be in addition to the loan(s) being assumed, for example an assumption of a $40,000 loan, a second trust deed to the seller for $40,000 and $20,000 cash downpayment to reach the total price of $100,000. The note and deed of trust may instead be a so-called "all-inclusive" trust deed which wraps around or includes the existing loan(s), for example, $20,000 cash downpayment and a second trust deed to the seller for $80,000 to reach the total sales price of $100,000. The $80,000 second trust deed includes the existing $40,000 loan, to which the buyer agrees to take subject.

There are blanks to indicate the principal amount of the trust deed to the seller, whether it will be a first (no underlying loans), second or third trust deed, the monthly payments, the interest rate and the term. There are additional boxes and blanks to indicate whether the note and trust deed will include due on sale and/or late charge provisions, and requests for notice of default or sale for the benefit of seller and/or purchaser.

In the following example, the buyer is to make a $20,000 cash down-payment and execute an $80,000 second trust deed to the seller. The interest rate is 11%, term is 20 years and the monthly payments are approximately $826. There is to be no alienation clause but there will be a late fee of 3% on any payment not paid within ten days of the due date. Buyer requests notice of default.

Example:

F. Buyer to execute a NOTE SECURED BY a ☐ first, ☒ second, ☐ third DEED OF TRUST in the amount of .... $ 80,000.00
IN FAVOR OF SELLER payable monthly at $ 826.00 ☒ or more, including interest at 11 % all due 20 years from date of origination, ☐ or upon sale or transfer of subject property. A late charge of 3% shall be due on any installment not paid within 10 days of the due date.
☒ Deed of Trust to contain a request for notice of default or sale for the benefit of Seller. Buyer ☒ will, ☐ will not execute a request for notice of delinquency. Additional terms ______

Subparagraph 1. I. is applicable in any transaction where the buyer either takes subject to or assumes an existing loan. The purpose of this clause is to give the buyer an opportunity to review the terms of the underlying loan(s) to see whether they are acceptable. For example, an underlying loan may have a $50,000 balloon payment which falls due in two years. If there is no apparent way for the seller to accumulate the $50,000 before the due date, the buyer would not want to take subject to the loan. A default on the underlying loan if the seller fails to make his/her balloon payment would result in a foreclosure which would also extinguish the buyer's interest in the property. The buyer would be given a few days to review the documents after receiving them and perhaps to confer with an attorney. If the buyer does not file a written objection within the allowed time period, the buyer is deemed to have agreed to accept and take subject to or assume (as appropriate) the existing trust deed(s).

The final sentence in Subparagraph 1. I. provides for adjustment if the loan to be assumed or taken subject to has a balance at closing which is different than the estimated balance. For example, suppose the buyer has agreed to pay $100,000 for the house by paying $20,000 in cash and assuming an existing trust deed which has an approximate balance of $80,000. At closing, information from the underlying lender indicates that the existing balance is only $79,000, not $80,000. Does this mean that the buyer has to pay $21,000 instead of $20,000 down or does it mean that the sales price is to be reduced to $99,000, or is there another way? The three possible methods are to adjust the downpayment (cash adjustment), adjust the sales price, or adjust the amount of a purchase money trust deed to the seller. Increasing the downpayment may be disagreeable or even financially impossible for the buyer. Lowering the sales price may be unacceptable to the seller. If there is any carry back financing, adjusting the amount of the trust deed to the seller is usually the most acceptable. Regardless of how the matter is to be resolved, it should be discussed and an arrangement made any time the transaction involves assumption or taking subject to an existing loan, since the outstanding balance at close of escrow is seldom exactly what the broker and/or the seller have estimated.

Even if the form you use is designed for seller-financed transactions or has a detailed section which is designed for seller-financed transactions, as does the CAR form, it is extremely important to make sure that the preprinted clauses are applicable to the particular transaction being negotiated. In some cases the preprinted provisions may be contrary to what the parties intend and in others there simply may not be enough blank space provided to fully set forth the terms of the agreement. In such situations, attach an addendum with the agreed upon payment terms clearly expressed. Remember to reference the addendum on the face of the deposit receipt form and to have the parties sign or initial and date the attachment.

The following examples of seller financing terms are intended to illustrate some provisions frequently used in seller-financed transactions, but they may not be applicable to a particular set of facts in a particular transaction. If there is any doubt as to the sufficiency of the written provisions for a particular transaction, competent legal counsel should be sought.

Transactions Where Seller Has Clear Title

The simplest seller-financed transactions are those in which the seller has clear title to the property. By clear title, it is meant that there are no outstanding trust deeds, judgment liens, or other liens which will continue against the property after closing. So the buyer does not have to take subject to or agree to assume any underlying loans, contracts or other liens. The seller and buyer need only come to an agreement as to the downpayment and the terms for paying off the remainder of the purchase price. On the CAR form, Subparagraph 1. F. could be used to write this type of financing arrangement.

Purchase money deed of trust. With purchase money trust deed financing, the buyer signs a promissory note and deed of trust in favor of the seller. The note contains the buyer's promise to pay the seller the money, spells out the size and frequency of payments and the interest rate. It also usually contains some provisions relating to defaults, such as, allowing the seller to accelerate the debt in the event of default and providing for a reasonable attorney's fee and other reasonable costs of collection incurred by the seller if the buyer defaults.

The promissory note, then, is the basic promise of the buyer to pay the money. The deed of trust is the security for that promise. The trust deed gives the seller (or other holder of the note if the seller later transfers the note to someone else) the right to force the sale of the property (at a trustee's sale) to pay the debt if the buyer fails to do so according to the terms contained in the note and trust deed.

If there is just a note and no trust deed, the debt (promise to pay) is unsecured. The seller would have nothing other than the buyer's promise to pay. If the buyer failed to make the payments, the seller would have to sue the buyer, get a judgment, and then enforce the judgment lien. In almost all cases the seller would want the security of a trust deed along with the note. If the standard clauses in your form do not provide for both a note and deed of trust (the CAR form does provide that the buyer will execute both), care should be taken that any provision you add does state that the buyer will execute both a note and a deed of trust. Failure to do so could have a disastrous effect on the seller's legal position in the event of default by the buyer and could easily result in a suit by the seller against whoever prepared the deposit receipt and omitted that important provision.

Terms of sale. If the parties agree that the purchase price is to be $100,000, with the buyer paying 20% down and the remainder on a 20-year, fully amortized note and trust deed, with interest at the rate of 12%, and monthly payments of $881, the method of payment provision might read as shown in the following example.

Example:

F. Buyer to execute a NOTE SECURED BY a [X] first, [ ] second, [ ] third DEED OF TRUST in the amount of .... $ 80,000.00
IN FAVOR OF SELLER payable monthly at $ 881.00 [X] or more, including interest at 12 % all due
20 years from date of origination, [ ] or upon sale or transfer of subject property. A late charge of 3%
shall be due on any installment not paid within 10 days of the due date.

A few matters should be discussed here which are relevant to many seller-financed transactions.

It is normally a good idea to attach to the deposit receipt copies of the form of the promissory note and trust deed that the buyer will execute at closing. This will insure that the parties have actually reached a specific agreement as to the financing terms. For example, the promissory note the buyer is asked to sign at closing may contain provisions for late payment penalties if the installment payments are made more than a certain number of days after the due date. If the terms set out in the deposit receipt made no reference to late payment penalties (or increased interest rate after default or provision for the seller to recover collection costs and attorneys' fees), the buyer may object that those provisions were not part of the agreement and should not be added at closing. In this regard, the REALTORS® form has pre-printed provisions for inserting a late payment penalty and blank lines for writing in other terms for the note and/or trust deed.

Prepayment. It is advisable to have an agreement as to whether the buyer has the option of paying off the debt early. For example, a clause might be entered which provides that:

"The purchaser has the right to prepay the unpaid principal balance, in whole or in part, without penalty, at any time."

This would give the purchaser the right to pay off the loan early without having to pay any additional costs or penalties for such early prepayment. In most cases, sellers have no objection to prepayment and may, in fact, prefer that the debt be paid off early. However, it is not uncommon for the seller to desire that the payments be spread over a number of years. This is usually to spread out the capital gain to the seller for federal income tax purposes. In such cases, rather than providing that the buyer has the right to prepay the principal without penalty, a clause would be included to prevent the buyer from paying off the entire balance before a certain date or to require that no more than a certain percentage of the principal balance be paid in any one year.

For transactions involving residential property with one to four units, California law restricts a lender's ability to prohibit or penalize prepayment. As a general rule, a residential borrower has the right to prepay at any time. But during the first five years of the loan term, the lender can impose a penalty if the borrower prepays more than 20% of the original loan amount in one year. The penalty cannot exceed six months' interest on the amount of prepayment over 20%. These rules apply to seller financing, with one exception: a home seller who carries back a purchase money loan can prevent any prepayment during the year of the sale (unless the seller carries back four or more residential trust deeds in one year).

Examples:

Prohibitions on Prepayment

"It is understood and agreed that purchaser shall not pay more than twenty thousand dollars ($20,000) of the principal balance prior to January 1, 1991."

"It is understood and agreed that purchaser shall be charged a penalty of three percent (3%) on any amount exceeding twenty percent (20%) of the original principal balance prepaid in any one calendar year during the first five years of the loan term."

The examples above contemplate a fully amortized 20-year payment plan. Often, however, the seller is unwilling to agree to any kind of long-term plan, but is willing to accept a short-term payment schedule of three to five years. It is expected that in that time the buyer will be able to obtain a loan from an institutional lender and pay off the seller.

A word of caution is in order here. As recent events in many parts of the country have shown, sometimes property values do not increase rapidly in a three to five-year period, sometimes interest rates do not come down significantly, and sometimes the buyer's income does not increase significantly. In short, sometimes many of the circumstances relied upon in the expectation that the buyer will be able to get a loan within the next three to five years to pay off the seller do not occur. California requires detailed **disclosures** to be made whenever seller financing is used in a residential transaction. Those disclosure requirements are covered in some detail in the chapter on finance disclosures (Chapter Nine).

The short- or medium-term payment plans (one to five years) may be structured as **fully amortized**, **partially amortized** or **interest only** payment schedules. A fully amortized plan would have equal monthly payments which would completely pay off (liquidate) the debt during the amortization period without any balloon payment at the end of the term. Both partially amortized plans and interest only payment plans require a **balloon payment** at the end of the term to pay off the debt. Most of these one- to five-year trust deeds to the seller have partially amortized or interest only payment schedules in order to keep the buyer's monthly payments at a minimum until he or she gets the institutional loan. It is the institutional loan that will be used to make the balloon payment and satisfy the buyer's obligation to the seller.

For example, if the $80,000 debt to the seller were to be paid off in an interest only, five-year note, the buyer would make payments of $800 per month, or interest only payments. (12% interest on $80,000 is $800 per month). By contrast, a fully amortized five-year note for the same amount would require monthly payments of $1,779.56.

Example:

Balloon Payment

"The entire principal balance and accrued interest shall be paid in full no later than five (5) years from date of close of escrow."

On an interest only payment schedule, no payment at all would be made to principal during the five years of monthly payments; after five years, the buyer would still owe the entire $80,000. The last payment, the balloon payment, would be $80,800, the entire principal balance, plus the last month's interest.

Partially amortized plans are usually written so that the monthly payment is based on a long-term amortization schedule, usually 30 years, but the entire outstanding balance is due at the end of the one- to five-year loan term.

Example:

Partially Amortized Loan

"a) Monthly payments of principal and interest in the amount of $822.89, or more at purchaser's option, said monthly payment amount being based upon a thirty (30) year amortization;

b) Interest at the rate of twelve percent (12%) per annum calculated on the declining principal balance;

c) The entire unpaid principal balance and accrued interest must be paid in full no later than five (5) years from date of close of escrow."

Partially amortized schedules have payments slightly larger than interest only schedules and, accordingly, result in some reduction of principal during the loan term, although this reduction is not substantial within the first five years of a 30-year schedule. By way of comparison, the outstanding principal balance at the end of the five-year term in the example directly above would be $78,160, instead of the $80,000 on the interest only plan.

Interest only plans and partially amortized plans are often used in connection with an assumption or taking subject to an existing loan where the buyer does not have enough cash to completely cash out the owner's equity in the property. The buyer then gives the seller a cash downpayment and short-term note for the remainder of the seller's equity.

> **NOTE:** In some cases, the seller agrees to take a second mortgage or trust deed for part of the downpayment and the buyer intends to obtain a loan from an institutional lender for the majority of the sales price. For example, a sale might be financed by a 10% cash downpayment, a 10% second trust deed to the seller, and an 80% loan from a savings and loan association. In those types of transactions, the second trust deed to the seller should have a term of at least five years. A second trust deed to the seller with a term of less than five years often makes it very difficult for the buyer to get a first trust deed loan from a bank or savings and loan. Institutional lenders feel that the increased financial pressure on the buyer to pay off the second trust deed in less than five years increases the likelihood of default on both loans.

Assumption or Subject to the Seller's Loan

The basic difference between a buyer assuming the seller's loan and taking subject to it is whether the buyer assumes personal responsibility for paying the debt. If the buyer takes "subject to" an existing loan, the buyer has agreed to accept the property encumbered by the lien of the seller's loan, but has not agreed to take personal responsibility for paying the loan.

The agreement may call for the buyer to pay the lender directly, it may call for the buyer to make payments to the seller who then pays the lender, or it may call for the buyer to make payments to a third party collection or escrow agent who then makes payments to the lender. If the payments to the seller's lender are not made, the lender can foreclose against the property. The lender could also hold the seller personally liable for the debt or, in some cases, for the deficiency if the property does not bring enough at the foreclosure sale to pay off the debt to the lender. The lender, though, cannot hold the buyer personally liable for the debt or for any shortfall after foreclosure because the buyer has never agreed to be personally responsible for the debt.

If the buyer "assumes" the seller's loan, the buyer does agree to take on personal responsibility for the loan. In that case, the lender could hold the buyer personally responsible for the debt or, depending on the circumstances, for any deficiency after a foreclosure sale. If the buyer assumes the loan, the buyer becomes primarily liable for paying off the loan. The seller remains secondarily liable, unless a release from liability is obtained from the lender. This means that if the lender is unable to get enough money from the buyer or from the property after default, the lender may then attempt to collect from the seller (who was the original borrower). It should be noted at this point that the California **anti-deficiency rule** will protect the buyer and seller from liability for deficiencies if the loan is purchase money financing for residential property used for the owner's personal residence. So, as a practical matter, there is little chance in a typical home sale for either the seller (original borrower) or buyer (assuming borrower) to be held personally liable for a deficiency.

The seller may escape this secondary liability by obtaining a "release from liability" or "substitution of liability" from the lender. The lender then agrees to release the seller from liability and accept the buyer as the sole person responsible for the debt. This is, in effect, a "novation" in that the original loan agreement is replaced by agreement with the buyer to repay the loan.

Obtaining a release from liability may entail what amounts to a new loan application by the buyer. This may negate many of the advantages of seller financing. Even if a release from liability (or substitution of liability) is not requested, lender approval may be required for the sale. Many conventional trust deeds contain "due on sale" or "alienation" clauses. The wording and effect of these clauses varies but the general effect is to give the lender the right to demand full payment of the loan or to increase the interest rate (or to choose between increasing the interest rate and demanding full payment) if the property is transferred.

If the underlying trust deed has a due on sale or alienation clause, steps will have to be taken to see whether acceleration of the debt or increase in interest rate will be demanded by the lender. Provision may be made in the deposit receipt to make the purchase and sale agreement contingent upon obtaining the lender's approval.

For example, suppose a transaction involves the sale of a home for $100,000. The seller has an outstanding trust deed of $55,000, with monthly payments of $595 for principal and interest, and an annual interest rate of 10½%. The buyer agrees to pay cash down to the seller's equity. (This type of transaction is not really seller financing, since the seller will not be actually financing any of the purchase price, but it is generally classified as seller financing because there is no new institutional loan involved.)

Example:

E. Buyer ☒ to assume, ☐ to take title subject to an EXISTING FIRST LOAN with an approximate balance of . . . . $ 55,000.00
in favor of 1st National Ban payable monthly at $ 595.00 including interest at 10.5% ☒ fixed rate,
☐ other ________ . Fees not to exceed $200.00 .
Disposition of impound account Buyer will assume Seller's impound account and
XXXXXXXXXX reimburse Seller at close of escrow .

In cases where the underlying loan has some sort of due on sale clause or alienation clause and you are not absolutely certain that the lender will permit the assumption at the existing interest rate and without assumption or other fees, it is best to include a paragraph to provide for the lender's approval, associated costs, and possible increases in the interest rate.

Example:

Lender's Approval of Assumption

"It is understood and agreed that lender's approval of purchaser's assumption of the underlying first trust deed may be required and

> purchaser agrees to provide the information reasonably required by lender to obtain such approval. This agreement is contingent upon purchaser's obtaining such approval. It is further understood and agreed that there may be an adjustment in interest rate. Purchaser agrees to such adjustment provided that the adjusted rate of interest does not exceed ______ % per annum. Purchaser further agrees to pay any assumption fee required by lender not to exceed ________________ ."

In some cases, the seller (and the buyer) may prefer that the buyer take subject to the existing loan rather than assume it. This may eliminate some of the procedures or cost required by the lender for an assumption.

The buyer may make payments directly to the seller's lender or may make payments to the seller who then pays the underlying lender. The buyer usually prefers to make the payments directly to the lender, as opposed to making payments to the seller who then makes payments to the lender. By making payments directly to the lender, the buyer can be assured that the payments are in fact being made to the lender. If payments are made directly to the seller with an agreement for the seller to make payments to the lender (e.g., "purchaser agrees to make all payments to seller on or before the first day of each month. Seller agrees to make all payments on the underlying obligation"), there is, of course, the possibility that the seller, for one reason or another, will not make the payments and the lender will foreclose, even though the buyer has been faithfully making the payments to the seller on the first of every month.

Second trust deed. In many transactions, the buyer does not have enough cash to fully cash out the seller's equity, so the buyer assumes or takes subject to the seller's loan, makes a cash downpayment, and gives the seller a note and trust deed for the remainder. Suppose that the purchase price is $100,000, with buyer to pay $20,000 in cash, assume the seller's existing $55,000 first trust deed and give the seller a second trust deed for the remainder ($25,000). This second trust deed could be fully amortized, partially amortized with a balloon payment, or interest only with a balloon payment.

Example:

E. Buyer [X] to assume, [ ] to take title subject to an EXISTING FIRST LOAN with an approximate balance of .... $ 55,000.00
in favor of 1st Nat'l Bank payable monthly at $ 595.00 including interest at 10.5% [XX] fixed rate,
[ ] other ______. Fees not to exceed $200.00.
Disposition of impound account Buyer will assume Seller's impound account and reimburse
~~Additional terms~~ XXXXXXXXXX seller at close of escrow.

F. Buyer to execute a NOTE SECURED BY a [ ] first, [X] second, [ ] third DEED OF TRUST in the amount of .... $ 25,000.00
IN FAVOR OF SELLER payable monthly at $ 250.00 [XX] or more, including interest at 12% all due
5 years from date of origination, [XX] or upon sale or transfer of subject property. A late charge of 3%
shall be due on any installment not paid within 10 days of the due date.
[XX] Deed of Trust to contain a request for notice of default or sale for the benefit of Seller. Buyer [X] will, [ ] will not execute a request for notice of delinquency. Additional terms Note is an interest only note with entire
$25,000 principal due 5 years from close of escrow.

All-Inclusive Trust Deeds

In "all-inclusive," or "wraparound," financing, the buyer makes a downpayment and gives the seller a trust deed for the rest of the purchase price. The all-inclusive trust deed includes, or "wraps around," any underlying liens. For example, if the purchase price is $100,000, there is an underlying $55,000 trust deed, and the buyer makes a $20,000 downpayment, the all-inclusive trust deed will be $80,000 ($100,000 – 20,000 = $80,000). In most cases, the buyer will make payments to the seller on the $80,000 second trust deed and the seller will continue to make payments on the underlying $55,000 first trust deed. The buyer takes subject to the underlying loan.

This type of arrangement has several advantages. As mentioned earlier, some of the procedures and costs may be less for the buyer than with an assumption. The primary advantage, though, is that the all-inclusive trust deed may provide the seller with a very attractive rate of return on his or her equity and at the same time provide low interest rate financing to the buyer.

How can that be possible? Take the above example. Assume that the interest rate on the underlying $55,000 trust deed is 10½%, that the interest rate on the all-inclusive $80,000 trust deed is 11%, and that the market interest rate is 11½%. The buyer profits because he or she is paying below market interest rates. The seller profits because he or she is collecting 11% interest on $80,000 but is really only financing $25,000.

This is the amount of the seller's equity ($100,000 – $20,000 cash downpayment – $55,000 existing trust deed lien = $25,000 seller's equity). So, the seller is collecting interest on $80,000 at the rate of 11% per year and paying interest on $55,000 at the rate of 10½% per year.

Looking at it another way, the seller is collecting 11% interest on his or her own $25,000 of equity and is also making ½% interest on the $55,000 underlying loan (the difference between the 11% being received from the buyer and the 10½% being paid to the bank).

In this particular case, the seller winds up with a return of approximately 12.1% on his or her equity.

11% of $25,000 =	$ 2,750.00
½% of $55,000 =	$ 275.00
net interest income =	$3,025.00

$3,025 ÷ 25,000 = .121 or 12.1%

As you can see, it is often possible to structure a wraparound transaction so that it is favorable to both parties.

Some Pitfalls

There are several potential pitfalls in seller-financed transactions. Some are easily avoided. For example, make sure that, if a fully amortized payment plan is intended, that the payments will in fact amortize the debt. This may seem pretty simple, but even in this day of amortization tables and inexpensive pocket calculators which are preprogrammed to find the proper payments for almost any principal amount, interest rate and term, people still write purchase and sale agreements with monthly payments that will never pay off the debt (or at least not pay it off within the lifetime of anyone now living). There is, of course, nothing wrong with payment plans that are not fully amortized, as long as the parties understand what the arrangement is and as long as there is an agreement for finally paying of any existing principal and interest.

There is another similar, and also simple to avoid, pitfall. Make sure that there is proper timing with any underlying loan. For example, if there is an all-inclusive trust deed with a fully amortized 20-year term and the underlying first trust deed still has 23 years left of an original 30-year term, there is a potential problem. In 20 years, the buyer will have completely paid off the purchase price. The seller, however, still has a couple of years to go on the first trust deed. This may require a large payment to be made by the seller to satisfy the underlying obligation or it may result in a problem (or litigation) because the buyer has paid the full price and has not received clear title. This can be avoided by structuring the all-inclusive financing so that any underlying liens are fully paid off before the final payment is made on the wraparound loan. A clause may also be added which states that if the principal balance on the all-inclusive trust deed ever falls below the principal balance on the underlying loan, that the entire amount of payments on the all-inclusive trust deed shall be applied to the underlying loan until such time as the balance on that debt is again smaller than the balance on the all-inclusive trust deed.

Somewhat more difficult situations arise in transactions in which there are a number of underlying trust deeds. This frequently occurs when the property is sold several times through various seller-financed arrangements without ever paying off any of the preceding notes and trust deeds. There are several matters to concern the buyer here. One is to make sure that all the underlying payments are in fact being made. This can be accomplished by making payments directly to the underlying lenders and/or sellers or, more commonly, by establishing an escrow or collection account. The buyer then makes payments to the escrow or collection agent who is given instructions to first satisfy any obligations due on the underlying loans and then to remit the remainder to the seller.

Example:

> "Purchaser's monthly payments to seller shall be paid by purchaser into a collection account at a bank of seller's choice. Said collection agent shall be instructed to disburse purchaser's payments first to the payments on the underlying indebtedness

against the property, and the balance shall be disbursed to seller's account. Cost of said collection account shall be paid equally by purchaser and seller."

Another, and probably more serious, problem, may arise if one (or more) of the underlying loans or contracts has a cash out or balloon payment clause. For example, if the seller is going to have to make a balloon payment of $8,000 in three years to his or her seller, the present buyer is going to want to know where that $8,000 is going to come from. If the buyer is obligated to make a $10,000 balloon payment the month before the seller is to make the $8,000 payment, the situation appears to be under control. On the other hand, if the seller has agreed to sell to the buyer on a 20-year fully amortized trust deed, there is reason for concern. Failure of the seller to make the balloon payment on the underlying loan may result in a foreclosure with the buyer losing the property. To avoid that kind of calamity, the buyer may want to have an interest-bearing escrow or trust account established to accumulate the $8,000. This, of course, is feasible only if the buyer's payments are large enough to meet the current obligations on any underlying loan(s) and also properly fund the trust account to meet the balloon payment.

"Zero Down" Seller Financing

There are various arrangements under which the buyer can buy the property without making any cash payment out of his or her own resources. Some of these plans may result in the seller actually being paid a cash downpayment at closing and in some, the buyer receives cash. How can it be possible for the buyer to not only buy the property "zero down" but to also receive cash from the transaction? The basic plan is for the buyer to take out a loan from a third party lender. The downpayment to the seller is made from part of that loan; the buyer keeps the remainder. The buyer gives the seller a note and trust deed for the remainder of the purchase price. The seller agrees to **subordinate** his or her lien to the third party loan.

For one example, suppose that the sales price is $100,000. There is an existing trust deed with an approximate balance of $30,000. The buyer agrees to assume and pay the existing $30,000 loan, to pay the seller $20,000 in cash and to give the seller a note and trust deed for the remaining $50,000. The seller agrees to subordinate the purchase money trust deed from the buyer to a loan which the buyer intends to obtain from a third party lender. The buyer then obtains a new loan for $45,000. The property now is encumbered by the two institutional loans (the seller's existing loan and the buyer's new loan) to 75% of value. The buyer pays the seller $20,000 and keeps the remaining $25,000 from the new loan. The seller holds what is now a third trust deed from the buyer. The technique is essentially a plan by which the buyer cashes out the owner's equity in the property. If the buyer defaults, it is unlikely that the seller will be able to recover much, if anything from a foreclosure because the property is encumbered by two senior liens and there is little value left to secure the purchase money trust deed to the seller.

There are numerous variations on this technique. The seller may be asked to refinance the property to 80% of value with the purchaser to assume the loan and to receive most, if not all, of the cash from that loan. The purchaser then gives the seller a cash downpayment (with cash from the loan proceeds) and/or another trust deed for the rest of the price. In some cases the seller is given no downpayment or "closing costs" down (the buyer pays the seller's closing costs). The buyer then gives the seller a note and trust deed for the entire purchase price. As in other variations, the seller subordinates the purchase money trust deed to a loan which the buyer obtains from a third party lender. The agreement may or may not stipulate that the buyer's third party loan is to be for construction or home improvement purposes. The purchase money trust deed to the seller may or may not involve any regular payments. Sometimes it provides for a one time balloon payment in three to five years at which time all principal and interest will be paid; in the interim, no payments of any kind are made to the seller.

Without spending a lot of time discussing almost innumerable variations on the basic theme (zero cash investment by the buyer, a third party loan which will provide cash to the buyer, and purchase money trust deed to the seller which will be subordinated to the third party lien(s)), suffice it to say that there are many possible ways in which the seller can, in effect, allow the buyer to cash out most or all of his or her equity in the property with little security for the buyer's promise to pay.

There are, of course, many legitimate transactions involving zero down purchases with subordination agreements. The buyer, for example, may in fact need a construction loan to make improvements so that the property may be sold at a profit and may need the seller to subordinate in order for the buyer to obtain the construction or home improvement financing.

Unfortunately, though, these techniques have been used in a manner which constitutes an abuse or even fraud in many transactions, leading to a fair amount of bad publicity and disapproval by persons in the industry (including the Department of Real Estate). When one of these transactions goes bad, often everybody in sight gets sued by the seller: the escrow officer, the mortgage broker if any, and of course any real estate broker or agent involved as listing or selling agent. Therefore, any time an agent is asked to write an offer based on any of these formats, he or she should make absolutely certain that all the disclosures required by law are made (the seller financing disclosures required under California Civil Code § §2956-2967, discussed in the finance disclosures chapter) and should also insure that the seller in fact understands what it means to be in a junior lien position, that it is possible that the property could be lost and the seller receive little or no money if the buyer defaults and the property is sold. California law requires deeds of trust with subordination provisions to have SUBORDINATED TRUST DEED printed in large, bold type at the top of the document, and to contain certain warnings about the risks involved in subordination. But those requirements do not apply when the subordinating loan (the later loan) will be for more than $25,000.

In order to protect the seller, the purchase and sale agreement and subordination agreement should include:

1) the maximum amount of the buyer's intended loan to which the seller agrees to subordinate;
2) the maximum interest rate, maximum and minimum term, and manner of payment, including, of course, any balloon payment;
3) the purpose of the loan (for example, the seller agrees to subordinate to a loan obtained by the buyer for improvement purposes, to the extent that funds are actually expended on the home for improvement purposes);

4) the right of the seller to review the buyer's loan prior to executing the subordination agreement (similar to the right given the buyer in Subparagraph 1. I. of the CAR deposit receipt form when the buyer takes subject to an existing loan).

The seller might want to insist that the loan be made by an institutional lender. An institutional lender's procedures for qualifying the buyer would help ensure that the buyer is able to afford both the payments owed to that lender and the payments owed to the seller. If the loan is for improvement purposes, the seller could require that the lender establish a program of periodic inspections and disbursements, to confirm that the loan is actually being spent on improvements to the property.

Checklist

Type of Document

- Note and trust deed (most frequently used in California)
- Note and mortgage
- Installment contract (land contract)
- Other (e.g., long term lease-purchase agreement)

Condition of Seller's Title

- Clear
- Underlying liens
- To assume
- To take subject to

General Provisions

- Payment of purchase price
- Deposit
    - downpayment
- Financing terms
    - Type of financing

  - Assume seller's financing
  - Take subject to seller's financing
  - Interest rate
  - Loan term
  - Amortization/balloon payments
  - Payment schedule
  - Prepayment provisions
  - Late payment penalties
  - Due on sale clause
  - Assignability
- Escrow provisions
- Consequences of default
- Payment of taxes
- Payment of insurance
- Consequences of condemnation
- Waste
- Payment of underlying encumbrances
- Special provisions desired by either party
- Credit report for buyer

For Underlying Liens to be Assumed or Taken Subject to

- General
- Buyer will assume
- Buyer will take subject to
- Lender approval required
- Release from liability to be obtained
- Amount

- Payments
- Lienholder (e.g., bank or judgment creditor)
- Location, volume and page where lien recorded
- Acknowledgment from lienholder that amount of debt is correct and that it is not in default
- Whether payments are to be made directly to lender
- Maximum assumption fee to be paid by buyer
- Maximum permissible increase in interest rate to be paid by buyer, if lender has right to increase rate on transfer

Pitfalls to Avoid (Not a Complete List!)

- Disclosures
  - Compliance with California's statutory disclosure requirements in seller-financed transactions
  - For "zero down" transactions or other transactions involving subordination agreements by the seller, insure that seller understands effect and potential consequences of taking subordinate lien position
- Make sure payments will pay off the debt (check amortization tables or use calculator)
- Make sure seller's underlying obligation(s) will be paid off by the time buyer finishes paying seller
- If the underlying lien will require a balloon payment, consider where money will be coming from to meet that balloon payment

Chapter Seventeen

Deposit Receipt: Conditions and Contingencies

Definition

Many deposit receipts are enforceable only after the happening of some event. Such events are called conditions or contingencies; the terms are interchangeable. If the specified event occurs, then both parties are bound to perform according to the terms of the contract. If the specified event does not occur, the agreement may be terminated and, in most cases, the buyer is entitled to a refund of any deposit or downpayment which has been paid.

Why Contingencies Are Used

In most cases, conditions in a real estate deposit receipt are inserted at the request of and for the benefit of the buyer. The buyer does not want to be legally obligated to buy the property if he or she cannot get a loan, or if the property cannot be subdivided, or if the property is infested with termites, or if some other condition is not met. Common examples include contracts contingent upon: the buyer obtaining a certain type of loan; satisfactory pest, soil, septic, well, or structural inspections; obtaining approval for a rezone, variance or subdivision from the local government; and upon the buyer obtaining some sort of license necessary to operate the establishment (such as a liquor license). Although most conditions are for the benefit of the buyer, some conditions protect both parties, and in some cases it is a bit difficult to figure out whom the condition is intended to benefit.

How Contingencies Work

Contingencies are usually placed in contracts for the benefit of only one party. If the specified condition does not come about, that party has the choice of being released from the contract or of waiving the condition and proceeding with the agreement. For example, suppose a contract is contingent upon the buyer obtaining a loan on specified terms (e.g., a 30-year, fixed-rate loan, fully amortized with interest rate not to exceed 12% per annum, for 80% of the purchase price) within 30 days of the seller's acceptance of the offer. If the buyer gets the loan within the time allowed, the buyer is obligated to buy the property. If the buyer refuses to perform under the contract after obtaining the loan, it would constitute a breach of contract and the seller would be able to retain the buyer's deposit or, depending upon the agreement and circumstances, sue the buyer for specific performance or for actual damages.

On the other hand, if the buyer did not get the loan, the buyer could take one of two actions. The buyer could give the seller notice that the condition had not been met and be released from the agreement and entitled to a refund of the deposit; or, the buyer could decide to waive the financing contingency and continue with the transaction. In such a case, the buyer would notify the seller that the condition was not met but would be waived, and that the buyer would continue with the transaction without the financing contingency. This would mean that the buyer would be obligated to buy and the seller obligated to sell whether or not the buyer got the loan. The buyer, then, would have to come up with the purchase price by the specified closing date from some source or forfeit the deposit if unable to perform according to the terms of the agreement.

Since the condition was for the benefit of the buyer, the seller could not refuse to go through with the sale simply because the condition was not met. It would be up to the buyer to decide whether to take advantage of the condition and get out of the contract or to waive it and go through with the sale even though the condition is not met. If the condition is intended to benefit both parties, it can be waived only with the consent of both. In other words, if the condition is not met, either of the parties would have the option to terminate the contract.

Conditions Within the Control of One of the Parties

Generally, if action by one of the parties is required in order for the condition to be met, such as applying for a loan or ordering an inspection, and that party makes no effort to meet the condition, then the condition is dropped from the contract and that party (usually the buyer) is bound even though the condition is not met. This would mean that the seller could keep the deposit if the buyer fails to perform the contract even if the buyer has not obtained the specified loan or satisfactory inspection report, for example.

There is an implied obligation to make a reasonable effort to meet the condition, even if the agreement does not specifically state that such an effort will be made. Otherwise, the agreement might lack mutuality. For example, if the buyer does not have to buy unless a certain loan is obtained and there is no obligation to try to get the loan, there is really no obligation on the part of the buyer and the contract may be void for that lack of mutuality of obligation. Although there is an implied obligation in law to make a reasonable effort to meet a contract condition (and in fact in California there is an obligation to exercise good faith even if the condition is based on the sole discretion of one party), it is advisable to spell out that the buyer (or seller, as the case may be) has an express obligation to take steps to meet the conditions.

Many deposit receipt forms, including the California REALTORS® form, expressly require the buyer to make a diligent effort to apply for and obtain the contemplated financing.

Example:

J. Buyer agrees to act diligently and in good faith to obtain all applicable financing.

If your form has no such agreement as part of the pre-printed clauses, either for a financing condition or for other conditions, an express obligation to attempt to meet the contingency (financing or other contingency) may be easily added.

Example:

"Buyer agrees to make written application for such loan within three days of seller's acceptance of this offer."

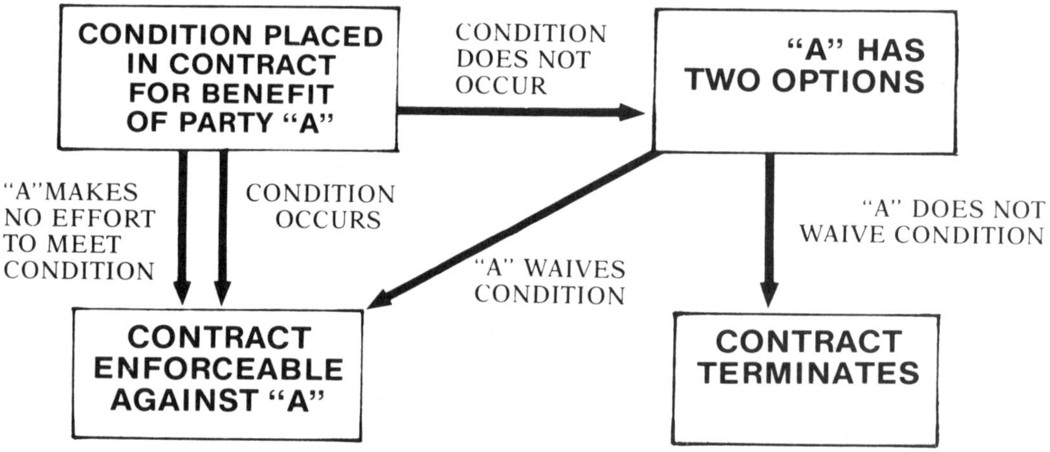

Elements of a Contingency Clause

Any type of contingency, whether a financing contingency or some other type of condition, should contain the following elements:

1) a clear statement of exactly what the condition is and **what has to be done** to meet the condition;

2) the **procedure for notifying** the other party of waiver or satisfaction of the condition;

3) a stated **time** by which the condition must be met or waived; and,

4) the **rights of the parties** in the event that the condition is not met or waived prior to the specified date.

In writing contingency clauses, it is best to avoid the phrase "subject to" in favor of other terms, such as, "contingent upon" or "conditioned upon." The phrase "subject to" is technically used in reference to a transaction in which the buyer agrees to take title subject to an existing lien or liens but does not agree to take personal liability for the debt(s) (does not "assume" the loan(s)). The use of the words "subject to" to draft a contingency clause may then lead to confusion and unforeseen problems.

Example 1: Termite Inspection Contingency

"Seller shall, within 15 days of acceptance of this offer, provide a current inspection report from a licensed or certified termite inspector, stating that there is no visible evidence of active termite infestation or visible damage to the structure requiring repair. If said report is not delivered to Buyer at Buyer's address shown above within the stated time limit, Buyer may rescind this agreement at Buyer's sole option by written notice to Seller at Seller's address shown above. Failure of Buyer to provide such notice within three days shall constitute a waiver of this condition."

Example 2: Termite Inspection Contingency

"Buyer shall, within 15 days of Seller's acceptance, obtain a report from a licensed or certified termite inspector. If said report indicates any active termite infestation or visible structural damage requiring repair, Seller agrees to remedy the infestation or damage at Seller's sole expense and to provide Buyer with verification thereof in the form of a follow-up inspection report from a licensed or certified termite inspector. Failure of Seller to complete such actions within 30 days of receipt of Buyer's inspection report shall result in termina-

> tion of this agreement, and Seller shall refund any earnest money or other deposits made by Buyer to Seller under this agreement."

It should be apparent from reading the two preceding examples that there are many ways to structure a contingency. However, regardless of how the contingency is written, it should always contain the four elements indicated above. In Example 1, the first element requires the seller to obtain a clear inspection report. The condition cannot be met if there is any damage indicated by the report. In Example 2, the buyer is required to obtain the report. The sale is contingent upon the seller repairing any damage that may exist; the mere fact that the inspection report indicates damage will not prevent performance of the contract.

With regard to the second element, notice procedures, Example 1 requires the seller to deliver a current inspection report to the buyer. However, if the seller fails to deliver the report within the specified time frame, the buyer must give written notice to the seller of an intention to rescind the agreement. Otherwise, the termite inspection contingency is deemed to be waived by the buyer. In Example 2, the buyer must first give the seller a copy of the report. The seller must then complete any repairs and deliver to the buyer a follow-up inspection report verifying that any infestation or damage has been remedied.

Example 1 sets a time limit of 15 days for meeting the contingency, and allows three days thereafter for the buyer to choose whether to waive the contingency. Example 2 allows the buyer 15 days to obtain a report, and gives the seller another 30 days to remedy any problems indicated by the report.

Finally, the buyer has the option to rescind the agreement in Example 1 if the contingency is not met, while Example 2 spells out the fact that the seller must refund the buyer's deposit unless he or she satisfies the contingency. Although the term "rescind" implies that the deposit will be refunded, it is probably better practice to state this expressly in the written contingency as was done in Example 2.

FINANCING CONTINGENCIES

Pre-printed clauses. Virtually all residential deposit receipts are contingent upon the buyer obtaining financing on satisfactory terms, either from an outside lender or from the seller. Standard form contracts often include a pre-printed financing contingency clause, although some forms merely provide space to insert such conditions. The California REALTORS® deposit receipt form has a financing contingency as part of the FINANCING paragraph. The contingency clause is divided. The first sentence of the FINANCING paragraph is a statement that the agreement is contingent upon the buyer obtaining the financing described. The rest of the condition is found near the end of the FINANCING paragraph, subparagraph 1. J. (1. F. on the DL-14 form which does not have pre-printed financing provisions).

Although there appears to be sufficient space in one or the other of the two variations of the REALTORS® forms to clearly set out most financing contingencies, some forms do not provide enough space to fill in a contingency clause which expresses the understanding of the parties. **It is best to be as specific as possible.** If the contingency cannot be clearly stated in the space provided on your form, an addendum should be attached.

Purpose of financing contingencies. The primary purpose of a financing contingency is to give the buyer the right to be released from the agreement and to receive a refund of the deposit if the buyer is unable to obtain a satisfactory loan for all or part of the purchase price. The buyer wants the contract to be contingent upon a financing arrangement which the buyer can afford and/or is willing to accept. With financing contingencies (and probably with other contingency clauses, too), the buyer often wants to give him or herself as many outs as possible.

The seller, on the other hand, wants to be able to hold the buyer to the agreement and sell the property or keep the deposit. The seller, then, does not want a contingency clause which describes a type of loan which the buyer is unlikely to be able to obtain.

Elements of a financing contingency. In order to clearly state the condition, a financing contingency should contain:

1) the **principal amount** of the loan (dollar amount or percentage of the purchase price);
2) the loan **term**;
3) the **interest rate**, and whether the rate is fixed or variable (if variable, the buyer may want an indication of the maximum initial rate and maximum rate for the life of the loan);
4) the **amortization period** of the loan; and,
5) the **party to pay the costs** and fees associated with the loan application.

The buyer may want a maximum **monthly payment** to be shown. If the type of financing is one in which points are likely to be required, the clause should indicate the maximum number of **points the seller is willing to pay**, if any, in order to assist the buyer in obtaining financing.

Financing clauses in form documents. The financing contingency clauses in many of the deposit receipt forms currently used by real estate brokers and salespersons do not have blanks for all the information listed above and do not have enough blank space to write it in. All but one of the five items are provided for in the FINANCING contingency clause in the REALTORS® form.

Subparagraph 1. D. and 1. H. are financing condition clauses in the CAR deposit receipt form. Subparagraph 1. D. states the terms for a condition based on the buyer's obtaining a new first loan to finance the purchase. There is, at the end of the first line in the paragraph, a blank to show the principal amount of the intended loan. There are then blanks or boxes to indicate the approximate monthly payments for principal and interest, the initial interest rate and whether that rate is to be fixed or variable and the term of the loan. The next sentence has blanks for the maximum loan fee to be paid by the buyer and the maximum FHA or VA discount points to be paid by the lender. At the end of the paragraph are a couple of blank lines to write in any additional terms. For example, the seller might agree to pay points on a conventional loan, the buyer might want to specify that he or she is applying for an FHA loan (or VA loan) instead of a conventional loan, or the buyer might want to include the maximum lifetime interest rate for an adjustable rate loan and the maximum adjustments at each adjustment period. It might be stated either here or in Subparagraph 1. K. ADDITIONAL FINANCING TERMS that the buyer agrees to pay the costs connected with the loan application.

Subparagraph 1. H. is substantially the same as Subparagraph 1. D., with the following exceptions: Subparagraph 1. D. states that the condition is that the buyer obtain a **first** loan and Subparagraph 1. H. is for a condition on a **second** loan; Subparagraph 1. D. provides a blank for the seller's agreement to pay FHA/VA discount points and there is no such pre-printed agreement in Subparagraph 1. H.

Fixed-rate, fully amortized loans. The pre-printed financing contingencies in most standard deposit receipt forms are satisfactory to effectively set out a financing contingency for a fixed-rate, fully amortized conventional, FHA or VA loan.

For example, assume that the purchase price is $90,000. The buyer wishes to obtain an FHA loan in the maximum amount and wants the seller to pay three points for the financing so that the loan will have a fixed interest rate of not over 10% and a term of 30 years. Assume that the minimum downpayment would be $4,000, including a $1,000 deposit made with the offer and the monthly principal and interest payments would be approximately $755. The following example illustrates how this contingency might be written on the CAR standard form:

1. **FINANCING:** The obtaining of Buyer's financing is a contingency of this agreement.
   A. DEPOSIT upon acceptance, to be deposited into Broker's Trust Account ______ $ 1,000.00
   B. INCREASED DEPOSIT within ______ days of acceptance to be deposited into ______ $ ______
   C. BALANCE OF DOWN PAYMENT to be deposited into Escrow ______ on or before November 1, 1990 $ 3,000.00
   D. Buyer to apply, qualify for and obtain a NEW FIRST LOAN in the amount of . . . . $ 86,000.00
   payable monthly at approximately $ 755.00 including interest at origination not to exceed 10 %,
   [X] fixed rate, [ ] other ______ all due 30 years from date of origination. Loan fee not to exceed 1% . Seller agrees to pay a maximum of 3% FHA/VA discount points.
   Additional terms Loan to be FHA 203b
   ______

For the purchase price of $100,000 with a contingency based on a zero down VA loan, 10% fixed-rate, 30 years, monthly payments of approximately $878 with the seller to pay three points, a contingency clause might be phrased as in the following example:

1. **FINANCING:** The obtaining of Buyer's financing is a contingency of this agreement.
   A. DEPOSIT upon acceptance, to be deposited into Broker's Trust Account .... $ ________
   B. INCREASED DEPOSIT within ________ days of acceptance to be deposited into ________ $ ________
   C. BALANCE OF DOWN PAYMENT to be deposited into ________ on or before ________ $ ________
   D. Buyer to apply, qualify for and obtain a NEW FIRST LOAN in the amount of .... $ 100,000.00
   payable monthly at approximately $ 878.00 including interest at origination not to exceed 10 %,
   [X] fixed rate, [ ] other ________ all due 30 years from date of origination. Loan fee not to
   exceed ________. Seller agrees to pay a maximum of ________ FHA/VA discount points.
   Additional terms Buyer to pay 1.25% VA funding fee in addition to 1% loan fee and all costs associated with loan application.

The following example illustrates the CAR form with a conventional loan financing contingency. The purchase price is $100,000, 20% down, including a $2,000 deposit, maximum interest rate of 11% fixed-rate, 30-year term, buyer to pay a loan fee of no more than 1½% and seller to pay no points.

1. **FINANCING:** The obtaining of Buyer's financing is a contingency of this agreement.
   A. DEPOSIT upon acceptance, to be deposited into Broker's Trust Account .... $ 2,000.00
   B. INCREASED DEPOSIT within ________ days of acceptance to be deposited into ________ $ ________
   C. BALANCE OF DOWN PAYMENT to be deposited into Escrow on or before November 10, 1990 $ 18,000.00
   D. Buyer to apply, qualify for and obtain a NEW FIRST LOAN in the amount of .... $ 80,000.00
   payable monthly at approximately $ 762.00 including interest at origination not to exceed 11 %,
   [X] fixed rate, [ ] other ________ all due 30 years from date of origination. Loan fee not to
   exceed 1.5. Seller agrees to pay a maximum of -0- FHA/VA discount points.
   Additional terms ________

Alternative financing. It is often difficult to fit all the terms of an adjustable rate loan (ARM) into one of the pre-printed clauses. The fact that an alternative type of loan, such as a variable rate loan, is planned should be indicated on the form to show that the parties did contemplate application for that type of financing, rather than traditional fixed-rate financing. The REALTORS® form does provide boxes to be checked to show whether the buyer intends to obtain a fixed-rate or variable rate loan. If the buyer wants to specify some terms which are not part of the pre-printed clause, such as a maximum overall rate as well as a maximum initial rate, some space is provided in the "ADDITIONAL TERMS . . ." blank at the end of subparagraph 1. D. If that space is not sufficient, attach an addendum.

Example: ARM Loan

"Purchaser makes this offer contingent upon obtaining an adjustable rate loan for the purchase of the above described property for not less than ninety percent (90%) of the purchase price, with a term of not less than 30 years, an initial interest rate not to exceed eight percent (8%) per annum and the maximum permissible interest rate for any period of the loan not to exceed thirteen percent (13%) per annum, computed on the diminishing principal balance. Said loan is to be fully amortized over the term of the loan. Purchaser agrees to pay a loan fee not to exceed one and one half percent (1½%) of the loan amount and to pay all costs required by lender in connection with the loan application. Purchaser agrees to make written application for such financing within three (3) business days of seller's acceptance of this offer and to deliver to seller a written firm commitment from the lender for such financing within thirty (30) days of seller's acceptance of offer. If buyer fails to obtain financing as indicated by the stated date or to waive buyer's rights under this clause, then either party may cancel this contract and buyer's deposit will be returned."

To recapitulate, then, a clearly written, unambiguous financing condition containing all material terms would set out the following:

1) a clear statement of the general terms of the financing, which would include the **principal** amount, the maximum **interest rate** and whether the rate is fixed or variable (if variable, probably a maximum initial rate and maximum rate for the term of the loan), the loan **term**, whether fully **amortized** or not, and possibly the maximum monthly **payment**;

2) an obligation of the buyer to make application for the loan, and a time limit for making the application (normally a matter of a couple of days);

3) provisions for paying the costs of the loan application, including items such as credit reports and appraisals (normally paid by the buyer);

4) an indication of the maximum points and/or costs (such as

repairs required by the lender or loan insurer) that the seller is willing to pay in order to assist the buyer in obtaining the desired financing;

5) a final date by which the condition must be satisfied;

6) provision for notifying the seller that the condition has been met (such as delivering the bank's written commitment to the seller at the seller's address); and,

7) the rights of the parties in the event that the condition is not met.

Sale of Buyer's Property

The most common contingency in residential transactions is the financing contingency, discussed above. A second very common contingency is a condition based upon the sale of some property owned by the buyer, most often the buyer's present home. The buyer is unwilling or unable to go through with the purchase unless he or she is able to sell some presently owned property and obtain a certain minimum amount of cash from that sale. In the most common case, the buyer simply does not have enough cash to make the downpayment in the present purchase unless the expected cash is received from the sale of his or her present home.

Depending upon the facts in a particular transaction and the provisions of the written contract, this situation may involve what is sometimes referred to as a "hidden contingency." This means that the purchase is actually contingent upon the sale of the buyer's home but that contingency is not expressly stated in the deposit receipt. For example, suppose that the deposit receipt does spell out that the purchase is contingent upon the buyer obtaining a loan from a third party lender. At the time the buyer makes an application for a loan, he or she does not have enough cash for the downpayment for the type of loan requested. The lender processes the application with the condition that the loan commitment is contingent upon the buyer obtaining the necessary cash prior to closing. If the buyer is unable to sell the home, he or she is unable to get the necessary cash for the downpayment and the lender refuses to make the loan. Since the buyer did not obtain the financing specified in the deposit receipt, the financing contingency is not met, and the transaction fails.

Pre-printed clauses. Some deposit receipt forms contain pre-printed clauses to be completed to show that the offer is contingent upon the sale of the buyer's home. If the buyer does, in fact, need to sell his or her own home (or other property) in order to have enough cash to complete the present purchase, then the seller should be advised and it should be included in the written agreement. Otherwise, the seller may be misled into believing that the buyer has far more cash and a much better chance of getting the necessary loan prior to the closing date than is really the case. If the transaction fails to close because the buyer is unable to sell the home and get the loan, the seller may later object that the agent had misrepresented (through nondisclosure) material facts regarding the buyer's financial ability to complete the purchase (the "able" buyer).

Essential elements. If the form does not contain a pre-printed clause covering a contingency on the sale of the buyer's home, any such contingency which is written in or added should spell out **what must occur**. Is the transaction to be contingent upon the buyer's acceptance of an offer to buy his or her present home, upon closing of that transaction, or both? In order to eliminate some of the waiting for the seller, it is probably best to make the condition based on the buyer's acceptance of an offer within a certain time period. If the buyer is unable to get an offer for the property within a certain time period, then the current transaction would be terminated. The buyer will most likely want the condition to also depend upon the actual closing of his or her sale and the receipt of sufficient cash from that sale to meet the cash requirements for this purchase.

The condition should also specify the **date** or dates for meeting the condition(s) (acceptance of offer and closing of sale) and indicate the **method of notifying** the seller that the condition has been met.

Example: Contingency of Sale of Purchaser's Residence

> "This deposit receipt is contingent upon purchaser's accepting an offer to buy purchaser's present residence located at 1015 Arbor Avenue, Avocado City, California. Purchaser must notify seller in writing within sixty (60) days of the date of seller's signature on this agreement that purchaser has accepted a written offer to buy purchaser's residence. The price and payment terms of that sales agreement must be such that the purchaser under this agreement will receive sufficient net proceeds to enable him or her to complete this transaction. If purchaser fails to provide seller with such notice within said sixty (60) day period, then this deposit receipt shall become null and void and purchaser's earnest money shall be refunded. This deposit receipt is also conditioned upon the closing of and distribution of the proceeds from the sale of purchaser's residence on or before the closing date of this agreement. If the sale of purchaser's residence fails to close by such date through no fault of purchaser, then this agreement shall become null and void and purchaser's deposit shall be refunded."

Some care must be taken in deciding what time periods or dates to include for the condition to be met. There is an inherent conflict here. The buyer wants as much time as possible, so that his or her house may be marketed for the highest possible price. The seller, on the other hand, wants the present transaction to close as soon as possible, so that he or she can get the money from the sale. To a certain extent, the "bump" clauses discussed below are intended to resolve some of this conflict. So, some date or time period must be chosen which will give the buyer a reasonable length of time to market the property but which also will not extend the present transaction too long without some kind of resolution, either a successful closing or failure of the condition.

It is extremely important to make sure that the dates within the agreement itself are in harmony. For example, a condition should not give the buyer 120 days to sell his or her home if the present transaction is supposed to close within 90 days. Reference to a calendar may be advisable.

Bump Clauses

When a deposit receipt contains a provision which makes the transaction contingent on the sale of the buyer's personal residence, it is common to include some sort of clause which gives the seller the right to keep the house on the market and to accept another offer. These provisions, often called "bump clauses" may be used any time the buyer's offer is contingent but they are most commonly used in connection with offers contingent upon the sale of the buyer's home because offers of that type are generally considered less secure than other contingent offers.

If the seller receives a second offer prior to the sale of the buyer's home, the seller can demand that the buyer meet or waive the contingency or cancel the deal. The buyer is given a certain period of time (often a very short period of time) in which to either sell the house or choose to proceed with the transaction without the protection of the contingency (to waive the contingency). If the buyer chooses to proceed and is ultimately unable to complete the purchase because his or her present home is not sold, the deposit would be forfeited.

A provision of this type enables the seller to accept an offer which is unsure at best (contingent upon the sale of the buyer's home) without having to remove the house from the market. While it may be possible, to some extent, to predict whether or not a buyer will be able to get a loan, it is almost impossible to predict whether or not a buyer will be able to sell his or her home by a certain date and on terms which will generate a certain amount of cash.

There is some variation in the working and effect of these clauses, so it is important that, if such a clause is part of the agreement, the parties read it carefully to make sure that it accurately states their intention. If they do not understand what it says, they may need to seek professional legal counsel. If they understand it and do not like it, they may want it changed. The clause reproduced on the next page is a California REALTORS® standard addendum for the REALTORS® deposit receipt form.

CALIFORNIA ASSOCIATION OF REALTORS

CONTINGENCY RELEASE CLAUSE ADDENDUM

THIS IS INTENDED TO BE A LEGALLY BINDING CONTRACT. READ IT CAREFULLY.

CALIFORNIA ASSOCIATION OF REALTORS® STANDARD FORM

This addendum is a part of the Real Estate Purchase Contract and Receipt for Deposit dated ____________________

Between ____ (Buyer)

and ____ (Seller)

regarding the real property described as ____

____

Seller shall have the right to continue to offer subject property for sale.

Should a subsequent written offer be accepted by Seller, conditioned upon above named Buyer's rights,

Buyer shall have ____________________ hours ____________________ days

following receipt of notice to **remove and waive** in writing the following condition(s) ____________________

____

____

____

In the event Buyer(s) shall fail to remove the condition(s) within the above time limit, the Real Estate Purchase Contract and Receipt for Deposit and this agreement shall terminate and become null and void and Buyer's deposit shall be returned to Buyer.

Notice to Buyer to remove condition(s) shall be deemed to have been received by Buyer when Buyer, or his agent, has received notice by delivery in person or by certified mail and addressed to ______________________

____

If notice is given by mail Buyer shall have until 6:00 PM of the third day following the date of mailing, unless the notice provides otherwise, to deliver to Seller or Seller's agent Buyer's written agreement to remove and waive the contingencies.

The undersigned acknowledges receipt of a copy hereof.

RECEIPT IF DELIVERED IN PERSON

Receipt of this notice is acknowledged:

Dated ______________________ Buyer ______________________

Buyer ______________________

Dated ______________________ Seller ______________________

Seller ______________________

FORM CRC-11

EQUAL HOUSING OPPORTUNITY

TT-L5-FG

MB-E6-MB/1

The CONTINGENCY RELEASE CLAUSE ADDENDUM may be used in any transaction which has a condition. The first few lines have blanks to identify the transaction in which the addendum is included. The date of the deposit receipt, the names of the parties and the property description would be entered.

The next lines provide that the seller has the right to keep the property on the market. If the seller receives another written offer the buyer is given a specified number of hours and/or days after receiving a notice from the seller to remove the listed condition(s). If the buyer waives the condition(s), the deposit receipt continues in effect, but the buyer no longer has the protection of the condition. If the buyer fails to complete the transaction, he or she would not normally be entitled to a refund of the deposit. If the buyer does not waive the condition(s) within the specified time limit, the agreement becomes null and void and the buyer's deposit is returned. The seller may then continue with the second deposit receipt.

The next two paragraphs provide for the procedure of giving notice and state that if notice is given by mail, the buyer has until 6:00 p.m. of the third day following mailing to deliver to seller the notice to waive the condition(s), unless the seller's notice specifies some other time period. REALTORS® forms for both the seller's notice to the buyer to remove and waive the condition(s) and the buyer's written notice to the seller to remove and waive the condition(s) are reproduced below.

Condition on Termination and Release of Prior Contract

Whenever a seller has entered into a deposit receipt which is not consummated and the seller wishes to sell to a second buyer under a subsequent contract, it is advisable to have the parties under the first contract sign a document which serves as a release of that first contract. Most often, this situation arises when the buyer under the first agreement is unable or unwilling to perform. For example, the buyer may not have obtained loan approval or may not have been able to sell his or her home within the time allotted under the deposit receipt. In some cases, the seller may have already entered a second deposit receipt agreement which is conditioned upon the buyer's failure to perform under the first agreement. Because of uncertainties regarding the respective rights and obligations of the buyer and seller under the first agreement, even in cases where the buyer has apparently breached the contract, the seller should not proceed with any subsequent sale without first clearly establishing that the first agreement is terminated and that the buyer has no right to enforce that earlier agreement. Any so-called "back up" offer which the seller intends to accept should be expressly conditioned both on the failure of the first agreement and on the seller's obtaining a written release from the buyer under that first agreement.

Example:

> "Seller has entered an earlier agreement to sell the property described in this agreement. That agreement is dated ________; the buyer under that agreement is ______________. Seller's acceptance of this offer is expressly conditioned upon:
>
> 1. the failure of the buyer under that earlier agreement, dated ______________ to perform on or before ______________;
> 2. seller's obtaining a written release from the buyer under the above described contract of all claims or demands against the seller under that contract and any right, title or interest in the described property."

Printed forms for the release of deposit receipt contracts are widely available. Such forms usually state that the contract is released or rescinded and that the parties mutually release each other from any claims or obligations under the contract. There are also generally blanks to indicate the parties' intentions as to the disbursement of the buyer's deposit. The CAR RELEASE OF CONTRACT form is reproduced below as an example of such a form.

Some other common types of conditions, such as inspection contingencies are frequently found in deposit receipts. There are several preprinted clauses of this type in the CAR deposit receipt form and those should be reviewed.

CALIFORNIA ASSOCIATION OF REALTORS

NOTICE TO BUYER TO REMOVE AND WAIVE CONTINGENCIES

CALIFORNIA ASSOCIATION OF REALTORS® STANDARD FORM

TO: ______________________________

____

____

In accordance with the Contingency Release Clause Addendum to Real Estate Purchase Contract

and Deposit Receipt dated ______________________________

between ______________________________ (Buyer)

and ______________________________ (Seller)

regarding real property described as ______________________________

____

You are hereby notified that Seller has accepted a written offer conditioned upon your rights to remove the contingencies outlined in the Contingency Clause Addendum.

Under the terms of the Addendum, you have until ______________________________
at 6:00 PM to remove said contingencies. In the event of your failure to remove the contingencies within the time limit specified, the Real Estate Purchase Contract and Deposit Receipt and all of the rights and obligations thereunder shall terminate and become null and void and your deposit shall be returned.

Dated ____________________ SELLER ______________________________

SELLER ______________________________

RECEIPT IF DELIVERED IN PERSON

Receipt of this notice is acknowledged:

Dated ____________________ BUYER ______________________________

BUYER ______________________________

FORM CRCN-11

EQUAL HOUSING OPPORTUNITY
MB-E6-MB/1

TT-L5-FG

CALIFORNIA ASSOCIATION OF REALTORS

CONTINGENCY REMOVAL

CALIFORNIA ASSOCIATION OF REALTORS® STANDARD FORM

This addendum is a part of the Real Estate Purchase Contract and Receipt for Deposit dated ____________________

between ____ (Buyer)

and ____ (Seller)

regarding the real property described as ____

____

The undersigned, hereby waives the following condition(s)

____

____

____

____

____

and agrees to purchase the property in accordance with all the other terms and conditions.

The undersigned acknowledges receipt of a copy hereof.

DATED: ____________________ BUYER ______________________________

BUYER ______________________________

RECEIPT BY SELLER

Receipt of a copy of the above waiver is hereby acknowledged.

DATED: ____________________ SELLER ______________________________

SELLER ______________________________

THIS STANDARDIZED DOCUMENT FOR USE IN SIMPLE TRANSACTIONS HAS BEEN APPROVED BY THE CALIFORNIA ASSOCIATION OF REALTORS® IN FORM ONLY. NO REPRESENTATION IS MADE AS TO THE APPROVAL OF THE FORM OF ANY SUPPLEMENTS NOT CURRENTLY PUBLISHED BY THE CALIFORNIA ASSOCIATION OF REALTORS® OR THE LEGAL VALIDITY OR ADEQUACY OF ANY PROVISION IN ANY SPECIFIC TRANSACTION. IT SHOULD NOT BE USED IN COMPLEX TRANSACTIONS OR WITH EXTENSIVE RIDERS OR ADDITIONS.

A REAL ESTATE BROKER IS THE PERSON QUALIFIED TO ADVISE ON REAL ESTATE TRANSACTIONS. IF YOU DESIRE LEGAL OR TAX ADVICE, CONSULT AN APPROPRIATE PROFESSIONAL

This form is available for use by the entire real estate industry. The use of this form is not intended to identify the user as a REALTOR® REALTOR® is a registered collective membership mark which may be used only by real estate licensees who are members of the NATIONAL ASSOCIATION OF REALTORS® and who subscribe to its Code of Ethics.

To order, contact—California Association of Realtors®
525 S. Virgil Ave., Los Angeles, California 90020

OFFICE USE ONLY

Reviewed by Broker or Designee ________

Date ________________

FORM CRCR-11

EQUAL HOUSING OPPORTUNITY
SF-Jan-88

CALIFORNIA ASSOCIATION OF REALTORS

☐

RELEASE OF CONTRACT

THIS IS INTENDED TO BE A LEGALLY BINDING CONTRACT. READ IT CAREFULLY.
CALIFORNIA ASSOCIATION OF REALTORS® (CAR) STANDARD FORM

The undersigned Buyer and Seller (or exchange party(ies), if applicable), the parties to that certain:
(Check all that apply):

☐ Real Estate Purchase Contract and Receipt for Deposit
☐ Mobile Home Purchase Contract and Receipt for Deposit
☐ Business Purchase Contract and Receipt for Deposit
☐ Escrow instructions
☐ Other ______________________________,

(hereinafter, "Contract"), covering the following described property:

____

____

____

____

____

____

____

hereby mutually release each other from all further obligation to buy, sell, or exchange under the Contract and all related documents, and from all claims, actions, and demands which each may have against the other(s) by reason of said Contract. It is the intent of this Agreement that all rights and obligations arising out of said Contract are null and void.

______________________________ is hereby instructed to cancel Escrow Number ____________.
(Name of Escrow Holder)

________________________, holder of the deposit under the terms of said Contract, is hereby
(Name of Broker or Escrow Holder)

instructed to disburse said deposit in the following manner:

$ ____________ TO ________________________
$ ____________ TO ________________________
$ ____________ TO ________________________
$ ____________ TO ________________________

Dated ____________	Dated ____________
Buyer ____________	Seller ____________
Buyer ____________	Seller ____________
Dated ____________	Dated ____________
Broker ____________	Broker ____________
By ____________	By ____________

THIS STANDARDIZED DOCUMENT FOR USE IN SIMPLE TRANSACTIONS HAS BEEN APPROVED BY THE CALIFORNIA ASSOCIATION OF REALTORS® IN FORM ONLY. NO REPRESENTATION IS MADE AS TO THE APPROVAL OF THE FORM OF ANY SUPPLEMENTS NOT CURRENTLY PUBLISHED BY THE CALIFORNIA ASSOCIATION OF REALTORS® OR THE LEGAL VALIDITY OR ADEQUACY OF ANY PROVISION IN ANY SPECIFIC TRANSACTION. IT SHOULD NOT BE USED IN COMPLEX TRANSACTIONS OR WITH EXTENSIVE RIDERS OR ADDITIONS.

A REAL ESTATE BROKER IS THE PERSON QUALIFIED TO ADVISE ON REAL ESTATE TRANSACTIONS. IF YOU DESIRE LEGAL OR TAX ADVICE, CONSULT AN APPROPRIATE PROFESSIONAL.

This form is available for use by the entire real estate industry. The use of this form is not intended to identify the user as a REALTOR®. REALTOR® is a registered collective membership mark which may be used only by real estate licensees who are members of the NATIONAL ASSOCIATION OF REALTORS® and who subscribe to its Code of Ethics.

FORM RC-11

OFFICE USE ONLY

Reviewed by Broker or Designee ________
Date ____________

EQUAL HOUSING OPPORTUNITY
M-SC-MAR-91

Checklist

In General

- Clear statement of the condition (What must happen in order for the condition to be met?)
- Party obligated to take steps to meet the condition (e.g., buyer to make written application for loan)
- Time by which the process for meeting the condition must be initiated (e.g., applying for the loan)
- Time by which the condition must be met or waived (Make sure this date is prior to the date set for close of escrow)
- Procedure for notifying the other party that the condition has been met or waived
- Who pays the costs or fees associated with meeting the condition (e.g., loan fee or inspection fee)
- Rights of the parties if the condition is neither met nor waived (e.g., contract terminated and deposit refunded to buyer)

Financing Contingency

- Clear description of the type of loan applied for
  - FHA, Conventional, VA
  - Principal amount (dollar amount or percentage of sales price)
  - Fixed or variable interest rate
  - If fixed rate, maximum interest rate
  - If variable rate, maximum initial rate and maximum overall rate, if any
  - Term of loan
  - Fully amortized or not
  - Maximum monthly payment

    - Number of points seller is willing to pay, if any
    - Number of points buyer is willing to pay, if any
- Stated obligation of buyer to make application for loan
- Time by which application must be made
- Specification of which party is to pay loan application costs (application fee, appraisal, credit report, inspections required by lender)
- Maximum repair costs to be paid by seller, if any
- Time by which loan approval must be obtained
- Provision for notifying seller that condition has been met (e.g., delivering lender's written commitment to seller)
- Rights of parties in the event that the loan is not obtained

Contingent on Sale of Buyer's Property

- Clear statement of the condition
    - Definition of sale
        - Acceptance of written offer (contingent or non-contingent?)
        - When buyer's sale closes
        - Both
    - Minimum sales price or net proceeds from sale
    - Obligation of buyer to attempt to sell his or her property
        - List with broker
        - Advertise
        - Other
- Review "bump" clause, if any, with:
    - Seller
    - Buyer
- Time by whch buyer must begin marketing property

- Date(s) by which condition must be met (acceptance of offer, closing of sale, or both)
- Procedure for notifying seller that condition has been met or waived
- Rights of parties if the condition is neither met nor waived by the specified date

Inspections

- Clear statement of the condition
    - Type of inspection
    - Who shall perform inspection
    - Definition of "satisfactory inspection"
        - To buyer's satisfaction
        - To inspector's satisfaction
        - Damage not to exceed certain dollar amount or percentage of sales price
        - No active infestation or damage in need of repair
- Time by which steps must be taken to meet the condition (ordering the inspection)
- Time by which inspection must be completed and report obtained
- Party to pay for inspection
- Consequences if inspection reveals damage or other problem
    - Seller obligated to repair, up to certain dollar amount or percentage of sales price
    - Buyer may rescind agreement
    - Other
- Procedure for notifying other party that condition has been met or waived

Chapter Eighteen

Deposit Receipts: Standard Provisions

This chapter will cover the provisions in Paragraphs 2 through 22 of the California Association of REALTORS® Deposit Receipt Form.

Paragraph 2. OCCUPANCY

Paragraph 2 provides two boxes to indicate whether or not the buyer intends to occupy the property as his or her primary residence. The buyer's intention to occupy the property as a personal residence may affect a number of matters including: the application of some laws such as the anti-deficiency rule; the availability of certain loan programs; and, in the case of seller carry back financing, the seller's decision regarding acceptable financing terms.

Paragraph 3. SUPPLEMENTS

Paragraph 3 serves to reference and incorporate supplements to the basic deposit receipt form. Any such referenced supplements would become a part of the purchase and sale contract along with the provisions in the pre-printed basic form. There are boxes to check to indicate incorporation of the REALTORS® standard forms for an Interim Occupancy Agreement, Residential Lease Agreement After Sale and VA and FHA Amendments. There are also three blank lines to reference other addenda, such as the Contingency Release Clause Addendum discussed in the last chapter.

The Interim Occupancy Agreement, or a similar rental agreement, should be used in situations where the buyer is to take possession of the property before close of escrow and conveyance of title. The Residential Lease Agreement After Sale is intended to be used when the seller is to remain in possession following close of escrow. Whether one of these forms or some other form is used, it is advisable to have a specific written agreement covering the rights and obligations of the buyer and seller any time that possession is to be delivered at some time other than close of escrow.

Copies of the CAR standard forms for Interim Occupancy Agreement and Residential Lease Agreement After Sale are reproduced on the following pages.

The VA/FHA Amendment form referred to in Paragraph 3 was covered earlier in the materials on third party financing.

Paragraph 4. ESCROW

In Paragraph 4, the escrow holder is named and the parties agree as to:

1) the time for delivery of escrow instructions to the escrow holder;
2) the time for close of escrow; and,
3) the division of escrow fees.

In choosing the time to be allowed for close of escrow, the agent preparing the deposit receipt must take into consideration the length of time needed to accomplish all conditions. In most cases, the seller must obtain a preliminary title report and the buyer must get a loan. Other conditions, such as inspections or sale of the buyer's home may also have to be met. It is necessary for the agent to have current knowledge of such matters as how long it takes to get loan approval for conventional, FHA and VA loans in order to be able to give competent advice regarding the closing date.

If, as time passes, it becomes apparent that it is unlikely that the closing date will be met, it is important to advise the parties as early as possible so that they may enter a written extension agreement. For example, if the closing date is set for October 15, and the agent learns on October 10 that the loan committee has still not received employment verification for the loan applicant, it is extremely unlikely that the loan will be approved and the escrow agent able to finalize the transaction in the next four or five days. The agent should advise the parties of the reason for the delay and check with the employer to find out the cause of the delay in providing employment verification. In some large corporations, a routine request like this may take a few weeks. After finding out the reason for the delay and getting some kind of rough estimate as to the length of time needed to clear up the problem (employment verification or apparent problem with seller's record title, for example), the parties may agree to an extension of a few days or a few weeks.

In some areas, there are specific forms available for extension agreements. If no particular extension agreement form is available, a standard addendum form may be used. The purchase and sale agreement is referenced on the addendum and an addendum is written to the effect that all terms and conditions remain the same except that "the time for close of escrow has been extended to ____________________."

The final lines of Paragraph 4 provide space to write the parties' agreement as to payment of the escrow fee. This is a matter which can, in most transactions, be decided by the parties even though there are local customs as to who usually pays: the buyer, the seller or divided between them.

Paragraph 5. TITLE

The TITLE paragraph has three separate provisions:

1) a warranty of the seller as to the condition of title;
2) an agreement to pay for the title insurance premium; and,
3) a contingency based on the condition of title.

CALIFORNIA ASSOCIATION OF REALTORS®

INTERIM OCCUPANCY AGREEMENT

(Buyer in Possession)

THIS IS INTENDED TO BE A LEGALLY BINDING AGREEMENT — READ IT CAREFULLY.

CALIFORNIA ASSOCIATION OF REALTORS® (CAR) STANDARD FORM

______________________, California ______________________________, 19____.

____, "LESSOR" and

____, "LESSEE" agree:

1. On ________________, 19____, LESSOR as SELLER and LESSEE as BUYER entered into an agreement for the sale and purchase of the real property commonly known as ______________________________, ______________________, California ("Premises") and the escrow thereof is scheduled to close on or before ______________________, ______________________, 19____.
2. Pending completion of sale and close of escrow, LESSEE is to be given immediate occupancy of the premises in accordance with the terms of this agreement.
3. LESSEE acknowledges an inspection of, and has found the premises in satisfactory condition and ready for occupancy, except as follows: ____
____
____
____.
4. LESSEE shall pay to LESSOR for the occupancy of said premises the sum of $____________ per ____________ (day/week/month)

   commencing ________________, 19____, to and including ______________________ (specific date/other)

   ______________________. Said sum shall be paid ______________________ (weekly/monthly) in advance.

   Prorations, if any, shall be predicated upon a 30 day month. As additional consideration, LESSEE shall pay for all utilities and services based upon occupancy of the premises and the following charges: ______________________ except ______________________ which shall be paid by LESSOR.
5. If the purchase and sale agreement between LESSOR and LESSEE is not completed within its designated term, or any written extension thereof through no fault of LESSOR, LESSEE agrees to vacate the premises upon service of a written notice in the form and manner provided by law. Any holding over thereafter shall create a day-to-day tenancy with a fair rental value of $________________ per day. Except as to daily rent and tenancy, all other covenants and conditions herein contained shall remain in full force and effect.
6. Except as provided by law LESSEE shall keep the premises and yards clean, sanitary, and in good order and repair during the term hereof and shall surrender the same in like condition if the said sale is not completed, reasonable wear and tear excepted.

Additionally, LESSEE shall save and hold LESSOR harmless from any and all claims, demands, damages or liabilities arising out of LESSEE's occupancy of the premises caused or permitted by LESSEE, LESSEE'S family, agents, servants, employees, guests and invitees.

7. As additional consideration passing from LESSEE to LESSOR, LESSEE shall obtain and maintain during the term of this agreement public liability insurance naming both LESSOR and LESSEE as co-insureds in the amount of not less than $__________ for injury to one person; $__________ for injury to a group; and $__________ for property damage. If permitted, LESSOR agrees to retain his fire insurance on the premises until close of escrow. Otherwise, LESSEE shall obtain fire insurance on the premises in a sum of not less than that designated as the sales price of the subject property.

8. The premises are to be used as a residence only by LESSEE and his immedate family and no animal, bird or pet except ____________________ shall be kept on or about the premises without LESSOR'S prior written consent. LESSEE shall not violate any law or ordinance in the use of the premises, nor permit waste or nuisance upon or about the premises and, except as provided by law, LESSEE shall not make any additions, alterations, or repairs to the premises without the prior written consent of LESSOR.

9. $__________ as security has been deposited. LESSOR may use therefrom such amounts as are reasonably necessary to remedy LESSEE defaults in the payment of rent, to repair damages caused by LESSEE, or to clean the premises if necessary upon the termination of tenancy. If used toward rent or damages during the term of this agreement, LESSEE agrees to reinstate said total security deposit upon 5 days written notice delivered to LESSEE in person or by mail. The balance of the security deposit, if any, shall be mailed to LESSEE'S last known address within 14 days of surrender of premises. Alternatively, and upon completion of sale, said security deposit shall be mailed to LESSEE at the subject premises within 10 days of close of escrow.

10. In the event of any action or proceeding between LESSOR and LESSEE under this agreement, the prevailing party shall be entitled to recover reasonable attorney's fees and costs.

11. The right to occupy the premises as granted LESSEE herein is personal to LESSEE and any attempt to assign, transfer, or hypothecate the same shall be null and void.

12. The undersigned LESSEE acknowledges having read the foregoing and receipt of a copy.

LESSOR and LESSEE have executed this agreement on the day and year above written.

Lessor ____________________ Lessee ____________________

Lessor ____________________ Lessee ____________________

THIS STANDARDIZED DOCUMENT FOR USE IN SIMPLE TRANSACTIONS HAS BEEN APPROVED BY THE CALIFORNIA ASSOCIATION OF REALTORS® IN FORM ONLY. NO REPRESENTATION IS MADE AS TO THE APPROVAL OF THE FORM OR ANY SUPPLEMENTS NOT CURRENTLY PUBLISHED BY THE CALIFORNIA ASSOCIATION OF REALTORS® OR THE LEGAL VALIDITY OR ADEQUACY OF ANY PROVISION IN ANY SPECIFIC TRANSACTION. IT SHOULD NOT BE USED IN COMPLEX TRANSACTIONS OR WITH EXTENSIVE RIDERS OR ADDITIONS.

A REAL ESTATE BROKER IS THE PERSON QUALIFIED TO ADVISE ON REAL ESTATE TRANSACTIONS. IF YOU DESIRE LEGAL OR TAX ADVICE, CONSULT AN APPROPRIATE PROFESSIONAL.

This form is available for use by the entire real estate industry. The use of this form is not intended to identify the user as a REALTOR®. REALTOR® is a registered collective membership mark which may be used only by real estate licensees who are members of the NATIONAL ASSOCIATION OF REALTORS® and who subscribe to its Code of Ethics.

OFFICE USE ONLY

Reviewed by Broker or Designee __________

Date __________

EQUAL HOUSING OPPORTUNITY

RESIDENTIAL LEASE AGREEMENT AFTER SALE

THIS IS INTENDED TO BE A LEGALLY BINDING AGREEMENT—READ IT CAREFULLY.

CALIFORNIA ASSOCIATION OF REALTORS® STANDARD FORM

(Possession Retained by Seller)

______________________, California, ______________________________________, 19 ____.

____, "LESSOR" and

____, "LESSEE"

agree:

1. On ______________, 19 ____, LESSOR as Buyer and LESSEE as Seller entered into an agreement for the sale and purchase of the real property commonly known as ____,
________________________________, California ("Premises"), wherein escrow is designated to close on or about ____________________, 19 ____.

2. LESSOR leases to LESSEE the premises as LESSEE'S personal residence in accordance with the terms of this lease.

3. Occupancy shall commence on the day following close of escrow and terminate ____________________ thereafter
days/weeks/months
at which time the permises shall be vacated and possession surrendered to LESSOR.

4. LESSEE shall pay to LESSOR as rent for the said premises the sum of $ __________ per ______________
commencing __________________, 19 ____ to and including ________________________________. Said sum shall be paid ____________________ in advance. Prorations, if any, shall be predicated upon a 30 day month. Additionally,
weekly/monthly
LESSEE shall pay for all utilities and services based upon occupancy of the premises and the following charges: ____________
except, ________________________ which shall be paid by LESSOR. Any holding over without the express written consent of other covenants and conditions herein contained shall remain in full force and effect.

5. As part of the consideration passing from LESSEE to LESSOR, but for which LESSOR would not have entered into this agreement, except as provided by law, LESSEE shall maintain the premises and yards and all real and personal property as conveyed by LESSEE to LESSOR in clean, sanitary, operable condition and repair, reasonable wear and tear excluded, at LESSEE'S sole cost and expense, LESSEE further agrees upon surrendering possession that said premises shall otherwise be in the same condition as required of LESSEE to have delivered them to LESSOR at close of escrow.

6. $ ______________ as security has been deposited. LESSOR may use therefrom such amounts as are reasonably necessary to remedy LESSEE'S defaults in the payment of rent, to repair damage caused by LESSEE, or clean the premises if necessary upon the termination of tenancy. If used toward rent or damages during the term of this agreement, LESSEE agrees to reinstate said total security deposit upon 5 days written notice delivered to LESSEE in person or by mail. The balance of the security deposit, if any, shall be mailed to LESSEE'S last known address within 14 days of surrender of the premises.

7. As additional consideration passing from LESSEE to LESSOR, LESSEE shall obtain and maintain during the term of this lease, public liability insurance naming both LESSOR and LESSEE as co-insureds in the amount of not less than $ ______________ for injury to one person; $ ______________ for any injury to a group, and $ ______________ for property damage. If permitted, LESSEE agrees to retain his fire insurance on the premises in a sum of not less than designated as the sales price of the subject property.

8. In the event of any action or proceeding between LESSOR and LESSEE under this agreement, the prevailing party shall be entitled to recover reasonable attorney's fees and costs.

9. The undersigned LESSEE acknowledges having read the foregoing and receipt of a copy.

LESSOR and LESSEE have executed this lease on the day and year above written.

LESSOR ______________________________ LESSEE ______________________________

LESSOR ______________________________ LESSEE ______________________________

NO REPRESENTATION IS MADE AS TO THE LEGAL VALIDITY OF ANY PROVISION OR THE ADEQUACY OF ANY PROVISION IN ANY SPECIFIC TRANSACTION. A REAL ESTATE BROKER IS THE PERSON QUALIFIED TO ADVISE ON REAL ESTATE. IF YOU DESIRE LEGAL ADVICE CONSULT YOUR ATTORNEY.

To order, contact—California Association of Realtors®
525 S. Virgil Avenue, Los Angeles, California 90020

FORM RLAS-11

EQUAL HOUSING OPPORTUNITY

TT-L5-FG

MB-E6-MB/1

CONTRACT SUPPLEMENT/ADDENDUM

THIS IS INTENDED TO BE A LEGALLY BINDING CONTRACT—READ IT CAREFULLY.

CALIFORNIA ASSOCIATION OF REALTORS® STANDARD FORM

The following terms and conditions are hereby incorporated in and made part of the: ☒ Real Estate Purchase Contract and Receipt for Deposit, ☐ Mobile Home Purchase Contract and Receipt for Deposit, ☐ Business Purchase Contract and Receipt for Deposit, ☐ other ____________

dated October 10, , 19___, on property known as: 1521 Orange Blvd., Costa Verde, Calif.
in which Margaret Aresteguy is referred to as buyer
and Martin Estevez is referred to as seller.

All terms and conditions remain the same, except that the time for close of escrow is extended to 120 calendar days from the date of seller's acceptance.

The undersigned acknowledge receipt of a copy of this page, which constitutes Page ________ of ________ Pages..

Date ____________	Date ____________
Buyer ____________	Seller ____________
Buyer ____________	Seller ____________

To order, contact—California Association of Realtors®
525 S. Virgil Ave., Los Angeles, California 90020

DS-14

This form is available for use by the entire real estate industry. The use of this form is not intended to identify the user as a REALTOR® REALTOR® is a registered collective membership mark which may be used only by real estate licensees who are members of the NATIONAL ASSOCIATION OF REALTORS® and who subscribe to its Code of Ethics.

EQUAL HOUSING OPPORTUNITY
MB-E6-MB/1

The buyer is entitled to "marketable title" whether or not that is expressly stated in the purchase contract. Marketable title is title which is sufficiently free from doubt that a reasonable purchaser who was informed as to the facts and their legal effect, and who was exercising ordinary business prudence, would accept. Certain encumbrances are not considered to render title unmarketable. Examples of these include visible easements (on the theory that the parties must have been aware of the encumbrance and entered the contract with the encumbrance in mind) and governmental restrictions, such as zoning ordinances (on the theory that the parties are considered to have been aware of the applicable local law and entered the contract with that law in mind). Some examples of encumbrances which generally do affect marketability of title include: recorded easements which are not visible (such as a buried pipeline or a road or access easement which has not been developed), judgment liens; mechanics' liens; mortgages and trust deeds; covenants, conditions and restrictions; tax and assessment liens; and rights of adverse possessors or tenants under leases.

The general practice is to order a preliminary title report to get an idea of the existing encumbrances of record. The buyer may then review the report to see if there are any encumbrances which would destroy marketability and decide whether or not to accept title as it is if the seller is unable or unwilling to clear the defect(s).

Paragraph 5 in the CAR deposit receipt form first states that title is to be free of such recorded encumbrances or other encumbrances known to the seller, with some exceptions. Current property taxes are to be excepted. Also, recorded private restrictions and public utility easements are to be excepted if they do not interfere with the buyer's intended use. The buyer is to be given a specified number of days to review the preliminary title report and give a written objection to any such encumbrances. There is then a blank to indicate who is to pay for the preliminary title report. The final blank in this sentence provides some space to write in any encumbrances which the buyer will assume or take subject to, for example delinquent taxes or the seller's existing loan which the buyer will assume and pay.

In the next sentence the title insurance company is named and it is agreed who will pay for the CLTA title insurance policy that the seller is to provide to the buyer. (Without such a provision, there is no implied obligation of the seller to provide title insurance or to pay for it.) In Northern California, the buyer usuallly pays for the title insurance and in Southern California, the seller usually pays, but this expense is one which may be decided by agreement of the parties.

The final two sentences of the TITLE paragraph govern the consequences of defects in title. If the seller is unable to convey title as represented in the first sentence of the paragraph or if the seller is unable or unwilling to cure any encumbrances objected to by the buyer after reviewing the preliminary title report, then the buyer may terminate the agreement and receive a refund of the deposit.

Paragraph 6. VESTING

Insert in Paragraph 6 the name(s) of the person(s) who will take title and the form of title. There is a bold face warning that the manner of taking title can have important legal, financial and tax consequences. Accordingly, real estate agents who are not licensed or professionally competent in those areas should avoid giving advice on how to take title. Brokers and salespersons should be able to describe to buyers the fundamental differences among taking title in severalty, joint tenancy, tenancy in common, community property and separate property but should refer buyers to professional counsel if they need detailed advice as to the best form for their particular circumstances.

Some common forms of taking title are shown in the examples below.

Examples:

VESTING TITLE

"Erik Larsen and Minna Larsen, husband and wife, as their community property."

"Peter Larsen, an unmarried man, as his separate property."

> "Minna Larsen, a married woman, as her separate property."
>
> "Arturo Sanchez and Alberta Doran, as joint tenants."
>
> "Arturo Sanchez and Alberta Doran, as tenants in common, in undivided equal interests."
>
> "Arturo Sanchez and Alberta Doran, as tenants in common, in undivided interests as follows: Arturo Sanchez, sixty-five percent (65%); Alberta Doran, thirty-five percent (35%)."

Paragraph 7. PRORATIONS

The first sentence in the PRORATIONS paragraph lists several expenses to be prorated, provides a blank to describe other expenses to be prorated and a blank to indicate the proration date. Usually, these items are prorated as of close of escrow or transfer of possession.

The second sentence deals with special assessments. These assessments are often paid in installments and often lead to misunderstandings. The buyer often assumes that the seller will pay off the lien because it is an encumbrance and the seller often feels that the buyer should take over the installment payments. This sentence is completed to show whether the bond or assessment lien(s) will be discharged by the seller at close of escrow or assumed and paid by the buyer.

There are then two sentences to indicate who will pay the applicable transfer taxes. The seller usually pays the state documentary transfer tax; custom regarding payment of local transfer taxes varies from county to county.

Then there is a bold print sentence which notifies the buyer that transfer of title will probably result in a change of valuation for the purpose of ad valorem real property tax assessments. A supplemental tax bill will be issued to be paid by the buyer for the period after close of escrow and by the seller for the period prior to close of escrow. Any tax bill that is issued after close of escrow can be handled directly between the buyer and seller.

Paragraph 8. POSSESSION

Paragraph 8 states the agreement as to delivery of possession. In most transactions, possession is transferred as of close of escrow and transfer of title, but it is not unusual for the seller to request a short delay to allow time to vacate. In some cases, particularly if the property is vacant and if it appears likely that the buyer will be able to qualify for the anticipated loan, the buyer and seller may agree to the buyer taking possession prior to close of escrow.

Remember, in any transaction where possession is transferred at some time other than close of escrow, the parties should enter a separate written rental agreement clearly delineating their respective rights and duties during that period and spelling out consequences if they fail to vacate when agreed. The attached agreement should be referenced here in the blank line provided (it is also referenced on page one of the deposit receipt in Paragraph 3).

Paragraph 9. KEYS

This is just an express statement that the seller is obligated to give the buyer the keys to the property when possession is transferred to the buyer.

Paragraph 10. PERSONAL PROPERTY
Paragraph 11. FIXTURES

One of the potential problems in contracts to buy and sell real estate is that the contracts are often pretty vague as to exactly what is included in the sale. The description of the property to be sold is usually a description only of the boundaries of the land. Items such as fences, garages, tool sheds and even the house itself are generally not mentioned in the contract or the deed. If at all, such items are usually simply referred to in a general phrase, such as, "including all permanently attached fixtures and appurtenances."

The general rule is that fixtures are included in the sale even if not mentioned in the contract or deed. Fixtures are items which were originally personal property but which have become real property by being permanently attached to real property through a physical or legal (constructive) attachment. The problem is that the definition of a "fixture" is anything but crystal clear. Houses, fences, garages, and other outbuildings are almost always considered fixtures. However, there have been cases in which particular buildings which were resting on blocks or on the ground without being permanently attached to a foundation have been ruled to be personal property, not fixtures.

Personal property is not included in the sale unless agreed to by the parties. The California REALTORS® form has a paragraph (Paragraph 10) which provides space to list personal property which is to be included in the sale.

What is a Fixture?

In deciding what is a fixture (that is, what is real property and therefore presumed to be included in the sale), the courts apply various tests, such as the method of attachment, the intention of the parties, and whether the item is particularly adapted to the property or necessary for its use. If the item is permanently attached by cement, screws or nails so that it would be difficult to remove and/or its removal would damage the remaining property, it is more likely to be considered a fixture. For example, Section 660 of the California Civil Code defines a fixture as follows: "A thing is deemed to be affixed to land when it is attached to it by roots, as in the case of trees, vines or shrubs; or imbedded in it, as in the case of walls; or permanently resting upon it, as in the case of buildings; or permanently attached to what is thus permanent, as by means of cement, plaster, nails, bolts or screws . . ."

If the party who attached it appears to have intended for it to permanently remain, then it is more likely to be considered a fixture. An agreement between the parties that a particular item is a fixture or is not a fixture may be a deciding factor. The relationship between the parties is also important. Items installed by property owners are more likely to be considered fixtures than items, even the same items, installed by tenants. It is generally assumed that tenants do not have any intention of permanently improving the property of the landlord, but rather install items for their own use only and intend to remove them at the end of the lease. On the other hand, it is generally assumed that property owners do have a desire to permanently improve their own property.

The various tests, the infinite variety of particular fact situations, and the gradually changing law, have resulted in thousands of court decisions concerning fixtures, many of them apparently hard to categorize into general rules. For instance, plumbing pipes and wiring generally fall into the category of fixtures. Central heating furnaces are usually fixtures; however, there is at least one case where radiators were held to be personal property. Sinks, toilets and bathtubs are usually fixtures (although there have been some cases holding sinks and bathtubs to be personal property). Wall-to-wall carpeting has usually (but not always) been held to be a fixture. Storm doors and windows, particularly if they have been built to fit the doors and windows on the property, are usually considered fixtures, even if they are not physically attached to the house at the time of sale (a spring or summer sale). Permanent lighting fixtures, such as chandeliers, are usually fixtures.

On the other hand, electric and gas ranges, refrigerators, washers and dryers in single family residences are usually considered to be personal property (however, several cases involving the sale of apartment houses have held ranges and refrigerators in the apartments to be fixtures). Window-mounted air conditioning units are usually considered personal property.

As you can see, this is an area of great uncertainty, even though there are some items on which there is general agreement. Most people would agree that the house and garage go with the sale, as do growing trees and shrubs and any central heating and cooling equipment. Most people would also agree that the seller's house furniture and lawn furniture, floor and table lamps, and mirrors hanging on walls by wire and hook like pictures (but maybe not mirrors attached to the wall by screws) are personal property items which could be removed by the seller.

However, there are a great number of items which give rise to disagreement, the seller normally thinking the particular item is removable personal property ("I put it here and I should be able to take it with me") and the buyer thinking that it is a fixture. For example, consider free standing fireplaces or fireplace inserts, wood stoves, light bulbs in the light fixtures, built in ranges and dishwashers, garbage disposal units, swimming pool cleaners and garage door openers. There are, of course, many other similar items where there would be differences of opinion as to whether the item should be included in the sale.

Fixtures and Personal Property Clauses in Pre-printed Forms

Many printed contract forms include a clause which lists certain items which are to be included in the sale and/or provides blanks for the parties to list fixtures or personal property to be included or not included in the sale. The California REALTORS® form has two such clauses: Paragraphs 10 and 11.

Paragraph 10 addresses personal property items to be included in the sale. It is first stated that the personal property is to be transferred free of any liens (such as UCC security interests) and without any warranty by the seller as to the condition of the items. There are then several blank lines to describe the items. Personal property items should be described as clearly as possible so that there will be no mistake as to the identity of the items. For example, appliances should be listed and described individually by make, by model number if possible, and current location on the property. You should certainly avoid vague phrases, such as, "All appliances are included." Such imprecise terms are nothing but an invitation to misunderstandings and trouble.

Example:

10. **PERSONAL PROPERTY:** The following items of personal property, free of liens and without warranty of condition, are included:
GE washer and dryer currently located in utility room. GE refrigerator, electric
range, and dishwasher currently located in kitchen.

If the space provided in Paragraph 10 of the REALTORS® form, or your own form, if different, is not sufficient to properly list and describe the personal property items to be included in the sale, you may attach a separate list of the personal property as an addendum or exhibit. The addendum would be labeled and then referenced on the contract form. All parties should initial and date the attached addendum.

Example:

10. PERSONAL PROPERTY: The following items of personal property, free of liens and without warranty of condition, are included:
For personal property items to be included in the sale refer to the inventory in
Exhibit 2, which is attached and incorporated in this agreement by this reference.

Paragraph 11 states that all fixtures are to be included in the sale and then lists a number of examples of fixtures. There are a couple of blanks to write in particular articles which are to be included in the sale even though not specifically listed in the paragraph (and perhaps not fixtures at all) and/or to specify particular items which are not to be included in the sale even though they may be fixtures and/or may be listed in the paragraph. Remember the general rule of contract interpretation that any terms typed or written on the form supersede any contrary terms which are part of the pre-printed form.

Clauses such as Paragraph 11 are found in most standard deposit receipt forms. These clauses have a certain similarity from form to form in that they all state that fixtures are included in the sale and then go on to list a number of examples of fixtures. In general, the items which are specifically mentioned are items which have frequently caused disagreements between buyers and sellers in the past and have been included in the form in order to avoid disagreements as to whether they are fixtures or not. There are, though, significant differences from one form to another in the items which are specifically listed.

Regardless of whether you use this form or some other standard form in your practice, you should become very familiar with this pre-printed list of included items. You should also review it with both buyer and seller so that both have a clear understanding of what the contract says is included and not included. If the sellers intend to take anything with them that is listed among the included items, the form will have to be amended or completed to indicate that the sellers, for example, will remove the crystal chandelier in the dining room or the rose bushes in the front yard or whatever other item or items they wish to take with them. Often, sellers have installed some articles on the property (such as heirloom chandeliers or mirrors) which they always intended to remove and take with them to their next home.

If there is anything that the buyers want that is not absolutely and clearly a fixture (like the house) that is not listed specifically in that clause, it should be listed separately, either in a blank on the form or on an addendum. For example, the form specifically includes built in appliances, but not other appliances. The refrigerator, range, dishwasher, dryer and other household appliances are probably personal property items if not built in and should be listed as included in the sale if the buyer is to receive them. This form does not specifically list water softeners or filters, fireplace inserts or the control boxes for directional TV antennas. They are probably all fixtures and included in the sale without specific mention but it would be best to avoid disputes by including them in the written agreement.

This whole subject of fixtures and other items to be included in the sale is an area which, probably as much as any other, results in disputes and bad feelings in residential transactions. There are often good faith, but mistaken ideas, as to what is or is not included in the sale of the property. As the short discussion of some items considered by courts illustrates, there is little uniformity. Even within one region, the result may be different if the facts are in any way different from an earlier case, different relationships are involved (mortgagor and mortgagee instead of vendor and vendee, for example) or simply from passage of time and changing ideas as to what a reasonable person would expect to be included in the sale. Real estate agents should take care to insure that the parties agree on what is included and what is not. It is not only good service to the clients and customers and the professional thing to do, it is often the best action to take in order to protect your own self-interest: referrals for the future and the commission for the present. In a large number of these cases, disputes as to TV antennas, chandeliers, rose bushes, and the like are settled by having the real estate agent(s) involved purchase a replacement out of a portion of the commission.

To avoid problems, the agent should inspect the property with a thorough knowledge of the provisions of the form to be used and an eye to potential misunderstandings. Seller and buyer should be asked whether particular items are to be included if there appears to be a possibility of differences of opinion. In addition to some items mentioned earlier, some examples of potential problems you might want to consider are: fireplace inserts; free standing fireplaces or wood stoves; above ground swimming pools; portable or semi-portable kennels, sheds or other enclosures or structures which are not fastened to a foundation or embedded in the ground; and satellite dish TV antennas.

Paragraph 12. SMOKE DETECTORS

In Paragraph 12, the seller agrees to provide a written statement of compliance with state and local smoke detector laws. California law requires all homes to be equipped with one or more smoke detectors in working order.

Paragraph 13. TRANSFER DISCLOSURE

This provision reminds the parties that the California Civil Code requires the seller to provide the buyer with a Real Estate Transfer Disclosure Statement. This document contains the seller's disclosures of the property's condition, the condition of the various systems, and structural changes made without appropriate permits. The parties are to indicate whether the buyer has received the form, and if not, when the seller will deliver it. After receiving the form, the buyer has three days (if it is delivered in person) or five days (if it is mailed) to terminate the agreement by written notice. (For more on the disclosure statement, see Chapter 4.)

Paragraph 14. TAX WITHHOLDING

This paragraph alerts the parties to certain provisions of the tax laws. The federal tax code requires buyers to withhold 10% of the price in some purchases when the seller is a foreign person. (Residential sales are exempt if the purchase price is $300,000 or less and the buyers plan to use the home as their primary residence for the next two years.) The state tax code requires buyers to withhold 3⅓% of the price if the money is being collected by an intermediary or if the seller has an out-of-state address. (A transaction is exempt from the state law if the seller had a homeowner's property tax exemption in the year of sale, or if the price is $100,000 or less.)

Paragraph 15. MULTIPLE LISTING SERVICE

Paragraph 15 gives the broker, if he or she is a member of a multiple listing service, the authorization to distribute information regarding the price and terms of this transaction to other members.

Paragraph 16. ADDITIONAL TERMS AND CONDITIONS

Paragraph 16 consists of 11 subparagraphs. These provisions may be incorporated in and made a part of the deposit receipt contract by filling in the blanks, if any, to complete the particular provision and having the parties initial in the spaces preceding the subparagraph(s). Some of these provisions would apply to and be included in most residential transactions and others would have a much more limited applicability. It is unlikely that any one transaction would include all 11 provisions.

If a provision is not applicable to a particular transaction, this fact should be indicated by deleting the provision or by writing "N/A" (not applicable) in the appropriate blank(s).

Paragraph 16. A. PHYSICAL AND GEOLOGICAL INSPECTION

It is quite common for purchasers to request that an inspection contingency of some sort be incorporated in the purchase and sale contract to allow the purchaser to have the structure and/or premises inspected for termite or other pest damage, dry rot, leaks, foundation soundness or other indications of structural soundness or damage, as well as inspections of plumbing and electrical systems, wells and septic systems and soil structure or stability tests. The CAR deposit receipt form addresses these matters in Subparagraph 16 A.

This provision gives the buyer the right to have the property inspected by a professional within a specified number of days for defects or problems occurring on the property, including defects or conditions in the structure, systems, appliances and soil. (There is a separate time limit for geological inspections). It is best to keep the time period permitted for the inspection relatively brief. The buyer should be given enough time to order the inspection and have it done, taking into consideration the current local availability of professional contractors or inspectors and the length of time normally required to have an inspection performed and report prepared. However, this should not be one of the last matters to be resolved when the parties are waiting to close escrow. It is quite possible that the inspection will result in items which will require further negotiation and agreement between the parties and should, therefore, be scheduled and taken care of as soon as possible after signing the deposit receipt, instead of waiting until after the buyer qualifies for the loan or meets some other condition(s).

The buyer is to be responsible for the costs of the inspection and for any damages, liability, expenses or liens (such as mechanics' liens) caused by the inspection. The seller agrees to make the premises available for inspection.

Any defects or other problem conditions must be set out in a written report and copies provided to the seller at no cost. If the buyer does not notify the seller in writing of unacceptable defects or conditions discovered by the inspection, the buyer is deemed to have approved the condition of the property. If the defect(s) will interfere with or affect the buyer's intended use of the property, the seller is not required to correct them. However, if the seller is unwilling or unable to correct defects which are unacceptable to the buyer then the buyer may terminate the agreement.

There is no specific objective standard which is set out in this contingency which states exactly what kind or degree of defects are considered unacceptable, such as "defects or conditions for which repair costs would exceed $500." A straight reading of the condition would then seem to give the buyer absolute discretion in deciding whether anything discovered by the inspection would render the property "unsatisfactory." Remember, though, that California law imposes on the buyer a duty to exercise that discretion in good faith and a reasonable manner.

Also remember that, whether or not an inspection is ordered or whether or not the seller makes any warranties as to the condition of the property, if the seller and/or the agent is aware of any defect or condition in the property or any other matter which would substantially affect the market value of the property, the seller and/or the agent(s) involved are required to make a full disclosure to the buyer. Reliance on "as is" clauses is generally ineffective if the seller or agent has reason to believe that there is a matter which should be disclosed to the buyer (anything with significant impact on market value). The Real Estate Transfer Disclosure Statement (discussed in Chapter 4) sets out the seller's and the agent's information regarding the condition of the property. The statement is intended to contain all the disclosures required by law; it must be used in any sale of one- to four-unit residential property.

Some deposit receipt forms contain a representation that the buyer has inspected the property and agrees to accept it as is, with the exception of items which are specifically noted. For example: "Buyer agrees that he has made a visual inspection of the property and accepts it in its present physical condition except as otherwise noted herein."

Pre-printed clauses in which the buyer acknowledges that a visual inspection has been conducted and that the buyer agrees to accept the property "as is" may lead to some misunderstanding. In California, this sort of provision would normally mean only that the buyer agreed to accept those defects which would be discovered through a visual inspection by the average home buyer. This means obvious or apparent defects, such as broken windows, loose stairs, and other defects which could be easily seen in a relatively careful inspection. However, items not apparent to visual inspection, such as plumbing and wiring problems, and hidden structural problems, such as termites and dry rot damage are excluded.

So, the phrase "as is" on a pre-printed form may not mean what it seems to mean. If the seller believes that there may be some hidden defect, it is safer to include a clause which specifically deals with the issue, rather than relying upon a pre-printed clause, which may result in problems caused by misunderstanding as to its effect.

If the seller or agent has any knowledge of any matter which might materially affect the value of the property, it must be disclosed to the buyer. Neither the seller nor the agent may rely upon an "as is" clause or other attempt to disclaim responsibility for the condition of the property.

Further, for a one- to four-unit residential property, not only does the agent have to disclose any known defects, the agent must make a reasonably competent inspection of the property looking for defects for the benefit of the purchaser.

Paragraph 16. B. CONDITION OF PROPERTY

Paragraph 16. B. is titled "CONDITION OF PROPERTY," but does not actually deal in a comprehensive way with the condition of the property. Instead it contains a few warranties or guarantees made by the seller. First, the seller promises to maintain the property in its present condition at the time of signing the deposit receipt until closing (but makes no express warranty as to what the present condition is). Second, the seller guarantees that the roof does not leak. Third, the seller warrants that the major systems and built-in appliances are all operative. Fourth, the seller promises to replace any broken or cracked glass. There is a final blank for any further warranties to be made by the seller. For example, the buyer may request a warranty that the property contains a certain number of acres or square feet.

Paragraph 16. C. SELLER REPRESENTATION

In this clause, the seller states that to his/her knowledge there are no violations of any applicable local, state or federal laws or ordinances governing the property.

Paragraph 16. D. PEST CONTROL

In keeping with California's extensive statutory regulation of pest control operators, there is a detailed pest control contingency in the deposit receipt form. The first sentence serves to specify the number of days allowed for obtaining an inspection and written report, the party who is to pay for the inspection and report, and the name of the licensed inspector who will conduct the inspection. It also identifies which parts of the property will be inspected.

The inspector may determine that there is no infestation or damage. In that case, the report will include a certification as required by state law. If the inspector discovers an infestation, the work required to clear up the problem may be performed at the buyer's expense or the seller's expense, depending on which box is checked in section (4) of Paragraph 16. D. Even if there is no infestation yet, the inspection may reveal conditions that are likely to lead to an infestation. The parties can indicate whether the buyer or the seller will cover the cost of remedying those conditions in section (5) of Paragraph 16. D. That work would be performed only if the buyer requests it.

If the report recommends that inaccessible areas be inspected, the buyer has the choice of accepting the report without having those areas inspected or requesting that the areas be opened and inspected. In the latter case, the buyer becomes responsible for the additional costs if no infestation is found. But if an infestation or conditions likely to lead to infestation are discovered, the repair costs will be paid as agreed in section (4) or (5).

In almost all transactions involving institutional loans, a pest inspection report will be required and in many other transactions the buyer will request an inspection. Regardless of whether an inspection is conducted, the seller and agent have an obligation to disclose to the buyer any knowledge of infestation and/or pest damage.

Paragraph 16. E. FLOOD HAZARD AREA DISCLOSURE

Paragraph 16. E. is applicable if the property is located in a flood zone. If the property is located in a designated Special Flood Hazard Area, flood insurance will be required if the buyer intends to get an institutional loan.

Paragraph 16. F. SPECIAL STUDIES ZONE DISCLOSURE

This paragraph is a notice to the buyer that the property is located in a "Special Studies Zone" under the Alquist-Priolo Special Studies Zone Act. "Special studies zones" include all recently active and potential earthquake fault areas. A number of restrictions may apply to structures or to construction within such zones. The buyer is given a specified number of days to make necessary inquiries to find out if the property will be suitable for his or her intended purposes. If not, the buyer may terminate the agreement. If the buyer fails to notify the seller within the allowed time period that the property is unsatisfactory, the buyer will be deemed to have approved the property.

Paragraph 16. G. ENERGY CONSERVATION RETROFIT

Paragraph 16. G. establishes which party will pay for energy conservation measures required by local law when property is transferred. In some areas, the work need not be completed prior to close of escrow; the buyer may be credited at escrow with an amount sufficient to cover the costs of the required work.

Paragraph 16. H. HOME PROTECTION PLAN

This paragraph is intended to document that the buyer and seller have been advised as to the availability of home protection plans or home warranty insurance. Such insurance plans cover certain repairs which may be needed after the property is transferred to the buyer. Coverages vary and premiums vary depending upon coverage, but examples of items covered by most policies include plumbing, wiring, heating and appliances included in the sale. The insurance is intended to cover the cost of repairs for problems that occur after the buyer takes possession of the home and may help avoid claims that the real estate agent and/or the seller should pay for fixing the kitchen range or furnace when something goes wrong three months after close of escrow. The paragraph provides boxes and blanks to indicate whether or not the parties intend to purchase this type of insurance and who is to pay for it.

Real estate agents need not recommend particular insurers or even recommend that the insurance be obtained, but in order to properly serve their clients and customers, they should definitely make sure that the parties are advised as to the nature and availability of these policies.

Paragraph 16. I. CONDOMINIUM/PUD

This paragraph is applicable if the property is a unit within a condominium or planned unit development. If so, there are blanks to show exactly what is included with the unit and the current monthly assessment. The seller is to provide the buyer with all applicable documents and give the buyer a specified number of days to review the articles, by-laws and other relevant documents. If the documents disclose conditions, restrictions, rules or other information which the buyer considers to be unacceptable, the buyer may notify the seller within the allotted time and terminate the agreement. As with the other contingencies of this nature discussed above, if the buyer fails to notify the seller in writing, the buyer is deemed to have accepted the property and will be held to the agreement.

Paragraph 16. J. LIQUIDATED DAMAGES

Paragraph 16. J. is titled "LIQUIDATED DAMAGES" but actually it permits the parties to decide between limiting the seller's remedies to liquidated damages, which is the most common, or allowing the seller to sue on the contract for the usual contract remedies: damages (a legal remedy) or specific performance (an equitable remedy). California law provides that if the property is a one- to four-unit residential property intended as the buyer's residence, that the amount retained as liquidated damages may not exceed three percent of the purchase price. The liquidated damages provision must be in bold print and separately initialed by the parties, as is done in this paragraph. These requirements also apply to any further deposits made which may serve as a source of liquidated damages, such as an increased deposit by the buyer after signing the deposit receipt. The CAR form for a receipt for an increased deposit contains another bold print liquidated damages paragraph similar to the one reproduced above.

The phrase in parentheses at the end of the paragraph serves to advise the seller that, if there is a dispute and the seller wants to retain the buyer's deposit as liquidated damages, it is unlikely that the escrow holder will release the funds without the consent of the buyer. It may be necessary to first bring a legal action or submit the matter to arbitration (see Paragraph 16. K.) to establish that the buyer is in default and that the seller is entitled to the liquidated damages.

The liquidated damages provisions only apply to the seller's remedy; there is, in this form, no right to liquidated damages for the buyer. The buyer may sue on the contract for the normal common law remedies of monetary damages or specific performance.

Paragraph 16. K. ARBITRATION

This provision gives the buyer and seller the option of having any dispute that arises between them decided by arbitration. If they initial this provision, any dispute the parties cannot resolve must be arbitrated; they give up the right to sue and have the matter decided by a judge or a jury. The arbitration will be conducted according to the rules of the American Arbitration Association, and the arbitrator's decision will be legally binding on the parties. The notice printed in capital letters is required by state law; it warns the parties that they are giving up their rights to litigate and to appeal, and that they can be compelled to submit to arbitration.

Paragraph 17. OTHER TERMS AND CONDITIONS

Paragraph 17 provides a couple of blank lines to write in any terms or conditions of this agreement that are not included in the printed form. If there is insufficient space provided, the terms or conditions may be written on an addendum and referenced here.

Paragraph 18. ATTORNEY'S FEES

This paragraph gives the prevailing party the right to recover attorney's fees and costs from the losing party in any legal action or proceeding (including arbitration) arising out of the deposit receipt agreement.

Paragraph 19. ENTIRE CONTRACT

Paragraph 20. CAPTIONS

Paragraphs 19 and 20 set out some provisions which relate to the nature of the contract as a whole and to its form.

The first statement in Paragraph 19 is a "time is of the essence" provision. This means that timely performance on or before the exact dates set out in the deposit receipt is one of the essential elements of the contract. Failure to perform on time is a major breach of the contract. Although clauses of this nature are included in most deposit receipt forms, they may or may not have any effect. In order to be enforceable, the parties must in fact insist upon timely performance. Waiver of timely performance or escrow instructions contrary to the provisions of the deposit receipt may cause a court to refuse to enforce the timely performance requirements of this paragraph.

The remainder of Paragraph 19 is what is known as an "integration clause." This provision has the effect of terminating any and all prior agreements that are not set forth in this deposit receipt, which is said to contain the entire agreement between the parties. It is intended to eliminate any later claims that there were other written or oral agreements between the parties.

Paragraph 20 relates to the form of the pre-printed contract. It advises the parties that the bold print captions preceding each paragraph are intended only to serve as a means of reference to particular provisions in the deposit receipt, but the captions themselves are not a part of the agreement.

Paragraph 21. AGENCY CONFIRMATION

This paragraph is in keeping with the state's concern that buyers and sellers know exactly who the real estate agent is representing. This is to help prevent possibilities of misrepresentation and undisclosed dual agency. Both the listing agent and the selling agent are required to disclose exactly who they represent: the seller, the buyer, or both.

Paragraph 22. AMENDMENTS

This provision is related to Paragraph 19 (the ENTIRE CONTRACT clause). Paragraph 22 states that this agreement may not be amended or changed in any way except by another written agreement signed by the buyer and the seller.

Paragraph 23. OFFER

Paragraph 23 indicates that the deposit receipt form constitutes an offer to buy the property and give the seller a certain number of days to accept that offer by delivering a signed copy to the buyer or to a representative named in the blank. If the signed copy is not delivered to the buyer within the allotted time, the offer is deemed revoked and the buyer's deposit is to be returned. There is also an acknowledgment that the buyer has been given a signed copy of the offer, as required by the California real estate license law.

SIGNATURE LINES

Following the last of the provisions of the offer are signature lines for the broker, normally signed by the salesperson of the broker who is the selling agent on the "by" line, and for the buyer(s). There are also blanks for addresses and phone numbers of the agent and buyer(s).

The agent is then obligated to present the offer to the seller as soon as reasonably possible. If the seller accepts the offer as presented, the ACCEPTANCE paragraph would then be signed.

ACCEPTANCE

The paragraph entitled ACCEPTANCE actually has only one sentence that deals strictly with acceptance of the offer. That is the first sentence, which simply states that the seller accepts the buyer's offer on the terms and conditions written above.

Most of the rest of the paragraph concerns the broker's right to a commission. In most transactions, this commission agreement would be a reaffirmation of an earlier promise in the listing agreement.

There are then signature lines for the seller(s) and for the broker(s) or their sales agents.

Counteroffer

Frequently, the seller is unwilling to accept the purchaser's offer as written, but would be willing to sell the property on slightly different terms. For example, the purchaser may offer to buy the property for $98,000, with a 10% cash downpayment to the seller, assumption of the seller's existing trust deed of $45,000 and a second trust deed to the seller with a term of 20 years, fully amortized, and interest at the rate of 11% per annum. The seller is generally favorable to the offer but would want the price to be raised to $102,000 and the interest rate on the second trust deed increased to 12%. The seller is willing to accept the remaining terms of the purchaser's offer as written.

Some agents simply cross out the appropriate figures on the purchaser's offer, replace them with the seller's figures and then have the seller sign the agreement and initial and date the changes. The agreement is then taken back to the purchaser to initial and date the changes and accept the seller's counteroffer. This approach may work if the changes are relatively minor and there is sufficient space to clearly indicate the changes and for the parties to initial the changes. Some problems with this approach are that often the agreement becomes illegible (particularly if the purchaser makes another change) and that sometimes agents fail to get every change initialed, leading to questions as to whether the parties ever reached an agreement on all the terms.

It is clearer and more professional to write any counter proposal on another form or separate addendum. In many areas, real estate agents use forms such as the one reproduced on the following pages which are specifically designed for this purpose.

When a Licensee is a Party

California license law requires a licensed real estate broker or salesperson who is a party to a real estate transaction to disclose that fact to all parties involved.

A licensee who holds a direct or indirect interest in a partnership, corporation or other entity that is a party to the transaction must also make a disclosure of that fact. A licensee acting as an agent for the other party in the transaction or who is in a fiduciary position with the other party to the transaction should insure that a full and complete disclosure is made of the nature of the interest held by the licensee. For example, a broker who merely disclosed that he held stock in a corporation buying the property was held to have breached his fiduciary duties of disclosure to the seller when it was later learned that the broker and his wife were the only two stockholders in the corporation.

Example:

> "Seller (or buyer) has been informed and acknowledges that (name of licensee) is a licensed real estate (broker or salesperson)."

> "Seller (or buyer) has been informed and acknowledges that (name of broker or salesperson) is a licensed real estate (broker or salesperson) and that he/she holds (here specify the nature and extent of the interest held, such as "one of 15 limited partnership interests" or "5% of the outstanding shares of stock") in (the name of the partnership or corporation) which is the buyer (or seller)."

Checklist

Deposit Receipt

- Parties and signatures
  - Names, addresses and phone numbers of ALL parties
  - Indication of marital status
  - Signatures of ALL necessary parties (including spouses)
  - Date(s) of signature(s)
- Description of property
- FULL purchase price
- Method of payment
  - Cash
  - Conventional loan
  - FHA loan
  - VA loan
  - CAL- VET loan
  - Seller financing
    - Deed of trust or installment contract
    - Credit report for buyer
    - Method of payment of taxes and/or insurance
    - Method of payment of underlying liens and/or encumbrances
- Financing terms
  - Principal amount
  - Interest rate (fixed or variable)
  - Amortization
  - Term of loan
  - Monthly payments

CALIFORNIA ASSOCIATION OF REALTORS®

COUNTER OFFER

THIS IS INTENDED TO BE A LEGALLY BINDING AGREEMENT – READ IT CAREFULLY.
CALIFORNIA ASSOCIATION OF REALTORS® (CAR) STANDARD FORM

This is a counter offer to the: ☐ Real Estate Purchase Contract and Receipt for Deposit, ☐ Mobile Home Purchase Contract and Receipt for Deposit, ☐ Business Purchase Contract and Receipt for Deposit, ☐ Other ____________ dated ____________, 19 ____, on property known as: ____________ in which ____________ is referred to as Buyer and ____________ is referred to as Seller.

Seller accepts all of the terms and conditions in the above designated agreement with the following changes or amendments:

____
____
____
____
____
____
____
____
____
____
____
____
____
____
____
____
____
____
____
____
____
____

The Seller reserves the right to continue to offer the herein described property for sale and accept any offer acceptable to Seller at any time prior to personal receipt by Seller or ____________, Seller's authorized agent, of a copy of this counter offer, duly accepted and signed by Buyer. "Accept," as used herein, includes delivery in person, by mail, or by facsimile.

Unless this counter offer is accepted on or before ____________, 19 ____ at ____________ AM/PM, it shall be deemed revoked and deposit shall be returned to the Buyer. Seller's acceptance of another offer shall revoke this counter offer. This counter offer and any supplement, addendum, or modification relating hereto, including any photocopy or facsimile thereof, may be executed in two or more counterparts, all of which shall constitute one and the same writing.

Receipt of a copy is acknowledged.

Date ______________________ 19____ Seller ______________________

Time ______________________ Seller ______________________

☐ The undersigned Buyer accepts the above counter offer, **OR**
☐ The undersigned Buyer accepts the above counter offer with the following changes or amendments:

Unless the following changes or amendments are accepted and a copy duly accepted and signed by Seller is personally delivered to Buyer or ______________________, the agent obtaining the offer on or before ______________, 19____ at ________AM/PM, it shall be deemed revoked and deposit shall be returned to Buyer. Receipt of a copy is acknowledged.

____

____

____

____

____

Date ______________________ 19____ Buyer ______________________

Time ______________________ Buyer ______________________

Receipt of signed copy on ______________, 19____ at ________AM/PM, by Seller ____________ (Initials)
or Seller's authorized Agent ____________ (Initials) is acknowledged.

THE FOLLOWING IS REQUIRED ONLY IF BUYER HAS MADE CHANGES OR AMENDMENTS ABOVE:
Seller accepts Buyer's changes or amendments to Seller's counter offer and agrees to sell on the above terms and conditions. Seller acknowledges receipt of a copy and authorizes Broker(s) to deliver a signed copy to Buyer.

Date ______________________ 19____ Seller ______________________

Time ______________________ Seller ______________________

THIS STANDARDIZED DOCUMENT FOR USE IN SIMPLE TRANSACTIONS HAS BEEN APPROVED BY THE CALIFORNIA ASSOCIATION OF REALTORS® IN FORM ONLY. NO REPRESENTATION IS MADE AS TO THE APPROVAL OF THE FORM OF ANY SUPPLEMENTS NOT CURRENTLY PUBLISHED BY THE CALIFORNIA ASSOCIATION OF REALTORS® OR THE LEGAL VALIDITY OR ADEQUACY OF ANY PROVISION IN ANY SPECIFIC TRANSACTION. IT SHOULD NOT BE USED IN COMPLEX TRANSACTIONS OR WITH EXTENSIVE RIDERS OR ADDITIONS.

A REAL ESTATE BROKER IS THE PERSON QUALIFIED TO ADVISE ON REAL ESTATE TRANSACTIONS. IF YOU DESIRE LEGAL OR TAX ADVICE, CONSULT AN APPROPRIATE PROFESSIONAL.

This form is available for use by the entire real estate industry. The use of this form is not intended to identify the user as a REALTOR®. REALTOR® is a registered collective membership mark which may be used only by real estate licensees who are members of the NATIONAL ASSOCIATION OF REALTORS® and who subscribe to its Code of Ethics.

OFFICE USE ONLY
Reviewed by Broker or Designee ________
Date ____________

EQUAL HOUSING OPPORTUNITY

CO-14

- Conditions or contingencies (financing, inspection, sale of buyer's home)
    - Clear statement of condition
    - Time by which condition must be met or waived
    - Notification procedures
    - Rights of parties if condition is not met
- Items included in sale and those which would normally be included but which seller intends to exclude (e.g., shrubbery, fixtures)
- Possession/risk of loss
- Encumbrances/condition of title
    - Seller to clear
    - Buyer to personally assume
    - Buyer to take subject to
- Special assessments
    - Buyer's liability
    - Seller's liability

Chapter Nineteen

Escrow

The real estate agent's job does not end with the signing of the purchase and sale agreement. Many matters must be taken care of before the sale can be finalized and a commission paid to the agent. The service provided by the agent during the closing process is every bit as important as the agent's marketing efforts prior to the sale. Careful shepherding of the parties through closing will prevent unnecessary delays and gain the agent a reputation for professionalism.

As you will recall from the discussion of deposit receipts, real estate sales transactions typically involve a number of contingencies or conditions. If a buyer and seller could simply sit down across a table and exchange the payment for the deed, there would be no need for the escrow process. (California does not require the use of escrows.) This is rarely, if ever, the case.

The reasons for using an escrow vary according to the perspectives of the parties. The buyer will want assurances that the seller will deliver a deed conveying marketable title before paying the purchase price. This will involve a title search and issuance of a title insurance policy, preparation of the deed itself, and often a payoff and release of existing encumbrances.

The seller wants to be sure that the buyer has the necessary funds for the purchase before conveying title. In most cases, this means that the buyer must qualify for and obtain a loan from a third party lender. The lender for its part will not want to disburse any loan funds until it is assured of a valid security interest in the property.

The broker(s) will be concerned with obtaining payment of any commissions due from the proceeds of the sale. And finally, provision must be made for satisfying the demands of various taxing authorities on the state and local levels.

For all of these reasons, the escrow process is indispensable. Escrow allows the concerns of all parties to be met simultaneously. This is accomplished through conditional delivery of all the necessary documents and funds to a neutral third party depository, who then disburses the documents and funds when all the conditions of the escrow are satisfied.

Definition of Escrow

The State of California defines escrow as "any transaction wherein one person, for the purpose of effecting the sale, transfer, encumbering, or leasing of real property to another person, delivers any written instrument, money, evidence of title to real or personal property, or other thing of value to a third person to be held by such third person until the happening of a specified event or the performance of a prescribed condition, when it is then delivered by such third person to a grantee, grantor, promisee, promisor, obligee, obligor, bailee, bailor, or any agent or employee of any of the latter."

There are two essential requirements for the creation of a valid escrow. First there must be a legally binding and enforceable **contract between the parties**. This contract may take the form of a purchase and sale agreement, escrow instructions signed by the buyer and seller, or a combination of the two. Escrow instructions will be discussed later in this chapter.

The second requirement of a valid escrow is **conditional delivery with relinquishment of control**. This means simply that the parties must deposit funds or documents with a third party along with instructions to disburse the funds or deliver the documents only upon the happening of a specified event. If the parties retain any control over the deposited items, there is no valid escrow and the closing will be legally ineffective.

Parties

Escrowees

An escrowee is the neutral third party who holds the items deposited by the parties and disburses them after the conditions of the escrow are satisfied. The escrowee also performs additional services such as preparing documents, calculating settlement costs and recording. Factors which may influence the choice of an escrowee include cost of service, professional reputation, and requirements of the third party lender. (Designation of a closing agent by a lender is regulated by RESPA, discussed below.)

Title companies are the most common escrowees in northern California. In the southern part of the State, independent escrow companies also close a large number of transactions. Many institutional lenders (banks, savings & loan associations and insurance companies) have their own escrow departments which are used as closing agents for transactions financed by such lenders. Under certain limited circumstances, attorneys and real estate brokers may also act as escrowees.

Escrow companies are required to be licensed by the State Department of Corporations under the **Escrow Law**; only corporations may be licensed as escrow companies, individuals are not eligible. Exempted from this licensing requirement are banks, S&Ls, insurance companies, attorneys and real estate brokers, all of whom are regulated by other agencies.

Real estate brokers are **exempt** from the Escrow Law "while performing acts in the course of or incidental to a real estate transaction in which the broker is an agent or a party to the transaction and in which the broker is performing an act for which a real estate license is required." The intent of this exemption is to permit brokers to provide certain services to their clients without becoming subject to regulation from another agency. The exemption does not permit brokers to operate as escrow agents in transactions where they have no bona fide interest other than that of providing escrow services.

Brokers who desire to perform escrow services should be aware that the Corporations Commissioner and the Attorney General take a dim view of arrangements which attempt to circumvent the intent of the Escrow Law. Independent escrow companies are subject to much more stringent regulations of escrow services than are brokers under the Real Estate Law. Schemes such as "broker-escrow cooperatives" — where two or more brokers operate a joint branch location which performs escrow services — and accepting a nominal commission split in exchange for performance of escrow services, may subject the errant broker to civil and criminal penalties, as well as loss of license. The simple fact that a referral fee is paid to a real estate broker in exchange for referral of escrow business constitutes evidence that the person or company receiving the referral is subject to the license requirement of the Escrow Law.

It should also be noted in this context that acceptance of "kickbacks" or similar compensation for referral of customers to an escrow business is grounds for suspension or revocation of a real estate license under the Real Estate Law.

Other Persons Involved in the Escrow Process

The typical escrow involves many functionaries who contribute to the overall service performed by the escrowee. In addition to the parties (buyer, seller, lender, escrow agent) and the real estate broker, important functions are performed by title companies, notaries public, local county recording officials and structural pest inspectors.

A **notary public** is an individual who is commissioned by the California Secretary of State with the power to administer oaths and grant official approval of documents. In real estate transactions, notaries are most commonly employed to witness and verify the signature and acknowledgement of documents which are to be recorded. Acknowledgement, accompanied by notarization, is a prerequisite for the recording of any document affecting title to real estate. The notarization process serves as a protection against forgeries.

The requirements for becoming a notary are relatively simple, and the commission is valid for four years. Real estate agents may be commissioned as notaries, and in fact virtually every real estate office will have at least one agent who is also a notary public. The ability to provide the service of a notary can be a very valuable service to clients, greatly facilitating the execution of the many documents involved in a real estate transaction. Agents should be aware, however, that notaries may not have any direct financial interest in the effect of any document they notarize. This limitation does not prevent the agent from notarizing documents where the agent's only interest is the receipt of a commission, but could create problems in situations where the agent has a more substantial role in the transaction.

Recording of documents is one of the key functions of an escrow. The recording system is designed to protect interests in real estate by establishing the relative priority of various interested parties. Any document relating to real estate ownership (deed, deed of trust, lien, real estate contract, etc.) can and should be recorded.

Each county in the State has its own set of records covering the real estate located in the county. The records are kept at the office of the **County Auditor** or **Recorder**. At the close of escrow, each party is charged for the recording fees applicable to the recording of documents which benefit that party. For example, sellers pay the cost of recording lien releases; buyers pay for recording of deeds. The charges for recording are imposed on a 'per page' basis, usually a few dollars for the first page of a document and a lesser amount for each additional page.

These charges help to pay for indexing the documents and maintaining the actual records.

In addition to protecting title and other interests in real estate, the recording system is a source of information for any member of the general public. Copies of any recorded document may be obtained for a nominal fee. Although the documents in the recorder's office could be searched to determine the state of title to a particular parcel of real estate, in practice the process of 'searching title' is normally performed by a title company on the basis of its own records or 'title plant.' However, the source of the title companies' records is ultimately the county record system.

One of the most common contingencies in a sale of real estate is a **structural pest inspection**. These inspections are required by many buyers, lenders and insuring agencies to determine that the security property is in good repair and free from damaging infestation. For a fee ranging from about $75 to $150 or more, a licensed inspector will prepare a written report of the property's condition, noting any repairs that need to be made. The responsibility for the inspection fee and the cost of needed repairs may be negotiated between the buyer and seller, but is commonly charged to the seller in most areas. It is a good practice for the agent to obtain a signed receipt from the buyer upon delivery of the inspection report. This will provide proof that the buyer was informed of any defects in the property. Remember that the Real Estate Law requires agents to disclose to buyers any known defects which may materially affect the value of the property.

The California State Structural Pest Control Board maintains records in Sacramento of all inspection reports and repair completion certificates. These records are open to inspection by the general public. For a modest fee, a person may request certified copies of all such documents filed within the preceding two years.

The Escrow Process

Although not usually called upon to perform escrow procedures, agents must be aware of the steps in the escrow process. Such an awareness will allow agents to advise their clients effectively and to expedite closings by anticipating the needs of the escrowee. Much of the information needed in escrow can and should be provided by the real estate agent.

The following discussion will cover the steps involved in a typical real estate escrow for a single family residential sale. The agent should be aware, however, that escrow customs vary significantly in some respects from one area of the State to another. Who will perform the escrow, the type of escrow instructions to be used, the timing of the escrow, and the allocation of closing costs are all subject to variation based on local custom.

Any escrow will involve certain essential steps:

- gathering of information necessary to prepare escrow instructions;
- a preliminary title report from the title company;
- satisfaction of existing loans secured by the property;
- preparation of documents such as escrow instructions, loan documents, deeds, etc.;
- deposit of funds by the buyer (and seller if necessary);
- proration of expenses and allocation of closing costs;
- preparation of a Uniform Settlement Statement;
- issuance of title insurance policies for buyer and lender;
- recording of necessary documents; and
- disbursal of funds and delivery of documents.

Escrow Instructions

The timing of escrow depends on local custom. In northern California, escrow instructions are typically prepared at a much later stage in the transaction than is the case in southern California. In southern counties, where escrows are often handled by escrow companies, the parties typically meet with the escrow agent shortly after the purchase and sale agreement is executed. The escrow instructions are prepared from information obtained by the escrow agent from the parties in this interview, and the terms of the deposit receipt itself are made a part of the escrow instructions. Joint escrow instructions (a single set of instructions for both buyer and seller) are preferred in southern California, and are normally executed shortly after the deposit receipt is signed.

In northern California counties, escrow instructions are often prepared only when the transaction is almost ready to close. Real estate agents play a much greater role in the escrow process in northern California, gathering much of the information needed by the escrowee (usually a title company). The escrowee has little if any direct contact with the parties, so it is up to the agent to insure that all the necessary information is forwarded in a timely manner to the escrowee. Separate escrow instructions for the buyer and seller are more common in northern California. The buyer's instructions are often signed at the same time the buyer makes his or her deposit of funds into the escrow and also signs the other documents of the transaction such as the note and deed of trust.

Whether joint or separate, escrow instructions are usually **pre-printed form documents** provided by the escrow agent or the lender. Generally speaking, separate escrow instructions tend to be simpler than joint instructions. The advantage of joint instructions is that they eliminate the possibility of conflicts between the instructions received from the buyer and the seller. On the other hand, separate instructions allow one party to keep certain information (for example, the amount of the commission) confidential from the other party.

Escrow Progress Chart

It is good practice for agents to utilize an **escrow progress chart** such as the form reproduced below in order to keep track of the status of the escrow. The chart will enable the agent to inform the buyer or seller of the current status of escrow, and is also a handy reminder for the agent of items which may still need to be attended to in order to close the transaction. One or more of the agents associated with the transaction will generally be responsible for coordinating the assembly of documents and information required by the escrowee. When more than one agent is involved, it is best for the agents to agree among themselves as to who shall have the responsibility of dealing directly with the escrowee in order to prevent confusion and duplication of effort. However, each agent should stay apprised of the process as the escrow progresses.

The first step in the escrow procedure is to **open the escrow**. This is done by providing the escrowee with the information needed to prepare preliminary escrow instructions. Once the instructions are signed and returned to the escrowee, the escrowee will order a **preliminary title report** showing the condition of title to the property. This information will be forwarded to the buyer's lender, along with a copy of the **escrow instructions**. Note that the escrow instructions must correspond to the terms of the loan which the lender is willing to make. Any discrepancy in the loan amount or terms (such as interest rate, repayment period or discount points) will necessitate the signing of amended escrow instructions, since the lender will not disburse any loan funds into the escrow (or even approve the loan) until the instructions correspond to the terms of the loan.

Early in the escrow process, the escrowee will also contact the seller's lender to obtain a **payoff figure** for the seller's loan. This is accomplished by sending a 'demand for payoff' or 'request for beneficiary's statement' to the lender, who then returns copies of the completed form to the escrowee and the title company. **Structural pest inspections**

ESCROW PROGRESS CHART

	Sch. Date	Actual Date	Escrow Operations
1			Notice of Sale to multiple listing service
2			Buyer's deposit increased to $
3			Escrow opened with
4			Preliminary title searched
5			Clouds on title eliminated
6			Credit report ordered from
7			Credit report received
8			Report of residential record ordered
9			Report of residential record received
10			Pest control inspection ordered
11			Pest control report received; work —
12			Pest control report accepted by seller
13			Pest control work ordered
14			Pest control work completed
15			Other inspections ordered
16			Report received; work —
17			Report accepted by
18			Special contingencies eliminated
19			Payoff or beneficiary statement ordered
20			Payoff or beneficiary statement received
21			Payoff or beneficiary statement ordered
22			Payoff or beneficiary statement received

23			1st loan commitment ordered from
24			Received: @ % Fee Pts.
25			2nd loan commitment ordered from
26			Received: @ % Fee Pts.
27			Loan application submitted to
28			Loan application approved
29			Loan/assumption papers received by escrow
30			Hazard insurance placed with
31			Escrow closing instructions requested
32			Client called for closing appointment
33			Closing papers signed
34			Closing papers to escrow holder
35			Funds ordered
36			Deed recorded

After Close of Escrow

Received	Delivered	
		Final adjusted closing statement
		Check of seller's proceeds
		Check of buyer's refund
		Commission check
		Seller's "Loss Payee" insurance policy
		Recorded deed
		Title insurance policy

Notations

are also ordered as soon as possible to avoid delays in closing which may be caused by the need to repair the property.

When the buyer's loan is approved, the lender will forward the **loan documents** (note, deed of trust and Truth-in-Lending statement) to the escrowee. At this point, the buyer is in a position to complete his or her part of the transaction by depositing the necessary funds into escrow and signing the loan documents, which are then forwarded to the lender.

The seller will be ready to close when the escrowee receives the payoff figures from the seller's lender and the pest control inspection detailing any repairs to be performed. This information will allow a reasonably accurate determination of the seller's proceeds from the sale. The pest control inspection, along with notices of completion of any required repairs, may also be forwarded to the buyer's lender if necessary.

Hazard insurance is another item which is common to most escrows. The new hazard insurance policy for the buyer, or an assignment of the seller's existing policy, must be forwarded to the new lender prior to disbursal of the loan funds. Before escrow can close, any other contingencies of the sale, such as sale of the buyer's existing home, must be satisfied or waived.

Once all contingencies have been satisfied, the lender will **disburse the loan funds** to the title company. The escrowee will have also sent the seller's grant deed to the title company for recording upon receipt of the loan funds. The title company will record the deed, deed of trust, reconveyance deed and other documents, and then provide the escrowee with the information (final payoff of the seller's loan, title and recording fees, etc.) necessary to prepare the final closing statements. The title company then gives the loan funds to the escrowee. The escrowee prepares the statements and makes the necessary disbursements of funds to the seller, broker and other entities. At this time, the title insurance policy is issued, and the buyer will also receive copies of the completed loan documents, insurance policies and inspection reports.

Closing Costs and Settlement Statements

A settlement statement is a listing of all the amounts payable by or to one of the parties in the transaction. Settlement statements are prepared for both buyer and seller, or a single statement may list charges and credits for both parties. In sales of residential property financed by institutional lenders, a Uniform Settlement Statement form such as the one shown below must be prepared.

Items on the settlement statement are listed as either **debits** or **credits**. A debit is a charge payable by a particular party; for example, the purchase price is a debit to the buyer, the sales commission a debit to the seller. Credits are items payable to a party; the buyer would be credited for his or her new loan, the seller for the purchase price. Think of the settlement statement as a check register for a bank account: debits are like checks written against the account, credits are the equivalent of deposits into the account. When the transaction closes, the balances in the buyer's and seller's accounts should equal zero.

Although it is virtually impossible to calculate the exact closing costs for a transaction until the time of closing, a reasonably accurate estimate can be prepared in advance. Agents are often called upon to make such an estimate of the buyer's cash requirements and the seller's net proceeds from the sale. Worksheets such as the forms shown below are commonly used for this purpose.

Buyer's Costs

Obviously, the main cost for the buyer will be the **purchase price**, which will be listed as a debit on the buyer's statement. In most transactions, the purchase price will be offset by some form of financing, either an institutional loan or seller financing. New loans from an institutional lender or from the seller, or assumptions of existing loans, are listed as credits for the buyer. The difference between the sales price and the financing is the downpayment. Some worksheet forms utilize

A. **Settlement Statement**

U.S. Department of Housing and Urban Development

OMB Approval No. 2502-0265

B. Type of Loan	6. File Number	7. Loan Number	8. Mortgage Insurance Case Number
1. ☐ FHA 2. ☐ FmHA 3. ☐ Conv. Unins. 4. ☐ VA 5. ☐ Conv. Ins.			

C. Note: This form is furnished to give you a statement of actual settlement costs. Amounts paid to and by the settlement agent are shown. Items marked "(p.o.c.)" were paid outside the closing; they are shown here for informational purposes and are not included in the totals.

D. Name and Address of Borrower	E. Name and Address of Seller	F. Name and Address of Lender

G. Property Location	H. Settlement Agent	
	Place of Settlement	I. Settlement Date

J. Summary of Borrower's Transaction		K. Summary of Seller's Transaction	
100. Gross Amount Due From Borrower		**400. Gross Amount Due To Seller**	
101. Contract sales price		401. Contract sales price	
102. Personal property		402. Personal property	
103. Settlement charges to borrower (line 1400)		403.	
104.		404.	
105.		405.	
Adjustments for items paid by seller in advance		**Adjustments for items paid by seller in advance**	
106. City/town taxes to		406. City/town taxes to	
107. County taxes to		407. County taxes to	
108. Assessments to		408. Assessments to	
109.		409.	
110.		410.	
111.		411.	
112.		412.	
120. Gross Amount Due From Borrower		**420. Gross Amount Due To Seller**	

200. Amounts Paid By Or In Behalf Of Borrower		500. Reductions In Amount Due To Seller	
201. Deposit or earnest money		501. Excess deposit (see instructions)	
202. Principal amount of new loan(s)		502. Settlement charges to seller (line 1400)	
203. Existing loan(s) taken subject to		503. Existing loan(s) taken subject to	
204.		504. Payoff of first mortgage loan	
205.		505. Payoff of second mortgage loan	
206.		506.	
207.		507.	
208.		508.	
209.		509.	
Adjustments for items unpaid by seller		**Adjustments for items unpaid by seller**	
210. City/town taxes to		510. City/town taxes to	
211. County taxes to		511. County taxes to	
212. Assessments to		512. Assessments to	
213.		513.	
214.		514.	
215.		515.	
216.		516.	
217.		517.	
218.		518.	
219.		519.	
220. Total Paid By/For Borrower		**520. Total Reduction Amount Due Seller**	
300. Cash At Settlement From/To Borrower		**600. Cash At Settlement To/From Seller**	
301. Gross Amount due from borrower (line 120)		601. Gross amount due to seller (line 420)	
302. Less amounts paid by/for borrower (line 220)	( )	602. Less reductions in amt. due seller (line 520)	( )
303. Cash ☐ **From** ☐ **To Borrower**		**603. Cash** ☐ **To** ☐ **From Seller**	

Previous Edition Is Obsolete

HUD-1 (3-86)
RESPA, HB 4305.2

L. Settlement Charges			Paid From Borrowers Funds at Settlement	Paid From Seller's Funds at Settlement
700. Total Sales/Broker's Commission based on price $	@	% =		
Division of Commission (line 700) as follows:				
701. $	to			
702. $	to			
703. Commission paid at Settlement				
704.				
800. Items Payable In Connection With Loan				
801. Loan Origination Fee	%			
802. Loan Discount	%			
803. Appraisal Fee	to			
804. Credit Report	to			
805. Lender's Inspection Fee				
806. Mortgage Insurance Application Fee to				
807. Assumption Fee				
808.				
809.				
810.				
811.				
900. Items Required By Lender To Be Paid In Advance				
901. Interest from to	@$	/day		
902. Mortgage Insurance Premium for		months to		
903. Hazard Insurance Premium for		years to		
904.		years to		
905.				
1000. Reserves Deposited With Lender				
1001. Hazard insurance	months@$	per month		
1002. Mortgage insurance	months@$	per month		
1003. City property taxes	months@$	per month		
1004. County property taxes	months@$	per month		
1005. Annual assessments	months@$	per month		
1006.	months@$	per month		
1007.	months@$	per month		
1008.	months@$	per month		
1100. Title Charges				
1101. Settlement or closing fee	to			
1102. Abstract or title search	to			

1103. Title examination to		
1104. Title insurance binder to		
1105. Document preparation to		
1106. Notary fees to		
1107. Attorney's fees to		
(includes above items numbers:)		
1108. Title insurance to		
(includes above items numbers:)		
1109. Lender's coverage $		
1110. Owner's coverage $		
1111.		
1112.		
1113.		
1200. Government Recording and Transfer Charges		
1201. Recording fees: Deed $; Mortgage $; Releases $		
1202. City/county tax/stamps: Deed $; Mortgage $		
1203. State tax/stamps: Deed $; Mortgage $		
1204.		
1205.		
1300. Additional Settlement Charges		
1301. Survey to		
1302. Pest inspection to		
1303.		
1304.		
1305.		
1400. Total Settlement Charges (enter on lines 103, Section J and 502, Section K)		

Public Reporting Burden for this collection of information is estimated to average 0.25 hours per response, including the time for reviewing instructions, searching existing data sources, gathering and maintaining the data needed, and completing and reviewing the collection of information. Send comments regarding this burden estimate or any other aspect of this collection of information, including suggestions for reducing this burden, to the Reports Management Officer, Office of Information Policies and Systems, U.S. Department of Housing and Urban Development, Washington, D.C. 20410-3600; and to the Office of Management and Budget, Paperwork Reduction Project (2502-0265), Washington, D.C. 20503

U.S. GOVERNMENT PRINTING OFFICE 1989 0—944-245

the figure for the downpayment in calculating the buyer's costs, rather than listing the purchase price and loan amounts separately. Either method will yield the same result.

After the purchase price, the largest debit to the buyer at closing is typically the **loan fee**. This is a percentage of the loan amount (usually 1-2%) charged by the lender to cover the administrative costs of making the loan. To calculate the loan origination fee, simply multiply the loan amount (not the purchase price) by the percentage of the fee.

The lender may also charge **discount points** (points) in connection with the loan. These are a percentage of the loan amount charged in order to increase the lender's yield on the loan. The seller often pays some or all of the loan discount, but (except in VA loans) the buyer may be responsible for the points. If the buyer pays the points, they should be shown as a debit on the buyer's statement.

Several other loan costs are customarily charged to the buyer in a real estate sale. These include the **appraisal fee, credit report fee,** amounts for impound or reserve accounts for **taxes and insurance**, lender's **title insurance premium**, and **prepaid interest**. The appraisal fee and credit report fee are usually set at a flat rate, which may vary depending on the location of the property and the person or firm preparing the appraisal or credit report. Residential appraisals cost a few hundred dollars; credit reports are normally less than $100. The title insurance fee depends on the amount of the loan and may be obtained from the title company or a rate chart. It will normally be in the range of $500 to $1,000.

Impound or reserve accounts are trust accounts maintained by the lender to pay property taxes and hazard insurance premiums. The borrower pays a portion (1/12 of the annual amount) of these expenses each month along with the principal and interest payment; when the taxes or insurance premium become payable, the lender pays them out of the reserve account. When the loan is originated, the lender may ask the borrower to deposit an initial amount into the reserve account. This is usually in the range of six months' to one year's worth of the taxes and insurance premium. The borrower's monthly deposits will then maintain a positive balance in the account as the items are paid.

Prepaid or interim interest is the amount of interest due on the new loan during the first (partial) month of the loan term. Interest on real estate loans is normally paid in arrears, that is, the interest for a given month is paid at the end of the month. However, when a new loan is made, the interest is paid in advance for the month of closing. For example, if closing occurs on June 15, interest for the period June 15 through June 30 is paid at closing. The first regular payment on the loan is then due on August 1 and covers the interest due for the month of July (payment in arrears). To calculate the amount of interim interest that will be due, multiply the daily interest rate (1/365 of the annual rate) times the number of days between the closing date and the end of the month times the amount of the loan.

Other items which are typically charged to the buyer in a real estate sale include: **attorney fees, notary fees,** a share of the **escrow fee** and **recording fees.** Depending on the agreement of the parties or local custom, the buyer may also be charged for all or a portion of the **owner's title insurance policy.** (This expense is paid by the seller in most southern California counties; in most northern counties it is either paid by the buyer or the cost is split between buyer and seller. Note, however, that the parties are free to ignore local custom and allocate this expense by agreement in the deposit receipt or escrow instructions if they so desire.) If a **pest control inspection** and/or **repairs** are one of the contingencies to the sale, the buyer may also be responsible for all or part of this expense, depending on the allocation agreed to by the parties. Finally, the buyer will be charged for **any special costs** incurred by the buyer, such as the cost of a home warranty contract.

Depending on the status of the property taxes, the buyer may be due a credit or may owe an amount to the seller. If the property taxes have been paid for a period after the closing date, the buyer will have to reimburse the seller for taxes applicable to the time after the closing date. On the other hand, if taxes are in arrears, the seller will owe the buyer for the amount of arrears. For example, assume that the closing date is June

ESTIMATED BUYER'S COST

CALIFORNIA ASSOCIATION OF REALTORS® (CAR) STANDARD FORM

BUYER ______________________________ DATE ______________

PROPERTY ADDRESS ______________________________

This estimate is based on costs associated with ______________________________ type of financing.

LOAN AMOUNT $ ____________ INTEREST RATE ________ % ☐ FIXED ☐ ADJUSTABLE •☐ OTHER

PROPOSED PURCHASE PRICE $ ____________ PROJECTED CLOSING DATE ____________

ESTIMATED BUYER'S EXPENSE:

Loan Origination Fee	$ ________
Processing Fee	________
Funding Fee	________
Lender's Prepaid Interest	
Days ________	________
Appraisal Fee	________
Credit Report	________
PMI/MIP	________
Other Lender Fees	________
Tax Service	________
Tax Impounds	________
Pro Rated Taxes	________
Hazard Insurance	________
Pro Rated Insurance	________
Insurance Impounds	________
Title Insurance (Owners)	________
Title Insurance (Lenders)	________
Escrow Fee	________

ESTIMATED CREDITS:

Prorated Taxes	$ ________
Rent	________
Security Deposits	________
Other	________
Other	________
Other	________
TOTAL CREDITS	$ ________

ESTIMATED CASH REQUIRED:

Expenses	$ ________
Down Payment	________
Less Credits	— ________
ESTIMATED TOTAL CASH REQUIRED	$ ________

Sub-Escrow Fee ____________
Recording Fees ____________

Notary Fees ____________
Preparation of Documents ____________
Structural Pest Control Inspection ____________
Structural Pest Control Repairs ____________
Physical Inspection Fee ____________
Other Inspection Fees ____________
Home Protection Policy ____________
Home Owners Transfer Fees ____________
Brokerage Fee ____________
Other ____________

TOTAL ESTIMATED EXPENSES $ ____________

ESTIMATED MONTHLY PAYMENTS

Prin. & Int.* $ ____________
(at origination)
Taxes ____________
Insurance ____________
Other ____________
Total ____________

*Buyer is aware that with regard to adjustable rate loans, the monthly payment may increase at various times over the life of the loan. Buyer should confirm directly with lender all terms and conditions of said loan.

This estimate based upon the above proposed purchase price, type of financing, and projected closing date has been prepared to assist Buyer in computing his/her costs. Lenders, title companies and escrow holders may vary in their charges. Expenses will also vary according to expenses for required repairs, if any, and other items. Therefore, these figures cannot be guaranteed by the broker or his/her representatives. All estimates and information are from sources believed reliable but not guaranteed.

I have read the above figures and acknowledge receipt of a copy of this form.

BUYER ____________________ Date ____________

BUYER ____________________ Date ____________

Firm: ____________________

Presented by: ____________________

Address: ____________________

Telephone No. ____________________

OFFICE USE ONLY
Reviewed by Broker or Designee ________
Date ____________

EQUAL HOUSING OPPORTUNITY
SF-Mar-89

FORM EBC-14

CALIFORNIA ASSOCIATION OF REALTORS®

ESTIMATED SELLER'S PROCEEDS

CALIFORNIA ASSOCIATION OF REALTORS® (CAR) STANDARD FORM

SELLER________________________________ DATE______________

PROPERTY ADDRESS ____

This estimate is based on costs associated with ______________________ type of financing.

PROJECTED CLOSING DATE ______________ ESTIMATED SELLING PRICE $______________

ESTIMATED COSTS

Escrow Fee	$ ________
Drawing, Recording, Notary	________
Title Insurance Policy	________
Transfer Tax	________
Documentary Transfer Tax	________
Prepayment Penalty	________
Bene/Demand Fee	________
Prorated Interest (all loans)	________
Reconveyance Deed	________
Misc. Lender Fees	________
Appraisal Fee	________
VA/FHA Discount______ Points	________
Preparation of Documents	________
Misc. VA/FHA Fees	________
Prorated Taxes	________
Structural Pest Control Inspection	________
Structural Pest Control Repairs	________
Other Required Repairs	________
Home Protection Policy	________

ENCUMBRANCES (Approximate):

First Trust Deed	$ ________
Second Trust Deed	________
Bonds, Liens	________
Other Encumbrances	________
TOTAL	$ ________
GROSS EQUITY	$ ________

APPROXIMATE CREDITS:

Prorated Taxes	$ ________
Prorated Insurance	________
Impound Accounts	________
Other	________
Other	________
TOTAL	$ ________

RECAP:

ESTIMATED SELLING PRICE	$ ________
LESS:	
Total Encumbrances	– ________
Estimated Costs	– ________
Sub-Total	$ ________

Brokerage Fee ______
Buyer's Closing Costs ______

Security Deposits ______
Prorated Rents ______
Other Fees/Costs ______
______ ______
______ ______
______ ______

ESTIMATED TOTAL COSTS $ ______

PLUS:
Approximate Credits + ______

ESTIMATED SELLERS PROCEEDS $ ______

LESS:
Purchase Money Note (If carried by seller) − ______

PLUS:
Proceeds From Sale of Purchase Money Note + ______

ESTIMATED SELLERS CASH PROCEEDS $ ______

This estimate is based upon the above projected selling price, type of financing, and projected closing date, has been prepared to assist the seller in computing his/her costs and proceeds. Lenders, title companies and escrow holders will vary in their charges. Expenses will also vary depending upon any required repairs, differences in unpaid loan balances, bond assessments, other liens, impound account, if any, and other items. Therefore, these figures cannot be guaranteed by the broker or his/her representatives. All estimates and information are from sources believed reliable but not guaranteed.

I have read the above figures and acknowledge receipt of a copy of this form.

SELLER ______ Date ______

SELLER ______ Date ______

Firm: ______

Presented by: ______

Address: ______

Phone No.: ______

This form is available for use by the entire real estate industry. The use of this form is not intended to identify the user as a REALTOR®. REALTOR® is a registered collective membership mark which may be used only by real estate licensees who are members of the NATIONAL ASSOCIATION OF REALTORS® and who subscribe to its Code of Ethics.

OFFICE USE ONLY
Reviewed by Broker or Designee ______
Date ______

EQUAL HOUSING OPPORTUNITY
SF-Sept-88

FORM ESP-14

15, and that taxes have been paid through the end of June. In this case the buyer would owe the seller an amount equal to the tax for the last half of June. If the closing date were July 15, the seller would owe the buyer a half month's property tax.

In calculating the amount of tax payable by or to the seller or buyer, it is necessary to know the daily rate of the tax and the number of days for which each party is responsible. The expense can then be prorated (allocated) between the parties. The process of proration is also used to allocate such items as interest on assumed loans, premiums on assumed insurance policies, and rents for income property.

Example:

Assume that the annual property taxes are $3,600 and have been paid through the end of June for the current year. If the sale is to close on April 17, the taxes would be prorated as follows.

Step 1: Calculate the daily rate of the expense by dividing the annual rate by 360 (for monthly expenses, divide by 30).

$3600 ÷ 360 = $10 daily rate of tax

NOTE: Although it is more accurate to use the actual number of days in the year or month (365 or 366 days per year; 28, 29, 30 or 31 days per month), it is easier and sufficiently accurate for the purposes of estimation to assume that each month contains 30 days, for a 360-day year.

Step 2: Calculate the number of days for which each party is responsible for the expense.

In this case, the taxes are paid in advance, so the buyer must reimburse the seller for taxes which pertain to the period April 17 through June 30. (The buyer is responsible for taxes that apply to the date of closing.)

14 days in April (30 – 16 = 14)
30 days in May
30 days in June
74 days total

Step 3: Multiply the daily rate times the number of days.

$10 x 74 = $740 prorated amount of taxes

The buyer will owe the seller approximately $740 for property taxes at closing. This amount will be listed as a debit for the buyer and a credit for the seller.

Buyer's Credits

To determine the amount that the buyer will owe at closing, certain credits must be deducted from the buyer's closing costs. For example, the buyer is credited for the amount of the **good faith (earnest money) deposit** and for any **deposit** given to the lender to cover the initial loan costs such as the appraisal and credit report. The buyer may also be due a credit for **prorated taxes** or **rents**. The cash needed by the buyer for closing can then be calculated as follows:

total of closing costs payable by buyer
– total of credits due to buyer
+ downpayment
cash required to close

Seller's Costs

The seller's primary cost at closing is normally the **payoff of any existing loans**. The seller may also be charged a **prepayment penalty** in connection with the payoff, and will be responsible for the **interest** due for the month of closing. The interest due may be calculated using the proration formula: daily rate times number of days equals prorated expense.

The seller will be responsible for payment of the **sales commission** and also for **attorney fees, escrow fee, notary fees** and **recording fees.** Depending on custom or agreement, the seller may also be responsible for the **owner's title insurance premium,** the **structural pest control inspection** and/or **repairs,** the buyer's **loan discount** and such miscellaneous items as a home warranty contract. If the **property taxes** are in arrears, the seller will also owe for the prorated tax due up to the date of closing.

Documentary transfer taxes are normally paid by the seller. This is a state tax that applies to the transfer of real estate. It is charged at the rate of 55¢ for each $500 of the purchase price.

Example:

sales price: $100,000

$100,000 ÷ 500 = 200

200 x .55 = $110 transfer tax

NOTE: The documentary transfer tax does not apply to the amount of any assumed loans or loans which the buyer takes subject to. If the buyer in the example above had assumed the seller's existing $70,000 loan, the tax would be due on only the $30,000 difference between the sales price and the assumed loan.

Seller's Credits

In addition to the purchase price, the seller may be due credits for such items as prorated taxes and insurance premiums, and the balances in any impound accounts in connection with existing loans. If the property is income property, there may be a credit (or a debit) for prorated rents. The seller's net proceeds from the sale can then be calculated as follows:

  purchase price
– existing loans (to be paid/assumed/taken subject to)
– seller financing (if any)
– seller's closing costs
\+ seller's credits
  net cash to seller

Seller financing. When the seller takes back a note from the buyer as part of the purchase price, or when the buyer assumes or takes subject to the seller's existing loan(s), the amounts of such financing are listed as credits to the buyer and debits to the seller. In the case of an assumption, the buyer is debited and the seller credited for any reserve account balances in connection with the assumed loan. If there is an assumption fee charged by the lender, it may be debited to either party, or shared, depending upon their agreement in the deposit receipt or escrow instructions.

Income property. When income property is sold, it is necessary to prorate the rents from the property. If rents are paid in advance, the buyer will be due a credit, and the seller a debit, for the amount of rents applicable to the time after closing. If rents are in arrears, the reverse is true: the seller is due a credit and the buyer is debited for the arrears applicable to the time the seller owned the property. If the seller is holding security deposits for the tenants, the amount of the deposits will be a credit to the buyer and a debit to the seller, since the deposits will be transferred to the new owner of the property.

RESPA

The Real Estate Settlement Procedures Act, commonly known as RESPA, applies to most sales of one- to four-unit residential property (including condominiums, co-ops and mobile homes) involving institutional financing where the purchase loan is secured by a first mortgage on the property. The Act does not apply to loans used to finance the purchase

	BUYER'S STATEMENT		SELLER'S STATEMENT	
	DEBIT	CREDIT	DEBIT	CREDIT
Purchase Price	X			X
Deposit		X		
Excise Tax			X	
Sales Commission			X	
Pay-Off Existing Loan			X	
Assume Existing Loan		X	X	
New Loan		X		
Purchase Money Loan		X	X	
Title Search	X			
Owner's Title Insur.			X	
Lender's Title Insur.	X			
Loan Discount (Points)			X	
Loan Fee	X			
Property Taxes				
Arrears		X	X	
Current/Not Due		X	X	
Prepaid	X			X

Insurance				
Assume Policy	X			X
New Policy	X			
Interest				
Pay-off Exist. Loan			X	
Assume Exist. Loan		X	X	
New Loan	X			
Reserve Accounts				
Pay-off Exist. Loan				X
Assumption	X			X
Credit Report	X			
Survey	X			
Appraisal	X			
Escrow Fee (Varies)	X		X	
Sale of Chattels	X			X
Misc. Recording Fees	X		X	
Balance Due From Buyer		X		
Balance Due Seller			X	
TOTALS	X	X	X	X

An Equal Housing Lender

GOOD FAITH ESTIMATE OF SETTLEMENT CHARGES AND ITEMIZATION OF AMOUNT FINANCED

Listed below is the Good Faith Estimate of Settlement Charges made pursuant to the requirements of the Real Estate Settlement Procedures Act (RESPA). Loan types: ☐ CONV ☐ Fixed Rate ☐ ARM ☐ GEM ☐ FHA ☐ VA ☐ Assumption ☐ Substitution of Liability.

This Good Faith Estimate is provided, based upon your application for a loan of $ __________ for ______ years, with a requested interest rate of ______ %. (______ % of Loan to Value). This Loan has a ______ year call option.

Branch __________ Number ______ Purchaser __________
Prepared by __________ Date ______ __________
Application # __________ Prop. Address __________
____
Mailing Address __________
____

ESTIMATED SETTLEMENT CHARGES*

Estimate Closing Date __________

Amount Paid to You Directly		$ ______
Amount Paid to Your Account		$ ______
Amount Paid to Others on Your Behalf		
Credit Reporting Agency	$ ______	
Appraisal	$ ______	
Title Company ______	$ ______	
Reconveyance ______	$ ______	
Public Officials	$ ______	
Settlement Fee to Lender	$ ______	
Inspection Fee ______	$ ______	
Attorney Review Fee ______	$ ______	
Real Estate Taxes ______	$ ______	
Real Estate Tax Reserve to Lender	$ ______	
Hazard Insurance Reserve to Lender	$ ______	
______	$ ______	

Loan Amount		$ ______
Prepaid Finance Charges		
Loan Fee	$ ______	
Loan Discount (Paid by Borrower)	$ ______	
Buy Down Fee (Paid by Borrower)	$ ______	
Tax registration	$ ______	
Private Mtge. Insur. Prem.	$ ______	
Insurance Reserve PMI/FHA	$ ______	
Interim Interest $ ______ per Day	$ ______ ++	
Review Fee	$ ______	
Total Prepaid Finance Charges		$ ______ (2)
Total Amount Financed (Loan Amount - Prepaid Finance Charges)		$ ______

______________________	$ ______
______________________	$ ______
______________________	$ ______
Total Amount Paid to Others	$ __________ (1)

This is a notice to you as required by the Right to Financial Privacy Act of 1978 that the Veterans Administration Loan Guaranty Service or Division/Federal Housing Administration has right of access to financial records held by a financial institution in connection with the consideration or administration of assistance to you. Financial records involving your transaction will be available to the Veterans Administration Loan Guaranty Service or Division/Federal Housing Administration without further notice or authorization but will not be disclosed or released to another Government agency or department without your consent except as required or permitted by law.

***"THIS FORM DOES NOT COVER ALL ITEMS YOU WILL BE REQUIRED TO PAY IN CASH AT SETTLEMENT. FOR EXAMPLE, DEPOSIT IN ESCROW FOR REAL ESTATE TAXES AND INSURANCE. YOU MAY WISH TO INQUIRE AS TO THE AMOUNTS OF SUCH OTHER ITEMS. YOU MAY BE REQUIRED TO PAY OTHER ADDITIONAL AMOUNTS AT SETTLEMENT," (FOR FURTHER EXPLANATION OF THESE CHARGES CONSULT YOUR BOOKLET ON SETTLEMENT COSTS.)**

++This interest calculation represents the greatest amount of interest you could be required to pay at settlement. The actual amount will be determined by the day of the month on which your settlement is concluded.

Principal & Interest	$ ______ **	Purchase Price	$ ______	Total to Close	$ ______
Mtg. Ins. Prem.	$ ______	Less Loan Amount	$ ______	Less Monies Paid	$ ______
1/12 Annual R/E Taxes	$ ______	Down Payment	$ ______	Est. Funds to CLOSE	$ ______
1/12 Hazard Ins.	$ ______	Plus:	$ ______	Source of Funds to CLOSE:	
Homeowner's Dues	$ ______	C/C Etc. (1&2 Above)	$ ______		
Other	$ ______			______________	
EST. MONTHLY PMT.	$ ______				

**Principal and Interest Amounts for GPM's, GEM's and Buydown (years)
Annual percentage increase in payment ______%.

1st $ ______	2nd $ ______	3rd $ ______
4th $ ______	5th $ ______	6th $ ______
7th $ ______	8th $ ______	9th $ ______
10th $ ______	11th $ ______	12th $ ______

☐ Adjustable Rate Mortgage: Payment Rate ______% Index ______ Chg. Rate: Pmt. ______ mos. Int. ______ mos.

The undersigned hereby acknowledges receipt of a photocopy of this page and a HUD Guide to Settlement Costs booklet.

______________________ (Borrower) ______________________ (Co-Borrower)

RL-040 8-89

of 25 acres or more, loans for the purchase of vacant land, or transactions where the buyer assumes or takes subject to an existing first lien loan.

In transactions subject to RESPA, the lender must give the borrower a **good faith estimate of the closing costs** at the time of the loan application (see form below). The lender is also required to give the borrower a booklet published by the Department of Housing and Urban Development which describes closing costs, settlement procedures and the borrower's rights. The entity handling the closing must prepare the settlement statement on a HUD form called a **Uniform Settlement Statement**, and the buyer must be allowed to inspect the statement on the day before closing if requested. (There is an exception to the inspection requirement when the buyer or his or her agent does not attend the settlement or when the escrowee does not require a meeting of the parties. Thus the inspection provision does not apply to most escrows in California. In these circumstances, the escrowee is required to mail the statement to the borrower as soon as possible after closing.)

RESPA also **prohibits kickbacks** and **unearned fees** in connection with covered transactions, and provides for criminal penalties and triple damages in the event of a violation. This provision does not apply to referral fees paid between real estate brokers, but will apply to any other fees received by a broker other than the commission; such fees must be earned.

Other important RESPA provisions concern providers of services. If the lender requires the use of a particular closing agent, it must disclose any business relationship between the lender and the agent, and give an estimate of the agent's charges for the service. Also, the sale may not be conditioned on the use of a particular title insurer or escrow company chosen by the seller.

Chapter Twenty

Tax Aspects of Real Estate Practice

Introduction: The Federal Income Tax System

The impact of income taxation affects to a greater or lesser degree all transactions in real estate. In some cases, the income tax consequences are a major factor in deciding how to structure the transaction or whether to enter the transaction at all. Therefore, even though real estate brokers and salespersons are not normally qualified to provide professional tax counsel and advice, it is necessary that they have a general understanding of some basic income tax concepts and of the provisions of federal income tax law which affect the most common real estate transactions.

Federal income tax is a progressive tax. Taxes may be "proportional," "progressive" or "regressive." A tax is proportional if the tax rate is the same for all levels of income. For example, one taxpayer has $20,000 of taxable income and pays $4,000 in taxes, and a second taxpayer has $60,000 of taxable income and pays $12,000 in taxes. Both taxpayers paid income taxes equal to 20% of taxable income, or paid taxes directly in proportion to their incomes. If the same rate (in this example, 20%) is applied to all levels of income throughout the tax rate structure, then the tax is proportional. Under a regressive tax rate structure, a smaller tax rate would be applied to higher levels of income.

The federal income tax and most state income taxes have tax rate structures which are progressive. In a progressive tax structure a higher tax rate is applied as taxable income increases. For example, in the 1988 tax year, the tax rate for a married couple filing jointly was 15% for the first $29,750 of taxable income and 28% for the next $42,150 of taxable income (up to $71,900 of taxable income).

Income, Realization, Recognition and Deferral

Before discussing particular provisions of the Internal Revenue Code, it may be helpful to cover a few income tax concepts which are basic to the operation of all sections of the code. Familiarity with the federal income taxation concepts of **income, realization, recognition** and **deferral** is a prerequisite to understanding the application of the particular code sections which affect real estate transactions.

Income. Income may be broadly defined as any economic benefit that is realized (see below) by the taxpayer and which is not specifically excluded by the tax code. The Internal Revenue Code has a sweeping definition of income for tax purposes:

> "Except as otherwise provided in this subtitle, gross income means all income from whatever source derived."

The general approach under the tax code is that all income is gross income for tax purposes unless there is some specific provision in the tax code which excludes it from income. For example, some items of income which are excluded from gross income for tax purposes are: gifts, payments on account of injury or sickness, some employee fringe benefits, interest on state and local government obligations (municipal bonds) and up to $125,000 of the gain on the sale of a principal residence by a taxpayer who is at least 55 years of age.

Some presumptions under the tax code which are applied in determining taxable income are:

1) all income is gross income for tax purposes unless there is a

specific exclusion in the tax code;

2) all income is taxable unless there is a specific provision to the contrary;

3) no expenses are deductible from income for the purpose of determining taxable income unless there is a specific provision in the tax code permitting the deduction.

Realization. While the tax code takes a broad view of what is to be considered gross income for income tax purposes, it does not define "income" and not all economic gain is considered income. The concept of income for income tax purposes is based on the principal of "realization."

Realization of income by an individual occurs when there is: 1) some sort of exchange of goods, other property and/or services between the individual and another individual, group or business entity and, 2) the assets received by the individual in the exchange may be objectively valued. For example, income would be realized in a sale or exchange of real or personal property where an individual gives up property and receives money or other property in exchange.

However, there is no realization of income through the mere appreciation in value of assets owned by the individual when there is no sale or exchange. For example, if a taxpayer owns a home which increases in value $5,000 over the course of the year, the taxpayer may be in a better financial position but there has been no realization of income since there has been no exchange or disposition which separates the gain or profit from the property. In order for income to be "derived" in the words of the code, the profit or value must be severed from the property and available for the recipient's separate use. In real estate, this usually occurs with the sale or exchange of the property.

Recognition. Income which is realized is subject to tax in the year it is recognized. The general rule is that any gain which is "realized" is "recognized" (that is, taxable) in the same year it is realized unless there is a specific provision of the tax code which permits deferral or other nonrecognition.

While gains are almost always recognized (taxable) sooner or later, the same is not true of losses. A loss which is recognized is deductible for income tax purposes and a loss which cannot be recognized for income tax purposes is not deductible. Usually losses realized on the sale or exchange of personal residences and other personal property (property which is not used in business or held for investment or production of income) are not recognized (may not be deducted for income tax purposes). In general, only losses which are incurred in connection with activities carried on with a profit motive (investment, production of income, use in trade or business) are deductible. Another way of looking at it is that losses are deductible for income tax purposes only when the losses are suffered in activities or transactions which might produce taxable income.

Nonrecognition and deferral. Some provisions of the tax code permit a taxpayer to postpone recognition of realized gain until a subsequent year. Some real estate examples include installment sales, exchange of like kind properties and the sale of a personal residence, all of which permit the taxpayer to defer recognition (taxes) on realized gains until some later year, assuming that all conditions of the relevant code provisions are met.

Classifications of Real Property

Frequently the availability of favorable tax treatment, such as deferral of gain, exclusion of gain from income and cost recovery deductions, is dependent upon the class of property involved. For example, the reinvestment deferral available when a taxpayer's principal residence is sold and a replacement residence is purchased is available only on the sale and replacement of a principal residence. If either the property sold or the property purchased is income producing property (such as a nonowner occupied single or multifamily residence) the deferral is not available; the gain would be recognized for tax purposes in the year realized.

On the other hand, tax-free exchange treatment is permitted only for the exchange of investment, income producing or trade or business property. An exchange of a principal residence or for a principal residence does not qualify. If, for example, the taxpayer traded an income producing duplex (which was not occupied by the taxpayer) for a single family residence which the taxpayer moved into as his/her principal residence the transaction would not be eligible for tax-free exchange treatment (or for the reinvestment deferral for the sale and replacement of a principal residence); the gain would be recognized in the year realized.

For the purposes of determining the availability of favorable tax treatment (primarily eligibility for depreciation or cost recovery deductions or for certain tax deferred transactions) real property may be divided into the following classes:

1) principal residence property;
2) unimproved investment property;
3) property held for the production of income;
4) property used in a trade or business; and,
5) dealer property.

Principal residence property. Principal residence property is the home in which the taxpayer lives. If the taxpayer has two homes and lives in both of them, the one in which he or she lives most of the time is the principal residence. A taxpayer may have only one principal residence. Principal residence property is eligible for a number of benefits under tax law including deductibility of interest on the mortgage, deferral of gain on sale and reinvestment in another principal residence, and exclusion of gain on sale by an owner who is at least 55 years of age.

A principal residence may be a single family residence, a condominium, cooperative apartment, mobile home, duplex, row house, house on a farm, an apartment in a multifamily apartment house if the apartment is occupied by the taxpayer, or an apartment over a store or other business, if occupied by the taxpayer. The determining factor is whether the residence is actually occupied by the taxpayer as his or her residence.

The residence may include land surrounding the house, if the land is used for residential purposes. In fact, the land may be considered part of the residence for purposes of nonrecognition, even if the land is not all sold at the same time as the home, if there are a series of transactions and the house is sold as part of the series. For example, in one case, the taxpayer owned a home on ten acres of land. The home was sold along with three acres in one transaction and an additional two acres were sold later. The two acre parcel was considered part of the old principal residence and the gain on that sale eligible for nonrecognition reinvestment treatment.

On the other hand, land by itself may not be considered a principal residence. If land is sold and the house is not sold, it does not qualify as a principal residence. Also, if part of the land is used for business or agricultural purposes, only the part of the land not so used may be considered part of the residence.

A similar rule applies any time part of the property is used for a principal residence and part of the property is devoted to other uses. For example, an apartment over a store, or an owner occupied apartment within a multifamily apartment house. On sale, only the portion of the gain attributable to the part of the property actually used as a principal residence is eligible for favorable tax treatment; on acquisition only the portion of the cost which could be allocated to the part of the property actually used as a principal residence is eligible.

Unimproved investment property. Unimproved investment property is vacant land which produces no rental income. It is held for capital growth. Favorable tax treatment for investment property includes deductibility of interest and "tax-free" exchanges for like kind property.

Property held for the production of income. Property held for the production of income includes residential, commercial and industrial rental property held for the production of rental income to the owner. Such property is eligible for mortgage interest deductions, depreciation or cost recovery deductions, and "tax-free" exchanges for like kind property.

Property used in a trade or business. Property used in a trade or business includes land and buildings, such as factories and business sites, used in the taxpayer's trade or business. Such property is eligible for mortgage interest deductions, depreciation or cost recovery deductions, and "tax-free" exchanges for like kind property.

Dealer property. "Dealer property" is property which is held primarily for sale to customers. Such property is not eligible for tax-free exchange treatment or depreciation/cost recovery deductions. Classification of the property as dealer property may therefore have serious adverse consequences for the owner. As with many other areas of the tax law, there is often no clear distinction between dealer property and property held for investment and there have been numerous cases arising from disputes between owners and the Internal Revenue Service as to whether the gains from particular transactions could be reported as long term capital gains or whether the gains were to be treated as ordinary income.

Some factors which are considered in making a determination include:

1) the frequency and number of sales;
2) subdivision or improvements to make the property more marketable;
3) the extent to which the owner is involved in the sales and marketing;
4) the length of time the property is held;
5) the proportion of income received from real property sales in relation to the taxpayer's income from other sources (this is less relevant if the taxpayer has large property sales income in only one year but is more important if the taxpayer has a large proportion of income from property sales over a number of years);
6) the nature of the taxpayer's business;
7) the extent of advertising or other sales efforts;

8) the purpose for which the taxpayer originally acquired the property;

9) whether or not the property is listed with a real estate broker.

A real estate broker or salesperson may or may not be a dealer. The normal brokerage activities involve representing others in real estate transactions and not acting as a dealer. However, real estate brokers frequently buy and sell property for their own account. In these transactions they may be classified as dealers and courts may be more strict in applying the guidelines to real estate brokers (and real estate lawyers) in deciding whether to classify the property as dealer property or investment property. For many taxpayers, the elimination of the long term capital gains exclusion under the Tax Reform Act of 1986 may lessen the importance of this distinction.

CLASSIFICATIONS OF REAL PROPERTY AND ELIGIBILITY FOR FAVORABLE INCOME TAX TREATMENT

Real Property Classification	Installment Sales Reporting of Gain	Tax-Free Exchange	Recovery Deductions
Principal Residence	Yes	No	No
Unimproved Investment	Yes	Yes	No
Trade or Business	Yes	Yes	Yes
Production of Income	Yes	Yes	Yes
Dealer	**No**	No	No

Gains and Losses

Sale or exchange of an asset normally results in either a gain or a loss. Gains are normally taxable. Unless there is a provision in the tax code permitting exclusion or deferral, the gain is taxable in the year realized. A realized loss may or may not be recognizable (that is, deductible) for income tax purposes depending upon the class of property sold or otherwise disposed of.

The gain or loss realized on a transaction is the difference between the amount realized on the sale or other disposition and the adjusted basis of the property:

  Amount realized
– Adjusted basis
  Gain/loss

Amount realized. The amount realized consists of any money or other property received and the amount of any mortgage debt disposed of. For example, if a property owner sells a property which is subject to a $30,000 mortgage to a buyer for $50,000 cash, the amount realized is $80,000 ($50,000 cash + the $30,000 mortgage disposed of). It makes no difference whether the buyer formally assumes liability for the mortgage debt or merely takes the property subject to the mortgage. The amount realized is reduced by the selling expenses, such as commissions.

  Money received
+ Fair market value of other property received
+ Mortgage or other debt in connection with property disposed of
– Selling expenses
Amount Realized

Adjusted basis. In most cases, the original or initial basis for property is the price paid for the property (the cost basis). The original cost basis of the property may be increased by capital expenditures and reduced by depreciation/cost recovery deductions to reach the adjusted basis.

Original basis
\+ Capital expenditures
– Depreciation/Cost recovery deductions
Adjusted Basis

Capital expenditures are expenditures which increase the value of property or significantly extend its useful life. For example, a new room addition, new deck or patio would be a capital expenditure. The effect of a capital expenditure would be to increase the basis and therefore reduce the gain on sale of the property. Maintenance expenses, such as routine repairs and repainting, are not capital expenditures and do not increase the cost basis.

Depreciation and cost recovery deductions are allowable expenses for income tax purposes to permit the owner to recover the cost of the property. The length of time and the rate of allowable deductions (and whether any such deduction is allowable at all) depends both upon the class of property and the time the property was acquired. Depreciation and cost recovery deductions and their effect on adjusted basis are covered in greater detail later in this chapter. In general, though, allowable depreciation or cost recovery deductions would have the effect of reducing basis and increasing the gain on sale of the property.

Capital gains and losses. Prior to 1987 the gain on disposition of certain assets, including most types of real estate other than dealer property, held for longer than six months was eligible for long term capital gains treatment. This favorable tax treatment permitted the taxpayer to exclude 60% of the gain from income. For example, if a gain of $100,000 was eligible for long term capital gains treatment, 60% of the gain ($60,000) would be excluded from income and only 40% ($40,000) would have been included in the taxpayer's taxable income. This tax benefit of real property ownership is no longer available; it was eliminated by the Tax Reform Act of 1986 for dispositions after January 1, 1987.

Nonrecognition and Deferral Transactions

The Internal Revenue Code allows a taxpayer in some cases to defer recognition of a realized gain to a later year or later transaction. Transactions in which gain may be deferred or not recognized in the year realized include **installment sales, sale of a principal residence, involuntary conversions, sale of low-income housing**, and **"tax-free" exchanges**. With the exception of a limited exclusion of gain on the sale of a principal residence by an owner of at least 55 years of age, these code provisions are not really "tax-free" transactions. The intent is that the realized gain will be recognized and taxed in a subsequent year.

The rationale for most nonrecognition provisions in the tax code is based on the so-called "wherewithal" concept: the taxpayer does not have the wherewithal to pay the taxes in the year the gain is realized so taxes are deferred until a later year or transaction when the taxpayer does have cash to pay the taxes.

For example, in the sale and replacement of a personal residence, the taxpayer does not have the money to pay taxes on the gain because it is assumed that all the proceeds of the sale will be needed by most taxpayers to pay for the new residence. The taxes are deferred until a time when the taxpayer sells a residence and does not replace it. Money is then available to pay the taxes. (If the taxpayer waits until the age 55, the gain may be completely exempt from taxes.)

In other nonrecognition transactions, much the same reasoning applies. In an involuntary conversion, the taxpayer cannot use the insurance or condemnation proceeds to pay taxes because all the money is needed to buy a replacement. In an exchange of property for like kind property, the taxpayer receives only property, not money, so again there is no money to pay taxes and they are deferred until there is a sale. Similarly, in the installment sale deferral discussed directly below, the taxpayer does not have the money to pay all of the taxes in the year of sale because not all the money is received in the year of sale. The taxes are deferred and paid as the profits are received.

Installment sales.

An installment sale occurs when less than one hundred percent of the sales price is received in the year of sale. Installment sale reporting allows the taxpayer to defer recognition of a portion of the gain to the year(s) in which the profit is received.

All types of real property are eligible for installment sale reporting, with the exception of dealer property. As a general rule, dealer property is not eligible. However, certain dealer property—timeshares and residential subdivision lots—can become eligible for installment sale reporting if the dealer/taxpayer chooses to comply with special rules.

On installment sale reporting, the gain recognized in any year is that proportion of the installment payment received which the gross profit bears to the total contract price. For installment sales, then, it is necessary to calculate the gross profit percentage. The gross profit is the difference between the sales price and the adjusted basis. For installment sales, commissions and other selling expenses paid by the seller are added to the adjusted basis.

Example:

$150,000	Sales price
$90,000	Seller's basis
+ 10,000	Commission and other selling expenses
$100,000	Adjusted basis
$150,000	
- 100,000	
$ 50,000	Gross profit

The percentage of gross profit is applied to the payments received in each year to determine how much of the amount received is gain to be taxed for that year. The gross profit percentage is the relationship between the amount of profit and the "contract price." The contract price is the total of all principal payments the seller will receive on the sale. In most cases, unless the buyer assumes an existing loan, the contract price is the same as the sales price.

Example:

Gross profit ratio = Gross profit ÷ Contract price
Gross profit ratio = $50,000 ÷ $150,000
Gross profit ratio = .3333

This percentage would be applied to the principal payments received each year to find the amount of capital gain to be subject to tax that year. All interest payments received would be reported as ordinary income

If the seller in the above example received a $30,000 downpayment, $500 in principal installment payments and $5,400 in interest the first year, the taxable gain would be calculated:

$30,000	downpayment
+ 500	installment principal payments
$30,500	total payments received on principal
$30,500	
× .3333	
$10,166	capital gains income
+ 5,400	interest income as ordinary income
$15,566	total taxable income in the year of sale

In some circumstances, the seller will be deemed to have received payments even though the buyer makes no direct payment to the seller and the contract price for tax reporting purposes may be less than the sales price, resulting in a higher profit percentage. This occurs in transactions in which the buyer assumes an existing mortgage which is larger than the seller's basis in the property (e.g., the buyer assumes an existing mortgage of $50,000 and the seller's adjusted basis in the property is only $30,000). In such transactions the excess is treated as a payment received in the year of sale and the contract price is regarded as the same as the gross profit, resulting in a gross profit ratio of 100%.

Also, if the seller uses an installment obligation of more than $150,000 as collateral to borrow money, the money borrowed is treated as payments received in that year. This is known as the pledge rule.

If the property is subject to recapture provisions because of depreciation or cost recovery deductions (discussed later in this chapter) the amount recaptured is also treated as a payment received in the year of sale.

Reinvestment deferral on sale of principal residence.

A deferral of gain is permitted a taxpayer who sells his or her principal residence and replaces that residence by buying another or building and occupying a new one within two years. The gain is deferred to the extent that it is reinvested in a replacement home. This means that if the acquisition cost of the replacement home is larger than the amount realized on the sale then the entire gain is deferred.

Example:

$90,000	amount realized on sale after selling expenses
– 80,000	taxpayer's basis in home
$10,000	gain realized on sale of principal residence

If the taxpayer buys a replacement residence which costs $100,000, the entire $10,000 gain would be deferred. The taxpayer's basis in the replacement home is reduced by the amount of the deferred gain. In this case, the basis in the new home would be $90,000 ($100,000 less the $10,000 deferred gain), not the $100,000 actually paid for the home.

If the acquisition cost of the new home is less than the sales price of the old home, the gain is deferred only to the extent of the price of the new home. Excess gain is taxable in the year of sale.

Example:

A taxpayer has a gain of $10,000 on the sale of his home. The adjusted sales price and amount realized are both $90,000. A new home is purchased for $85,000.

If the adjusted sales price exceeds the cost of the new home, the gain is taxable to that extent. In this case, the adjusted sales price exceeds the cost of the new home by $5,000, so $5,000 of the gain would be taxable in the year of sale. The other $5,000 of gain would be deferred and would reduce the cost basis of the new home to $80,000.

Exclusion on sale of principal residence by taxpayer over 55.

Anytime a taxpayer sells a principal residence and replaces it, he or she is entitled to the **deferral** of gain discussed above. **Once in a lifetime** a taxpayer is entitled to an **exclusion** of gain of up to $125,000 on the sale of a principal residence. The maximum exclusion is $62,500 for a married taxpayer filing separately. This is one of the few provisions of the tax code which permits a taxpayer to realize gain which will never be subject to taxation.

In order to qualify for the exclusion, the following conditions must be met:

1) the taxpayer must be at least 55 years of age (for a married couple only one spouse must be 55);

2) the property must have been used as the taxpayer's principal residence for at least three of the last five years.

Involuntary conversions.

Involuntary conversions occur when an asset is destroyed, condemned or otherwise lost and is then replaced with the insurance proceeds or condemnation award. Often a gain is realized on such replacements. For example, suppose a taxpayer owns a small warehouse with a cost basis of $50,000, which is now worth $100,000 and is insured for full market value. If the warehouse is completely destroyed and the taxpayer receives $100,000 in insurance proceeds, he or she will have realized a gain of $50,000 on the destruction of the property. If the taxpayer replaces the warehouse with similar property within two years of its destruction, the gain is not recognized to the extent that the proceeds are invested in the replacement property. This deferral provision is similar to the principal residence reinvestment deferral discussed above, except that it is available for any type of property and the basis of the replacement property is the same as the taxpayer's basis in the property lost or destroyed.

Sale of low-income housing.

An owner of certain qualified low-income housing may sell such housing and reinvest the proceeds in similar housing within one year without recognizing gain on the sale. Gain which is not reinvested in similar property is recognized and taxable in the year of sale.

"Tax-free" exchanges.

A "tax-free" exchange is really a tax deferred exchange. If investment property, income property or property used in a trade or business is exchanged for **like kind** property, any realized gain may be deferred to the extent that only like kind property is received. Principal residence property and dealer property are not eligible for this deferral.

In meeting the requirements for this deferral, the property received must be "like kind." This refers to the nature of the property rather than its quality. Most real estate is considered to be of like kind for the purposes of the exchange deferral without regard to whether it is improved or unimproved, city or rural property, encumbered or unencumbered or whether the taxpayer owns a full or only a partial interest.

If nothing other than like kind property is received, no gain or loss is recognized and the taxpayer's basis in the property received is the same as the property transferred. However, if anything other than like kind property is received, it is regarded as **boot**. If real estate is the like kind property, examples of boot might include cash, stock or property other than like kind real estate, and differences in mortgage balances. For example, if a taxpayer trades a property which has an outstanding trust deed of $50,000 for a property which has an outstanding trust deed of $30,000, there would be $20,000 of boot, regardless of whether there is a formal assumption of the loan. If any boot is received, gain is recognized to the extent of the boot received. In this example, the taxpayer would recognize $20,000 of gain, just as if he or she had received $20,000 in cash.

The taxpayer's old basis is transferred to the property received in the trade. If nothing other than like kind property is traded, no adjustments are necessary. However, if boot is involved, adjustments to the basis may be required for boot paid or received and gain or loss recognized. The basis in the new property is adjusted upward for any boot paid or gain recognized and downward for any boot received and for any loss recognized on boot paid.

The following formula may be used for calculating the new basis:

Adjusted basis of old property	
Additions:	
+ Cash or other boot given	
+ Gain recognized	
TOTAL	
Deductions:	
- Cash or other boot received	
- Loss recognized on boot given	
BASIS OF NEW PROPERTY	

Example:

A taxpayer trades property with a basis of $250,000 for other investment or income property with a fair market value of $140,000 plus a home (which the taxpayer will occupy as her personal residence) with a value of $100,000 and $50,000 cash (total of $290,000). The taxpayer would realize a gain of $40,000, all of which would be recognized as $150,000 of boot was received. The new basis would be $140,000:

Adjusted basis of old property	$250,000
+ Gain recognized	+ 40,000
	$290,000
- Cash and other boot received	- 150,000
NEW BASIS	$140,000

Tax-free exchanges can be advantageous because current tax expenses can be reduced or eliminated and property acquired which it would not be possible to buy with the after-tax proceeds from the sale of existing property.

Depreciation and Cost Recovery Deductions

Depreciation and cost recovery deductions are allowable deductions from income to permit a taxpayer to recover the cost of an asset used for the **production of income** or **used in a trade or business**. In general, only property which wears out and must be replaced is eligible for depreciation or cost recovery. Examples of such property include: apartment buildings, business or plant equipment and commercial fruit orchards. Land does not wear out and is not depreciable property. Also, as the depreciation and cost recovery deductions are deductions from income, they are allowable only for income producing property. **Principal residence** property, **land** and **dealer property** are not eligible for the deductions.

The entire expense of acquiring the asset may not be deducted in the year the expense is incurred as is permitted with many business expenses (such as wages, supplies, utilities) but the expense of acquiring the asset may be deducted over a number of years (from 15 to 31½ years for most real estate, depending on the type of real estate and when it was placed in service). The number of years permitted is a reflection of legislative policy and has little if any relationship to the actual length of time that the property may be economically useful. The whole field of depreciation and cost recovery deductions has been subject to frequent modification by congress. There are now five different systems in use. Real estate agents need some familiarity with all depreciation/cost recovery methods because all are in effect.

Depreciation and cost recovery methods.

Which of the five possible systems is to be used depends upon when the property was placed in service. Within each system are several allowable methods, depending on the type of property. The time periods determining the applicable system are:

1) before January 1, 1981;

2) between January 1, 1981 and March 15, 1984;

3) between March 16, 1984 and March 8, 1985;

4) between March 9, 1985 and December 31, 1986; and,

5) after December 31, 1986.

Property acquired before January 1, 1981.

For property acquired before January 1, 1981, depreciation deductions are allowed based upon the presumed **useful life** of the asset. The estimated **salvage value** is deducted from the basis to determine the amount which may be depreciated. The method to be used and the number of years of useful life depend upon the type of property, whether it was new at the time of acquisition, and the taxpayer's choice. There are five different methods commonly used to calculate the annual depreciation. Useful life periods for real property range from 20-40 years. It is beyond the scope of this text to cover in detail which methods and which time periods are allowable for particular classes of real property. Following is a brief discussion of the five depreciation methods: one "straight line" method and four "accelerated" methods. The **five methods** are:

1) straight line;

2) 200% declining balance (accelerated method);

3) 150% declining balance (accelerated method);

4) 125% declining balance (accelerated method); and,

5) sum-of-the-years'-digits (accelerated method).

In a straight line method, the same amount is deducted for depreciation each year of the asset's useful life. In an accelerated method, larger depreciation deductions are taken in the earlier years of the asset's life and smaller deductions in the later years.

Straight line. Under the straight line method, the same amount is deducted each year as a depreciation deduction.

Example:

Property cost	$120,000
Land value	20,000
Salvage value	– 10,000
Depreciable value	$ 90,000

Estimated useful life: 20 years

$90,000 ÷ 20 = $4,500 depreciation deduction per year

The depreciation deduction may also be calculated through use of percentages.

Example:

100% ÷ 20 = 5% per year
$90,000 x .05 = $4,500 per year

200% declining balance. The 200% declining balance method (often called the double declining balance method) is an **accelerated method** with larger depreciation deductions taken in the early years of the useful life and smaller deductions in later years than would be taken under the straight line method.

With this method, the depreciation deduction for the first year is twice what would be taken under the straight line method. A percentage equal to double the straight line percentage is used. For example, if the percentage under the straight line method would be 5% per year, the percentage under the 200% declining balance method would be 10%. The amount taken as a depreciation deduction is subtracted from the original base to determine the declining balance to be used the next year.

With the 200% declining balance and with other declining balance methods, the salvage value is not used in calculating the depreciation deduction. However, the salvage value must be known because the property may not be depreciated below the salvage value.

Example:

Depreciation base: \$100,000 (salvage value not used in calculations)

20-year life:
200% ÷ 20 years = 10% per year

Year 1:
\$100,000 × .10 = \$10,000 depreciation deduction

Year 2:
\$100,000 – 10,000 deduction for Year 1 = \$90,000 base for Year 2
\$90,000 × .10 = \$9,000 deduction

Year 3:
\$90,000 – 9,000 = \$81,000 base for Year 3
\$81,000 × .10 = \$8,100 depreciation deduction for Year 3

150% and 125% declining balance. The 150% and 125% declining balance methods are essentially the same as the 200% declining balance method, with the exception that the percentage rate applied to the depreciation base each year is calculated using the number of years in the useful life and a percentage rate of 150% or 125%, as applicable, instead of 200%.

Example:

20-year life, 150% declining balance
\$100,000 initial depreciation base

150% ÷ 20 = 7.5%

Year 1:
\$100,000 x .075 = \$7,500 depreciation deduction

Year 2:
\$100,000 – 7,500 = \$92,500 base for Year 2
\$92,500 x .075 = \$6,937.50 deduction for Year 2

Year 3:
\$92,500 − 6,937.50 = \$85,562.50
\$85,562.50 x .075 = \$6,417.19 deduction for Year 3

Sum-of-the-years'-digits. The sum-of-the-years'-digits is an accelerated method in which a fraction is used to calculate the depreciation deduction for each year. The bottom number (denominator) of the fraction is the sum of the years of the useful life.

Example:

20-year life
1+2+3+4+5+6+7+8+9+10+11+12+13+14+15+16+17+18+19+20=210

Or the following formula may be used:

$$\text{Sum} = \frac{\text{Number of Years} \times (\text{Number of Years} + 1)}{2}$$

$$\text{Sum} = \frac{20 \times (20 + 1)}{2}$$

$$\text{Sum} = \frac{20 \times 21}{2} = \frac{420}{2} = 210$$

The denominator stays the same each year. The numerator (the top number) changes each year. The numerator each year is the number of years remaining in the useful life. In our example using a 20-year useful life, the numerator would be 20 the first year, 19 the second year, 18 the third year, and so on.

Example:

20-year life, sum-of-the-years'-digits
\$90,000 depreciable basis (salvage value used in calculations)

$$\text{Sum-of-years'-digits} = \frac{\text{life} \times (1 + \text{life})}{2}$$

$$\text{Sum} = \frac{20 \times (1 + 20)}{2}$$

Sum (denominator) = 210

Year 1:

$$\$90{,}000 \times \frac{20}{210} = \$8{,}571.43 \text{ first year deduction}$$

Year 2:

$$\$90{,}000 \times \frac{19}{210} = \$8{,}142.86 \text{ deduction for Year 2}$$

Property placed in service January 1, 1981 - December 31, 1986.

The Economic Tax and Recovery Act of 1981 replaced the depreciation methods discussed above with a simpler system of **cost recovery**. The **accelerated cost recovery system (ACRS)** available under that act permitted much more rapid cost recovery than was available under previous methods.

The cost recovery deduction for each year is determined by multiplying the basis of the property times a statutory percentage. Salvage value is not used in the calculations. The appropriate percentage is determined by reference to tables provided by the Internal Revenue Service. The percentage (and proper IRS table) to be used depends upon the class of property and when it was placed in service. A sample table for real property other than low-income housing, placed in service between January 1, 1981 and March 15, 1984 is shown below. The cost basis of the asset is recovered over a 15-year period without allowance for salvage value.

The taxpayer may elect to use a **straight line** method instead of the accelerated percentages from the tables. If a straight line method is used, the number of years in the recovery period is divided into the basis (without allowance for salvage value) to find the annual deduction. The allowable recovery periods depend on the class of property and when it was placed in service.

ACRS Table for Real Property (Other Than Low-Income Housing) Placed in Service After December 31, 1980

Find the applicable percentage under the month in which the property was first placed in service.

Recovery Year	*Month* 1	2	3	4	5	6	7	8	9	10	11	12
1	12%	11%	10%	9%	8%	7%	6%	5%	4%	3%	2%	1%
2	10	10	11	11	11	11	11	11	11	11	11	12
3	9	9	9	9	10	10	10	10	10	10	10	10
4	8	8	8	8	8	8	9	9	9	9	9	9
5	7	7	7	7	7	7	8	8	8	8	8	8
6	6	6	6	6	7	7	7	7	7	7	7	7
7	6	6	6	6	6	6	6	6	6	6	6	6
8	6	6	6	6	6	6	5	6	6	6	6	6
9	6	6	6	6	5	6	5	5	5	6	6	6
10	5	6	5	6	5	5	5	5	5	5	6	5
11	5	5	5	5	5	5	5	5	5	5	5	5
12	5	5	5	5	5	5	5	5	5	5	5	5
13	5	5	5	5	5	5	5	5	5	5	5	5
14	5	5	5	5	5	5	5	5	5	5	5	5
15	5	5	5	5	5	5	5	5	5	5	5	5
16	-	-	1	1	2	2	3	3	4	4	4	5

Property placed in service January 1, 1981 - March 15, 1984.

For most real property, other than low-income housing, acquired and placed in service between January 1, 1981 and March 15, 1984, the recovery period is 15 years with ACRS percentages as shown on the sample table. Low-income housing is also in a 15-year class, but different percentages are used which permit a more rapid recovery of cost than is permitted for other buildings. Manufactured homes have a 10-year recovery period.

If the taxpayer elects to use a straight line recovery, the owner may choose from recovery periods of 15, 35 and 45 years.

Example:

$100,000 depreciable asset (no deduction for salvage value)
15-year life

ACRS System (Refer to table for appropriate percentages). Assume asset was placed in service January 1 for full year's deduction:

Year 1:
$100,000 x .12 = $12,000 ACRS deduction

Year 2:
$100,000 x .10 = $10,000 ACRS deduction

Year 3:
$100,000 x .09= $9,000 ACRS deduction

Straight line:

$100,000 ÷ 15 = $6,666.67 cost recovery per year

Or use percentage:
100% ÷ 15 = 6.667% per year

Property placed in service March 16, 1984 - May 8, 1985.

Cost recovery treatment for property placed in service between March 16, 1984 and May 8, 1985 is substantially the same as discussed directly above. The major difference is that the minimum recovery period for most buildings other than low-income housing is 18 years instead of 15 years. Calculation of the annual deduction is the same as the example above, except that the 18-year ACRS table is used instead of the 15-year table. A taxpayer electing straight line cost recovery may use recovery periods of 18, 35 or 45 years.

Property placed in service May 9, 1985 - December 31, 1986.

Cost recovery treatment for property placed in service during this time period is essentially the same as that discussed above, except that the minimum recovery period is increased to 19 years and the 19-year ACRS table would be used for taxpayers electing the accelerated cost recovery method. The minimum straight line recovery period would also be 19 years.

Property placed in service after December 31, 1986.

The Tax Reform Act of 1986 establishes a completely new system of cost recovery for property placed in service beginning January 1, 1987. Only straight line deductions are allowed; there is no provision for any accelerated depreciation or cost recovery. For residential property, the recovery period is 27½ years; for nonresidential real property, the recovery period is 31½ years.

Example:

$100,000 depreciable residential property

$100,000 ÷ 27.5 = $3,636.36 cost recovery deduction per year

Or use a percentage:

Residential property:
100% ÷ 27.5 = 3.636% per year deduction

Nonresidential property:
100% ÷ 31.5 = 3.175% per year deduction

Effect of depreciation or cost recovery deductions on recognized gain.

Any depreciation or cost recovery deductions allowed or allowable reduce the adjusted basis of the property and, consequently, increase the recognized gain on resale.

Example:

$120,000	original cost basis of property
- 27,100	depreciation taken under 200% declining balance method
$ 92,900	new adjusted cost basis of property
$135,000	net sales price
- 92,900	adjusted basis
$ 42,100	gain

Deductions

An allowable income tax **deduction** is subtracted from the taxpayer's income before taxation. A deduction reduces the taxable income and thereby reduces the income tax owed by the taxpayer. There are a number of income tax deductions permitted to owners of real property. Some deductions were greatly restricted or eliminated by the Tax Reform Act of 1986.

Depreciation and cost recovery deductions. Depreciation and cost recovery deductions are discussed directly above. The Tax Reform Act of 1986 reduced the annual allowable deductions by increasing the cost recovery periods to 27½ or 31½ years from the 15- to 19-year periods permitted for property placed in service 1981-1986.

Repair deductions. For most properties other than personal residences, expenditures for repairs are deductible in the year paid as an expense if they are made to keep the property in ordinary, efficient, operating condition and not to add to its value or prolong its life.

Repairs should be contrasted with improvements and alterations which are **capital expenditures**. Capital expenditures add to the value of the property and frequently prolong its economic life. Capital expenditures are not deductible in the year made, but are added to the property's basis. The resulting increase in the cost basis of the property will affect the gain or loss on the sale of the property and will also increase the allowable cost recovery deductions (since the basis is larger) if the property is eligible for depreciation or cost recovery.

Taxes. Real property taxes are deductible. Federal income taxes are not deductible.

Mortgage Interest. Mortgage interest is deductible for most property other than personal residences subject to some restrictions. The Tax Reform Act of 1986 and subsequent amendments to the Tax Reform Act placed some limitations on interest deductions for personal residences (which is the only consumer interest deductible under the new tax law). A taxpayer may deduct the interest payments on a loan of up to one million dollars used to buy or improve a residence. For other home loans (home equity loans for purposes other than acquisition or improvement), interest on loans of up to $100,000 can be deducted by a couple filing a joint return without regard to the purpose of the loan or whether the loan exceeds the original acquisition cost of the home, plus capital improvements. Taxpayers filing separate returns can deduct interest on up to $60,000 of debt.

Limitations on deductibility of "passive losses." Under the Tax Reform Act of 1986, losses from passive activities, such as rental properties, can no longer be offset against income from wages, salaries, interest, dividends or royalties. Losses from passive activities can only be offset against income from other passive activities. For example, if a taxpayer had $30,000 salary income and owned one rental property, which had a net loss of $2,000 for the year, the $2,000 net loss could not be deducted from the $30,000 salary income. However, the loss can be carried forward and used when the taxpayer does have positive income from a passive activity. Also, for property acquired before October 22, 1986, there is four-year phase-in of the rule before it becomes fully effective. For the tax year 1987, 65% of the passive loss may be deducted from other income, for 1988 — 40%, for 1989 — 20%, and for 1990 — 10%. Beginning in 1991, none of the passive loss may be deducted from other income.

There is **one exception** in favor of **individuals** who **actively participate** in the rental property activity and whose adjusted gross income does not exceed $100,000. For these taxpayers, the losses from rental property of up to $25,000 may be offset against their other income. The requirement for "active participation" is met if the owner actually excercises some control over the management of the rental property, for example by selecting tenants, setting rental terms or authorizing repairs and maintenance work. This exception is only available to individuals; it may not be used by an investor who is a limited partner in a limited partnership which owns the property or by an owner who owns less than a 10% interest in the property. There is a further limitation based on income. If the taxpayer's adjusted gross income is more than $100,000, the maximum $25,000 deduction is reduced by 50¢ for every $1 of income over the $100,000 limit. So, a taxpayer whose adjusted gross income exceeded $150,000 would not be able to take any advantage of this limited exception.

INDEX